International Humanitarian Law Facing New Challenges

Wolff Heintschel von Heinegg
Volker Epping
Editors

International Humanitarian Law Facing New Challenges

Symposium in Honour of KNUT IPSEN

Springer

Professor Dr. Wolff Heintschel von Heinegg
Europa-Universität Viadrina,
Lehrstuhl für Öffentliches Recht,
insbesondere Völkerrecht, Europarecht
und ausländisches Verfassungsrecht
August-Bebel-Straße 12
15234 Frankfurt/Oder
Germany
heinegg@euv-frankfurt-o.de

Professor Dr. Volker Epping
Leibniz Universität Hannover,
Juristische Fakultät,
Lehrstuhl für Öffentliches Recht,
Völker- und Europarecht
Königsworther Platz 1
30167 Hannover
Germany
epping@jura.uni-hannover.de

Library of Congress Control Number: 2006939132

ISBN 978-3-540-49089-0 Springer Berlin Heidelberg New York

Springer is part of Springer Science+Business Media

springer.com

Production: LE-TeX Jelonek, Schmidt & Vöckler GbR, Leipzig
Cover-design: WMX Design GmbH, Heidelberg

SPIN 11927525 64/3100YL - 5 4 3 2 1 0 Printed on acid-free paper

Foreword

There should be no doubt about the necessity of principles and rules of international law applicable to situations in which States and other actors have – for whatever reasons or motives, whether legally justified or not – decided to resort to the use of armed force. The principles and rules applicable to international armed conflicts, first codified in the 19th century and since then constantly developed in international conventions, are, for the most part, recognized as customary in character. The law applicable to non-international armed conflicts is less elaborated. However, there are many who believe that under customary international law the differences between the law governing international armed conflicts and the law governing non-international armed conflicts have decreased. They claim that the two bodies have more or less merged into a single body of rules applicable to both kinds of conflicts. While this position has not remained unchallenged – it may be added: rightly so – the core problem we are facing today is not the question of whether there has been a merger of the principles and rules applicable to international and to non-international armed conflicts. Rather, the alleged asymmetries of modern armed conflicts could shake the well-established legal regime governing armed hostilities.

Indeed, recent armed conflicts, whether international or non-international in character, are in many respects characterized by a variety of asymmetries. One may not like that characterization because it may be overstressed, sometimes even abused, and ultimately virtually meaningless. Still, the said asymmetries – either as such or in conjunction with other developments – seem to challenge the law of armed conflicts or: international humanitarian law. These challenges may very well compromise the very function of that body of law, which is to mitigate as far as possible the calamities of war. Thus, the law of armed conflict may be deprived of its fundamental function as an order of necessity because its legally binding directives will increasingly be disregarded for the sake of allegedly superior values. Even if, however, the law of armed conflict retains that fundamental function we may witness a remodelling of that law insofar as there will or may be what could be characterized a renaissance of military necessity. Especially the said asymmetries – that are not new phenomena typical or even exclusive for 21st century armed conflicts – are sometimes used to doubt the wisdom of the existing law and the underlying compromise between considerations of military necessity and considerations of humanity.

Against these findings or rather apprehensions some may raise objections by hinting at the indeed fast-paced development of criminal international law. That law, they will maintain, gives clear evidence of the preparedness of the international community to reaffirm the law of armed conflict and to even improve its enforcement. While the appropriateness of criminal international law as one enforcement mechanism of the law of armed conflict is not doubted here the question remains whether its very existence may not lead to a shift of responsibilities from the State level to the individual level. In view of the so-called CNN effect it may prove more profitable to have the individual wrongdoer in the spotlight and thus to distract from the international responsibility of the State whose organ the wrongdoer is.

Moreover, we still witness a lack of dissemination of the law of armed conflict. Of course, small States, developing countries and countries in transition are in most cases not in a position to comply with their duty to effectively disseminate that law neither among their armed forces nor among the population. However, there are some incidents that seem to give evidence of a poorly developed dissemination mechanism in advanced and rich countries as well.

With regard to the alleged or real asymmetries the focus is very often laid on the fact of an increased involvement of non-State actors in armed hostilities. All too often it is, however, forgotten that private individuals have always – indirectly or directly – participated in armed hostilities – either with or without the blessing of the respective government. It suffices here to mention partisan warfare during the Second World War and to the fact that that asymmetry lead to an increased disregard of the law. However, it would fall short of reality if the partisans of those days were put on par with those individuals that today participate in international and non-international armed conflicts. Very often those non-State actors are well-trained and equipped and, moreover, organized in a way that seems to indicate that they more resemble transnational terrorists than individuals who have decided to intervene into an armed conflict for purely patriotic or similar reasons.

Another aspect contributing to an asymmetric character of modern armed conflicts are private contractors and other civilians increasingly performing military functions that used to be the exclusive monopoly of the State and its organs. Private military firms, e.g., are entrusted with a variety of tasks ranging from mere supply and technical support to the provision of data, training, and to close air support or even to fighting the war altogether.

A further asymmetry that is all too often left aside or even forgotten is the increasing technology gap. It suffices to mention the advanced state of the US in weapons and electronic technology. Again, it would fall short of reality if the ensuing technology gap between the US and the vast majority of other States were merely taken for justifying the claim that technologically advanced States are under a legal obligation to only make use of high-precision weaponry. An adversary confronted with highly advanced armed forces equipped with highly sophisticated weapons and other systems may well be inclined to disregard the law by alleging that its very survival is at stake. It needs to be emphasized in this context that the problem not only lies in the possible use of poorly developed weapons of mass destruction. Only remember Somalia, only remember Iraq and the tactics used in those countries against an overwhelming enemy military power. There is, however, the reverse of the technology gap we should not forget either. Technological supremacy creates new vulnerabilities that will certainly induce the adversary to undertake everything feasible to make military or political use of them. The possible effects are not yet thoroughly scrutinized and may very well have negative impacts on the principle of distinction.

The said asymmetries may not only result in a renaissance of considerations of military necessity, they may not only have a negative impact on the principle of distinction, but they may moreover brush aside the achievements of the past 150 years in which the law of armed conflict has been developed to a rather sophisticated legal order that is very much in line with the fundamental values of modern civilized States.

In order to discuss these and other questions a most distinguished group of experts in the field of the law of armed conflicts gathered in Berlin in June 2005. Their contributions reveal that they do not agree on every assessment. Still, the discussions were guided by mutual respect and by the common goal to find operable solutions for contemporary problems and challenges.

The Berlin Symposium was dedicated to celebrate the 70th birthday of *Knut Ipsen*. Of course, it would not do justice to *Knut Ipsen* to reduce his academic and professional work to the field of the law of armed conflict. As a member of the German delegation to the Geneva conference on the reaffirmation and progressive development of international humanitarian law applicable to armed conflicts (1974-1977) and to the United Nations Conference on conventional weapons (1978-1980) he has, however, like no other German international lawyer of the second half of the 20th century, contributed to the progressive development of the law of armed conflicts. As the President of the German Red Cross (1994-2003) his impact on that development may have been indirect but it has certainly been lasting and effective.

The editors express their gratitude to the Fritz-Thyssen Foundation for their contribution which made the symposium possible. They also thank the German Red Cross for making available their premises that enabled the participants to pursue their goals in a most pleasant atmosphere. They owe gratitude to the "Verein zur Förderung der Rechtswissenschaften e.V. (Bochum)" and the "Förderkreis Europa-Universität VIADRINA e.V." whose contributions enabled them to publish the results of the symposium. Finally, the editors would like to thank Mr. Tobias Gries for his never-tiring work in organizing the symposium and in preparing the present publication.

Frankfurt (Oder)/Hannover, November 2006

Wolff Heintschel von Heinegg Volker Epping

Table of Contents

The System of Status Groups

The Relationship between Individual and State Responsibility

Dissemination and Monitoring Compliance

Introduction

Confronting New Challenges Knut Ipsen and International Humanitarian Law

Volker Epping

Gottfried Wilhelm Leibniz University of Hannover

Knut Ipsen, born on 9th June, 1935, was *Eberhard Menzel*'s assistant at Christian-Albrechts-University Kiel, under whom he obtained his doctorate[1] and qualified in 1973 as a university lecturer with a habilitation thesis on biological and chemical weapons in international law[2]. After this, it did not take him long to receive an offer for the chair for Public and Public International Law from the law department at Ruhr-University Bochum. He remained faithful to both his university and to international humanitarian law. This is illustrated not only by his central article on armed conflicts in the textbook on international law he took over from *Menzel* and which is now in its fifth edition[3]. Also the multitude of his publications shows his unfaltering commitment to international humanitarian law. His publications include works on the employment of A-, B-, and C-weapons[4], on combatant status[5]

---

1 The doctoral dissertation was completed in 1967 and treated the legal bases and the internationalisation of Atlantic-West European defence: Rechtsgrundlagen und Institutionalisierung der atlantisch-westeuropäischen Verteidigung, Kiel/Hamburg 1967.

2 Biologische und chemische Kampfmittel im Völkerrecht, Kiel 1973.

3 *K. Ipsen* (ed.), Völkerrecht, 5th ed., Munich 2004.

4 BC-Waffen im Völkerrecht, in: E. v. Weizsäcker (ed.), BC-Waffen und Friedenspolitik, Stuttgart/Munich 1970, pp. 42-61; Sicherheitspolitische und völkerrechtliche Aspekte der biologischen und chemischen Kampfmittel, in: Europa-Archiv 27 (1972), pp. 589-600; Prävention oder Reaktion? Sicherheitsmaßnahmen und Sicherheitsstandards im Rahmen der Internationalen Atomenergie-Organisation und die Konvention über kerntechnische Unfälle vom 26.9.1986, in: U. Hüffler/K. Ipsen/P. J. Tettinger (eds.), Berg- und Energierecht vor den Fragen der Gegenwart, Festschrift für Fritz Fabricius zum 70. Geburtstag, Stuttgart/Munich/Hannover 1989, pp. 357-376; A Nuclear-Weapon-Free World: Legal Problems, in: J. Rotblat/F. Blackaby (eds.), Towards a Secure World in the 21st Century, Annals of Pugwash 1990, London 1991, pp. 98-108; The Verification of the Biological Weapons Convention and International Law, in: O. Thränert (ed.), The Verification of the Biological Weapons Convention: Problems and Perspectives, Bonn 1992, pp. 31-37.

5 Kombattantenstatus oder völkerrechtlicher Sonderstatus der Polizei? Stand und Entwicklungstendenzen des in internationalen bewaffneten Konflikten anwendbaren Völkerrechts, in: Zeitschrift für den Bundesgrenzschutz 22.12 (1972), pp. 6-8; Die Kampfführungsbestimmungen des I. Protokolls unter besonderer Berücksichtigung des Kombattantenstatus, in: Neue Zeitschrift für Wehrrecht 21 (1979), pp. 98-100; Rules of National Law Relating to Combatant Status – Introductory Report, in: M. Bothe/P. Macalister-Smith/Th. Kurzidem (eds.), National Implementation of International Humani-

and laws and customs of warfare[6], and of course time and again on topical problems relating to the renewed Geneva and Hague Conventions. Those problems arose in part out of events, such as the Second Gulf War in 1992[7] and the NATO Kosovo mission in 1999[8]. With regard to the conference, the publications on international criminal law – on the Tokyo Trial to be more precise[9] – are also worth mentioning. Despite this academic approach, *Knut Ipsen* has never lived in a university ivory tower. Quite to the contrary, he took part in the practical development of international humanitarian law. From 1975 to 1977, he was member of and counsellor on public international law to the German government's delegation to the Geneva Conference on International Humanitarian Law applicable in Armed Conflicts[10]. From 1978 to 1980, he performed the same functions at the Conference on Prohibitions or Restrictions on the Use of Certain Conventional Weapons. Moreover, he founded the interdisciplinary Institute for International Law of Peace and Armed Conflict.

This short overview presents only a small – if central – part of *Knut Ipsen*'s work. Nevertheless, it is not surprising that this birthday symposium is dedicated to the new challenges international humanitarian law is facing due to current events. International humanitarian law has been confronted with challenges be-

---

tarian Law, Dordrecht/Boston 1990, pp. 113-116; Kombattanten und Kriegsgefangene, in: H. Schöttler/B. Hoffmann (eds.), Die Genfer Zusatzprotokolle – Kommentare und Analysen, Bonn 1993, pp. 136-156.

6 Zum Begriff des "internationalen bewaffneten Konflikts", in: J. Delbrück/K. Ipsen/D. Rauschning (eds.), Recht im Dienst des Friedens, Festschrift für Eberhard Menzel zum 65. Geburtstag, Berlin 1975, pp. 405-425; Die Kennzeichnung ziviler Krankenhäuser mit dem Emblem des Roten Kreuzes, in: Humanitäres Völkerrecht – Informationsschriften 1.1 (1988), pp. 4-13; "Perfidy", in: R. Bernhardt (ed.), Encyclopedia of Public International Law, Vol. III, Amsterdam/Lausanne/New York/Oxford/Shannon/Singapore/Tokyo 1997, pp. 978-981; Neue Entwicklungen im Humanitären Völkerrecht, in: W. Voit (ed.), Vereinte Nationen und humanitäres Völkerrecht – Rechtsentwicklung und Rechtsanwendung…, Bochum 1997, pp. 3-18; Relativierung des "absoluten" Gewaltverbots? Zur Problematik der Erstanwendung zwischenstaatlicher Waffengewalt, in: K. Ipsen/Chr. Raap/T. Stein/A. A. Steinkamm (eds.), Wehrrecht und Friedenssicherung, Festschrift für Klaus Dau zum 65. Geburtstag, Neuwied/Kriftel 1999, pp. 103-120.

7 Auswirkungen des Golfkriegs auf das humanitäre Völkerrecht, in: W. Voit (ed.), Das humanitäre Völkerrecht im Golfkrieg und andere Rotkreuz-Fragen, Bochm 1992, pp. 29-48.

8 Der Kosovo-Einsatz – Illegal? Gerechtfertigt? Entschuldbar?, in: Friedenswarte 74 (1999), pp. 19-23.

9 A Review of the Main Legal Aspects of the Tokyo Trial and Their Influence on the Development of International Law, in: Ch. Hosoya/N. Ando/Y. Onuma/R. Minear (eds.), The Tokyo War Crimes Trial: An International Symposium, Tokyo 1986, pp. 37-44; Das "Tokyo Trial" im Lichte des seinerzeit geltenden Völkerrechts, in: R. D. Herzberg (ed.), Festschrift für Dietrich Ohler zum 65. Geburtstag, Cologne/Berlin/Bonn/Munich 1985, pp. 505-515.

10 See *M. Bothe/K. Ipsen/K. J. Partsch*, Die Genfer Konferenz über humanitäres Völkerrecht – Verlauf und Ergebnisse, in: Zeitschrift für ausländisches öffentliches Recht und Völkerrecht 38 (1978), pp. 1-159.

fore. For instance, the four Geneva Conventions of 1949 had to assimilate the experiences from the Second World War. The aforementioned conference on the two additional protocols *Knut Ipsen* participated in had to deal with the effects post-World War developments had had on international humanitarian law.

The first additional protocol, relating to the protection of victims of international armed conflicts, had to come to terms with liberation movements that had obtained de facto authority in their respective territories. These liberation movements consequently had to be integrated into international humanitarian law, since otherwise they would not be bound by it. In addition, the protection by the Geneva Conventions had to be extended to include wounded, sick and shipwrecked civilians, civilian medical personnel and units, and religious personnel. Apart from regulations concerning missing and dead persons and concerning the protection of civilian population, new weapons and their development had to be subjected to the prohibitory provisions of the protocol and other relevant international regulations.[11]

These developments were complemented by efforts in favour of the protection of victims of non-international armed conflicts, leading from article 3 common to the Geneva Conventions to the second additional protocol. The draft by the International Committee of the Red Cross (ICRC) included an expansion similar to that of the first additional protocol. However, numerous states objected to this for fear of interference with their internal affairs, resulting in no agreement on the draft relating to the protection of civilians, but only on the protection of the wounded, sick and shipwrecked, and of medical and religious personnel. Also, they agreed on a more precise definition of what should be considered "humane treatment".[12]

Looking at the renewals international humanitarian law underwent in the seventies, the question arises what challenges the international community is facing today.

One of those challenges is represented by the asymmetries of warfare. International humanitarian law is based on the assumption that equal parties or at least two states face each other. Modern conflicts, however, are characterised by strong asymmetries of military capabilities. In asymmetric conflicts the threat of reciprocity is a merely weak one. Thus, in certain constellations, the stronger party may infringe the laws and customs of war without risking their own soldiers or civilians to fall victims to a violation of international humanitarian law, and the weaker party may see its only way to overcome the other party's strength by taking recourse to unlawful methods. Infringement of the laws and customs of war then leads to military advantages.[13]

---

11 Supra note 10, pp. 7-10, 14-20, 22-24.

12 Supra note 10, pp. 69-70, 72-81.

13 *R. Barnett*, Asymmetrical Warfare: Today's Challenge to U.S. Military Power, Washington 2003; *R. Kolb*, Perspektiven des "humanitären Völkerrechts", in: Jusletter 16 September 2002, para. 14; *T. Pfanner*, Asymmetrical warfare from the perspective of humanitarian law and humanitarian action, in: International Review of the Red Cross 87 (2005), pp. 151-153; see the contribution of *Michael N. Schmitt* to this volume, pp. 11 et seq.

Another challenge to the international community is the impact of modern warfare on international humanitarian law. The duty to distinguish between military and civilian targets and not to attack the latter represents one of the leading principles in international humanitarian law. This victim-oriented approach is increasingly replaced by an operation-oriented approach. So-called zero death-strategies, as employed by the United States, are aimed at minimising the death risk for the own soldiers. For instance, air raids are carried out from great heights, so as not to be in reach of adversary air defence. Consequently, aiming precision decreases and there are more errors, stray bombs, and unintended collateral damage. During the Kosovo conflict, for example, NATO accidentally destroyed the Chinese embassy in Belgrade. The term "collateral damage" gained such notoriety that it even became German "Buzz word of the Year 1999"[14].

Military interests tend to overpower the laws and customs of war. This constitutes a very real risk of long-term damage to international humanitarian law. It is regrettable that of all states it is western democracies that show less and less scruples when it comes to the use of force.[15]

The definition of status groups in international humanitarian law confronts the international community with topical problems, too. Some states believe international humanitarian law to be against their own vital interests. For instance, the rights granted to prisoners of war according to the Third and Fourth Geneva Conventions are considered inconvenient. To prevent international humanitarian law from being applicable and thus being able to act free from the boundaries of it, some states simply alter the definition of what constitutes a prisoner of war.

The camp in Guantánamo Bay is one example for this practice. The United States deny Guantánamo Bay captives the status of prisoners of war because article 17 of the Third Geneva Convention restricts the questioning of prisoners of war. Instead, they are termed "unlawful combatants". The location of the camp makes it impossible for captives to take legal actions before U.S. courts, which they would be able to do if detained on U.S. territory. As a consequence, according to United States policy, neither international humanitarian law nor U.S. laws apply to Guantánamo Bay captives. Even the U.S. Supreme Court voiced doubts as to the lawfulness of this. Nevertheless, the international community is rather hesitant in raising objections.[16]

---

14 See at http://www.unwortdesjahres.org/unwoerter.htm.

15 *R. Kolb*, supra note 13, para. 13; *M. Lippmann*, Aerial Attacks on Civilians and the Humanitarian Law of War: Technology and Terror from World War I to Afghanistan, in: California Western International Law Journal 33 (2002/2003), p. 67; *M. N. Schmitt*, Precision attack and international humanitarian law, in: International Review of the Red Cross 87 (2005), p. 462; *V. Wiebe*, Footprints of Death: Cluster Bombs as Indiscriminate Weapons under International Humanitarian Law, in: Michigan Journal of International Law 22 (2000/2001), p. 104; see the contribution of *William Hays Parks* to this volume, pp. 65 et seq.

16 *S. R. Shapiro*, The Role of the Courts in the War Against Terrorism: A Preliminary Assessment, in: Fletcher Forum of World Affairs 29.1 (2005), p. 107-116; *J. Wieczorek*, Unrechtmäßige Kombattanten und humanitäres Völkerrecht, Berlin 2005; *A. de Zayas*,

Prisoners of war are just one of many different status groups in international humanitarian law.[17]

During the past ten years, numerous means for prosecuting severe crimes against international law have been created. The most prominent ones are certainly the International Criminal Tribunals for the former Yugoslavia and Rwanda and the International Criminal Court in The Hague. Their main purpose is a broader and more effective implementation of international humanitarian law by building up tremendous pressure through personal liability for war crimes. But this development comprises risks which must not be underestimated, though. Today's omnipresent emphasis on personal liability may well lead to the undermining of state responsibility. And numerous questions regarding the relationship between personal criminal responsibility and state responsibility are still unanswered.[18]

The most basic precondition of implementing international humanitarian law is the knowledge of the law itself. First and foremost, this is true for states and their organs. In armed conflicts, it is therefore crucial for soldiers to know the law. The past decades have shown, however, that dissemination of international humanitarian law has been neglected somewhat by the states. The cause of this might be found partly in a poorly developed judicial infrastructure of the armed forces. At the same time, the lack of knowledge might also result from the fact that states experience humanitarian law more and more as no more than a burdensome duty, rather than a moral commitment.[19]

The underlying problem to all of the aforementioned challenges is an increasing acceptance of war as a means of law enforcement. Often, the war-waging parties even refer to public international law when it comes to justifying their actions. In this context, it is most alarming that to obey international humanitarian law seems to have become something of a replacement for the observance of the principle of the prohibition of force. Some states foster the impression that non-violation of international humanitarian law legitimises the use of force. International humanitarian law, ius in bello, thrusts aside the principle of prohibition of force, ius contra bellum. This development constitutes a dramatic weakening of the law on war prevention as it is laid down in article 2, section 4 UN Charter. Hence, one could observe that at the present time, the concept of a just war experiences a creeping renaissance. Particularly the Great Powers may never have been thrilled at seeing their capacities to act restricted by a narrow interpretation of the principle of the prohibition of the threat or use of force. However, since the beginning of the nineties, this principle has become ever weaker. Freed from the impediments of the Cold War and the balance of powers, some states are turning more and more directly to the use of force to achieve their aims. If they expect the UN Security

The Statuts of Guantánamo Bay and the Status of the Detainees, in: University of British Columbia Law Review 37 (2004), p. 277.

17 See the contribution of *Yoram Dinstein* to this volume, pp. 145 et seq.

18 See the contribution of *Dieter Fleck* to this volume, pp. 171 et seq.

19 See the contribution of *Knut Dörmann* to this volume, pp. 227 et seq.

Council not to give the go-ahead, they simply defy it, as happened in the Kosovo conflict and the war on Iraq.[20]

It is the intent of this volume to contribute to the understanding of contemporary challenges to international humanitarian law. Access to the matter is hereby provided by distinguished experts in their field of research or profession, whose contributions are in the continuity of the work of *Knut Ipsen*.

---

20 *Chr. Enemark/Chr. Michaelsen*, Just War Doctrine and the Invasion of Iraq, in: Australian Journal of Politics and History 51 (2005), pp. 545-563; *M. Glennon*, Why the Security Council Failed, in: Foreign Affairs 82.2 (2003), p. 16; *R. Kolb*, supra note 13, para. 11; *W. M. Reisman*, Assessing Claims to Revise the Laws of War, in: American Journal of International Law 97 (2003), p. 90; *J.-A. Schulze*, Der Irak-Krieg 2003 im Lichte der Wiederkehr des gerechten Krieges, Berlin 2005.

Asymmetries with regard to Methods and Means of Warfare

Asymmetrical Warfare and International Humanitarian Law

Michael N. Schmitt

George C. Marshall European Center for Security Studies, Garmisch-Partenkirchen

In much the same way the notion of "revolutions in military affairs" dominated the attention of military thinkers in the last decade, "asymmetry" has now become the catch-phrase *du jour*. Yet, asymmetry hardly represents a radically new operational model, for it is in the very nature of warfare to seek strategies, tactics, and weapons that either leverage one's own strengths (positive asymmetry) or exploit the enemy's weaknesses (negative asymmetry), or both. *Sun Tzu* understood this two and a half millennia ago when he proclaimed "an army may be likened to water, for just as flowing water avoids the heights and hastens to the lowlands, so an army avoids strengths and strikes weaknesses."[1] Centuries later, General *Curtis E. LeMay*, who, while the USAF Chief of Staff in 1964, famously set out his asymmetrical recipe for ending the Vietnam war: "They've got to draw in their horns and stop their aggression, or we're going to bomb them back into the Stone Age."[2] Modern foes also grasp the dynamics of asymmetry in warfare, a fact well illustrated by none other than Osama bin Laden.

"The difference between us and our adversaries in terms of military strength, manpower, and equipment is very huge. But, for the grace of God, the difference is also very huge in terms of psychological resources, faith, certainty, and reliance on the Almighty God. This difference between us and them is very, very huge and great."[3]

This article explores asymmetry's influence on the law governing methods and means of warfare. International humanitarian law (IHL) and war exist in a symbiotic relationship. Most typically, IHL reacts to shifts in the nature of warfare; indeed, most major humanitarian law treaties arrived on the heels of a major conflict

1 *Sun Tzu*, The Art of War, Oxford U.P., Samuel B. Griffith trans., 1971, p. 101.

2 *Curtis E. LeMay*, Mission with LeMay, Doubleday, 1965, p. 565.

3 Foreign Broadcast Information System, Al-Jazirah Airs 'Selected Portions' of Latest Al-Qa'ida Tape on 11 Sep. Attacks, Doha Al-Jazirah Satellite Channel Television in Arabic 1835 GMT 18 Apr. 02, Compilation of Usama Bin Laden Statements 1994-January 2004 (January 2004), at 191, 194.

in response to *post factum* concerns over particular aspects thereof.[4] As importantly, the nature of the hostilities in which belligerents find themselves shapes their attitude towards IHL. When they view law as serving their needs, for instance by protecting their civilians, fidelity to legal strictures is usually high. On the other hand, when belligerents see themselves as disadvantaged by normative boundaries, those boundaries may well be ignored.[5] This being so, in what ways does asymmetry in 21st century warfare affect application of IHL?[6]

Forms of Asymmetry

To grasp the normative consequences of asymmetry, it is necessary to conceive of the notion very broadly. *Steven Metz* and *Douglas Johnston* of the US Army War College have fashioned a particularly useful definition in this regard. According to *Metz* and *Johnson*,

---

4 The US Civil War motivated adoption of Professor *Francis Lieber*'s "set of regulations" (Lieber Code) as General Order No. 100, U.S. Dep't of Army, Instructions for the Government of Armies of the United States in the Field; the Battle of Solferino during the Italian War of Liberation, and the resulting monograph "Souvenir de Solferino" by *Henri Dunant* (1862), led to creation of the International Committee of the Red Cross; the Russo-Japanese War of 1904-05 was followed by the Geneva Convention of 1906 and the Hague Conventions of 1907; World War I was followed by the 1925 Gas Protocol and the 1929 Geneva Convention; World War II was followed by the Geneva Conventions of 1949 and the 1954 Cultural Property Convention; and Korea, Vietnam, and the "wars of national liberation" were followed by the Additional Protocols to the 1949 Geneva Conventions, the Environmental Modification Convention, and the Conventional Weapons Convention. Each of the aforementioned instruments is available on the ICRC IHL Documents Website, www.icrc.org/ihl.
There have been a few proactive attempts to limit methods or means of warfare, most notably the bans on blinding lasers and biological weapons. Additional Protocol to the Convention on the Prohibitions or Restrictions on the Use of Certain Conventional Weapons Which May Be Deemed to Be Excessively Injurious or to Have Indiscriminate Effects, Protocol on Blinding Laser Weapons (1995); Protocol for the Prohibition of the Use in War of Asphyxiating, Poisonous, or Other Gases, and of Bacteriological Methods of Warfare (1925); Convention on the Prohibition of the Development, Production and Stockpiling of Bacteriological (Biological) and Toxin Weapons and on Their Destruction (1972).

5 The recent US memos on torture illustrate this dynamic graphically. The memos are reproduced in *Mark Danner*, Torture and the Truth: America, Abu Ghraib, and the War on Terror, Granta Books, 2004; *Karen J. Greenberg/Joshua L. Dratel* (eds.), The Torture Papers: The Road to Abu Ghraib, Cambridge U.P., 2005, pp. 144, 145, 153-69. For a graphic description of mistreatment, see *Tim Golden*, In U.S. Report, Brutal Details of 2 Afghan Inmates' Deaths, in: New York Times, May 20, 2005, at A1.

6 For a recent discussion of this subject, see *Toni Pfanner*, Asymmetrical Warfare from the Perspective of Humanitarian Law and Humanitarian Action, in: International Review of the Red Cross, March 2005, p. 149.

"[i]n the realm of military affairs and national security, asymmetry is acting, organizing, and thinking differently than opponents in order to maximize one's own advantages, exploit an opponent's weaknesses, attain the initiative, or gain greater freedom of action. It can be political-strategic, military strategic, or a combination of these. It can entail different methods, technologies, values, organizations, time perspectives, or some combination of these. It can be short-term or long-term. It can be deliberate or by default. It can be discrete or pursued in combination with symmetric approaches. It can have both psychological and physical dimensions."[7]

As is apparent, asymmetry has many dimensions. It operates across the entire spectrum of conflict, from the tactical through the operational to the strategic levels of war.[8] For example, at the tactical level, troops with lightweight body armour

---

7 *Steven Metz/Douglas V. Johnson II*, Asymmetry and U.S. Military Strategy: Definition, Background, and Strategic Concepts, US Army War College, Strategic Studies Institute, January 2001. For an interesting argument that the concept of asymmetry has been "twisted beyond utility," see *Stephen J. Blank*, Rethinking Asymmetric Threats, US Army War College, Strategic Studies Institute, September 2003. Other useful material on asymmetry includes *Ivan Arrequin-Toft,* How the Weak Win Wars: A Theory of Asymmetric Conflict, in: International Security, Summer 2001, p. 19; *Steven J. Lambakis*, Reconsidering Asymmetric Warfare, in: Joint Force Quarterly, December 2004, p. 102; *Montgomery C. Meigs*, Unorthodox Thoughts about Asymmetric Warfare, in: Parameters, Summer 2003, p. 4; *R.V. Gusentine*, Asymmetric Warfare – On Our Terms, in: Proceedings of the United States naval Institute, August 2002, p. 58.

8 The Department of Defense "Dictionary of Military and Associated Terms" sets forth the following definitions for the levels of war:
"*Strategic Level of War*: The level of war at which a nation, often as a member of a group of nations, determines, national or multinational (alliance or coalition) security objectives and guidance, and develops and uses national resources to accomplish these objectives. Activities at this level establish national and multinational military objectives; sequence initiatives; define limits and assess risks for the use of military and other instruments of national power; develop global plans or theater war plans to achieve these objectives; and provide military forces and other capabilities in accordance with strategic plans.
Operational Level of War: The level of war at which campaigns and major operations are planned, conducted, and sustained to accomplish strategic objectives within theaters or other operational areas. Activities at this level link tactics and strategy by establishing operational objectives needed to accomplish the strategic objectives, sequencing events to achieve the operational objectives, initiating actions, and applying resources to bring about and sustain these events. These activities imply a broader dimension of time or space than do tactics; they ensure the logistic and administrative support of tactical forces, and provide the means by which tactical successes are exploited to achieve strategic objectives.
Tactical Level of War: The level of war at which battles and engagements are planned and executed to accomplish military objectives assigned to tactical units or task forces. Activities at this level focus on the ordered arrangement and maneuver of combat elements in relation to each other and to the enemy to achieve combat objectives."

have a distinct advantage over those without advanced protection. At the operational level, a networked force with real-time access to state-of-the-art C4ISR assets has a much better understanding of the battle. This allows it to act more quickly and decisively than does its enemy.[9] The strategic level of conflict has both military and political dimensions. At the military strategic level, asymmetry may itself become a strategy. Terrorism is the most compelling contemporary exemplar. Political strategies with military impact include the formation of alliances, crafting humanitarian law or arms control regimes, and other efforts to leverage diplomacy, law, information, and economics to enhance one's military wherewithal.[10]

Asymmetry not only acts at different levels, it also takes multiple forms. Most noticeable is technological asymmetry, which occurs when one side of a conflict possesses superior weapon systems and other military equipment (means of warfare).[11] Currently, the US military far outdistances all other armed forces in this regard. Other Western countries, primarily those in NATO, occupy a second tier of technological advantage. The militaries that remain have little hope of reaching such levels. This reality is unlikely to change anytime in the near future, for US investment in research and development dwarfs that of all other nations.[12] Of course, some technology will "trickle down", but those who benefit in this way are the least likely to find themselves at odds with the United States. The existing qualitative divide can only be expected to grow.

(Department of Defense Dictionary of Military and Associated Terms, Joint Publication 1-02, as amended through November 20, 2004, www.dtic.mil/ doctrine/jel/doddict/).

9 C4ISR: Command, control, communications, intelligence, surveillance, reconnaissance. Intelligence is "the *product* resulting from the collection, processing, integration, analysis, evaluation, and interpretation of available information concerning foreign countries or areas." Surveillance is the "*systematic observation* of aerospace, surface, or subsurface areas, places, persons, or things, by visual, aural, electronic, photographic, or other means." Reconnaissance is "a *mission* undertaken to obtain, by visual observation or other detection methods, information about the activities and resources of an enemy or potential enemy, or to secure data concerning the meteorological, hydrographic, or geographic characteristics of a particular area." DoD Dictionary, supra note 8.

10 Asymmetry can also relate to the level of violence in a conflict. In high-intensity conflict, technological advantage is usually more determinative than in low-intensity conflict. The impact of asymmetry can also be temporally determined. For instance, technological asymmetry, as demonstrated in Iraq, impacts the conflict more during the core hostilities, than during periods of occupation.

11 Technological asymmetry has become much more significant in modern warfare than numerical ones.

12 The US defence budget for 2003 (most recent comparative figures available) was 404.9 billion dollars. Compare this figure with: Germany, 35.1b$; UK, 42b$; France 45.7b$; China, 55.9b$; and Russia, 65.2b$. *International Institute of Strategic Studies*, Strategic Balance 2004-2005. The United States spent 26.2% of this amount on investment (research, development, acquisition). Available comparable figures for Germany and the UK are 18.5% and 24.4%, respectively. NATO Press Release 146 (2003).

A second form of military asymmetry involves methods of warfare, specifically doctrines.[13] For advanced Western militaries, effects-based operations (EBO) have replaced attrition warfare as the pre-eminent asymmetrical operational concept.[14] Effects-based operations are designed to generate defined effects on an opponent. Terrorism also constitutes an asymmetrical doctrinal concept.[15] Increasingly adopted by low-tech forces to counter the military pre-eminence of their opponents, it is analogous to, albeit more nefarious than, the guerrilla warfare that was so effective against US technological dominance in Vietnam.

Less obvious forms of asymmetry also influence the application of IHL. A conflict can be normatively asymmetrical when different legal or policy norms govern the belligerents. Normative asymmetry may even exist between allies. Conflicts can also be asymmetrical with regard to the participants therein. Although IHL is based on the premise of hostilities between armed forces (or militia and other groups that are similarly situated and meet set criteria), actors in modern warfare increasingly deviate from this paradigm. Finally, belligerents may be asymmetrically positioned by virtue of their *jus ad bellum* status or moral standing, real *or perceived.* Of course, when notions of legal or moral valence infuse the resort to arms, attitudes towards the application of IHL are inevitably shaped accordingly. It is to the impact of such asymmetries on international humanitarian law that we now turn.

---

13 Doctrine consists of "[f]undamental principles by which the military forces or elements thereof guide their actions in support of national objectives." DoD Dictionary, supra note 8.

14 The United States Air Force has expressly adopted asymmetry as a doctrine.
US military forces now employ sophisticated military capabilities to achieve national objectives and avoid costly force-on-force engagements that characterized the traditional strategies of attrition and annihilation that evolved from nineteenth century warfare. Airpower is particularly relevant to this new way of war or, as it is commonly referred to, "asymmetric force strategy". Asymmetric force strategy dictates applying US strengths against adversary vulnerabilities and enabling the US to directly attack an enemy's centers of gravity (COGs) without placing Americans or allies at risk unnecessarily.
United States Air Force, Air Warfare, Doctrine Document 2-1, January 22, 2000, at 3. For a concise description of EBO, see Department of Defense, Effects-based Operations Briefing, March 19, 2003, www.defenselink.mil/news/Mar2003/g030318-D-9085.html. On EBO and law, see *Michael N. Schmitt*, Aerial Effects-Based Operations and the Law of Armed Conflict, paper presented at a conference to mark the launch of the "UK Manual of the Law of Armed Conflict", Oxford University, July 2004.

15 Terrorism represents a form of EBO since the true targets are seldom an attack's immediate victims, but rather the attitudes of the population, political leaders, members of the armed forces, international community, and so forth.

Asymmetry and IHL

Each of the cited forms of asymmetry – technological, doctrinal, normative, participatory, and legal or moral standing – exerts measurable influence on the application of international humanitarian law. A disturbing example is mistreatment of detainees by members of the United States armed forces.[16] However, this paper limits itself to those aspects of IHL governing means (weapons) and methods (tactics) of warfare. Because technological asymmetry has the greatest relevance to the application and interpretation of IHL, most discussion will focus on that form.

Technological Asymmetry. The technological edge enjoyed by the United States and other advanced militaries is sometimes misunderstood. In wars of the last century, range, precision, and mobility were the dominant media of technological asymmetry, a reflection of the linear construct of the battlefield. With forces facing each other across a FEBA (forward edge of the battle area), the immediate objective of warfare was to weaken the enemy sufficiently to allow one's own forces to seize territory. You wore the enemy down through attrition warfare, the serial destruction of its military. Being able to shoot farther with greater accuracy than the other side was obviously useful in conducting attrition warfare. So was greater mobility, because it allowed your forces to avoid the enemy's assaults and strike at its weaker flanks.

Today, battlefields are multi-dimensional, i.e., technology has evolved to the point where the concept of a line marking the heart of the battle (with combat fading the greater the distance from that line) no longer makes sense. There may be ground forces facing each other, but the conflict is everywhere. Consider Operation Iraqi Freedom (OIF). During the campaign, there was literally no point within Iraq untouchable by Coalition forces. Indeed, the first blow of the war was not the crossing of the Iraqi border by an invasion force, but rather an attack by Tomahawk cruise missiles and F-117s designed to kill Saddam Hussein.

In this environment, an ability to rapidly gather, process, and react to information about an opponent, while hindering the enemy's efforts to do the same, is even more determinative than range, precision, and mobility. Using networked C4ISR unavailable to the other side, friendly forces seek to "get inside the enemy's observe-orient-decide-act (OODA) loop."[17] In other words, acting more

[16] To some extent, mistreatment of Afghan and Iraqi (and other nationality) prisoners was made "more acceptable" by the unlikelihood that US troops would be taken prisoner and mistreated in return. In other words, reciprocity did not operate as the incentive for compliance it usually acts as in IHL. No US soldiers were taken prisoner in Afghanistan. Nine were seized in Iraq, eight of which were rescued. CNN, War in Iraq, www.cnn.com/SPECIALS/2003/iraq/forces/pow.mia/.

[17] *Colonel J. Boyd*, USAF, coined the term. Operating within an opponent's OODA loop is a decision-making concept in which one party, maintaining constant situational awareness, assesses a situation and acts on it more rapidly than its opponent. When this happens, the opponent is forced into a reactive mode, thereby allowing the first party to maintain the initiative. As the process proceeds, the opponent eventually begins to react

quickly than the enemy forces him to become purely reactive, thereby allowing you to control the flow, pace, and direction of battle. Eventually he becomes so disoriented that paralysis ensues. In this style of warfare, the technological edge that matters most is C4ISR – and it is in C4ISR that the gap between the technological "haves" and "have-nots" is widest and still growing.

Operating inside an opponent's OODA loop requires: the ability to locate and accurately identify enemy forces quickly and reliably; weapon systems that are immediately available; sufficient command and control assets to monitor and direct fast-paced, changing engagements; and the capacity to conduct reliable battle damage assessment to determine if restrike is needed. Slowing the enemy's reaction time and blocking or distorting enemy information further enhances the effects of your own operations.

Modern technology fills these requirements. Today, the battlefield has become phenomenally transparent to those fielding advanced ISR assets. No longer are the obstacles that traditionally masked enemy activity – such as night, poor weather, range, terrain, and intelligence processing and distribution times – insurmountable. Moreover, today's advanced militaries draw on information from an amazing array of sources: imagery intelligence (IMINT); human intelligence (HUMINT); signals intelligence (SIGINT); measurement and signature intelligence (MASINT); open-source intelligence (OSINT); technical intelligence (TECHINT); and counterintelligence (CI).[18] This multi-source data can be fused and disseminated with such extraordinary speed that US air forces have developed a methodology (Time Sensitive Targeting – TST) to specifically leverage the narrowing sensor-to-shooter window.[19]

Of course, technology is fallible. For instance, US forces conducted 50 TST decapitation strikes against Iraqi leaders using cell phones fixes and human intelligence reporting. None succeeded.[20] Earlier, during Operation Allied Force (OAF), critics claimed that NATO air strikes against tanks "identified" through high-tech means often stuck decoys.[21] Despite these alleged failures, the fact remains that on

to actions that no longer bear on the immediate situation. The resulting confusion causes paralysis.

18 *Joint Chiefs of Staff*, Doctrine for Intelligence Support to Joint Operations, Joint Publication 2-0, March 9, 2000, Figure II-2.

19 On the topic, see *US Joint Forces Command Joint Warfighting Center*, Commander's Handbook for Joint Time-Sensitive Targeting, March 22, 2002, www.jwf.jte.osd.mil/pdf/tsthndbk.pdf. TST strikes were carried out during Operations Enduring Freedom and Iraqi Freedom. Although the process has been criticized, US forces continue to refine the methodology. *Leonard LaVella*, Operation Enduring Freedom Time Sensitive Targeting Process Study (prepared for USAF-ACC/DRY), August 25, 2003, on file with author.

20 *Human Rights Watch*, Off Target: The Conduct of the War and Civilian Casualties in Iraq, December 2003, pp. 21-40, www.hrw.org/reports/2003/usa1203/. On the legality of the strikes, see *Michael N. Schmitt*, The Conduct of Hostilities during Operation Iraqi Freedom: An International Humanitarian Law Assessment, in: Yearbook of International Humanitarian Law (2003), pp. 73 et seq.

21 For an assessment of strikes against mobile targets during Operation Allied Force, see *Department of Defense*, Report to Congress: Kosovo/Operation Allied Force After-Ac-

21st century battlefields, systems such as satellites, AWACS, JSTARS, UAVs, counter-battery radar, and night vision goggles – all of which are now commonplace in the battlespace – render an opponent's activities remarkably observable.[22]

The weapons systems on hand to exploit this information are equally impressive. Combat aircraft ranging from the F-16 to the B-52 now often launch without a set target, relying instead on the systems described above to feed data to powerful command and control assets that in turn vector them to the attack. They can fly and strike at night and during poor weather,[23] loiter for extended periods (espe-

tion Report, January 31, 2000, pp. 84-86; *Rebecca Grant*, The Kosovo Campaign: Aerospace Power Made it Work, Air Force Association, September 1999, p. 23.

22 The E-3 Sentry is an airborne warning and control system (AWACS) providing surveillance, command, weapons control, battle management, and communications services in the aerial environment. It is distinguishable by the large rotating radar dome (radome) mounted on its fuselage, which is capable of identifying and tracking low-altitude targets out to 400 kilometres, and medium and high altitude targets at significantly greater distances. Defensively, AWACS detects enemy aircraft or missiles and directs fighters to intercept them. Offensively, it can monitor the battlespace, providing real-time location and identification of enemy and friendly aircraft and naval vessels to users at the tactical, operational, and strategic levels of warfare.
The E-8C Joint Surveillance Target Attack Radar System (JSTARS) is an airborne battle management, command and control, intelligence, surveillance and reconnaissance aircraft that provides ground and air commanders with information that supports attacks on enemy ground forces. Its radar can cover a 50,000 square kilometre area and detect potential targets 250 kilometres away.
Unmanned Aerial vehicle (UAV) are aircraft without a human crew. The RQ-1 Predator provides surveillance, reconnaissance, and target acquisition services over long periods of time. Its detection capabilities include a TV camera, an infrared camera, and synthetic aperture radar for looking through smoke, clouds or haze. The MQ-1 variant is armed with two Hellfire missiles, thereby allowing it to directly engage targets. A third UAV in service is the Global Hawk. Unlike the Predator, which is a medium level system, the Global Hawk flies at high level (thereby enhancing survivability and extending its coverage). It has great range and loitering capability; for instance, it can fly to an interest area over 1,600 kilometres away and remain on station for 24 hours. Using synthetic aperture radar, a ground moving target indicator, and high-resolution electro-optical and infrared sensors, it collects information that is transmitted to users near real-time.
Counter-battery fire is merely fire delivered to suppress an enemy's fire (e.g., from mortars or artillery) after detecting its source. Aircraft or ground observers may identify the source. Today, radar is often used to calculate the source of an incoming shell.

23 For instance, F-15 and 16s rely on the Low Altitude Navigation and Targeting Infrared for Night (LANTIRN) to fly at night and in poor weather. Using terrain-following radar and an infrared sensor, the pod allows the aircraft to follow the contour of the earth at low level. High-resolution forward-looking infrared radar (FLIR) feeds the pilot an infrared target image, while a laser designator-rangefinder and target tracking software facilitate target identification and attack. A second precision targeting system is the LITENING pod, which is used day or night in all weather conditions. It employs high-resolution FLIR, a television camera for target imagery, automatic target tracking, and laser designation for acquiring multiple targets simultaneously. In addition to the F-15 and 16, it can be carried by the A-10 and B-52.

cially when tankers are available), and in many cases fire their weapons from beyond the threat envelope of enemy defences.[24] Precision systems dramatically increase the probability of damage (Pd) resulting from such attacks.[25] Today, modern weaponry has a circular error probable (CEP) measured in feet, tens of feet at worst.[26] The fielding of the JDAM is making precision weaponry widely available.[27]

Further, as attack aircraft penetrate heavily defended enemy territory, high-tech jamming, escort, and wild weasel aircraft effectively neutralize enemy defences.[28] The Operation Iraqi Freedom air campaign illustrates the value of defence suppression missions. Although flying 20,733 fighter/bomber sorties over territory with degraded, albeit still potent air defences, the Coalition lost only one aircraft to hostile fire, an A-10 Warthog.[29] Airframes such as cruise missiles, UAVs, and stealth aircraft limit the need for defence suppression, thereby freeing up aircraft that would otherwise perform such missions to conduct attacks themselves.

---

24 For example, the AGM (air-to-ground missile) 154 JSOW (Joint Stand-off Weapon) has the following ranges: unpowered low-altitude launch – 24 km; unpowered high-altitude launch – 64 km; powered launch – 200 km. GlobalSecurity.org, available at www.globalsecurity.org/military/systems/.

25 Probability of damage (Pd) is Pd is used to express the statistical probability (percentage or decimal) that specified damage criteria can be met assuming the probability of arrival. *United States Air Force*, Intelligence Targeting Guide, AF Pamphlet 14-210, February 1, 1998, pp. 59-60. For non-nuclear weapons, damage criteria include F-Kill (Fire-power kill), M-Kill (Mobility kill), K-Kill (Catastrophic Kill), FC-Kill (Fire Control Kill), PTO-Kill (Prevent Takeoff Kill), I-Kill (Interdiction Kill), SW-Kill (Seaworthiness Kill), Cut, and Block. Id., p. 58.

26 The two most frequently dropped guided weapons in Operation Iraqi Freedom were the GBU 12 laser-guided Bomb and the GBU 32 Joint Direct Attack Munition. Their CEP (radius of a circle within which 50% of the weapons will strike) is 9 and 13 meters respectively. GlobalSecurity.org, supra note 24.

27 The JDAM is an unguided free fall bomb to which a guidance tail kit has been attached. It has an unclassified CEP of approximately 13 meters from as far away as 15 miles (an upgrade will improve accuracy to 3 meters) based on global positioning system (satellite) and inertial navigation system guidance. What makes the JDAM unique are its price tag (roughly $20,000) and the fact that nearly all US combat aircraft can carry them. GlobalSecurity.org, supra note 24. 30 % of the 19,948 guided munitions employed in Operation Iraqi Freedom were JDAMs. *US Central Command Air Forces*, Assessment and Analysis Division, Operation Iraqi Freedom – By the Numbers, April 30, 2003, p. 11, at www.globalsecurity.org/military/library/report/2003/uscentaf_oif_report_30apr2003.pdf.

28 Wild weasel aircraft such as the F-16C use the AGM-88 HARM (high speed anti-radiation missile) to target enemy radar. The HARM contains a fixed antenna and seeker head that hones in on radar emissions. With a 30-mile range, it needs only a small 40-pound warhead to destroy its fragile target.

29 By the Numbers, supra note 27, pp. 3, 7-8; Losses also included four Apache and two Cobra helicopters. Id. Iraqi air defences had been degraded by Operations Northern Watch and Southern Watch air strikes prior to commencement of Operation Iraqi Freedom. These operations monitored the no-fly zones in northern and southern Iraq.

Most significant among the technological wizardry is a networked command and control system that links information, decision-makers, and shooters in real-time. Observing the unfolding battle, commanders are able to move the right assets to the right location at the right time, either to exploit an opportunity or defend vulnerabilities. In some cases, intelligence is fed directly to the cockpit, thereby bypassing commanders and other planners altogether, and collapsing decision-making timing dramatically. In the end, modern air forces typically enjoy not air superiority, but air supremacy.[30]

Technological asymmetry in ground-to-ground fighting is less exaggerated, but still impressive. Advanced ground forces directly linked to many of the sensors described above, particularly the JSTARS and UAVs, have a picture of the battlefield far more comprehensive, accurate, and timely than that of their opponents. Additionally, offensive systems can fire from ranges far in excess of the enemy's and with greater precision. For instance, computerized counter-battery radar systems are capable of identifying an incoming shell at the apex of its flight and immediately computing counter-fire data. Based on the computer-derived location, fire is returned quickly, presumably before the enemy has an opportunity to relocate.

And despite public controversy over protective armour for humvees in Iraq, Coalition vehicles are more survivable than their counterparts due to technological advances like the use of depleted uranium armour on tanks.[31] They are also faster and more manoeuvrable, and therefore capable of reacting more quickly to evolving situations.[32]

Soldiers are better equipped as well, sporting lightweight body armour, night vision goggles, global positioning systems, and individual weapons equipped with advanced sighting. They are able to communicate hands-free among each other even at the squad level. Secure, wireless laptops are deployed into the field with vertical and horizontal linkage and access to databases ranging from terrain charts to current enemy order-of-battle data. Helicopter or fixed wing air support is typically on-call and immediately available in the contact area.

Illustrative of the advantage is the Blue-Force Tracker, a satellite tracking and communication system that allows computerized integration and dissemination of data. With Blue-Force Tracker, all echelons of command and staff can follow a TIC (troops in contact) event and provide near simultaneous combat support. Us-

---

30 Air superiority is "that degree of dominance in the air battle of one force over another which permits the conduct of operations by the former … at a given time and place without prohibitive interference by the opposing force." Air supremacy is "that degree of air superiority wherein the opposing air force is incapable of effective interference." *NATO Standardization Agency*, NATO Glossary of Terms and Definitions (AAP-6) (2004).

31 E.g., on the US M1A1 Abrams main battle tank. Depleted uranium amour has a density two and a half times greater than steel. For a discussion of improvements on armoured fighting vehicles (AFV), see *Christopher F. Foss*, Making the Tough Tougher, in: Jane's Defence Weekly, June 6, 2001, Jane's On-line, available at www2.janes.com/K2/k2search.jsp.

32 The M1A1 moves at speeds of over 70 km/hour.

ing a combination of computer maps, real-time automated data updates (on friendly and enemy locations, as well as other battlefield information), and chat room coordination, troops engaging the enemy no longer have to rely on preplanned support or what happens to be "on-station" (in the vicinity). Instead, they can draw on the full range of theatre assets, near simultaneously.[33]

Of course, advanced forces remain vulnerable.[34] By May 2005, over 1500 US soldiers, sailors, airmen, and marines had died in Iraq, and nearly 12,000 had been wounded.[35] Nevertheless, in an otherwise equal fight, very few militaries can match units equipped with such technology. The Battle of Fallujah is an excellent example. Although the Iraqi insurgents enjoyed the positional advantage (defending an urban area), nearly 1200 were killed compared to approximately 50 US Marines.[36]

Growing technological asymmetry exerts a powerful influence on the application of international humanitarian law. On the one hand, there is little incentive for the asymmetrically advantaged side to deviate from IHL – at least until its opponent does.[37] During the combat phase of OIF, for instance, Coalition compliance with those components of IHL governing the conduct of hostilities was exceptional.[38] A number of concerns were expressed regarding the requirement to exercise precaution in attack, but such concerns generally evidenced a poor understanding of combat operations.[39] The sole colourable criticism was that certain of the decapitation targets and a few of the government and Ba'ath party facilities attacked did not meet the criteria for "combatant status" and "military objective"

---

33 Interview with senior US Army officer with recent combat experience.

34 Technological advantage is no panacea. Indeed, history demonstrates that disadvantaged sides often find ways to counter their opponent's superiority. For a fascinating article warning against false-confidence, see *Charles J. Dunlap, Jr.*, How We Lost the high-Tech War of 2007, in: The Weekly Standard, January 29, 1996, p. 22.

35 GlobalSecurity.org, US Casualties in Iraq, at www.globalsecurity.org/military/ops/iraq_casualties.htm.

36 Estimates of casualties vary somewhat. See, e.g., *Anthony Shadid*, Baghdad Suffers a Day of Attacks, in: Washington Post, November 21, 2004, p. A30; US Casualties Surge in Iraq, but Public Impact is Muffled, in: Agence France Presse, November 30, 2004; Iraq Coalition Casualty Count, www.icasualties.org/oif/Stats.aspx (filter by place and month).

37 For an interesting article on how the advanced technology of war is tied to legal and moral issues, see *Charles J. Dunlap, Jr.*, Technology: Recomplicating Moral Life for the Nation's Defenders, Parameters, Autumn 1999, p. 24.

38 The combat phase was from 20 March 2003, when strikes were first launched, through 1 May, 2003, the day on which President *Bush* announced, "major combat operations in Iraq have ended." *George W. Bush*, Remarks from the USS Abraham Lincoln, May 1, 2003, www.whitehouse.gov/news/releases/2003/05/iraq/2003501-15.html.

39 For instance, *Human Rights Watch* criticized decapitation strikes conducted by the US air forces on the ground that "the continued resort to decapitation strikes despite their complete lack of success and the significant civilian losses they caused can be seen as a failure to take 'all feasible precautions' in choice of means and methods of warfare in order to minimize civilian losses as required by international humanitarian law." Off Target, supra note 20, p. 40.

respectively. Such allegations are generally incorrect as a matter of law, but it is interesting to note that both decapitation and government facility strikes reflect the doctrinal asymmetry discussed infra.[40]

On the other hand, forces that are technologically disadvantaged have two basic problems – how to survive and how to effectively engage the enemy. Dealing first with the former, it is self-evident that the best way to survive is to frustrate the enemy's ability to locate and identify you. Many lawful techniques for doing so exist: encrypting transmissions, camouflage, ruses, manoeuvrability, jamming, meaconing, forcing the fight into a more advantageous environment such as an urban area, and so forth.[41]

The problem is that IHL is premised on a rough balance between humanitarian concerns and military necessity. States are generally only willing to accept those humanitarian limitations on their conduct of hostilities that neither enfeeble them militarily nor give their opponents a measurable advantage. When that balance is thrown off-kilter, as occurs when forces are asymmetrically equipped and capable, it is only natural that the weaker side seeks to compensate for the imbalance.

One way it often accomplishes this is by making it difficult to distinguish its forces from the civilian population.[42] Doing so turns the IHL principle of distinction on its head by incentivising its violation. Set forth in Article 48 of the 1977 Protocol Additional I, and clearly customary in nature, the principle provides that "[i]n order to ensure respect for and protection of the civilian population and civilian objects, the Parties to the conflict shall at all times distinguish between the civilian population and combatants and between civilian objects and military objectives and accordingly shall direct their operations only against military objectives."[43] The general principle is implemented through specific prohibitions on at-

---

40 See *Schmitt*, The Conduct of Hostilities, supra note 20.

41 Meaconing is "a system of receiving radio beacon signals and rebroadcasting them on the same frequency to confuse navigation. The meaconing stations cause inaccurate bearings to be obtained by aircraft or ground stations." DoD Dictionary, supra note 8. On urban warfare, see *James Blaker*, Urban Warfare: Advantage US, in: Christian Science Monitor, March 27, 2003, p. 11; *Alan Crowell*, House to House, in: New York Times, March 27, 2003, p. B12; *Joint Chiefs of Staff*, Doctrine for Joint Urban Operations, Joint Publication 3-06, September 16, 2002.

42 On the moral dimensions of this practice, see *Michael Skerker*, Just War Criteria and the New Face of War: Human Shields, Manufactured Martyrs, and Little Boys with Stones, in: 3(1) Journal of Military Ethics 27 (2004). On the legal dimensions, see *Michael N. Schmitt*, The Impact of High and Low-Tech Warfare on the Principle of Distinction, Harvard Program on Humanitarian Policy and Conflict Research, International Humanitarian Law Research Initiative Briefing Paper (November 2003), reprinted in International Humanitarian Law and the 21st Century's Conflicts: Changes and Challenges, Lausanne: Editions Interuniversitaires Suisses, Roberta Arnold/Pierre-Antoine Hildbrand (eds.), 2005.

43 Protocol Additional (I) to the Geneva Convention of 12 August 1949, and Relating to the Protection of Victims of International Armed Conflicts, December 12, 1977, 1125 UNTS 3, 16 International Legal Materials 1391 (1977) [hereinafter PI]. The obligation is contained in the recently released ICRC study, "Customary International Humanitarian Law". *Jean-Marie Henckaerts/Louise Doswald-Beck* (eds.), I Customary Interna-

tacking civilians, civilian objects, and specially protected individuals and objects, such as those who are *hors de combat* and medical facilities.[44]

Application of the proportionality principle and the requirement to take precautions in attack further effectuate distinction. Proportionality, a customary IHL principle appearing three times in Protocol Additional I, prohibits "launching an attack which may be expected to cause incidental loss of civilian life, injury to civilians, damage to civilian objects, or a combination thereof, which would be excessive in relation to the concrete and direct military advantage anticipated".[45] Requisite precautions in attack include, inter alia, doing "everything feasible" to verify that the target is not immune from attack; taking "all feasible precautions" when choosing weapons and tactics so as to minimize collateral damage and incidental injury; and selecting that target from among potential targets offering "similar military advantage", the attack on which causes the least collateral damage and incidental injury.[46]

The asymmetrically disadvantaged party either feigns protected status or uses proximity to protected individuals and objects to deter attacks. Facing a technologically dominant adversary, the Iraqi military (and others fighting alongside them) systematically resorted to these techniques. They had learned early in the conflict that meeting the Coalition forces in classic force-on-force action was nearly suicidal. Such tactics are an unfortunate, but logical, consequence of the Coalition's ability to kill them almost at will once they had been located and identified. To understand the dynamics of asymmetry, it is illustrative to explore a number of these methods of warfare and their legality.

---

tional Humanitarian Law, Cambridge U.P., 2005, Rule 7 [hereinafter CIHL]. Customary international law emerges when "a general practice accepted as law" exists. Statute of the International Court of Justice, art. 38.1(b). It is "looked for primarily in the actual practice and *opinio juris* of States" (*Continental Shelf (Libyan Arab Jamahiriya/Malta)*, Judgment, [1985] I.C.J. Reports, para. 27). See also *North Sea Continental Shelf cases*, Judgment, [1969], ICJ Reports 3, 44. For an excellent summary of the nature and sources of customary international humanitarian law, see *Jean-Marie Henckaerts*, Study on Customary International Humanitarian Law: A Contribution to the Understanding and Respect for the Rule of Law in Armed Conflict, in: 87:857 International Review of the Red Cross 175 (2005).

44 "The civilian population as such, as well as individual civilians, shall not be the object of attack." PI, supra note 43, art. 512. "Civilian objects shall not be the object of attack or of reprisals. Civilian objects are all objects which are not military objectives." PI, supra note 43, art. 52.1. CIHL suggests that the following are specially protected under customary IHL: medical and religious personnel and objects, humanitarian relief personnel and objects, journalists, protected zones, cultural property, works and installations containing dangerous forces, the natural environment, and those who are *hors de combat* (wounded, sick, shipwrecked, those who have surrendered, prisoners of war). CIHL, supra note 43, Parts II and V.

45 CIHL, supra note 43, Rule 14; PI, supra note 43, arts. 51.5(b); 57.2(a)(iii); 57.2(b).

46 CIHL, supra note 43, Rules 15-21; PI, supra note 43, art. 57.

During OIF, Iraqi regular and irregular forces repeatedly donned civilian clothes when Coalition forces might have otherwise identified them.[47] This practice flies in the face of the distinction principle's underlying goal of facilitating the recognition of civilians.[48] Undoubtedly, the practice weakens respect for the principle of distinction, thereby endangering civilians. Yet, despite Protocol Additional I's pronouncement in Article 44.3 that "combatants are obliged to distinguish themselves from the civilian population while they are engaged in an attack or in a military operation preparatory to an attack," failure to do so is not a violation of IHL. Instead, military personnel who wear civilian clothes merely lose lawful combatant status and its associated benefits.[49] An explanation of this oft-confused point is in order.

Members of the armed forces enjoy combatant status under Article 4A (1) of the Third Geneva Convention.[50] Implicit as criteria for combatant status are the

---

47 Off Target, supra note 20, at 78-79. Since the denial of combatant status to Taliban fighters and publication of photos of US Special Forces soldiers attired in indigenous clothing during Operation Enduring Freedom, the "requirement" to wear uniforms has evoked much discussion. See, e.g., *Michelle Kelly/Morten Rostrup*, Identify Yourselves: Coalition Soldiers in Afghanistan are Endangering Air Workers, in: Guardian, February 1, 2002, p. 19. For a comprehensive legal analysis of the subject, see *W. Hays Parks*, Special Forces' Wear of Non-Standard Uniforms, in: 4 Chicago Journal of International Law 493 (2003).

48 *Jean Pictet*, Commentary: III Geneva Convention 52 (ICRC, 1960); Commentary on the Additional Protocols of 8 June 1977 to the Geneva Conventions of 12 August 1949 (ICRC, Yves Sandoz/Christophe Swinarki/Bruno Zimmerman (eds.), 1987), paras. 1577-78.

49 See generally, *Yoram Dinstein*, The Conduct of Hostilities under the Law of International Armed Conflict, Cambridge U.P., 2004, Chapter 2.

50 The relevant provisions of Article 4 exclude the following from civilian status:
(1) Members of the armed forces of a Party to the conflict, as well as members of militias or volunteer corps forming part of such armed forces.
(2) Members of other militias and members of other volunteer corps, including those of organized resistance movements, belonging to a Party to the conflict and operating in or outside their own territory, even if this territory is occupied, provided that such militias or volunteer corps, including such organized resistance movements, fulfil the following conditions:
(a) that of being commanded by a person responsible for his subordinates;
(b) that of having a fixed distinctive sign recognizable at a distance;
(c) that of carrying arms openly;
(d) that of conducting their operations in accordance with the laws and customs of war.

Convention Relative to the Treatment of Prisoners of War, August 12, 1949, art. 142, 6 UST 3316, 75 UNTS 135 [hereinafter GCIII]. See also Regulations Respecting the Laws and Customs of War on Land, annex to Convention (No. IV) Respecting the Laws and Customs of War on Land, October 18, 1907, art. 1.2, 36 Stat. 2277, 1 Bevans 631 [hereinafter HIVR]; Convention for the Amelioration of the Condition of the Wounded and Sick in Armed Forces in the Field, August 12, 1949, art. 13(2)(b), 6 UST 3114, 75 UNTS 31 [hereinafter GCI]; Convention for the Amelioration of the Condi-

four cumulative conditions set forth in Article 4A (2), including "having a fixed distinctive sign recognizable at a distance".[51] The most common "distinctive sign" is a uniform. Protocol Additional I relaxes the uniform criterion somewhat, but because certain States, especially the United States, strongly object to this relaxation, it cannot be said to be customary law.[52]

The loss of combatant status through non-compliance with the uniform condition has two consequences. Those captured forfeit prisoner of war (POW) status and its protections.[53] Further, because military personnel in civilian clothes do not qualify for combatant status, they enjoy no combatant immunity for using force against the enemy. Attacking the enemy is not a war crime, but it may amount to a criminal offence (e.g., attempted murder) under the national law of the capturing Party. Absent combatant immunity, any State with subject matter and personal ju-

---

tion of the Wounded, Sick, and Shipwrecked Members of Armed Forces at Sea, August 12, 1949, art. 13(2)(b), 6 UST 3217, 75 UNTS 85 [hereinafter GCII].

51 Textually, these conditions appear in the provision applying only to members of a militia that do not form part of the armed forces (and members of other volunteer corps, including organized resistance movements). However, they are interpreted as being inherent in the term "armed forces". As noted by *Michael Bothe* (et. al.), "[i]t is generally assumed that these conditions were deemed, by the 1874 Brussels Conference and the 1899 and 1907 Hague Peace Conferences, to be inherent in the regular armed forces of States. Accordingly, it was considered unnecessary and redundant to spell them out in the Conventions." *Michael Bothe* et. al., New Rules for Victims of Armed Conflict, 1982, p. 234. See also discussion in CIHL, supra note 43, p. 15. Case law is supportive. See, e.g., *Mohammed Ali et al. v. Public Prosecutor* (1968), [1969] AC 430, 449; *Ex parte Quirin et. al.* 317 U.S. 1 (1942).

52 PI, supra note 43, art. 44.3.

In order to promote the protection of the civilian population from the effects of hostilities, combatants are obliged to distinguish themselves from the civilian population while they are engaged in an attack or in a military operation preparatory to an attack. Recognizing, however, that there are situations in armed conflicts where, owing to the nature of the hostilities an armed combatant cannot so distinguish himself, he shall retain his status as a combatant, provided that, in such situations, he carries his arms openly:

(a) during each military engagement, and

(b) during such time as he is visible to the adversary while he is engaged in a military deployment preceding the launching of an attack in which he is to participate.

Acts which comply with the requirements of this paragraph shall not be considered as perfidious within the meaning of Article 37, paragraph 1 (c).

It is not customary despite its appearance in CIHL, supra note 43, Rule 106. The US position on Protocol I is authoritatively set out in Memorandum for Assistant General Counsel (International), Office of the Secretary of Defense, 1977 Protocols Additional to the Geneva Conventions: Customary International Law Implications, May 8, 1986 (on-file with author) [hereinafter PI Memorandum]. See also *Michael J. Matheson*, The United States Position on the Relation of Customary International Law to the 1977 Protocols Additional to the 1949 Geneva Conventions, in: 2 American University Journal of International Law and Policy 419 (1987).

53 This point is reflected in CIHL, supra note 43, Rule 106.

risdiction may subject the non-uniformed soldier to domestic prosecution based on his or her combat actions, including attacking enemy combatants.[54]

Another technique commonly employed in Iraq to offset asymmetrical technological disadvantage is the use of civilians and civilian objects as shields.[55] In military jargon, such tactics are labelled "counter-targeting".[56]

Iraqi forces, especially the paramilitary Fedayeen, passively and actively exploited human shields to deter attacks. In the former case, they based themselves in locations where civilians were present; in the latter, they forcibly used civilians, including women and children, to physically shield their operations.[57]

Whether passive or active, human shielding expressly violates IHL. Article 51(7) of Protocol Additional I prohibits the use of "[t]he presence or movements of the civilian population or individual civilians ... to render certain points or areas immune from military operations, in particular in attempts to shield military objectives from attacks or to shield, favour or impede military operations."[58] The widespread condemnation that inevitably ensues whenever shields are used evidences the norm's customary character.[59]

---

[54] The classic article on the subject is *Richard R. Baxter*, So-called "Unprivileged Belligerency": Spies, Guerrillas and Saboteurs, in: 1952 British Yearbook of International Law 323, reprinted in Military Law review (Bicentennial Issue) 487 (1975).

[55] Off Target, supra note 20, pp. 67-73.

[56] Counter-targeting is "preventing or degrading detection, characterization, destruction, and post-strike assessment". *Defense Intelligence Agency*, Saddam's Use of Human Shields and Deceptive Sanctuaries: Special Briefing for the Pentagon Press Corps, February 26, 2003, www.defenselink.mil/news/Feb2003/g030226-D-9085M.html.

[57] *Todd S. Purdum*, Night Time Ambush in Iraqi City, in: New York Times, April 5, 2003, p. 1; *Dexter Filkins*, In the Field Choosing Targets: Iraqi Fighters Or Civilians? Hard Decision for Copters, in: New York Times, March 31, 2003, p. 5.

[58] This prescription tracks that found in the 1949 Fourth Geneva Convention, art. 28: "The presence of a protected person may not be used to render certain points or areas immune from military operations." The prohibition only applies vis-à-vis those who "find themselves ... in the hands of a Party, to the conflict or Occupying Party of which they are not nationals." It would not apply to Iraqi forces using Iraqis as shields. Convention Relative to the Protection of Civilian Persons in Time of War, August 12, 1949, art. 4, 6 UST 3516, 75 UNTS 287 [hereinafter GCIV].

[59] CIHL, supra note 43, Rule 97. See also US Navy, Marine Corp, Coast Guard, Commander's Handbook on the Law of Naval Operations, NWP 1-14M, MCWP 5-2.1, COMDTPUB P5800.7, para. 11.2, 1995, reprinted in its annotated version as Vol. 73 of the International Law Studies (US Naval War College, 1999); Rome Statute of the International Criminal Court, July 17,1998, art. 8.2(b)(xxiii), UN Doc. A/CONF. 183/9*, 37 International Legal Materials 1002 (1998), corrected through January 16, 2002, at http://www.icc-cpi.int/. The UN General Assembly labelled Iraq's use of human shields during the first Gulf War as a "most grave and blatant violation of Iraq's obligations under international law" GA Res. 46/134 (December 17, 1991). In May 1995, Bosnian Serbs seized UNPROFOR peacekeepers and used them as human shields against NATO air strikes. In response, the UN condemned the action, demanded release, and authorized the creation of a rapid reaction force to handle such situations. SC Res. 998 (June 16, 1995).

Mere presence of human shields does not prevent an attack (as a matter of law) unless it would otherwise violate the proportionality principle by causing incidental injury or collateral damage excessive in relation to the concrete and direct military advantage accruing to the attacker. There have been suggestions that involuntary shields should not be included in the calculation of incidental injury, lest lawbreakers benefit from their misconduct.[60] However, Article 51.8 of Protocol Additional I rejects this contention: "Any violation of these prohibitions [includes the prohibition on shielding] shall not release the Parties to the conflict from their legal obligations with respect to the civilian population and civilians ..." In other words, civilians never lose their IHL protection because of a belligerent's actions, but may chose to forfeit it by directly participating in hostilities.[61] Although IHL seeks to balance humanitarian concerns with military necessity, it was never intended to ensure a "fair fight" between belligerents.[62]

Human shielding is unlawful only when involuntary. *Voluntary* shields forfeit the protection they are entitled to as civilians by "directly participating" in hostili-

---

[60] Those taking the opposite stance reasonably and accurately point out that it creates an incentive for the use of shields because an opponent can effectively render a military objective immune from attack simply by placing enough civilians at risk (by virtue of operation of the proportionality principle). *APV Rogers* has argued that:
"... a tribunal considering whether a grave breach has been committed [a disproportionate attack] would be able to take into account when considering the rule of proportionality the extent to which the defenders had flouted their obligation to separate military objectives from civilian objects and to take precautions to protect the civilian population ... the proportionality approach taken by the tribunals should help to redress the balance which would otherwise be tilted in favour of the unscrupulous." (*A.P.V. Rogers*, Law on the Battlefield, 2d ed., Juris Publ., 2004, p. 129.)
See also *W. Hays Parks*, Air War and the Law of War, in: 32 Air Force Law Review 1, 163 (1992).

[61] On direct participation, see *Michael N. Schmitt*, Humanitarian Law and Direct Participation in Hostilities by Private Contractors or Civilian Employees, in: 5 Chicago Journal of International Law 511 (2005); *Michael N. Schmitt*, "Direct Participation in Hostilities" and 21st Century Armed Conflict, in: BWV, Horst Fischer et al (eds.), Crisis Management and Humanitarian Protection: Festschrift fur Dieter Fleck, 2004, pp. 505-529.

[62] The sole possible exception is the principle of belligerent reprisal. A belligerent reprisal is an unlawful, but proportionate, act taken to compel one's adversary to desist in its own unlawful course of conduct. But it is an extremely limited doctrine and one that is increasingly rejected as out of step with contemporary acceptable methods of warfare. Further, it is designed not to foster a fair (equal) fight, but rather to force the Party violating humanitarian law back into compliance. On reprisals, see *Frits Kalshoven*, Belligerent Reprisals, Sijthoff, 1971. Protocol Additional I went far beyond prior humanitarian law in prohibiting reprisals, a fact that led in part to US opposition to the treaty. See PI, supra note 43, arts. 51.6 (civilians and civilian population), 52.1 (civilian objects), 53 (cultural objects and places of worship), 54.4 (objects indispensable to the survival of the civilian population), 55.2 (the natural environment), and 56.4 (dams, dykes and nuclear electrical generating stations).

ties.[63] As noted in Article 51.3 of Protocol Additional I, "[c]ivilians shall enjoy the protection afforded by this Section, *unless and for such time as they take a direct part in hostilities.*"[64] Since they may therefore be attacked, they can shield nothing as a matter of law.[65]

Civilian objects may also be utilized to neutralize enemy technological advantages, through operation of law (proportionality principle), because policy concerns preclude attack, or simply as hiding places. For instance, Iraqi forces frequently placed military equipment and troops in or near civilian buildings (e.g., schools). They also used specially protected objects, such as medical and religious buildings and cultural property, as bases for military operations or supply depots.[66]

The IHL on using objects as shields is less explicit than that regarding human shields. Unlike Article 51, which deals only with protection of "the civilian population or individual civilians", Article 52, which addresses civilian objects, fails to mention shielding. Article 58 mitigates the omission somewhat by requiring defenders to "endeavour to remove the civilian population, individual civilians and civilian objects under their control from the vicinity of military objects; avoid locating military objectives within or near densely populated areas; [and] take the other necessary precautions to protect the civilian population, individual civilians

---

63 International volunteer shields travelled to Iraq prior to Operation Iraqi Freedom. All departed once they realized the seriousness of their actions and the Iraqi government's desire to use them as shields for military objectives.

64 The Rome Statute adopts this standard by making it a war crime to intentionally attack civilians unless they are "taking direct part in hostilities". Supra note 59, art. 8 .2(b)(i). The United States correctly takes the position that as direct participants, they become targetable (although there will seldom be any reason to directly attack them) and, more important, are excluded in the estimation of incidental injury when assessing proportionality.
"And then, the other target category that is a challenge for us is where the human shields that we've talked of before might be used. And you really have two types of human shields. You have people who volunteer to go and stand on a bridge or a power plant or a water works facility, and you have people that are placed in those areas not of their own free will. In the case of some of the previous use of human shields in Iraq, Saddam placed hostages, if you will, on sensitive sites in order to show that these were human shields, but, in fact, they were not there of their own free will. Two separate problems to deal with that, and it requires that we work very carefully with the intelligence community to determine what that situation might be at a particular location." (*Department of Defense*, Background Briefing on Targeting, March 5, 2003, www.defenselink.mil/news/Mar2003/t03052003_t305targ.html)
Human Rights Watch takes the opposite position. *Human Rights Watch*, International Humanitarian Law Issues in a Potential War in Iraq, February 20, 2002, www.hrw.org/backgrounder/arms/ iraq0202003.htm#1.

65 Children legally lack the mental capacity to form the intent to voluntarily shield military objectives. Israeli forces do not to use live ammunition against children. *Justus R. Weiner*, Co-existence Without Conflict: The Implementation of Legal Structures for Israeli-Palestinian Cooperation Pursuant to the Interim Peace Agreements, in: 26 Brooklyn Journal of International Law 591, at n. 407 (2000).

66 1 MEF Roots Out Paramilitaries, Destroys Several Ba'ath Party Headquarters, US Central Command News Release 03-04-13, April 1, 2003.

and civilian objects under their control against the dangers resulting from military operations."[67] While these obligations apply only "to the maximum extent feasible",[68] a contentious term in IHL interpretation, it is by definition always feasible to not intentionally deter attack by placing military objectives near civilian objects. This being so, intentional use of civilian objects to shield military objectives, as Iraqi forces did, amounts to a failure to comply with one's IHL obligations.

An additional way technologically inferior forces avoid attack is through misuse of specially protected objects. Human Rights Watch (HRW) documented many such incidents during hostilities in Iraq. For instance, "Off Target", HRW's report on the conflict, cited Fedayeen use of al-Nasiriyya Surgical Hospital, the Baghdad Red Crescent Maternity Hospital, the Imam Ali mosque in al-Najaf, and the Abu Hanifa mosque. The Iman Ali mosque is the holiest site in Iraq for Shia Muslims, whereas the Abu Hanifa mosque is an important shrine for Sunnis.[69]

These actions were clearly unlawful. The First Geneva Convention provides that "[t]he responsible authorities shall ensure that ... medical establishments and units are, as far as possible, situated in such a manner that attacks against military objectives cannot imperil their safety."[70] Protocol Additional I, Article 12.4, expresses the prohibition even more bluntly: "Under no circumstances shall medical units be used in an attempt to shield military objectives from attack." Article 53(b) sets forth a similar prohibition for "historic monuments, works of art or places of worship which constitute the cultural or spiritual heritage of peoples."[71] Both of the mosques cited by HRW meet the special significance criterion.

Unlawful tactics such as those described supra do not entirely neutralize a foe's technological superiority. The IHL provisions extending special protection to medical, religious, and cultural facilities include clauses removing protection upon misuse.[72] More generally, civilian objects may become military objectives because of their militarily significant *location*, through *use* for military actions, or when the enemy's intended future *purpose* for an object is military in nature.[73]

Even if the technologically weaker party can manage to avoid being attacked, at some point it must take offensive action against its enemy if it hopes to prevail.

---

67 See also CIHL, supra note 43, Chapter 6.

68 PI, supra note 43, art. 58. On the obligations of defenders, see discussion in *Marco Sassoli*, Targeting: the Scope and Utility of the Concept of "Military Objectives" for the Protection of Civilians in Contemporary Armed Conflicts, in: David Wippman/Matthew Evangelista (eds.), New Wars, New Laws?, Transnational Publ., 2005.

69 Off Target, supra note 20, p. 72-73. On misuse of religious locations, see also: Regime Shows Disregard for Historical, Religious Sites in Holy City, US Central Command News Release No. 03-04-28, April 2, 2003; Regime Use of Baghdad Mosques and Hospitals, US Central Command News Release No. 03-04-65, April 6, 2003.

70 GCI, supra note 50, art. 19.

71 See also HIVR, supra note 50, art. 4.

72 See also Rome Statute, supra note 59, art. 8.2(b)(ix).

73 PI, supra note 43, art. 52(2). For instance, an apartment building's use as a unit headquarters transforms it into an attackable military facility. Any collateral damage or incidental injury that might be caused during the attack would be governed by the principle of proportionality.

Guerrilla warfare is a classic response to this requirement. Increasingly, especially as the capabilities gap widens, so too are violations of IHL.

With advanced technology, it is becoming ever more difficult to get close enough to the enemy to mount an attack, let alone survive one. Perfidy, i.e., "killing or wounding treacherously individuals belonging to the hostile nation or army,"[74] has become a common tactic for doing so. The precise parameters of perfidy are unclear. The 1907 Hague IV Regulations reference "improper use of a flag of truce, of the national flag or of the military insignia and uniform of the enemy, as well as distinctive badges of the Geneva Convention,"[75] a prohibition that is now unquestionably customary.[76] Article 37.1 of Protocol Additional I is perfidy's most recent codification: "It is prohibited to kill, injure or capture an adversary by resort to perfidy. Acts inviting the confidence of an adversary to lead him to believe that he is entitled to, or is obliged to accord, protection under the rules of international law applicable in armed conflict, with the intent to betray that confidence, shall constitute perfidy."

Protocol Additional I proffers feigning civilian, non-combatant status as an example of perfidy.[77] Thus, when combatants don civilian clothing for the express purpose of attacking the enemy, they arguably violate the IHL prohibition on perfidy. Although disagreement exists over the prohibition's alleged customary character,[78] the weight of authority suggests it is customary. The ICRC's recently released "Customary International Humanitarian Law Study" includes it as a customary norm and the IHL manuals of many countries, including those of the United States,[79] characterize such actions as perfidious. The "San Remo Manual

---

74 Convention [No. II] with Respect to the Laws and Customs of War on Land, with annex of regulations, preamble, July 29, 1899, art. 23(b), 32 Stat. 1803, 1 Bevans 247 [hereinafter 1899 HR]; HIVR, supra note 50, art. 23(b). Perfidy is distinguished from ruses, which are acts intended to mislead an adversary and cause him to act recklessly, but which do not involve false claims of protected status. Ruses are lawful. HIVR, supra, art. 24; PI, supra note 43, art. 37.2.

75 HIVR, supra note 50, art. 23(f). The reference is to the Geneva Convention of 1864. Convention for the Amelioration of the Condition of the Wounded in Armies in the Field, August 22, 1864, 18 Martens Nouveau Recueil (le ser.) 612.

76 CIHL, supra note 43, Chapter 18; International Military Tribunal (Nuremberg), Judgment and Sentences (1946), 41 American Journal of International Law 172, 218 (1947).

77 PI, supra note 43, art. 37.1(c).

78 *Yoram Dinstein* has perceptively pointed out that elsewhere the Protocol Additional relaxes the requirement for uniform wear; this inconsistency renders characterization of feigned civilian status as perfidy "not … much more than lip-service". *Dinstein*, Conduct, supra note 49, p. 203. That perfidy constitutes a grave breach under Protocol Additional I, but feigning civilian status does not, further supports this position. PI, supra note 43, art. 85.3(f). But see *Parks*, Special Forces', supra note 47.

79 CIHL, supra note 43, p. 224; NWP 1-14M, supra note 59, para. 12.7; US Army Judge Advocate General's School, Law of War Handbook 192 (2005). See also UK Ministry of Defence, The Manual of the Law of Armed Conflict, Oxford, Oxford U.P., 2004, para. 5.9.2(c) (although because the UK is a party to Protocol, the manual's bearing on the existence of a customary norm is limited).

on International Law Applicable to Conflicts at Sea" does likewise.[80] Finally, according to the Official Record of the Diplomatic Conference that adopted Protocol Additional I, the Committee that drafted the article on perfidy "decided to limit itself to a brief list of particularly clear examples. Examples that were debatable or involved borderline cases were avoided."[81]

An unquestionably perfidious tactic is feigned surrender. Again, feigning surrender allows one to get close enough to attack the enemy, thereby compensating for the technological edge that would otherwise preclude attack. Feigning surrender to ambush Coalition forces was a recurring pattern of Iraqi behaviour during OIF.[82]

Article 37.1(a) of Additional Protocol I cites "the feigning of an intent to negotiate under a flag of truce or surrender" as an example of perfidy when carried out with the objective of capturing, injuring, or killing the enemy. A flag is not the sole means of communicating intent to surrender; any technique that so informs the enemy suffices. Surrendering forces are *hors de combat* and entitled to immunity from attack.[83] The "Customary International Law Study" includes the ban on perfidious surrender as a customary IHL norm.[84]

Another tactic for countering technological strength on the battlefield is misuse of protective emblems. During the recent conflict, Iraqi regular and irregular forces used marked ambulances to reach the battlefield, serve as scout vehicles, and attack Coalition forces. Additionally, the Ba'ath Party building in Basra was marked with the ICRC emblem. Party buildings were often employed as supply depots for military equipment and rallying points for militia.[85] As noted supra, Iraqi forces also conducted military operations from medical facilities.

Displaying the distinctive emblems of medical and religious personnel, transports, and units, or the personnel, property, and activities of the International Movement of the Red Cross and Red Crescent, for other than their intended purposes, is unlawful under IHL.[86] The misuse need not be intended to help capture, injure, or kill an opponent. This prohibition is one of the longest standing in IHL,

---

80 San Remo Manual on International Law Applicable to Armed Conflicts at Sea, Cambridge U.P., Louise Doswald-Beck (ed.), 1995, Rule 111.

81 Official Records, vol. XV, CDDH/236/Rev.1, para. 17.

82 See, e.g., *Glenn Collins*, Allied Advances, Tougher Iraqi Resistance, and a Hunt in the Tigris, in: New York Times, March 24, 2003, p. 1; *Brian Knowlton*, Bush Tells of 'Good Progress' But Says War has Just Begun, in: International Herald Tribune, March 24, 2003, p. 6.

83 Lieber Code, supra note 4, art. 71; Project of an International Declaration concerning the Laws and Customs of War (1874 Brussels Declaration), art. 13; The Laws of War on Land (1880 Oxford Manual), at 9(b); 1899 HR, supra note 74, art. 23(c); HIVR, supra note 50, art. 23(c); PI, supra note 43, art. 41.2(b). Violation is a grave breach pursuant to PI, supra, art. 85.3(e). The Brussels Declaration and Oxford Manual are at ICRC Treaty Database, www.icrc.org/ihl.

84 CIHL, supra note 43, Rule 65.

85 Off Target, supra note 20, at 70.

86 Permitted purposes are set forth in GCI, supra note 50, arts. 24-27, 38-44; GCII, supra note 50, arts. 22, 24-25, 27, 36-39, 41-44; GCIV, supra note 58, arts. 18-22; PI, supra note 43, arts. 8, 18, 22-23.

appearing in the 1863 Lieber Code; 1899 and 1907 Hague Regulations; 1906, 1929, and 1949 Geneva Conventions; Protocol Additional I; and the military manuals of many nations.[87] It is self-evidently customary in nature today.[88] When the purpose of the misuse goes beyond merely "hiding" from the enemy to the use of the emblem to treacherously attack, the separate violation of perfidy occurs.[89]

Suicide bombing is an asymmetrical technique to which the disadvantaged side increasingly resorts. For instance, in 2003, there were 20 suicide bombings in Iraq. The figure for 2003 was nearly 50, whereas suicide attacks in 2005 will exceed that figure appreciably. Such attacks are seldom isolated acts by religious or other fanatics. On the contrary, most suicide bombings are tied to an organized political or military campaign, usually one designed to "compel modern democracies to withdraw military forces from territory that the terrorists consider to be their homeland."[90]

Suicide bombing is not unlawful per se. The case of Japanese Kamikaze's during the World War II illustrates the point that lawful combatants can conduct suicide attacks against enemy combatants consistent with the principle of distinction.

However, the technique is unlawful as perfidious if conducted by combatants out of uniform (see discussion supra). More typically, though, civilians (unlawful combatants) carry out suicide attacks.[91] If they *intentionally* use their civilian appearance to enable them to get close enough to their target to detonate themselves, they have acted perfidiously. On the other hand, if that is not their intent, then they will have "directly participated" in hostilities, but not have violated IHL. Rather, as with combatants that wear civilian clothes, the consequences of their actions are that they lose civilian immunity from attack (i.e., they may lawfully be targeted) and may be prosecuted under the domestic law of any State with subject matter and personal jurisdiction.[92]

In each of the methods of warfare described above, the asymmetrically disadvantaged party engages in behaviour that either violates IHL norms designed to foster the distinction between combatants and civilians (and military objectives and civilian objects), or takes steps that otherwise weaken them. More reprehensi-

---

87 Lieber Code, supra note 4, art. 117. See also 1899 HR, supra note 74, art. 23(f); HIVR, supra note 50, art. 23(f); 1906 Geneva Convention, arts. 27-28, ICRC Treaty Database, www.icrc.org/ihl; 1929 Geneva Convention, arts. 24 & 28, ICRC Treaty Database, www.icrc.org/ihl; GCI, supra note 50, arts. 39, 44, 53, 54; GCII, supra note 50, arts. 41, 44, 45; PI, supra note 43, art. 38.1; NWP 1-14M, supra note 59, para. 11.9.6; British Manual, supra note 79, para. 5.10(a).

88 CIHL, supra note 43, Rule 59.

89 See, e.g., NWP 1-14M, supra note 59, para. 12.2.; Federal Ministry of Defense (Germany), Humanitarian Law in Armed Conflicts Manual (1992), sec. 640.

90 *Robert A. Pape*, Blowing Up an Assumption, in: International Herald Tribune, May 19, 2005, p. 8. *Pape* looked at 315 suicide bombings since 1980 in his research. See also *Robert A. Pape*, Dying to Win: The Strategic Logic of Suicide Terrorism, Random House, 2005.

91 Regarding use of the method in Iraq, see *Yoram Dinstein*, Jus in Bello Issues Arising in the Hostilities in Iraq in 2003, 34 Israel Yearbook on Human Rights 1, 4-5 (2004).

92 See *Schmitt*, Humanitarian Law and Direct Participation, supra note 61, p. 520-21.

bly, parties to a conflict may dispense with the norms altogether by directly attacking civilians and civilian objects. Unable to prevail on the battlefield (even using the tactics just discussed), the technologically weaker party takes the next logical step – moving the fight beyond the battlefield in the hope of prevailing indirectly. Perhaps the objective is to rupture a coalition, as in the Iraqi scud attacks against Israeli population centres in 1991.[93] Alternatively, the direct attacks may be designed to counteract the involvement of the international community, governmental or non-governmental, in a conflict, as with the suicide bombings of the UN and ICRC facilities in Iraq.[94] Current insurgent attacks against the Iraqi citizenry seek to both turn the population against the Coalition forces out of a sense that they were more secure before the war, and, more generally, intimidate the population into uncooperativeness with the Coalition.

Most frequently, attacks directly against protected objects and individuals are designed to strike at the key centre of gravity for democracies – its population. The attackers hope to alter the democracy's cost-benefit calculations enough to achieve their aims without having to defeat their enemy's superior military. The attacks of September 11th, although conducted outside the context of an armed conflict to which IHL applied, are the paradigmatic examples of this dynamic. All such actions are a direct violation of the customary law norms codified in Articles 51.2 and 52.1 of Protocol Additional I.[95] Sadly, they are a logical reaction to asymmetry on the battlefield.

Beyond *methods* of warfare, an asymmetrically disadvantaged opponent may resort to various *means* of warfare to counteract an opponent's dominance. One possibility is the computer, which enables attack on the enemy's computer networks (computer network attack – CNA). The beauty of CNA directed at a militarily stronger opponent is that the very technology representing the enemy's technological edge constitutes a highly exploitable vulnerability. Further, mounting a computer network attack is affordable, requiring little more than connectivity and hacker know-how.[96] It is a powerful counter to technological asymmetry.

---

93 During the Gulf War of 1990-91, Iraq sought to draw Israel into the conflict by targeting Israeli cities with SCUD missiles. It was hoped that this would rupture the Coalition, which included forces from States with an anti-Israel policy stance, such as Syria.

94 Recall the August 2003 attack on the UN's Headquarters in Baghdad which killed 23, including Sergio Vieira de Mello, the Secretary-General's Special Representative in Iraq. Two months later, a suicide bomber drove an explosive-packed ambulance into the ICRC compound, killing 18 bystanders. Many aid organizations, including the United Nations, withdrew or scaled back their staffs following the attacks. For a discussion of the subject, see *Nicholas de Torrente*, Humanitarian Actions under Attack: Reflections on the Iraq War, 17 Harvard Human Rights Journal 1(2004).

95 See text supra at fns. 43-44. See also CIHL, supra note 43, Rules 1-10. The United States specifically finds both provisions to be reflective of customary IHL. PI Memorandum, supra note 52.

96 On computer network attack, see *Michael N. Schmitt/Brian O'Donnell* (eds.), Computer Network Attack and International Law, Naval War College International Law Studies, 2002; *Michael N. Schmitt*, Wired Warfare: Computer Network Attack and International Law, 84 (No. 846) International Review of the Red Cross 365 (June 2002); *Michael N. Schmitt/Heather A. Harrison-Dinniss/Thomas C. Winfield*, Computers and War: The

There is nothing inherently unlawful about using computers to disrupt the enemy's networked military systems. However, because a military network is usually more difficult to hack into than civilian infrastructure, the latter is an attractive target set for a belligerent without the sophisticated dedicated information operations units fielded by the United States.[97] It must be noted that not all CNA targeting of civilian entities is prohibited; some operations will not qualify as an "attack" because the IHL term of art does not encompass mere inconvenience or hardship. That said, computer network attacks directed at civilians or civilian objects that cause death, injury, damage, or destruction would amount to an unlawful attack.

A more frightening prospect is an asymmetrically disadvantaged belligerent turning to weapons of mass destruction (WMD).[98] In the case of nuclear weapons, use for State survival is probably lawful per se (assuming compliance with the proportionality principle and precautions in attack requirements).[99] Yet, nuclear weapons might also be employed as a conflict's opening salvo against an asymmetrically advantaged opponent in the hope that the blow would be so devastating the adversary would surrender or otherwise accede to the objectives of the attacker. The express intention of North Korea to enhance its nuclear delivery capability is an apt illustration of how asymmetry can propel a weak State to think of nuclear weapons as compensatory in nature.[100] The legality of use for other than survival purposes is unsettled.[101]

Legal Battlespace, Harvard Program on Humanitarian Policy and Conflict Research, International Humanitarian Law Research Initiative Briefing Paper (June 2004), at www.ihlresearch.org/ihl/pdfs/schmittetal.pdf.

97 Such as the Air Force's 67th Information Operations Wing. See http://aia.lackland.af.mil/homepages/67iow/units.cfm.

98 This a strategic concern expressed by the United States in its National Defense Strategy:
"In the face of American dominance in *traditional* forms of warfare, some hostile forces are seeking to acquire *catastrophic* capabilities, particularly weapons of mass destruction (WMD). Porous international borders, weak international controls, and easy access to information related technologies facilitate these efforts. Particularly troublesome is the nexus of transnational terrorists, proliferation, and problem states that possess or seek WMD, increasing the risk of WMD attack against the United States." (Department of Defense, The National Defense Strategy of the United States, March 2005, p. 2).

99 The International Court of Justice implicitly recognized this in *Use of Nuclear Weapons*, when it refused to rule out affirmatively the possibility that the use of nuclear weapons would be legal if the survival of a State were at stake. Legality of the Threat or Use of Nuclear Weapons, Advisory Opinion, 1996 ICJ 226, 263 (July 8).

100 See, e.g., *James Brooke*, North Koreans Claim to Extract Weapons Grade Fuel for Bombs, in: New York Times, May 12, 2005, p. 1.

101 All of the nuclear powers argued that it was not in proceedings before the International Court of Justice in the *Use of Nuclear Weapons*. See discussion of the case in *Michael N. Schmitt*, The International Court of Justice and the Use of Nuclear Weapons, in: Naval War College Review, Spring 1998, at 91-116.

One nefarious possibility is that weaker States will fall back on chemical or biological weapons to compensate for the enemy's military wherewithal. Both are easier to surreptitiously develop, hide, and employ than nuclear weapons, and the source of a chemical or biological attack would be more difficult to ascertain. Any use would be unlawful. In the first place, even if directed against military objects, the effects of their use would probably be difficult to control, thereby violating the prohibition on the use of indiscriminate weapons.[102] Second, the most likely scenario is use against the civilian population because it would produce the greatest effect on the enemy's willingness to continue. This would violate the prohibition on attacking civilians and civilian objects. Third, use of biological and chemical weapons would violate express prohibitions for States Party to the 1925 Gas Protocol, 1972 Biological Weapons Convention, and 1993 Chemical Weapons Convention.[103] These proscriptions arguably extend even to non-Party States, at least to the extent they represent customary law.[104]

Beyond a disadvantaged party directly violating IHL in an effort to avoid defeat, asymmetry may well influence IHL's *interpretation* or *application*. For instance, outmatched on the battlefield, the weaker party has an incentive to broadly interpret the notions of "effective contribution to military action" and "definite military advantage" when identifying military objectives. Similarly, the US inclusion of "war-sustaining" objects (primarily economic in nature) within the scope of military objectives would appeal to a weaker side, for "war-sustaining" entities are of considerable value, but less well defended than typical military objectives.[105]

Application of the proportionality principle might also be affected. Ultimately, no objective means of valuing either incidental injury/collateral damage or military advantage exists.[106] Instead, it is the subjective perspective of the party carrying out the proportionality assessment that matters. A weaker party is likely to assess the military advantage accruing from its own attack as high. This is because when one chronically suffers defeats, any success looms large. Consider the opening days of the war in Iraq. Every downing of a Coalition helicopter or destruction of an armoured fighting vehicle was celebrated as a great victory. By contrast, Coalition forces almost effortlessly destroyed every Iraqi military vehicle

---

102 PI, art. 51.4(c) prohibits as indiscriminate attacks "which employ a method or means of combat the effects of which cannot be limited as required by this Protocol". Supra note 43. An example is a contagion that spreads randomly among a population.

103 Gas Protocol, supra note 4; Biological Weapons Convention, supra note 4; Convention on the Prohibition of the Development, Production, Stockpiling and Use of Chemical Weapons and on Their Destruction, January 13, 1993, 1974 UNTS 45, 32 International Legal Materials 800 (1993).

104 They are included in CIHL. Supra note 43, Rules 73 & 74.

105 See fn. 126 infra and accompanying discussion.

106 Now for distinguishing military advantage that is "concrete and direct" from that which is not. The official ICRC *Commentary* to the Protocol Additional indicates the expression "show[s] that the advantage concerned should be substantial and relatively close, and that advantages which are hardly perceptible and those which would only appear in the long term should be disregarded." PI Commentary, supra note 48, para. 2209.

(their air force never took off out of fear of immediate destruction) that dared challenge them. In such an environment, it is only natural that dissimilarly placed parties apply the proportionality principle dissimilarly.

The same dynamic applies to the other side of the calculation. To a belligerent facing military defeat, enemy civilian casualties are unlikely to have the weight they would to one assured of victory. The latter, for instance, will be far more concerned about public perceptions of its actions than the former. Coalition efforts to avoid causing collateral damage and incidental injury during OIF are illustrative. Of course, proportionality is always a contextual determination, but concerns about enemy civilian suffering inevitably erode the closer to defeat one comes.

As should be apparent, technological asymmetry exerts enormous influence on the willingness of belligerents to abide by international humanitarian law. It similarly affects how they interpret and apply it. However, technologically asymmetry is but one of numerous forms of asymmetry that affect the viability of international humanitarian law during conflict. A brief review of the others is instructive.

Doctrinal Asymmetry: In war, each side hopes to be technologically and tactically superior to its opponents. Both search for that doctrinal approach which best leverages their strengths and exploits the enemy's weaknesses. For advanced Western militaries, effects based-operations (EBO), which are made possible by technological asymmetry, represent the emerging prevailing approach. Because the lack of technological wherewithal precludes lesser-equipped forces from engaging in EBO, its application creates doctrinal asymmetry.[107]

In EBO, targeting is "focused on creating *specific effects* to achieve the joint force commander's campaign objectives or the subordinate component commander's supporting objectives".[108] Effects-based operations begin with identification of the effect(s) that the attacker hopes to create through attack. The enemy's systems are then deconstructed to identify those components that should be attacked to best realize the desired effect. As an example, EBO posits that it is unnecessary to destroy an enemy formation that can be rendered combat ineffective through computer network attack on its command and control system. In a real-world application of EBO, US forces engaged in a decapitation campaign during OIF designed to kill senior Iraqi leaders. Leadership is an attractive effects-based target set because, at least in theory, decapitation paralyzes enemy command and control (the effect), thereby avoiding the need to destroy the enemy armed forces.[109] Ultimately, the process addresses the causality between actions and their effects; concentrates on desired effects, both physical and behavioural; models the

---

[107] On the role of technology in enabling EBO, see, *Schmitt*, Aerial Effects-Based Operations, supra note 14.

[108] Joint Chiefs of Staff, Joint Doctrine for Targeting, Joint Publication 3-60, January 17, 2002, at I-1; *David A. Deptula*, Effects-Based Operations: Change in the Nature of War, Aerospace Education Foundation Defense and Airpower Series, 2001.

[109] Such strikes seek effects that "cascade". Presumably, the direct effects of removing key decision makers will ripple throughout subordinate echelons, with paralysis at one level cascading down to the next, and so forth. Types of effects are outlined in JP 3-60, supra note 108, at I-6.

enemy as a system of systems; and considers timing because the desirability of specific effects depends on the context in which they are created.

Effects may be direct or indirect. Direct effects are "the immediate, first order consequences of a military action unaltered by intervening events or mechanisms,"[110] for example, the results of the weapon's blast and fragmentation. By contrast, indirect effects are "the delayed and/or second- and third-order consequences of military action."[111] An example would be undermining enemy civilian morale by destroying the nation's military. The ultimate effects sought through an attack may be direct or indirect (or both).

EBO has the potential of enhancing the humanitarian ends of IHL with no detriment to military necessity. In particular, the approach fosters compliance with Article 57.3 of Protocol Additional I by systemizing the search for alternative targets.[112]

However, EBO may also negatively influence IHL compliance. This is apparent in the proposal of operational concepts urging a broad interpretation of military objectives. For instance, when technological asymmetry allows one party to a conflict to attack with almost complete impunity, coercing the other into engaging in (or ceasing) particular conduct becomes theoretically impossible. The advantaged party simply bombs its opponent into compliance with its wishes. Operation Allied Force serves as a classic example of a "coercive" campaign, for the intent was never to defeat President Slobodan Milosevic's army. Rather, it was to compel a return to the bargaining table and end systematic and widespread mistreatment of the Kosovar Albanian population.[113]

In a coercion campaign, the defining question is what to strike to force the enemy leadership into making the decision you desire.[114] Effects-based operations

---

110 Id.

111 Id.

112 "When a choice is possible between several military objectives for obtaining a similar military advantage, the objective to be selected shall be that the attack on which may be expected to cause the least danger to civilian lives and to civilian objects." See also CIHL, supra note 43, Rule 2, which repeats this formula verbatim (except for substitution of the word "must" for "shall").

113 The Statement of the Extraordinary Meeting of the North Atlantic Council on 12 April 1999, reaffirmed by the Heads of State and Government at Washington on 23 April, set forth NATO's demands. They included a cessation of military action, as well as ending violence and repression of the Kosovar Albanians; withdrawal from Kosovo of military, police, and paramilitary forces; an international military presence in Kosovo; safe return of refugees and displaced persons and unhindered access to them by humanitarian aid organizations; and the establishment of a political framework agreement on the basis of the Rambouillet Accords. Press Release M-NAC-1 (99) 51, April 12, 1999; Press Release S-1 (99) 62, April 23, 1999.

114 Coercion campaigns are also labelled "compellance campaigns". *Robert Pape* identifies three types of coercive military strategies. Punishment coercion campaigns cause "suffering on civilians, either directly or indirectly by damaging the target state's economy. Bombing or naval blockades can cause shortages of key supplies such as food and clothing or deprive residents of electrical power, water, and other essential services." They seek to quickly compel the enemy leadership to comply with demands or turn the

are tailor-made for such campaigns because they mandate a hunt for those targets most likely to compel the decision-maker. The problem vis-à-vis IHL is that military capability may not be sufficiently valued by the enemy leadership to force their hand by holding it at risk. In such cases, the logically remedy may be to strike something which is *not* military in nature.

Recall Lieutenant General *Michael Short*'s well-known comments as NATO air component commander for OAF: "I felt that on the first night the power should have gone off, and major bridges around Belgrade should have gone into the Danube, and the water should be cut off so the next morning the leading citizens of Belgrade would have got up and asked 'Why are we doing this?' and asked Milosevic the same question."[115] Short perceptively realized that weakening the Yugoslav military would not necessarily force Milosevic to accede to NATO demands. Rather, Milosevic feared losing the support of the population, and therefore his power base, far more.

Thus, the logic of EBO, particularly when applied in a coercive campaign, will sometimes lead planners towards targeting non-military objectives. Predictably, as EBO becomes increasingly possible due to technological asymmetry and doctrinal maturation, there have been calls for abandoning facets of the principle of distinction. For instance, one distinguished commentator has urged that:

"We need a new paradigm when using force against societies with malevolent propensities. We must hold at risk the very way of life that sustains their depredations, and we must threaten to destroy their world as they know it if they persist. This means the air weapon should be unleashed against entire new categories of property that current conceptions of LOAC put off-limits."[116]

Cited examples include "resorts, along with other entertainment, sports, and recreational facilities" and "factories, plants, stores, and shops that produce, sell, or distribute luxury products." This is EBO at its grandest, and it aptly illustrates how an asymmetrical doctrine may influence application of IHL.

---

population against that government. Risk coercion strategies gradually degrade civilian and economic targets "in order to convince the opponent that much more severe damage will follow if concessions are not made." Denial coercion strategies "target the opponent's military ability to achieve its territorial or other political objectives, thereby compelling concessions in order to avoid futile expenditure of further resources." *Robert Pape*, Bombing to Win: Airpower and Coercion in War, Cornell U.P., 1996, pp. 15-19. See also *Paul C. Strickland*, USAF Aerospace Power Doctrine: Decisive or Coercive, in: Aerospace Power Journal, Fall 2000, p. 13; *Daniel Byman/Matthew C. Waxman/Eric V. Larson*, Air Power as a Coercive Instrument, Rand, 1999.

115 *Craig R. Whitney*, The Commander; Air Wars Won't Stay Risk-Free, General Says, New York Times, June 18, 1999, at A1.

116 *Charles J. Dunlap, Jr.*, The End of Innocence: Rethinking Noncombatancy in the Post-Kosovo Era, Strategic Review 14 (Summer 2000). He would reserve such operations for societies with a "moral compass" that is "wildly askew". Nor would civilians or objects "genuinely indispensable to the survival of the noncombatant" be targeted. But "almost everything else would be fair game." Id.

On the other side of the doctrinal coin lies the informal but no less significant doctrine of intentionally resorting to violations of IHL and other methods of wearing away the distinction principle. As discussed supra, disadvantaged forces facing technologically superior forces will often resort to such tactics, either as a matter of survival or to effectively attack the enemy. But tactics become doctrine when they rise to the level of "[f]undamental principles by which the military forces or elements thereof guide their actions in support of national objectives."[117] That is certainly occurring in the context of IHL violations now that the technological divide has become so dramatic, particularly during conflicts involving the United States and its closest allies. As discussed, it is but a short jump from weakening the principle of distinction to discarding it through the direct targeting of civilians and civilian objects. Although these actions may occur on the tactical level, at a certain point the enemy can be so incapable of militarily engaging its adversaries, that targeting protected persons and objects becomes doctrine. Terrorism represents a paradigmatic example of this dynamic.[118] Utterly incapable of defeating its enemy in force-on-force engagements, terrorists strike at non-military centers of gravity. Faced with dramatic disparity of capabilities on the battlefield, military forces may come to find the same doctrinal approach rather rational. The insurgencies in Afghanistan and Iraq have sadly signalled this reality.[119]

---

117 DoD Dictionary, supra note 8. Tactics merely involve "the employment and ordered arrangement of forces in relation to each other." Id.

118 The United States has acknowledged this dynamic in the new National Defense Strategy. It has also noted the need to develop defence strategies to cope with asymmetrical challenges to its military dominance:
"*Irregular challenges*. Increasingly sophisticated *irregular* methods e.g., terrorism and insurgency challenge U.S. security interests. Adversaries employing irregular methods aim to erode U.S. influence, patience, and political will. Irregular opponents often take a long term approach, attempting to impose prohibitive human, material, financial, and political costs on the United States to compel strategic retreat from a key region or course of action. Two factors have intensified the danger of *irregular* challenges: the rise of extremist ideologies and the absence of effective governance. Political, religious, and ethnic extremism continues to fuel conflicts worldwide. The absence of effective governance in many parts of the world creates sanctuaries for terrorists, criminals, and insurgents. Many states are unable, and in some cases unwilling, to exercise effective control over their territory or frontiers, thus leaving areas open to hostile exploitation. Our experience in the war on terrorism points to the need to reorient our military capabilities to contend with such irregular challenges more effectively." (National Defense Strategy, supra note 98, p. 3.).

119 For a discussion of insurgency as an asymmetrical doctrine, see *Thomas X. Hammes*, Insurgency: Modern Warfare Evolves into a Fourth Generation, Strategic Forum (No. 214), January 2005. See also *J.G. Eaton*, The Beauty of Asymmetry: An Examination of the Context and Practice of Asymmetric and Unconventional Warfare from a Western/Centrist Perspective, 2(1) Defence Studies 51 (2002); *Robert M. Cassidy*, Why Great Powers Fight Small Wars Badly, in: Military Review, September-October 2000, p. 41; US Army, Counterinsurgency Operations, Field Manual (Interim) 3-07.22, October 1, 2004.

Normative Asymmetry: Since customary international humanitarian law, at least in theory, governs all States,[120] legal asymmetry, in which belligerents are bound by differing legal norms, generally derives from treaty Party status. Most multilateral conflicts present a complex maze of applicability. Consider the war in Iraq. All major belligerents were Party to the 1949 Geneva Conventions. Beyond those four agreements, neither the United States nor Iraq was Party to Protocol Additional I. The fact that the UK was a Party imposed no legal obligations on British forces because the protocol only applies between a Party and non-Party State when the latter "accepts and applies the provisions thereof."[121] Iraq had not. The 1907 Hague Convention (IV) respecting the Laws and Customs of War on Land (and its annexed Regulations) was inapplicable through operation of its general participation clause since Iraq was not a Party.[122] Although a number of other relevant IHL treaties avoid this result by providing that they remain operative between Parties thereto even if all belligerents are not Party, none applied on this basis.[123] Finally, the 1993 Chemical Weapons Convention did bind the UK and US despite Iraq's non-Party status because it prohibits using chemical weapons "under any circumstances."[124] So other than the Geneva Conventions, the only relevant treaties that formally constrained all three major belligerents were the 1925 Gas Protocol and the 1972 Biological Weapons Convention. Resultantly, in Iraq, customary law, not treaty law, governed the conduct of hostilities. Given the complicated schemes for applicability of treaties, this is likely to be the case more often than not.

Even when bound by the same customary and treaty law, asymmetry can result from differing *interpretations* thereof. Most well know in this regard is the US approach to the definition of "military objective". Article 52 of Protocol Additional I sets forth the classic definition: "objects which by their nature, location, purpose or use make an effective contribution to military action and whose total or partial

[120] For an excellent summary of the nature and sources of customary international humanitarian law, see *Jean-Marie Henckaerts*, Study on Customary International Humanitarian Law: A Contribution to the Understanding and Respect for the Rule of Law in Armed Conflict, 87:857 International Review of the Red Cross 175 (2005).

[121] PI, supra note 43, art. 96.

[122] HIVR, supra note 50, art. 2. A general participation clause (*clausula si omnes*) precludes application of the treaty when all belligerents are not party to the treaty. The intent is to avoid the creation of multiple legal regimes in the same conflict.

[123] E.g., Convention and Protocol for the Protection of Cultural Property in the Event of Armed Conflict, May 14, 1954, 249 UNTS 240 (US/UK not a Party, although signatories); Convention on the Prohibition of Military or Any Other Hostile Use of Environmental Modification Techniques, December 10, 1976, 31 UST 333, 16 International Legal Materials 88 (Iraq not a Party); Convention on Prohibitions or Restrictions on the Use of Certain Conventional Weapons Which May Be Deemed to Be Excessively Injurious or to Have Indiscriminate Effects, October 10, 1980, 19 International Legal Materials 1523 (1980) (Iraq not a Party); Convention on the Prohibition of the Use, Stockpiling, Production and Transfer of Anti-Personnel Mines and on Their Destruction, September 18, 1997, 36 International Legal Materials 1507 (1997) (Iraq and US are not parties).

[124] Chemical Weapons Convention, supra note 103, art. 1.1.

destruction, capture or neutralization, in the circumstances ruling at the time, offers a definite military advantage."[125] Although the United States accepts this textual formula, it adopts a broader interpretation in practice. In particular, the *Commander's Handbook on the Law of Naval Warfare*, the most current of the American law of war manuals, includes "war sustaining" activities within the scope of the phrase.[126] Or consider the 1949 Third Geneva Convention's obligation to convene an Article 5 tribunal to determine the status of detainees when doubt as to their entitlement to prisoner of war status arises.[127] The US agrees it is bound by this provision, but has made a blanket determination that no doubt exists about the status of any of the detainees at Guantanamo.[128] Some States disagree with this approach. Thus, *how* belligerents conduct themselves may be determined as much by their interpretation of the law as by the fact that the law binds them.

At times, asymmetry may actually drive the differing interpretations of IHL adopted by States. Take military objectives. To the extent a valued entity is vulnerable to enemy attack, there will be an incentive to exclude it from the ambit of military objectives. Conversely, the enemy has an incentive to include it. The de-

---

125 PI, supra note 43, art. 52(2). Protocols II and III of the Conventional Weapons Convention and the Second Protocol to the Cultural Property Convention, as well as many military manuals and training material (including those of the US), repeat this formula. Protocol on Prohibitions or Restrictions on the Use of Mines, Booby Traps and Other Devices (Protocol II), 1980, as amended, 1996, art. 2.6, 35 International Legal Materials 1206 (1980); Protocol on Prohibitions or Restrictions on the Use of Incendiary Weapons (Protocol III), 1980, art. 1.3, 1342 UNTS 171; Second Protocol to the Hague Convention of 1954 for Protection of Cultural Property in Event of Armed Conflict, 1996, art. 1(f), 38 International Legal Materials 769 (1999). For manuals and training material, see Judge Advocate General's School, Operational Law Handbook 12 (2004); NWP 1-14M, supra note 59, para. 8.1.1; UK Manual, supra note 79, para. 5.4.1; German Manual, supra note 89, sec. 442.

126 "Economic targets of the enemy that indirectly but effectively support and sustain the enemy's war-fighting capability may also be attacked." NWP 1-14M, supra note 59, para. 8.1.1. This assertion is labelled a "statement of customary international law". The Handbook cites General Counsel, Department of Defense, Letter of September 22, 1972, reprinted in 67 American Journal of International Law 123 (1973), as the basis for this characterization. US joint doctrine reinforces this approach by providing that "[c]ivilian objects consist of all civilian property and activities other than those used to support or sustain the adversary's warfighting capability." Joint Publication 3-60, supra note 108, at A-2. The term "war sustaining" also appears in the Instructions for the US Military Commission at Guantanamo. Department of Defense, Military Commission Instruction No. 2, Crimes and Elements for Trials by Military Commission, April 30, 2003, para. 5D.

127 "Should any doubt arise as to whether persons, having committed a belligerent act and having fallen into the hands of the enemy, belong to any of the categories enumerated in Article 4, such persons shall enjoy the protection of the present Convention until such time as their status has been determined by a competent tribunal." GCIII, supra note 50, art. 5.

128 *George Bush*, Memorandum, Humane Treatment of al Qaeda and Taliban Detainees, February 7, 2002.

bate over whether media stations are military objectives exemplifies this dynamic.[129]

Asymmetry in capabilities also powerfully influences *application* of IHL. This is primarily so with regard to the requirements for precautions in attack. Recall that the attacker must "do everything feasible to verify" the target's status as a military objective; select weapons and tactics with a view to minimizing collateral damage and incidental injury; apply the principle of proportionality; choose the target (from among potential targets offering similar military advantage) that poses the least danger to civilian lives and objects; and give "effective advance warning" of attacks, "unless circumstances do not permit".[130]

Technologically advanced militaries can achieve a far higher level of precautions than their opponents can. State-of-the-art ISR capabilities provide a fuller understanding of the target system and make possible a better estimate of likely collateral damage and incidental injury. Precision-guided munitions (PGM) limit unintended effects of a strike. Moreover, because PGMs are more accurate, the explosive charge needed to achieve desired results is typically smaller than in their unguided counterparts. Powerful C4ISR assets allow high-tech militaries to identify a greater number of potential targets and advanced forces posses weapons systems more capable of attacking them. Finally, because their advantages may be so dramatic that they can conduct operations with little risk, technologically superior forces have more opportunities to warn the civilian population of impending attack.

Of course, the legal standard that applies to belligerents is a constant. However, because they have greater ability to exercise precautions in attack, advanced militaries are held to a higher standard – as a matter of law – because more precautions are feasible. As the gap between "haves" and "have-nots" widens in 21st century warfare, this normative relativism will grow. In a sense, we are witnessing the birth of a capabilities-based IHL regime.

This is certainly apparent in the assessments produced in the aftermath of recent conflicts. The persistent refrain in each was a failure to exhaust the possibilities for precautions in attack. To illustrate the extent to which expectations have risen, recall that Human Rights Watch chose the title "*Off Target*" for OIF report – even though the air campaign was undoubtedly the most precise in the history of warfare and despite the fact that Iraqi forces engaged in widespread, systematic, and unambiguous IHL violations. Thus, asymmetry creates a paradoxical situation. The more a military is capable of conducting "clean" warfare, the greater its

---

[129] It has been a contentious subject since NATO struck Belgrade's Radio Televisija Srbije (RTS) facility during Operation Allied Force in 1999. Litigation in the European Court of Human Rights ensued, but was eventually dismissed on jurisdictional grounds. Bankovic & Others v. Belgium, the Czech Republic, Denmark, France, Germany, Greece, Hungary, Iceland, Italy, Luxembourg, the Netherlands, Norway, Poland, Portugal, Spain, Turkey and the United Kingdom, Eur. Ct. Hum. Rts. App. No. 52207/99. The issue resurfaced when Coalition forces struck media facilities during Operation Iraqi Freedom. On those strikes, see Schmitt, The Conduct of Hostilities during Operation Iraqi Freedom, supra note 20.

[130] PI, supra note 43, art. 57. See also CIHL, supra note 43, Rules 15-21.

legal obligations, and the more critical the international community will be of any instance of collateral damage and incidental injury (even when unavoidable).

The complexity of formal treaty applicability and interpretation is exacerbated by the fact that, as a matter of *policy*, States may require their troops to observe the terms of a treaty regardless of provisions therein that release them from compliance. It is, for example, difficult to imagine Germany, France, or the United Kingdom – all States that regularly deploy forces abroad – acquiescing to any violations of Protocol Additional I even in a conflict in which the agreement was inoperative.

Further, a belligerent may impose normative restrictions on its force's conduct that are not derivative of law, but instead based purely on policy. As an example, Coalition rules of engagement in Iraq during the ground war forbade soldiers from targeting "enemy infrastructure (public works, commercial communications facilities, dams) lines of communication (roads, highways, tunnels, bridges, railways) and economic objects (commercial storage facilities, pipelines) unless necessary for self-defense or if ordered by your Commander."[131] In IHL, the limiting standards are merely that the infrastructure qualifies as a military objective and can be attacked consistent with the principle of proportionality. For policy reasons, such as keeping critical infrastructure intact in order to ease post-conflict recovery, the rules of engagement were more restrictive than the law. Thus, normative asymmetry derives from both policy and law.

As a practical matter, normative asymmetry between coalition partners may be more significant than that between opposing belligerents. Consider Rules of Engagement (ROE). ROE represent guidance to the warfighter based on operational, policy, and legal concerns. To the extent that partners are bound by differing legal (or policy) standards, they have two options. First, they may operate using different use of force ROE. This situation complicates coalition command and control, can be dangerous to friendly forces, and poses significant risk to civilians.[132] Alternatively, because no member will accept ROE that violate national legal and policy positions, a coalition may adopt common ROE incorporating the most restrictive standards from among those applicable to the partners. In either event, normative asymmetry shapes the "rules of the game".

Such differences may even find their way into operational planning. As an example, during OAF, all NATO allies possessed the power to veto missions. On multiple occasions, France played the "red card" to block missions.[133] Legal concerns certainly influenced its decisions about when to exercise this authority. This experience led, in part, to the US decision to build a coalition of the willing *of its choice* for Operation Enduring Freedom, rather than accept the NATO offer of in-

---

[131] CFLCC ROE Card, Iraq, 2003, at para. 1e, reprinted in Operational Law Handbook, supra note 125, at 101.

[132] For an interesting discussion of the complications caused by forces operating with differing rules of engagement in the same area, see *F.M. Lorenz*, Rules of Engagement in Somalia: Were They Effective?, 42 Naval Law Review 62 (1995).

[133] BBC News Online, US General Condemns French "Red Card", October 22, 1999, at news.bbc.co.uk/1/hi/world/482015.stm.

volvement, and the unwieldy decision-making mechanism that would accompany it. Of course, aside from the formal right to veto a mission, the most restrictive approach may govern de facto merely because those bound by such norms will be hesitant to participate in a coalition where its partners act in a contrary manner, lest they be "tainted" through association. Therefore, survival of the coalition may dictate which norms apply.

Alternatively, legal and policy asymmetry may lead coalitions to turn to members with greater normative leeway to conduct certain missions. There may be good policy reasons for steering clear of being the coalition partner that executes the normatively sensitive operations, but such a scenario is nevertheless conceivable. One distinguished scholar has suggested that this is a likely prospect during maritime intercept operations (MIO).[134] In such operations, the nationality of warships is distinct and apparent. An intercept by one State's vessel is therefore less likely to be seen as "tainting" other States than would be the case in ground operations. Even ground-based situations can be imagined in which one coalition partner would take on tasks forbidden to its partners because the stakes are especially high or a national interest is specially affected for that State.

Participatory Asymmetry: The list of actors in the modern battlespace is becoming extraordinarily confusing. Many countries, most notably the United States, now employ private contractors to perform functions that were traditionally within the purview of military personnel.[135] Indeed, there are more contractors in Iraq today than all non-US Coalition forces combined.[136] At the same time, consider the variety of forces facing the Coalition: the regular army; Republican Guards; Special Republic Guards; Fedayeen Saddam paramilitary forces; civilians impressed into service; groups led by tribal leaders whose authority was at risk; religious zealots fighting the Christians; those who wanted a political voice (Sadr and his Mahdi Army); those who had a relative killed, wounded or insulted during the fighting; foreign jihadists; and pure criminals.[137]

Who is involved in a conflict will affect how the hostilities are conducted. This fact derives from two related factors: enforcement mechanisms and sanctions. First, many such participants are not subject to an internal disciplinary system designed to ensure compliance with IHL. Consider US civilians in Iraq. Government

---

134 Discussion under Chatham House Rules a conference entitled "The Law of Armed Conflict: Problems and Prospects", April 18-19, 2005, Royal Institute of International Affairs, London, UK. The proceedings are available at www.riia.org/pdf/research/il/ILParmedconflict.pdf.

135 See generally *Schmitt*, Humanitarian Law and Direct Participation, supra note 61.

136 Estimates on the number of contractors vary widely as there is no central registry documenting their presence. However, estimates are in the 50-100,000 range, with roughly 20,000 of these working for private security firms. Contractor Deaths in Iraq Prove Difficult to Track, USATODAY.com (Associated Press), May 21, 2005, at www.usatoday.com/news/world/iraq/2005-05-21-iraq-contractors_x.htm. There were 23,900 non-US Coalition troops in Iraq as of March 15, 2005. GlobalSecurity.org, Non-US Forces in Iraq – early December 2004, at www.globalsecurity.org/military/ops/iraq_orbat_coalition.htm.

137 Author interview with senior US military intelligence officer.

civil servants are subject to an administrative, but not judicial, disciplinary system. Contractor personnel are even less formally accountable. In their case, the contracting officer, not the military commander, exercises "supervisory" control. In the event of misconduct, the contracting officer may impose pecuniary penalties on the company, but has no authority vis-à-vis the employee. Rather, discipline is the company's responsibility.[138] Some States, including the United States, have responded to this void by extending criminal jurisdiction to their civilians on the battlefield.[139] However, even in such cases, the absence of a judicial system *in situ* is a significant impediment to full enforcement of IHL among one's own forces. As should be apparent from the catalogue of participants on the Iraqi side, it may be that there is no disciplinary oversight at all of those engaging in hostilities.

Moreover, consider sanctions. Individuals who do not qualify as combatants will not enjoy the protections that the status offers upon capture. In particular, they may be punished under the domestic law of their captor (or another State) for their actions, including having attacked combatants. If they have committed war crimes, international tribunals (with jurisdiction), as well as national courts vis-à-vis crimes for which universal jurisdiction exists, may also try them.[140] Yet, as a practical matter, the fact that they are already punishable for participating in the conflict diminishes the incentives for complying with IHL. In a sense, they have less to lose than lawful combatants in violating IHL. Therefore, the make-up of the forces opposing each other influences the extent to which the participants will abide by IHL.

Ad Bellum or Moral Asymmetry: It is a foundational tenet of international law that the *jus ad bellum* and *jus in bello* are separate bodies of law with no normative influence on each other.[141] The fact that a State acts in violation of the *jus ad*

---

138 See Letter from *Donald H. Rumsfeld*, Secretary of Defense, to The Honorable Ike Skelton, May 4, 2004, www.house.gov/skelton/5-4-04_Rumsfeld_letter_on_contractors.pdf. The lack of command and control over contract personnel invites abuses. Some US judge advocates have reportedly charged that contractors were used during interrogations of detainees in Iraq to limit knowledge of aggressive techniques. The claim was denied by a Pentagon spokesperson. *Joshua Chaffin*, Contract Interrogators Hired to Avoid Supervision, Financial Times, May 21, 2004, p. 9.

139 For instance, includes the Military Extraterritorial Jurisdiction Act, which subjects individuals employed by the US military abroad, whether directly or as contractors, to federal jurisdiction. Military Extraterritorial Jurisdiction Act, 10 USC § 3261 (2000). The Act was intended primarily to address crimes by contractors against US military personnel and their dependents abroad. Also providing possible jurisdiction is the War Crimes Act of 1996, 18 USC § 2441 (2004), and the federal torture statute, 18 USC § 2340A (2000).

140 On the principle of universality and war crimes, see *Yoram Dinstein*, The Universality Principle and War Crimes, in: Michael N. Schmitt/Leslie C. Green (eds.), The Law of Armed Conflict: Into the Next Millennium, 17 Naval War College International Law Studies, 1998.

141 The US Military Tribunal at Nuremberg made this point in US v. Wilhelm List et. al. (The Hostages Trial):
"We concur in the views expressed in the following text on the subject: 'Whatever may be the cause of a war that has broken out, and whether or no the cause be a so-called

bellum does not release its victim from adherence to the *jus in bello*. For instance, that the US and its Allies were acting in legitimate collective defence in Afghanistan,[142] does not excuse mistreatment of prisoners they took on the field of battle.

Despite this truism, the fact remains that in most conflicts one side acts unlawfully, the other lawfully, with regard to the resort to armed force; they are dissimilarly placed vis-à-vis the *jus ad bellum*. In practice, this asymmetry exerts a powerful influence on the willingness of parties to observe IHL. To the extent Country A believes itself to have been legally wronged by Country B, there is a natural (and historic) tendency for it to view B's soldiers and citizens as less worthy of IHL's benefits. After all, they represent lawlessness. Why should they enjoy the equal benefits of the law?

Of course, the problematic reality is that both sides usually contend that they comply with international law ... and the others do not.[143] Such claims, even in clear cases to the contrary, may well resonate with the aggressor's population, leadership, and military, and, at times, even with those outside the country. Perceptions are what matter in terms of shaping attitudes; attitudes often determine action.

Along the same lines, the parties may be morally asymmetrical. Despite justifiable discomfort with adjudging morality, the truth remains that in many conflicts one side acts immorally. Ethnic cleansing is a tragic contemporary example, one that led to claims that although the bombing of the Federal Republic of Yugosla-

just cause, the same rules of International Law are valid as to what must not be done, and must be done by the belligerents themselves in making war against each other; and as between the belligerents and neutral States. This is so, even if the declaration of war is *ipso facto* a violation of International Law, as when a belligerent declares war upon a neutral State for refusing passage to its troops, or when a State goes to war in patent violation of its obligations under the Covenant of the League or of the General Treaty for the Renunciation of War. To say that, because such a declaration of war is *ipso facto* a violation of International Law, it is 'inoperative in law and without any judicial significance,' is erroneous. The rules of International Law apply to war from whatever cause it originates. Oppenheim's *International Law,* II Lauterpacht, p. 174." (The United Nations War Crimes Commission, VIII Law Reports of the Trials of War Criminals 60 [1949]).

142 See analysis in *Michael N. Schmitt*, Counter-terrorism and the Use of Force in International Law, 32 Israel Yearbook on Human Rights 53 (2002).

143 The classic example is the Gulf War of 1990-91, in which the Iraqi Revolutionary Command Council justified the annexation of Kuwait as follows: "What has befallen other states in the Arab lands befell Iraq when colonialism divested it of a dear part of it, namely Kuwait, and kept Iraq away from the waters to prevent it from acquiring part of its tactical and strategic abilities, and thus kept part of its people and part of its wealth away from the origin and the wellspring." (Excerpts From Iraq's Statement on Kuwait, in: New York Times, August 9, 1990, p. A18.) The statement was issued six days following the Security Council's condemnation of the Iraqi attack as "breach of international peace and security." The vote was 14-0 (Yemen did not participate). SC Res. 660 (August 2, 1990).

via in 1999 may have been illegal, it was nevertheless legitimate.[144] Whatever the objective reality, States understandably often demonize their opponents in order to shore up civilian and military morale and garner international support. For better or worse, conflicts continue to be viewed in terms of "good" and "evil". The persistence into the 21st century of ancient notions such as just war and jihad evidences this dynamic.[145] Indeed, one prominent scholar-practitioner has suggested applying IHL differently to a belligerent whose "moral compass" is "wildly askew".[146] There is no basis for distinctions founded on legal or moral asymmetry in international humanitarian law, but the reality is that such differences, real or perceived, matter.[147]

Concluding Thoughts

This article has identified various forms of asymmetry that influence the application or interpretation of international humanitarian law in 21st century armed conflicts. Clearly, the most visible influence is that exerted by technological differences in the military power of opposing sides. However, other forms of asymmetry also drive the willingness of participants to abide by the norms of IHL, or, perhaps more precisely, deviate from them.

The real danger is that violations of IHL by one side usually lead to corresponding violations by the other, thereby initiating a vicious cycle of lawlessness. Recall that the willingness of States to abide by humanitarian law is in part based on the notion of reciprocity. Parties agree to limit their actions during hostilities because they will benefit when their opponent does the same; IHL presumes corresponding interests among the belligerents. Yet, when asymmetry disrupts the presumption and one side violates the agreed rules, the practical incentive for compliance by the other fades. Instead, IHL begins appearing as if it operates to the benefit of one's foes. When that happens, the dictates of the law appear out of step with reality, perhaps even "quaint".[148] So, the real danger is not so much that

---

144 And the opposite may hold as well. A State acting may be acting legally, but illegitimately. An example would be an enforcement operation authorized pursuant to Chapter VII of the United Nations Charter that illegitimately intruded into the affairs of the target State. To presume the moral infallibility of the Security Council would be naïve.

145 *Abu Musab al-Zarqawi* has reportedly justified the killing of innocents in suicide bombings against US forces on precisely this basis: "The killing of infidels by any method including martyrdom" has been "sanctified by many scholars even if it means killing innocent Muslims ... This legality has been agreed upon so as not to disrupt jihad ... These operations are our lethal weapons against the enemy." (Al Qaeda Defends Killings, International Herald Tribune, May 19, 2005, p. 4).

146 See supra fn. 116.

147 Interestingly, the international community seems more tolerant of IHL violations by the weaker side. One might cynically conclude that it seems more "moral" (or at least justifiable) to deviate from the rules of the game when one is at the disadvantage.

148 See *Alberto R. Gonzales*, Memorandum for the President, Decision Re Application of the Geneva Convention on Prisoners of War to the Conflict with Al Qaeda and the

the various forms of asymmetry will result in violations of IHL. Rather, it is that asymmetries may unleash a dynamic that undercuts the very foundations of this body of law.

Taliban, January 25, 2002, in which the White House Chief Counsel wrote that the war on terrorism "renders obsolete Geneva's strict limitations on questioning of enemy prisoners and renders quaint some of its provisions".

'The end justifies the means' – Should this be the philosophy?

William H. Boothby

Assistant Director Legal at the UK Joint Doctrine and Concepts Centre

This paper was presented as a reply to and comment on the paper entitled 'Asymmetrical Warfare and International Humanitarian Law' delivered by *Michael N Schmitt* in the first panel of the symposium.

Noting Mr *Schmitt*'s scholarly, comprehensive, wide ranging, well considered and well reasoned treatment of a complex and fundamentally important issue, one is left with seemingly little of significance to say. As one reads the document, one wonders 'so what' and imagines that that might be a profitable avenue to develop, so it is somewhat frustrating to note the final paragraph where Mr *Schmitt*, in the author's view correctly, sees the greatest risk of asymmetry as being the marginalisation of IHL.

Perhaps the right starting point is to ask if there is such a thing as symmetrical warfare, and if so is it a good thing? On one level, there is almost always a victor or some party with the upper hand in any conflict. If the stalemate trench warfare of WW1 is symmetry, perhaps that is not what we want. Alternatively we may be referring to symmetry of general approach to conflict, a kind of gentlemanly agreement as to the rules of the game and so on, rather like cricket. Clearly those days are long gone, particularly in relation to recent asymmetric conflicts.

Perhaps asymmetry is facilitated by our engagement in wars with wider objectives. No longer do we go to war simply to destroy our enemy. Our aims are now framed in terms of limited objectives and wider ideas of long term stability in a region and so on. Is it the fact that such wider aims are easier to frustrate by the techniques all too frequently employed by our inferior adversaries in these asymmetric conflicts that makes such an approach more attractive to them?

Mr *Schmitt*'s paper argues that the ability to gather, process and react to information about an opponent with the goal of disorienting him is determinative of the battle today. Surely our goal is typically minimal destruction, speedier re-construction, clinical warfare all coherent with our typical western technology loving mindset. Is it not time to reconstruct what we mean by 'the battle' and rather think in terms of all phases of the crisis including those which do not involve the military? Certainly we have the technology to destroy what we wish, but do we have insight? Yes we have information, but do we have understanding? Yes we have magnificent machines and control of the battle-space, but can we control the 13 year old whose mother we have killed and who needs vengeance. The better we say our weapons and doctrine are, the more that 13 year old believes we intended to kill his mother, and we have just recruited him and his school as our asymmetric enemies.

Violations of IHL are indeed a classic response to asymmetric inferiority. Increasingly we will see those violations coming with rhetoric that IHL is a peculiarly western construct to which those seeking to attack us feel no compulsion to adhere. This will be designed to turn its breach into a coherent part of their campaign.

Mr *Schmitt*'s analysis of the issue by reference to perfidy is spot on. It forces one to focus on the relevant point, namely that asymmetry generates breaches of very widely accepted principles. So we are talking about adversaries who feel themselves forced to do that which they themselves know and believe to be wrong. They are essentially performing these acts out of a belief that the end justifies the means. The end is the attack of nations, armies and interests which they profoundly believe to be evil. One can readily imagine that, in such a mindset, whatever moral baggage attaches to the breach of legal principles which you did not make but which you are broadly prepared to accept pales into insignificance against the need to contribute to the defeat of the evil one. The compelling logic here is proved by the willingness to re-define ethics basic to the inferior's moral or religious code where these conflict with the pressing need to act.

If therefore we accept that the behaviour which we have identified, and which we find so unacceptable is the logical reaction to asymmetry, the question which next arises is what do we do about it? The sensible approach would appear to be to break down the logic and, in an effects based way, to emphasise the logical weak points in the adversary's position. This implies that we should aim to:

1. show that the adversary's behaviour re-enforces opposition to him, hardens resolve and attracts allies to his opponents;
2. feed widely held revulsion back into his domestic populations to weaken support or promote controversy;
3. focus on the innocence of the victims of his attacks;
4. demonstrate that poverty is the inevitable consequence of his activities;
5. attack the argument that these adversaries have a monopoly on ethical and religious principle by demonstrating that IHL, with which we seek to comply, reflects our ethical position, a coherence absent on their side.

It follows that upholding the law is fundamental to our position and our chances of success. We must be seen to adhere to the principles we developed and to repress breaches. This is where expansive approaches to the definition of military objective may prove to be distinctly counter-productive.

So we must make the case on what we believe.

We must articulate and promulgate the moral dimension of what we believe.

We must state clearly why the conduct listed in Mr *Schmitt*'s paper repels us.

We must make the point that while we did develop the law, the principles it contains are universally accepted and that nobody has come up with a better formula if, that is, you accept that war should not descend every time into utter bar-

barity, wanton destruction and chaos. So perhaps we need to demand credit for the formulation of this body of law and to be more evangelical about it.

Later in the paper, Mr *Schmitt* suggests that lack of technological wherewithal precludes engagement in effects based operations. I am not sure this is really right. Al Qaeda handling of the media, the impact of the very unpredictability of their military activities and the mere fact of their diffuse structure would all suggest that they are indeed the masters of effects based operations.

There is a substantial effects based dividend to be acquired from being seen to comply with, for example, rules as to treatment of prisoners. If we are seen to breach those principles, we must be seen to investigate thoroughly and to bring the wrongdoers to justice. Such breaches erode the moral basis for our insistence on appropriate behaviour by an adversary. If we are seen to comply, we have at least a basis for complaint, we have some hope of inspiring the adversary to higher standards and we have a basis for using the media to his external and internal disadvantage if he does not comply. Similar potential for effects based advantage may exist in relation to human shielding, targeting, precautions in attack and so on.

Mr *Schmitt*'s paper also notes that, in a compellance campaign, the defining question is what to strike to force the enemy leadership into making the decision that you want. Perhaps, however, in a compellance campaign the really defining question is do I know enough about how my adversary's mind works, what his perspectives and priorities are to determine the correct approach to the problem WHICH MAY NOT BE MILITARY.

To the man with a hammer, every problem is a nail. To continue the analogy, when that man has a slight leak in his central heating system, his response destroys the system and produces a major flood. So the man with a hammer needs to start to invent and use a spanner. We need to get very lateral in our thinking and very integrated in our governmental response to crises. Developing thinking in the UK looks to strategically integrated responses to crises, and work is under way to achieve the degree of strategic coherence across government departments necessary to achieve this. Future conflicts will be multi-phased and the warfighting element is likely to be of limited duration. The establishment of a peaceful steady state will be the strategic objective and we will need to employ all levers of government in an appropriately structured and thought through mix in order to accomplish that aim.

Finally, Mr *Schmitt* discusses good and evil as a prism through which wars are viewed, but is this really so? The alternative view is that wars are too often viewed as an evil per se, that societies that lack clear moral principles will regard the war itself as the evil rather than the wrongdoing that gave rise to it.

My conclusion is that it is adherence to moral principle enshrined in IHL that defines us. To defend ourselves, we must continue to develop, to assert and to enforce that body of law. What Mr *Schmitt* has defined is a fact of contemporary life. We do not have to let it change who we are, what we believe and how we behave.

When I finished reading the piece, I had a philosophical question that would not go away, namely "Are we also impeded because nowadays weakness appears as moral strength in certain areas of the media, where strength is seen as in itself justifying the assault upon it?" Perhaps that would form the basis of an interesting future debate.

Comment: Is the Principle of Distinction Outdated?

Stefan Oeter

University of Hamburg, Germany

1. Introduction

Asymmetrical warfare is not a new phenomenon in military life, as *Michael Schmitt* rightly stresses in the introduction of his paper. Since time immemorial, military strategists reflect and argue about asymmetries in warfare, and since two centuries asymmetrical warfare is an explicit issue in military theory.[1] When the powerful army of Napoleonic France invaded Spain two hundred years ago, Spaniards took refuge to partisan tactics and established the notion of 'guerrilla' warfare. The French military had huge problems in finding an adequate answer to such strategy. The same happened in the German-French War of 1870/71 with the notorious 'franc-tireurs'. Late nineteenth-century military lawyers had to grapple with the problem of how to distinguish (acceptable) militias from such (illicit) 'franc-tireurs'. Practically all the colonial wars of late-nineteenth and twentieth century were asymmetrical wars. The savage partisan wars which the German occupying armies had to fight in Yugoslavia, Greece and Russia are notorious in military history, and some of the provisions of Art. 4 A of the IIIrd Geneva Convention, Art. 4 A para. 1 No. 2 in particular, were direct reactions to these experiences.[2] The problems of the U.S. armed forces in Vietnam as well as the problems of the Red Army in Afghanistan illustrate the same point. Thus asymmetry in itself has nothing revolutionary – just to the contrary, it is a classic of international humanitarian law.

Does this mean that there is no new challenge for IHL? Unfortunately there is, notwithstanding the long history of humanitarian law doctrine dealing with the issue of asymmetrical warfare.[3] Being a commentator to the seminal paper of *Michael N. Schmitt* is helpful here, since one might refer to the thorough description

---

1 See only *Herfried Münkler*, The Wars of the 21st Century, 85 International Review of the Red Cross 849 (2003), pp. 7-21.

2 See *Jean Pictet*, La Convention de Genève III, relative au traitement des prisonniers de guerre, Geneva 1958, pp. 59-65.

3 Comp. also *Toni Pfanner*, Asymmetrical Warfare from the Perspective of Humanitarian Law and Humanitarian Action, 87 International Review of the Red Cross 856 (2005), pp. 149 et seq.

of the state of the art in his paper, but constitutes a problem at the same time – a problem since one may come to different conclusions in certain regards, sees differences in assessment which are linked to the historical 'longue-durée' mentioned above.

2. The Phenomenon of Asymmetrical Warfare

The empirical part of *Michael Schmitt*'s paper, his description of the current asymmetries in military technology and resources and its repercussions on military strategies, are so thorough and dense that I find few points of disagreement.[4] Today, "battlefields are multidimensional", as *Michael Schmitt* has explained to us. Technology has evolved to the point where the concept of a line marking the heart of the battle no longer makes sense in too much a number of cases.[5] There may be similarities to traditional forms of asymmetrical warfare, in particular concerning partisan warfare in situations of military occupation, where clear frontlines also did not exist.[6] But the regular forces functioning as occupying power and the partisans were still facing each other directly, man to man in situations of ground combat. This is becoming more and more different, as a consequence of 'revolution in military affairs', in conventional warfare. There may be ground forces facing each other, like in the first phase of the Iraq invasion. "But the conflict is everywhere", as *Michael Schmitt* tells us. In modern warfare, at least if led by high-tech military like the U.S. forces, operations often are led over long distance.[7] Aerial attacks and cruise-missile raids can strike everywhere in enemy territory, and legitimate military objectives will be scattered over much of this territory. Distinguishing between military objectives and civilian objectives becomes much more complex in such a situation, but all the more important. It may be that an attacking force will attempt to stretch the notion of 'military objective', will try to extend it beyond military installations and infrastructure delivering a direct contribution to military efforts.[8] The number of 'dual-use objects' in a larger sense is nearly infinite – offices and housing of the political leadership, administrative buildings which house authorities controlling the country, radio and TV stations used in political propaganda, industrial installations which help the enemy in earning the

---

4 See, in addition, *Ivan Arrequin-Toft*, How the Weak Win Wars: A theory of Asymmetric Conflict, in: International Security (Summer 2001), pp. 19 et seq., and *Montgomery C. Meigs*, Unorthodox Thoughts about Asymmetric Warfare, in: Parameters (Summer 2003), pp. 4 et seq.

5 See *Michael N. Schmitt*, Targeting and Humanitarian law: Current Issues, 34 Israel Yearbook on Human Rights (2004), pp. 59-60.

6 See *Eyal Benvenisti*, The International Law of Occupation, 2nd ed. Princeton 2004.

7 See also *Michael N. Schmitt*, The Impact of High- and Low-Tech Warfare on the Principle of Distinction, Briefing Paper, International Humanitarian Law Research Initiative, Program on Humanitarian Policy and Conflict Research at Harvard University, http://www.ihlresearch.org/portal/ihli/alabama.php, at pp. 4-7.

8 Id., pp. 7-9.

foreign currency needed to sustain the war effort.[9] If you give up the traditional requirement of a 'direct contribution to military efforts', there is no trace of a clear criterion of distinction any more.

3. The Principle of Distinction – an Endangered Species?

Here the normative assumptions of IHL come into play. Should we simply accept, in a resignative mood, the fact that the process of blurring the traditional distinctions seems inevitable, impossible to stem? Should we accept such erosion of the principle of distinction as something unalterable, or do we still need the prescriptive approach of traditional IHL in order to stem the flood of escalating violence, create legal dams and try to channel all the potential forms of warfare into the bed of restricted, but legitimate means and methods of warfare? On a normative level – and we are lawyers – raising the question means answering it in the positive.[10] The traditional rules on means and methods of warfare may be in danger of eroding as a result of the described asymmetries, but this does not mean that we should give them up – just to the contrary, we need them all the more desperately.[11]
Accordingly, the principle of distinction is a species of rules particularly endangered in the course of asymmetrical warfare.[12] Not that this principle never had any challenges to cope with – it always belonged to the basic sets of rules which in practice were put into doubt by belligerents that were not willing to restrict their use of violence as soon as such restrictions were perceived as being harmful to one's strategies.[13] The principle of distinction always was perceived by armies with superior firing power as too restrictive, as an annoyance hindering them to end the war as soon as possible (which often was understood as being the ultimate

---

9 See *Yoram Dinstein*, Legitimate Military Objectives under the Current Jus in Bello, in: A.E. Wall (ed.), Legal and Ethical Lessons of NATO's Kosovo Campaign (U.S. Naval War College International Law Studies, vol. 78), Newport 2002, pp. 139 et seq.; see also *Marco Sassòli*, Targeting: The Scope and Utility of the Concept of 'Military Objectives' for the Protection of Civilians in Contemporary Armed Conflicts, in: David Wippman/Matthew Evangelista (eds.), New Wars, New Laws? Applying the Laws of War in 21st Century Conflicts, Ardsley, N.Y 2005, pp. 193-196.

10 See *Marco Sassòli*, supra note 9, pp. 194-195.

11 See *William J. Fenrick*, The Law Applicable to Targeting and Proportionality after Operation Allied Force: A View from the Outside, 2000 Yearbook of International Humanitarian Law, pp. 51 et seq.

12 See also *Christopher Greenwood*, International Law and the Conduct of Military Operations: Stocktaking at the Start of a New Millenium, in: Michael N. Schmitt (ed.), International law Across the Spectrum of Conflict (US Naval War College International law Studies, vol. 75), Newport 2000, pp. 139 et seq.

13 See only *Matthew Lippman*, Aerial Attacks on Civilians and the Humanitarian Law of War: Technology and Terror from World War I to Afghanistan, 33 California Western International Law Journal (2002), pp. 1 et seq.

humanitarian challenge).[14] If you want to compel the enemy politically to abide again by the law, you should hit him where he is most vulnerable, so goes the logic. Military installations will not always be the best target of attacks in that sense.[15] At the same time, with the other side being militarily inferior, the temptation always has been very great to use the civilian population as a kind of hostage, by hiding military installations amongst concentrations of civilians, and operating with the advantage of suspense from civilian camouflage. There even exists a temptation, as *Michael Schmitt* has pointed out in his paper, to disregard completely traditional concepts of distinction and make the civilian population the primary target of violence, in order to subvert the power and the authority of the party exercising control over a territory.[16] Accordingly, both sides in asymmetrical situations always were in danger of neglecting the principle of distinction.

Modern military asymmetry, however, threatens to brush aside the principle altogether. Historically, it was linked to the "concept of a line marking the heart of the battle" where use of force was clearly legitimate, as long as it was specifically directed to enemy combatants and other military objectives. If the conflict is everywhere, the traditional spatial limitation of legitimate force vanishes – force may be exercised everywhere where a 'military objective' may be found. The concept of 'military objective' accordingly becomes a cornerstone of limiting the use of force.[17] Asymmetry has its inherent temptations, however. The advantaged side possessing the overwhelming military technology and resources will inevitably be tempted to use its resources and technological dominance as massively as possible.

The current debate on the definition (and the limits) of 'military objectives' demonstrate such temptation. An issue of particular concern is the tendency of the U.S. military, in the context of the doctrine of 'effects based-operations', to extend the ambit of 'military objectives' to so-called 'war-sustaining' objects (primarily economic and political-administrative in nature).[18] Target of military operations here is not the military effort of the enemy any more, but the political command and control system and its resource basis. The requirement of a close nexus between the target and on-going military operations is given up in this approach.[19]

---

14 See also *Jeanne M. Meyer*, Tearing Down the Façade: A Critical Look at the Current Law on Targeting the Will of the enemy and Air Force Doctrine, 51 Air Force Law Review (2001), pp. 143, 180.

15 See *Michael N. Schmitt*, supra note 7, p. 8, and id., supra note 5, pp. 62-66.

16 See also *Thomas X. Hammes*, Insurgency: Modern Warfare Evolves into a Fourth Generation, Strategic Forum No. 214 (Jan. 2005).

17 See *Marco Sassòli*, supra note 9, pp. 184-190, and *Stefan Oeter*, Methods and Means of Combat, in: Dieter Fleck (ed.), The Handbook of Humanitarian Law in Armed Conflicts, Oxford 1995, pp. 105, 153-161.

18 See *Charles J. Dunlap, Jr.*, The End of Innocence: Rethinking Noncombatancy in the Post-Kosovo Era, in: Strategic Review (Summer 2000), pp. 11, 14 et seq.; *James A. Burger*, International Humanitarian Law and the Kosovo Crisis: Lessons Learned or to be Learned, 82 International Review of the Red Cross (2000), p. 132.

19 See also *Michael N. Schmitt*, supra note 7, p. 2, and *Yoram Dinstein*, supra note 9, p. 145.

The inherent revisionism towards traditional concepts of 'military objective' is most striking with an article of General *Dunlap* published in the aftermath of the Kosovo campaign.[20] General *Dunlap* advocates in this article "a new paradigm when using force against societies with malevolent propensities". Such paradigm is explained in drastic words: "We must hold at risk the very way of life that sustains their depredations, and we must threaten to destroy the world as they know it if they persist. This means the air weapon should be unleashed against entirely new categories of property" that current conceptions of air warfare put off-limits. As an example, he suggests "reducing the middle and upper classes to a subsistence level through the destruction of all but essential goods might pressure the very groups best positioned to effect the desired change". In his view, bombing a country 'back to stone-age' is just because the population bears some culpability for supporting the government, or at least failing to fulfil with a duty to oppose it. Politically, this argument is overly naïve – as if a dictator and the small clique profiting from his power could be influenced by a deterioration of general living conditions; Iraq sanctions should have told us the lesson. It also overstates the possibilities of even traditional middle and upper class members, administrative, economic and intellectual elites, to influence the political system. Living in a dictatorial regime like that of Saddam Hussein will be a traumatic experience in itself – a duty to oppose it cannot realistically be argued, since it might come near to a duty to commit suicide. Operating with such simplistic political arguments in order to argue an 'effects based-operations' doctrine means sacrificing all traditional conceptions of distinction on the altar of a missionary ideology of 'fighting for democracy'. He who pursues the right (political) objective is justified in any means, thus one might radicalise the fundament of such thinking.

4. The Collateral Damages to Proportionality

Blurring the line of distinction means eroding the principle of distinction as such, with the civilian population as the unavoidable victim of any such strategy.[21] A bit a comparable development seems to happen with the principle of proportionality and the prohibition of disproportionate collateral damages. The rule of proportionality between expected military advantages and damages always had an inherent weakness – the danger that the points of reference needed for relating advantages and damages get confused. Assessing proportionality always has been a contextual judgment. In principle all seems clear if you look into the usual handbooks and manuals – relevant damages for measuring proportionality are the potential losses under the civilian population and civilian objects.[22] A minimal military advantage which has as its price the loss of hundreds of civilians will not be proportionate in

---

[20] *Charles J. Dunlap*, supra note 18, p. 14.

[21] See also *Marco Sassòli*, supra note 9, pp. 195-196, but also *Michael N. Schmitt*, supra note 5, pp. 72-74.

[22] See *Stefan Oeter*, supra note 17, pp. 178-180.

these terms. But in practice the yardsticks are not that clear.[23] Concentrations of civilian population might be seen to resemble a military objective if the population has become radicalized ideologically, supports decidedly its regime and shields military objectives. Damages also will not be easily to predict, in particular if the target is a 'dual-use' installation of civilian infrastructure, like an electric power grid.[24] Destroying such an electrical grid might offer a decisive military advantage, but may at the same time have dramatic repercussions on civilian functions such as the water-distribution system, medical services etc.[25] Bearing in mind the ever-increasing dependence of modern societies on electrical systems, the risk of destroying such basic technical infrastructures may have serious consequences in a whole array of societal spheres, due to the societal interconnectivity of modern social networks. This means that at least reasonably foreseeable reverberating effects of destructions of such elementary civilian infrastructure must be included in the calculation of collateral damage.[26]

'Military advantage' might also shift. How do you equate losses of your own military personnel with potential losses under the enemy civilian population? Should you sacrifice the life of one of your own soldiers in order to save the life of one enemy civilian? For most military professionals this would seem completely counter-intuitive, not to say irrational. The more professionalized and technologically advanced military forces become, the more military commanders will perceive the life of their soldiers as a precious asset that should be sacrificed only when it becomes unavoidable. But is such a sacrifice unavoidable if you could safely reach your objective, with the price of sacrificing only some enemy civilians? Most military professionals will intuitively answer the question with a decided 'no' – it is not unavoidable, and accordingly you should not endanger the life of your subordinates. In legal terms this means: It is a decisive military advantage if you can spare the life of your own soldiers, an advantage that justifies a certain amount of collateral damages.[27] This, however, blurs decisively proportionality. Minimizing your own losses then justifies more and more collateral damages under civilians – a clear case of a sliding-scale. The more technological possibilities you have as a belligerent to avoid direct exposure of your own military personnel to enemy force, the more collateral damage you will tend to find justified and proportionate if it helps to spare the lives of your own soldiers. At the end of the sliding-scale you end up with Russian strategy in Grozny: Should we end up – so asked Russian generals – in urban house-to-house warfare, if we can overwhelm the enemy by erasing the whole city? There is not much left of the principle of distinction if you argue in that way.

---

23 See also *Yoram Dinstein*, Collateral Damage and the Principle of Proportionality, in: David Wippman/Matthew Evangelista (eds.), New Wars, New Laws? Applying the Laws of War in 21st Century Conflicts, Ardsley, N.Y 2005, pp. 211 et seq.

24 See *J.W. Crawford*, The Law of Noncombatant Immunity and the Targeting of National Electrical Power Systems, 21 Fletcher Forum of World Affairs (1997), pp. 101-102.

25 See *Michael N. Schmitt*, supra note 7, p. 10.

26 Id.

27 See also *Michael N. Schmitt*, supra note 7, pp. 10-11.

Precautions according to Art. 57 para. 2 AP I are another delicate issue. The basics are clear and undebatable. Let us look to Art. 57 para. 2 lit a (ii) AP I – a military commander shall choose the means and methods minimizing incidental injury and damage to civilian life and objects.[28] But what does this mean in practice? Is there any room left in times of precision-guided munitions for classical bombing, not to speak of area bombardments? If you could minimize losses by using the right technical options, shouldn't you do it? Of course, but ... – and the 'but' should not underestimated. Firstly, the option should be available in practice for the deciding military commander – if you do not have PGM's at hand, you cannot replace traditional forms of bombardment by them. As a result, technological asymmetry transforms into a legal asymmetry: The technologically advanced force is under much more stringent legal requirements to minimize potential collateral damages by choosing the right weaponry than the archaic third world army possessing only old-fashioned guns, mortars and rockets.[29]

Michael Schmitt has pointed to the fact that military asymmetry here also brings with it its temptations for the disadvantaged side. In order to restore a kind of balance, this side might be tempted to heighten the potential collateral damages by placing its forces and military installations in the midst of concentrations of civilian populations, or even to remove civilians to the vicinity of military installations in order to shield them from attacks.[30] One resulting question is the issue dealt with by *Michael Schmitt* when dealing with the civilians used as shield. Here I agree with him: Civilians voluntarily engaging in warfare lose their quality (and immunity) as civilians and become part of a legitimate 'military objective'. Their death accordingly will not be judged any more as a collateral damage strictu senso.[31] If civilians, however, are forcibly transferred to an installation, or the installation inmidst the civilians, they remain protected and risk of excessive losses under them might outlaw the potential attack on the installation.[32] This leads to a serious problem, if it creates a practical incentive to disregard the requirement of passive precautions.[33] The notorious case of a 'rogue regime' with no

---

28 See *Stefan Oeter*, supra note 17, pp. 181-186, and *Marco Sassòli*, supra note 9, pp. 205-206.

29 See *Michael N. Schmitt*, supra note 7, p. 11; see also *Stuart W. Belt*, Missile Over Kosovo: Emergence, Lex Lata, of a Customary Norm Requiring the Use of Precision Munitions in Urban Areas, 47 Naval Law Review (2000), pp. 115 et seq.

30 See also *Michael Skerker*, Just War Criteria and the New Face of War: Human Shields, Manufactured Martyrs, and Little Boys with Stones, 3 (1) Journal of Military Ethics (2004), pp. 27 et seq.

31 See *Michael N. Schmitt*, 'Direct Participation in Hostilities' and 21st Century Armed Conflict, in: Horst Fischer et al. (eds.), Crisis Management and Humanitarian Protection: Festschrift für Dieter Fleck, Berlin 2004, pp. 521-522, as well as *Michael N. Schmitt*, supra note 5, pp. 95-96.

32 See *Michael N. Schmitt*, supra note 31, p. 521, and id. supra note 5, pp. 91-95; see also *Emanuel Gross*, Use of Civilians as Human Shields: What Legal and Moral Restrictions Pertain to a War Waged by a Democratic State Against Terrorism?, 16 Emory International Law Review (2002), pp. 445 et seq.

33 See also *A.P.V. Rogers*, Law on the Battlefield, 2nd ed. 2004, p. 129; *W. Hays Parks*, Air War and the Law of War, 32 Air Force Law Review (1992), pp. 1, 163.

respect of the law may here get an advantage by strategically violating the law – an advantage which is difficult to counter under the existing rules.[34] I think, the legal set-up does not adequately respond to this problem, since international law here works with an asymmetrical construction itself – the commander ordering an attack leading to excessive collateral damages might be personally held accountable for a war crime, but not the politician (or military) violating the principle of passive precautions, although he might be as responsible for losses of civilian lives as the attacking force.[35]

5. Problems with the Distinction between Combatants and Civilians

A final remark might be dedicated to the problem of deliberately blurring the distinction between combatants and civilians as a reaction to military asymmetries. We know this problem since a long time from guerrilla warfare. Traditional laws of war were rather brute in that matter – the civilian taking part in hostilities while not wearing a uniform or distinctive sign as a member of a regular militia was summarily executed, and the regular military doing the same had to expect the same fate as a spy.[36] With the adoption of AP I, the international community tried to soften that approach a bit, treating also guerrilla fighters as combatants as long as they met certain minimum requirements.[37] This attempt to adapt IHL to new circumstances was heavily attacked by traditional military lawyers, in particular from the U.S. I can understand (and share) this criticism to a certain degree; nevertheless I think that the new rules of Art. 44 AP I make sense in political terms.[38] We have to cope with the fact that most armed conflicts fought in the world are civil wars or other non-international armed conflicts where fighters often do not fully comply with the requirements of being distinguishable openly as combatants. The same is true more and more also for international armed conflicts, as a result of the dramatic military asymmetries. Keeping all irregular fighters out of the vicinity of combatancy would mean to condemn these conflicts to lawlessness.

In political terms, I think it makes a lot of sense of sending out the signal that it is in the hands of even such irregulars whether they want to be treated as respect-

---

34 See also *Marco Sassòli*, supra note 9, pp. 206-209.

35 See *W. Hays Parks*, supra note 33, pp. 149-168.

36 As the classic in this regard see *Richard R. Baxter*, So-Called 'Unprivileged Belligerency': Spies, Guerrillas and Saboteurs, 28 British Yearbook of International Law (1952), pp. 323 et seq.; as to the ensuing problems concerning special forces see also *W. Hays Parks*, Special Forces' Wear of Non-Standard Uniforms, 4 Chicago Journal of International Law (2003), pp. 493 et seq.

37 See *Knut Ipsen*, Combatants and Non-Combatants, in: Dieter Fleck (ed.), The Handbook of Humanitarian Law in Armed Conflicts, Oxford 1995, pp. 77-79.

38 See *Stefan Oeter*, Terrorism and "Wars of National Liberation" from a Law of War Perspective, 49 Zeitschrift für ausländisches öffentliches Recht und Völkerrecht (1989), pp. 479-483.

able combatants or quasi-combatants or whether they want to act as criminals. It is simply not true that terrorists would be privileged under Art. 44 AP I. Just to the contrary, Art. 44 AP I gives a clear message that carrying arms openly while launching an attack is a basic precondition for legal respectability, and the respect for the principle of distinction another minimum requirement that must be observed even by such irregular fighters if they want to escape the fate as being dealt with as criminals.[39] It is true that Art. 44 para. 4 AP I extends a certain protection also to irregular fighters violating these minimum requirements – but they remain liable to individual criminal responsibility for their acts, since the classical combatant immunity is not extended to them. Resistance and guerrilla movements thus have to choose – do they want to be respected as military organizations or not? If they want to, they must accept the basic principles of IHL, under them the principle of distinction, and if they violate these rules, they become liable in criminal law terms. This is not compatible with terrorist strategies, just to the contrary, since AP I makes with utmost clarity the point that even regular militaries using terrorist tactics are personally liable as war criminals. I am not that sure whether it grants an advantage to being converted from an ordinary criminal into a war criminal, which is the only what might happen to irregular fighters directing their violence against civilians.

Counter-terrorism also raises its own challenges to the principle of distinction. Labeling the combat against terrorist crime a "war on terrorism" might finally mean brushing aside traditional concepts of policing terrorist crimes. In labelling counter-terrorism a war, a state might try in its operations against terrorists to get rid of inherited limitations to the use of violence. In particular 'extra-judicial killings' might then easily be declared to constitute military operations led against military objectives in an ongoing conflict.[40] But does this not give too much honour to terrorists? Are they really serious opponents in an armed conflict, or should they not better be treated as mere criminals, committing abhorrent acts against basic values of mankind? It may be that such a qualification might uphold certain limits to using force – like erasing a car with a suspected group of terrorists by firing a cruise-missile at them. But are we ready to accept collateral damage under civilians in such operations? Would we ever accept such terrorists to qualify as regular combatants? The two questions mark a friction that should be taken into consideration. It seems better blurring not too much the distinctions between armed operations in a military conflict and mere law-enforcement.

6. Conclusions

All in all, I think that modern IHL is well suited to cope with the challenges resulting from growing military asymmetries. Some adaptations in detail will be

39 See also *Stefan Oeter*, Terrorismus: Ein völkerrechtliches Verbrechen?, 76 Die Friedens-Warte (2001), pp. 23-26.

40 See only *Michael N. Schmitt*, supra note 5, pp. 81-89.

needed, like it always happens in law over time, but the intellectual reference frame that is underpinning the rules on methods and means of warfare is still valid. With growing military asymmetries, these rules of IHL become even more important. We will have to defend these rules against the temptations going along with asymmetry – temptations that come up on both sides of the technological divide. In order to do this, we should rebut all attempts to blur the critical distinctions on which the rules are based – and we will have to fight against some confusion that has accompanied the development of IHL during the last decades. Let us bear in mind an old experience: Rules on means and methods of warfare were never as precious an asset of law than in times of military asymmetries, just because it becomes much more difficult to apply them than in a conventional war between two nearly equal regular armed forces.

Asymmetries and the Identification of Legitimate Military Objectives

Asymmetries and the Identification of Legitimate Military Objectives

W. Hays Parks

Office of General Counsel, U.S. Department of Defense

I begin by thanking the German Red Cross and other conference sponsors for the opportunity to participate in honouring Professor *Knut Ipsen*. My predecessor in my former Army position, the late *Waldemar Solf*, worked with Professor *Ipsen* in the Diplomatic Conference that produced Additional Protocols I and II. Wally often spoke admiringly of those for whom he had great respect, and for their contributions to the success of the Diplomatic Conference. Professor *Ipsen* was one of those. So I speak not only for myself but for *Wally Solf* in honouring Professor *Ipsen*.

The task assigned this panel is to consider what may be regarded as a legitimate military objective. I am somewhat cautious in using the term "asymmetry", as it has several meanings in armed conflict. Often there is asymmetry between opposing forces. I once heard an international law professor state *proportionality* means that where there is asymmetry in forces, the superior force must engage his opponent on an even playing field, that is, with roughly equivalent forces. Fairness is not a law of war principle.

There may be an asymmetry in national military capabilities to attack particular military objectives. There may be an asymmetry in the political will of governments to approve attacks against a particular military objective. There may be an asymmetry in views as to priority of attack of military objectives, as occurred between the United Kingdom and United States regarding oil (U.S.) and transportation (U.K.) targets in the Strategic Bombing Offensive against Germany during the final year of World War Two.[1] I do not believe there is nor should there be any major asymmetry as to what constitutes a military objective under the law of war.

---

1 The British point of view is offered in *Solly Zuckerman*, From Apes to Warlords (1978), pp. 244, 306, 319, 344, 352, 422-424. *Zuckerman* was the architect and chief proponent of the British argument. The American view is contained in *W.W. Rostow*, Pre-Invasion Bombing Strategy (1981). Appendix 5 (pp. 420-421) of Professor *Zuckerman*'s book is an excerpt from the post-war British Bombing Survey Unit (BBSU) report, supporting the British (*Zuckerman*'s) position. *Zuckerman* neglects to note that he was the author of the BBSU conclusions. See *Sebastian Cox*, "Introduction", in British Bombing Survey Unit, in: The Strategic Air War Against Germany 1939-1945 (reprint ed., 1998), p. xviii. The British-American pre-D-Day debate became somewhat moot, as ultimately both transportation and oil targets were attacked by British and American forces. The debate

The law of war relating to legitimate military objectives is longstanding, and may be summarized in two basic points:

- Only legitimate military objectives may be intentionally attacked. An attacker is obligated to direct his attack at military objectives only, and not at civilian objects or civilians not taking a direct part in hostilities.
- Where legitimate military objectives are intermingled with civilian objects and the civilian population, collateral damage to civilian objects and incidental injury to civilians not taking a direct part in hostilities is a regrettable but not necessarily an unlawful result of attack of military objectives. The obligation to take reasonable measures to avoid collateral damage to civilian objects and incidental injury to civilians is shared by attacker and defender.

While each point reflects the long-standing law of war principle of *distinction*, as often is said, "The devil has been in the details." Nonetheless there is an identifiable road map for progression in definition through history. Some roads taken have been dead ends, regrettably now being re-visited by some as potential avenues. I will identify them without necessarily embracing them.

Before beginning this tour through history, it is necessary to note that prior to the 1977 Protocol I Additional to the 1949 Geneva Conventions, various terms were used to describe objects lawfully subject to attack. They included "targets," "military targets", "civilian targets", and "military objectives". The term *civilian target*, frequently seen in media reports, is an oxymoron. Additional Protocol I properly divides objects into *civilian objects* and *military objectives*. This paper will use *military objective* as codified and defined in Additional Protocol I except where other terms are used in a quotation.

Targeting contains two major categories: people and objects. Given the title of our panel, my focus is limited to the latter, with one observation as to a distinction between the two. Whereas a civilian may not be the object of direct attack "unless and for such time … [as he or she takes] a direct part in hostilities,"[2] a civilian object may become a military objective not only for such time as it is occupied or otherwise used by enemy military forces, but also if its seizure, neutralization or destruction, in the circumstances ruling at the time, offers a definite military advantage.[3] This distinction between people and objects is important. Targeting also

highlights the situational nature of targeting priorities, as it centred on which target set would have the greatest effect on preventing *Wehrmacht*counterattack of Allied forces as they landed at Normandy. Subsequently the issue was which target category would contribute to German defeat. The answer was both.

2 Article 51, para. 3, 1977 Protocol I Additional to the Geneva Conventions of August 12, 1949, contained in *Dietrich Schindler/Jiři Toman*, The Laws of Armed Conflicts (Fourth Rev. and Completed Ed., 2004), p. 651.

3 Article 27 of the Annex to Hague Convention IV contains language similar to the quoted language from Article 51, para. 3 of Additional Protocol I for certain civilian objects, declaring:
"In sieges and bombardments all necessary steps must be taken to spare, as far as possible, buildings dedicated to art, science, or charitable purposes, historic monuments, hos-

is subject to agreed restrictions afforded certain objects, such as cultural property, and precautions in attack in order to limit collateral damage to civilian objects and incidental injury to the civilian population as such and individual civilians not taking a direct part in hostilities. My focus is on what constitutes a *military objective* as that term applies to objects.

There have been a number of historic efforts at determining objects that may be attacked lawfully. In the course of the American Civil War (1861-1865), President *Abraham Lincoln* tasked *Dr. Francis Lieber* to prepare a law of war code for Union forces. General Orders No. 100[4] was the first modern statement of the law of war. Several of its articles bear directly on development of the law relating to defining *military objective.*

14. Military necessity, as understood by modern civilized nations, consists in the necessity of those measures which are indispensable for securing the ends of the war, and which are lawful according to the modern law and usages of war.
15. Military necessity admits of all direct destruction of life or limb of armed enemies, and of other persons whose destruction is incidentally unavoidable in the armed conflicts of war. ... it allows of all destruction of property, and obstruction of the ways and channels of traffic, travel, or communication, and of all withholding of sustenance or means of life from the enemy ...
20. Public war is a state of armed hostility between sovereign nations or governments. It is a law and requisite of civilized existence that men live in political, continuous societies, forming organized units, called states or nations, whose constituents bear, enjoy, and suffer, advance and retrograde together, in peace and war.
21. The citizen or native of a hostile country is thus an enemy, as one of constituents of the hostile state or nation, and as such is subjected to the hardships of war.
22. Nevertheless, as civilization has advanced during the last centuries, so has likewise steadily advanced, especially in war on land, the distinction between the private individual belonging to a hostile country and the hostile country itself, with its men in arms. The principle has been more and more acknowledged that the unarmed citizen is to be spared in person, property, and honor so much as the exigencies of war will admit.

In five paragraphs Professor *Lieber* identified and defined the law of war principles of *military necessity* and *distinction*, and identified some military objectives. Contrary to recent theories regarding "dual use" military objectives, the Lieber Code acknowledged that even where attacks are limited to military objectives, the civilian population of a warring nation likely will experience hardships. This is a natural consequence of war. His work product remained a leading law of war reference for the remainder of the Nineteenth Century, serving as a basis for the

pitals, and places where the sick and wounded are collected, *provided they are not being used at the time for military purposes.*" [emphasis provided]. Id., p. 84.

4 Id., pp. 3-20.

Project of an International Declaration Concerning the Laws and Customs of War produced by the 1874 Brussels Conference,[5] the Oxford Manual on the Laws of War on Land adopted by the Institute of International Law on September 9, 1880,[6] and Hague Convention (II) with Respect to the Laws of Customs of War on Land promulgated and adopted at the First Hague Peace Conference in 1899.[7]

Five years later representatives of seventeen nations met in St. Petersburg to draft what became the Declaration Renouncing the Use, in Time of War, of Explosive Projectiles Under 400 Grammes Weight.[8] Its preamble language states "The only legitimate object of which States should endeavour to accomplish during war is to weaken the military forces of the enemy." This language is vague, but less restrictive than first appears. It does not state "the only legitimate object is attack or destruction of the *military forces* of an enemy." Military objectives that support or sustain an enemy nation's ability to resist are integral to weakening its military forces.

The St. Petersburg Declaration applied only between States Parties. Its primary object – prohibition of explosive or incendiary projectiles weighing less than 400 grams – became obsolete shortly after its enactment. No reference was made to it or its provisions in the 1899 Hague Convention (II) with Respect to the Laws and Customs of War on Land or its successor, the 1907 Hague Convention (IV) of the same title.[9] The quoted clause is an historic anomaly. A restrictive interpretation would not be consistent with State practice in Twentieth Century or recent conflicts.[10]

---

5 *Schindler/Toman*, supra n. 2, pp. 21-28.

6 Id., pp. 29-40.

7 Id., pp. 55-97.

8 Id., pp. 91-93.

9 Id., pp. 55-97.

10 In a 1925 lecture at the U.S. Army War College, Major General *Mason Patrick*, Chief of the U.S. Army Air Corps, citing Captain *B.H. Liddell Hart*'s "Paris, or the Future of War" (1925), agreed with the British author's purported thesis that the main military objective in war is the "will of the enemy to fight" rather than defeat of his armed forces in the field.

Major General *Haywood S. Hansell, Jr.*, USAF, The Air Plan that Defeated Hitler (Privately published, 1972), p. 10.

That said, *Patrick*'s thesis was not *Liddell Hart*'s. *Liddell Hart* declared that the means to the moral objective, that is, the enemy's will to resist, was not limited to its military forces, but included its economic, political and social spheres which *Liddell Hart* then concluded "was outside our purview". Paris, or the Future of War, pp. 27, 28. Pre-World War II airpower focus on enemy morale incorrectly emphasized the political, economic and social – with emphasis on the latter – to the exclusion of attacks on enemy military forces.

Similarly, in pre-World War II lectures at the Air Corps Tactical School, a U.S. Army Air Corps officer stated:

"We find throughout the pages of military writings statements that the objective of war is the destruction on the field of battle of the enemy's main forces. Such a conclusion is a confusion of the means with the end. *The destruction of the military forces of the enemy is not now and never has been the objective of war; it has been merely a means to*

Wars following commencement of the Industrial Revolution recognized the necessity for attack of an enemy's ability to wage war, as well as its military forces. In the century preceding the first and second Hague Peace Conferences, an era limited to land and naval operations, *military objective* was not limited to tactical objectives. In the period between 1830 and 1870, for example, "railroads emerged as *the* decisive factor in modern war."[11] In the famous 1864-1865 march of Union forces through the South, General *William Techumseh Sherman* cut the Confederacy in half while destroying its railroads and industrial resources and denying it the ability to grow and export cotton to finance its war of secession.[12] Naval blockade to defeat an enemy nation's ability to wage war is historic, and would remain a principal method of war through World War II. It was a strategic method of warfare, often producing far greater civilian suffering than land operations; in World War I, an estimated 800,000 civilians died from starvation as a result of the Royal Navy blockade of Germany.[13] Historically *military objectives* have not been range-limited, or limited to strictly military forces, but have included objects related to a government's ability to wage war.

The First Hague Peace Conference. The First Hague Peace Conference convened in The Hague on May 18, 1899, with delegations from twenty-six nations.[14]

The conference adopted Convention II with Respect to the Laws and Customs of War on Land and its Annexed Regulations Respecting the Laws and Customs of War on Land.[15] Article 23(g) of the Annex provides: "It is especially prohibited ... to destroy or seize the enemy's property, unless such destruction or seizure be imperatively demanded by the necessities of war." Article 23(g) re-states articles 14 and 15 of the 1863 Lieber Code, opting to state the law in the negative rather than in the positive, as was done in the Lieber Code. This language is a fundamental corollary to the principle of *distinction*; that is, violence will be directed towards military objectives. Further, Article 25 prohibited "The attack or bombardment of towns, villages, habitations or buildings which are not defended." Cultural property, hospitals and similar civilian objects were protected from direct attack so long as they were not used for military purposes or there was no other

---

an end – merely the removal of an obstacle which lay in the path of overcoming the will to resist." [emphasis in original]. Captain (later Lieutenant General) *Harold E. George*, as quoted in *Hansell*, id., p. 33.

11 *Maurice Pearton*, Diplomacy, War and Technology Since 1830 (1984), p. 75 [emphasis in original].

12 See, for example, *Joseph T. Glatthaar*, The March to the Sea and Beyond (1985). *Sherman*'s attack of Confederate railroads was the model for the allied air offensive against Germany's rail lines eighty years later; see generally *A. C. Mierzejewski*, The Collapse of the Germany War Economy, 1944-1945 (1988).

13 See, for example, *Nigel Hawkins*, The Starvation Blockades: Naval Blockades of World War I (2001).

14 A general, excellent history of the First Hague Peace Conference is *Arthur Eyffinger*, The 1899 Hague Peace Conference (2001).

15 *Schindler/Toman*, supra n. 2, p. 55-87.

military necessity for their seizure or attack.[16] The intent of these articles was to codify existing practice, rather than create new law.[17]

The Second Hague Peace Conference. The Second Hague Peace Conference met from 15 June to 18 October 1907. Article 23(g) of 1899 Hague (II) was re-codified unchanged as Article 23(g) of the Annex to Hague Convention IV. The significant conference contribution for this panel's topic was Hague Convention IX Concerning Bombardment by Naval Forces in Time of War.[18] Hague Convention IX provided clearer rules – and authority – than did the 1907 Hague Convention IV. While repeating the restrictions on bombardment contained in Convention IV, article 2 of Hague IX identified particular military objectives that could be attacked. Hague Convention IX was significant in that it was the first treaty codification or acknowledgment that bombardment was related to the military value of the target rather than whether the city, town or village in which the target was located was defended. It provided the only list of military objectives contained in any adopted law of war treaty. While incomplete by later State practice, it constituted an improvement over previous treaties.

Article 2 lists as military objectives "military works, military or naval establishments, depots of arms or war materiel, workshops or plant(s) which could be utilized for the needs of the hostile fleet or army, and the ships of war in the harbor". Military objectives were not limited to objects purely military or naval in nature, but included industrial targets of value to an enemy war effort. The list was regarded by the head of the United States delegation to be declaratory of customary international law as it existed in 1907.[19] Nonetheless the issue of what constituted a *military objective* remained far from settled.

World War I. It is beyond the scope of this paper to describe or summarize the bombing and naval campaigns of World War I and development of the law through State practice. History suggests that law of war considerations received little attention, if any, other than as a tool for propaganda attributing indiscriminate attacks only to enemy actions. Nonetheless several observations may be offered:

- The practice of strategic bombing by the warring nations provided a fairly clear indication of the types of objects regarded as lawful targets: military and naval bases; warehouses, airfields, and docks; lines of communication; and industrial targets that offered a contribution to the enemy's war effort. The degree of perceived contribution established the priority of attack.

---

[16] Id., article 27.

[17] *James Brown Scott*, I The Hague Peace Conferences of 1899 and 1907 (1939), p. 537. For example, article 26 restates article 19 of the Lieber Code, while article 27 is a restatement of articles 35 and 36 of the Lieber Code.

[18] *Schindler/Toman*, supra n. 2, pp. 1079-1086.

[19] *J. Scott* (ed.), Instructions to the American Delegates to the Hague Peace Conferences and Their Official Reports (1916), p. 122.

- Attacks on civilian morale as such occurred. While often viewed as a consequence of aerial attack only, other means were employed. The German Paris Gun, with a range of seventy-five miles, could be aimed only at the centre of Paris. Used in conjunction with the March 1918 German offensive and air attacks on Paris, its purpose was to attack civilian morale.[20]
- Bombing had an effect upon civilian morale on both sides. German steel manufacturers reported a thirty per cent decrease in worker efficiency during the 1916 British air attacks on the Saar and Lorraine Luxemburg, while British Minister of Munitions *Winston S. Churchill*, in a War Cabinet meeting on October 1, 1917, asserted that German air raids on preceding nights had a pronounced effect on employee absenteeism and production at Woolwich Arsenal. The official British history reported "the loss of output was out of all proportion to the percentage of employees who stayed away from work". While views differed as to the efficacy of morale attacks, both sides in World War I gained information suggesting there was value in attacks on enemy morale. Such attacks were not regarded as illegal. This was to have a significant effect on air planning thereafter through World War II.

The Treaty of Versailles. The conclusion of World War I brought an attempt at unilateral disarmament – of the defeated. Under the Treaty of Versailles, Germany was to dispose of all aviation-related equipment; its military was to be disbanded; its navy scuttled or otherwise disposed of. Although Germany submitted to the Versailles Treaty, it did not acquiesce entirely. A game of legal and diplomatic intrigue followed. One historian commented, "[T]he Allies attempted to contain Germany's air potential through legal restraints that Germany assiduously tried to avoid".[21] Allied disarmament efforts against Germany became less successful in the years that followed.[22] My point is not to criticize Germany's resistance to its total disarmament, but to set the tone for postwar events that followed with respect to development of the law of war and the definition of *military objective*.

The Washington Conference on the Limitation of Armament of 1922. Efforts toward greater, multilateral disarmament began with the Washington Conference on the Limitation of Armament, popularly known as the Washington Naval Conference. In 1921, representatives of the United Kingdom, France, Italy, Japan and the United States initially considered a total prohibition on new methods of warfare, to include the machinegun, poisonous gas (chemical and bacteriological weapons), submarines and aircraft. In considering aircraft, the delegates turned to the possibility of "rules for control of new agencies of warfare", suggesting regu-

---

[20] *Henry W. Miller*, The Paris Gun (1930), pp. vii, viii, 68, 70.

[21] *Edward L. Homze*, Arming the Luftwaffe (1976), p. 3. See also *Barton Whaley*, Covert German Rearmament, 1919-1939 (1984).

[22] For a history of failed attempts to ban or regulate submarine warfare and covert German submarine rearmament between the wars, see this author's "Making Law of War Treaties: Lessons from Submarine Warfare Regulation" in: Michael N. Schmitt (ed.), International Law Across the Conflict Spectrum: Essays in Honor of Professor L. C. Green, Volume 75, Naval War College International Law Studies (2001).

lation rather than limitation or prohibition. With limited conference time, the delegates unanimously accepted a recommendation that military aircraft should operate within rules established by a subsequent conference of legal experts. That subsequent conference was charged with development of rules relating to radio use in war and air warfare. Issues identified as to the latter included the following:

- Do existing rules of international law adequately cover new methods of attack or defence resulting from the introduction or development, since the Hague Conference of 1907, of new agencies of warfare?
- If not so, what changes in existing rules ought to be adopted in consequence thereof as a part of the law of nations?

The Hague Commission of Jurists of 1922-1923. The Commission of Jurists and its Military and Naval Advisors convened in The Hague on December 11, 1922, with delegations from the United Kingdom, France, Italy, Japan, The Netherlands, and the United States.[23] The charter enjoined negotiators to consider, *inter alia*, the regulation of aviation in time of war, to include regulations for aerial bombardment. Discussion focused on the legality of targets and the depth of the extended battlefield. A U.S. proposal drew a distinction between military objectives within the "combat area" – the area of on-going ground force combat between the military forces of parties to the conflict – and military objectives not within the combat area. It was assumed that the civilian population would have removed themselves from the combat area. Accordingly, military objectives could be engaged without restriction. Beyond the combat area, aircraft attack of cities, towns, villages, dwellings or buildings was prohibited. Enemy forces, lines of communications and transportation, military or naval establishments, depots of arms or war material, and workshops, plants and factories used for war materiel manufacture remained subject to attack wherever located. However, delegations were unable to reach agreement.

British and American drafts differed in their approach in other ways. The British phrased its proposal in terms of attacks upon "military objectives", the term subsequently adopted in Additional Protocol I, while the U.S. draft identified illustrative objects which might be attacked (repeating the approach taken in the 1907 Hague Convention IX) while avoiding use of "military objective" or "military target". The British delegation set great store in "military objective" as having a limitative effect, while the U.S. delegation argued the phrase left too much to the discretion of the individual commander.

Subcommittee members were unanimous in accepting the principle that enemy forces, military works, lines of military communication, military or naval bases, and depots of arms, ammunition, or war materiel could be attacked. But no draft

---

[23] The official Commission records are "Commission of Jurists to Consider and Report Upon the Revision of the Rules of War" (1923). As was the case with the Washington Naval Conference, Germany was not invited. A comprehensive discussion of the conference and its results is *Heinz Marcuss Hanke*, The 1923 Hague Rules of Air Warfare, in: International Review of the Red Cross 292 (January-February 1993), pp. 12-44.

formula gained a majority of votes. A fundamental difficulty was "the determination of the conditions under which the bombardment of objects, intrinsically liable to attack, was to be forbidden, when they were found in centers of population."[24]

The Rules Concerning the Control of Wireless Telegraphy in Time of War and Air Warfare ultimately adopted by the Commission of Jurists contained comprehensive rules related to air warfare.[25] They included the following rules directly applicable to aerial bombardment and protection of the civilian population and civilian objects:

Art. 22. Any air bombardment for the purpose of terrorizing the civil population or destroying or damaging private property without military character or injuring non-combatants, is forbidden.
Art. 24. (1). An air bombardment is legitimate only when is directed against a military objective, i.e. an objective whereof the total or partial destruction would constitute an obvious military advantage for the belligerent.
(2) Such bombardment is legitimate only when directed exclusively against the following objectives: military forces, military works, military establishments or depots, manufacturing plants constituting important and well-known centres for the production of arms, ammunition or characterized military supplies, lines of communication or of transport which are used for military purposes.
(3) Any bombardment of cities, towns, villages, habitations and building which are not situated in the immediate vicinity of the operations of the land forces, is forbidden.[26]
(4) In the immediate vicinity of the operations of the land forces, the bombardment of cities, towns, villages, habitations and buildings is legitimate, provided there is a reasonable presumption that the military concentration is important enough to justify the bombardment, taking into account the danger to which the civil population will thus be exposed.

Professor *Jiří Toman* has concluded the 1923 Hague Air Rules "to a great extent ... correspond to the customary rules and general principles underlying the con-

---

24 *John Bassett Moore*, International Law and Some Current Illusions and Other Essays (1924), p. 197.

25 The rules in their entirety are contained in *Schindler/Toman*, supra n. 2, pp. 315-325. They are far more comprehensive than this discussion suggests, consisting of provisions related to external markings and other qualifications of belligerent aircraft; use by or against aircraft of incendiary or explosive projectiles; aircraft use for information warfare; aerial bombardment; the right of a State party to a conflict to establish exclusion zones and to warn off neutral aircraft; treatment of captured aircraft crews; relations with neutral states; and the law relating to visit, search, capture and condemnation in connection with the exercise of blockade and contraband. The rules are not and were not intended to be exhaustive.

26 While airpower proponents subsequently were critical of this provision, it was consistent with U.S. War Department policy at the time, which – deriving from U.S. World War I aviation experience – "denied the importance of 'independent' air operations beyond the immediate rear of the enemy ground forces". *Hansell*, supra n. 10, p. 7.

ventions on the law of war and at sea."[27] This conclusion is not consistent with State practice and the opinion of legal writers of that era as to the rules quoted. In contrast, *Sir Hersch Lauterpacht* observed that the 1923 Hague Air Rules were "of importance as an authoritative *attempt* to clarify and formulate rules of law governing the use of aircraft in war and they will doubtless prove a convenient starting point for any future steps in that direction."[28] Professor *Lauterpacht*'s assessment is closer to the mark.

The 1923 Hague Air Rules were not adopted by any nation, though governments on occasion prior to World War II announced they would act in accordance with them or otherwise made reference to them, particularly if or when it was in their interests to make such statements, as illustrated infra, but always subject to reciprocity.

Greatest military concern focused on the undefined term "military objective" in Article 24. The authors of the British official history of the World War Two strategic air offensive explained the dilemma:

"Part of the argument cantered upon the difference between 'military' and 'civilian' targets and developed along the lines of the conventions which had been attached to military and naval warfare. There was a school of thought which demanded that bombing should be restricted to 'military targets' which could be destroyed without undue risk to 'civilian' life or property. This argument turned upon what was meant by the term 'military target.' Clearly, a tank on the battlefield was a military target, but was a tank on the assembly line in a factory a civilian target? Clearly a soldier in the front line was a military target, but was a worker engaged in the manufacture of his rifle a civilian target? There was also the question of what constituted 'undue risk' to civilian life and property. A battleship at sea, it might be assumed, would be manned only by naval personnel and a badly aimed bomb would be unlikely to fall anywhere other than in the water. But the same battleship in port might have civilian workers on board and a badly aimed bomb might destroy anything from a warehouse to a church.

Obviously a strict interpretation of these obscure questions meant the absolute prohibition of strategic bombing and the confinement of all operations to the actual area of land fighting or to war ships at sea … In modern war between major powers there is, after all, practically nothing worth attacking which does not have some bearing upon the national war effort."[29]

The attempt at limitation on the attack of military objectives must be viewed through the eyes of airpower planners of the time. Writing five years after the 1923 Hague conference, Marshal of the Royal Air Force Lord *Trenchard* commented:

---

27 *Schindler/Toman*, supra n. 2, p. 315.

28 *H. Lauterpacht* (ed.), International Law by Oppenheim, Vol. II: Disputes, War and Neutrality (7th ed., 1952), p. 519 [emphasis provided].

29 *Sir Charles Webster/Noble Frankland*, The Strategic Air Offensive Against German 1939-1945 [hereinafter *SAOG*] (1961), Volume I, pp. 14-15.

"To attack the armed forces is … to attack the enemy at his strongest point. On the other hand, by attacking the source from which these armed forces are maintained infinitely more effect is obtained. In the course of a day's attack upon the aerodromes of the enemy perhaps 50 aeroplanes could be destroyed, whereas a modern industrial state will produce 100 in a day – production will far more than replace any destruction we can hope to do in the forward zone. On the other hand, by attacking the enemy's factories, then output is reduced by a much greater proportion."[30]

Writing in the same vein, also in 1928, Field Marshal *Sir George F. Milne*, Chief of the British Imperial General Staff, commented:

"[Military] objectives will, naturally, differ from time to time, and their relative importance can only be measured by the influence they happen to be exerting at any given moment. For instance, when an enemy is concentrating for an attack, the dislocation of his railways and other means of communication may produce results which will influence the course of the war far more than will the bombardment of some of his munitions factories."[31]

Lord *Trenchard* and *Sir George*'s statements were consistent with the law of war as it existed, in that they emphasized the efficient use of military force and the (to use language from Article 24(1) of the 1923 Hague Air Rules and Article 52(2) of Additional Protocol I) distinct or definite military advantage to be gained from an attack. Their comments also illustrated the dynamic nature of targeting, as the value of a potential military target may vary depending upon the circumstances ruling at the time. Lord *Trenchard* accomplished what the negotiators at The Hague failed to do. He defined *military objective* as "any objectives which will contribute effectively towards the destruction of the enemy's means of resistance and the lowering of his determination to fight".[32]

Lord *Trenchard* and others, whether international lawyers or military officers, identified deficiencies in the Hague Air Rules. Contemporary criticism of the rules was high, continuing up to World War II.[33] Writing in *The New Republic* in 1937, Jonathon Mitchell argued the Hague Air Rules' definition of "military objective" was at odds with contemporary views of total war. The Hague Air Rules "remain

---

30 Id., IV, p. 74.

31 Id., p. 78.

32 Id., p. 74.

33 *Elbridge Colby*, Aerial Law and War Targets, 19 Am. J. Int'l. L (1929), p. 713; *Frank E. Quindry*, Aerial Bombardment of Civilian and Military Objectives, 2 Journal of Air Law and Commerce (October 1931), pp. 474-509, at 484; *James Moloney Spaight*, Air Power and War Rights (1924), pp. 226-259; and *James Moloney Spaight*, The Chaotic State of International Law Governing Aerial Bombardment, in: The Air Force Quarterly 9 (1938), pp. 24-32.

unratified, and many American experts believe them too vague to be of practical importance".[34]

The Hague Air Rules were an improvement in that they abandoned the test as to whether a town was "undefended". The nature of the objective or the use to which it is being put at the time of its attack became the test. But critics argued the limited nature of the list of military objectives contained in Article 24(2) was inconsistent with the practice of nations in World War I, as well thinking of airpower advocates and other military planners. *James Moloney Spaight* identified deficiencies in the first edition of his authoritative *Air Power and War Rights*, published the year following the Hague conference.[35] He provided a three-page list of targets attacked during World War I, to include an aqueduct; blast furnaces; electric works; gas works; iron works and foundries; magneto works; motor works; steel works; and petroleum, oil and lubricant production, manufacturing, storage facilities, that arguably would have been immune from attack under Article 24(2) of the 1923 Hague Air Rules. Article 24(2)'s limiting attack to "*military* forces, *military* works, *military* establishments or depots, and factories constituting important and well-known centres engaged in the manufacture of arms, ammunition or distinctively *military* supplies" was contrary to State practice by both sides in World War I and emerging airpower theory. The Commission's effort to paint a picture of warfare at odds with military thinking did not escape criticism by international lawyers of that era, and undoubtedly contributed to failure of formal acceptance of the Hague Air Rules.

Much could be said of the 1923 Hague Air Rules. Emphasis has been placed on their effort to "kick the can down the road" with respect to what constitutes a *military objective*. There is no doubt they were ahead of the time. They were the first, last, and only formal effort at defining *military objective* until the 1974-1977 Diplomatic Conference that promulgated Additional Protocol I. Nations expressed interest in forms of restraint or constraint on subsequent occasions leading up to World War II, most associated with the Geneva Disarmament Conference, most illusory if not contrived. The details of this busy but legislatively unproductive period are provided elsewhere, and not directly germane to the issue at hand.[36]

Attacks on morale. In his recent article on the 1923 Hague Air Rules, *Heinz Marcus Hanke* notes that the prohibition of indiscriminate attacks was not new.[37] As he acknowledges, the prohibition suffered from a lack of definition, a shortfall that continued until *indiscriminate attacks* was defined in Article 51(4) and (5) of Additional Protocol I.

The prohibition ran afoul of the blind faith airpower advocates attached to "attacks on morale" from World War I through World War II. While originally an

---

[34] *Tami Davis Biddle*, Rhetoric and Reality in Air Warfare: The Evolution of British and American Ideas about Strategic Bombing, 1914-1945 (2002), p. 153.

[35] *Spaight*, Air Power and War Rights, supra n. 33, pp. 212-238.

[36] A leading account of this period is *Uri Bialer*, The Shadow of the Bomber: The Fear of Air Attack and British Politics 1932-1939 (1980).

[37] *Hanke*, supra n. 23, pp. 24-25.

observed effect of air attacks on enemy ground forces, civilian worker absenteeism resulting from World War I air raids expanded the idea of airpower's ability to attack enemy civilian morale as a war-ending tool. This was not an argument for indiscriminate attacks as such, but an essential indirect effect of strategic bombing of enemy industry. "Attacks on morale" became a shibboleth, a mantra, exhorted as a matter of blind faith by airpower advocates in behalf of aviation service survival and development in the post-World War I budget battles with land and naval forces.[38] It continued through the 1930s.[39]

An interesting facet regarding the advocacy of attacks on morale was that each side assumed it could take punishment better than its opponent. In the 1920s RAF Air Marshal *Sir Philip Joubert de la Ferté* "reiterated the standing, irrational belief, based on Germany's internal and military collapse in 1918, that the nation with the stouter hearts (the British) and the better leaders and equipment, would win wars against the weaker (the Germans), a false belief, with regard to morale, that before and during the Second World War, for ideological reasons, was shared in reverse by the Germans".[40] Thus in the 1930s, *Dr. Robert Knauss*, initially with the German Air Ministry before heading the new Air War College at Gatow, argued that a "totalitarian society like Nazi Germany would prove more capable of enduring bombing attacks than the fractured societies of Britain and France",[41] while a British writer in the early stages of World War II argued that German morale was extremely susceptible: "They [the German leadership] don't seem to realize that what merely stiffens our [British] backs flattens a German".[42] While somewhat of an aside, it is an important manifestation of the faith officials and the public placed on attacks on morale.

The most ardent advocate of attacks on civilian morale was Lord *Trenchard.* As early as 1916, he asserted that "[T]he moral effect produced by a hostile aeroplane ... is out of proportion to the damage it can inflict."[43] He argued that "the moral [morale] effects of bombing [including bombing the civilian population] is to the material to the ratio of twenty to one," prompting one airpower historian to observe that *Trenchard* was the master of the "wholly unfounded statistic."[44] Nonetheless it became British airpower dogma as early as March 1917.

The argument of *Trenchard* and other airpower advocates did not receive universal acceptance. Writing as Minister of Munitions in October 1917, *Winston S. Churchill* stated somewhat presciently:

"It is improbable that any terrorization of the civil population which could be achieved by air attack would compel the Government of a great nation to surren-

---

[38] An excellent summary is *Biddle*, supra n. 34, pp. 77-81.

[39] Id., p. 147.

[40] *Horst Boog*, A German View, in: Sir Arthur T. Harris, Despatch on War Operations, 23rd February 1942 to 8th May 1945 (Reprint ed., 1995), p. xi.

[41] *Williamson Murray*, Strategy for Defeat: The Luftwaffe 1933-1945 (1983), p. 10.

[42] *Mark Connelly*, Reaching for the Stars: A New History of Bomber Command in World War II (2001), p. 49.

[43] Id., p. 77.

[44] *Malcolm Smith*, British Air Strategy between the Wars (1984), p. 61.

der … In our own case we have seen the combative spirit of the people roused, not quelled, by the German air raids … Nothing that we have learned of the capacity of the German population to endure suffering justifies us in assuming that they would not be rendered more desperately resolved to them."[45]

Yet other factors gave continued life to this argument. In addition to constant repetition of the *Trenchardian* argument in official speeches, essays and articles, doctrine, and policy statements, the Royal Air Force had sustained its existence through use of its aircraft for 'policing' Somaliland, and, subsequently, Iraq, Palestine, India, South-west Arabia, and parts of its colonial empire in Africa. Indigenous tribes whose conduct strayed often returned to British colonial ways merely with a 'demonstration' bombing by RAF aircraft, profoundly shocked by this new method of warfare. If a mere demonstration was insufficient, attacks on villages and their populations followed, with significant military success notwithstanding dubious legality. These attacks validated the RAF concept of attacks on morale, as one RAF officer commented in 1923:

"The shocks and interruptions, the inconvenience and indignity if it all, will tell in the end. The civilized nation will go through the same three phases as did the semi-civilized tribe: alarm, indifference, weariness, followed ultimately by compliance with our will."[46]

The views of U.S. airpower advocates differed only slightly. U.S. Army aviators, seeking the independence the Royal Air Force enjoyed, and fighting similar post-World War I budget battles, took a similar approach. While early doctrine noted the potential for attacks on "population centers" to weaken enemy civilian morale, it also acknowledged that such attacks might be prohibited by the law of war.[47] Army Air Corps Major *William C. Sherman* hedged the issue in his 1926 treatise *Air Warfare*.[48] *Sherman* acknowledged that World War I aerial attacks by both sides were "practically indiscriminate," that "the civilian population nearly always suffered more casualties than military forces," that "nor was this result entirely accidental and unpremeditated," but "There can be no doubt that the effect on the civilian population was often the real motive of the attack." Continuing, he stated: "History then, contains no example of a serious major air campaign directed against the unarmed portion of the enemy's population," but continues by citing the argument of French Marshal *Ferdinand Foch* that aircraft in future conflicts could provide the "possibility of bringing such pressure to bear on civilian populations as to end war through the action of the air force alone." *Sherman* recog-

---

[45] *Biddle*, supra n. 34, p. 79.

[46] Wing-Commander *C. Edmonds*, RAF, at the Royal United Services Institution, December 12, 1923, as quoted in David E. Omissi, Air Power and Colonial Control: The Royal Air Force, 1919-1939 (1990), p. 107.

[47] *Biddle*, supra n. 34, p. 139.

[48] Major *Sherman* authored "Air Warfare" (1926), regarded at the time as a leading treatise on the subject, shortly before his death on November 22, 1927.

nized the "present trend of international law, as witnessed by tentative agreements among the major powers [the 1923 Hague Air Rules], definitely forbids the bombardment of civilians for the purposes of intimidation." He found the potential for constraint driven as much by the potential for what he termed "reprisal" – in all likelihood meaning retaliation, or escalation – as from the law of war, concluding that "any decision to bomb cities is necessarily political [rather than legal] in character." Where one of the parties to the conflict "is so situated that he can bomb the enemy's cities without fear of having to undergo the same punishment, international law will be subjected to its severest trial."[49] His views were adopted by the U.S. Army Air Corps Tactical School as doctrine, but were not necessarily accepted by all within the fledgling branch.[50] The line between bombing the civilian population of an enemy solely for the purpose of terrorizing it and bombing economic and industrial targets with an "incidental" attack on the morale of the civilian population was a thin one, with airpower advocates emphasizing the former while denying the latter. In some respects, this was an advance (however subtle) in the law. Denying that developing doctrine had as its purpose terrorization of the civilian population constituted somewhat of an acknowledgement that it was prohibited. Advocates of 'morale bombing' pushed the line to its breaking point.

British and American thinking was not unique. In May 1933, *Dr. Robert Knauss* completed a major study for Luftwaffe Field Marshal *Erhard Milch*, State Secretary for the new German Air Ministry. *Knauss* argued that not only should modern industrial centers be attacked in order to destroy an enemy nation's economic capability to wage war, but population centers offered the possibility of attacking civilian morale directly. *Knauss* suggested "the terrorizing of the enemy's chief cities and industrial regions through bombing would lead that much more quickly to a collapse of the social and political rifts that cleave his society."[51]

The story of thinking by airpower advocates between the wars has been reported at length by military historians.[52] To the extent there was official public disavowal of indiscriminate attack, and it was very limited, often it was countered by an analogy to siege warfare, or arguments as to the effects on civilians of 'total war' – in essence, accepting Articles 20 and 21 of the Lieber Code, while ignoring Article 22 thereof – and a reluctance to trust international agreements (ironically documents promulgated by the victorious World War I governments, with Germany intentionally excluded from participation) over an overt threat of retaliation in kind. Pessimism as to the value of treaties, public and official, was not limited

---

[49] Id., pp. 5, 210-214.

[50] *Tami Davis Biddle*, Air Power, in: Michael Howard/George J. Andreopoulos/Mark R. Shulman (eds.), The Laws of War: Constraints on Warfare in the Western World (1994), p. 151, citing: International Air Regulations, Air Corps Tactical School, 1933-1934. Air Force Historical Research Center, file no. 248.101-16. *Stephen L. McFarland*, America's Pursuit of Precision Bombing 1910-1945 (1995), p. 101, identifies key dissenters, many of whom were responsible for writing the U.S. World War II Air War Plan AWPD-1. On AWPD-1, see *Barry D. Watts*, The Foundations of Air Force Doctrine (1984), pp. 17-23.

[51] *Williamson Murray*, Luftwaffe (1985), pp. 8, 11.

[52] *Biddle*, supra n. 34, pp. 69-175.

to treaties relating to aerial bombardment, and increased with Japan's withdrawal from the League of Nations on 24 February 1933.

The wars of the 1930s. One may argue that World War II began as early as 1932, with Japan's war in China (1932 through 1945), continuing with the Italo-Abyssinian War (1935-1941), and the Spanish Civil War (1936-1938). Those conflicts contributed little to the definition of *military objective* and, for brevity's sake, will be by-passed.

The last days of peace: one government's actions. As the war clouds darkened over Europe, and with the experience of the wars in China, Spain and Ethiopia in mind, several last-ditch efforts were made to establish legal standards. Actions and statements of three governments – Great Britain, the United States and Germany – will be reviewed.

Great Britain. In a debate in the House of Commons on June 21, 1938, British Prime Minister *Neville Chamberlain* suggested three basic rules for bombing:

- It is against international law to bomb civilians as such and to make deliberate attacks upon civilian populations.
- Targets which are aimed at from the air must be legitimate military objectives and must be capable of distinction.
- Reasonable care must be taken in attacking those military objectives so that by carelessness a civilian population in the neighbourhood is not bombed.

I have been critical not only of the motivation for these 'rules', but also for their practical effect, other than perhaps the first.[53] But *Chamberlain* continued:

"We cannot too strongly condemn any declaration on the part of anybody, wherever it may be made and on whatever side it may be made, that it should be part of a deliberate policy to try to win a war by demoralizing the civilian population through a process of bombing from the air. That is absolutely contrary to international law."[54]

Prime Minister *Chamberlain*'s focus on constraint in aerial bombing was more political than humanitarian, and wholly inconsistent with British Air Ministry war plans promulgated less than a year earlier.[55] As *James Maloney Spaight* acknowl-

---

53 *Parks*, Air War and the Law of War, in: Air University Review 32, 1 (1990), pp. 36-37.

54 *Spaight*, Air Power and War Rights, 3rd ed. (1947), p. 257.

55 The preceding year, on October 1, 1937, the Air Ministry sent to Bomber Command a series of thirteen plans, called Western Air (W.A.) plans, with instructions to concentrate on the first three. Some relevant W.A. plans were:
W.A. 1: the attack on the German Air Striking Force and its maintenance organization, to which was added the German aircraft industry (originally listed under W.A. 6).

edged in "International Law of the Air, 1939-1945", an official confidential supplement to "Air Power and War Rights" prepared for the Air Historical Branch of the Air Ministry following the end of the European War:

"Our policy before the war and from the first nine months of the war was inspired by the consideration that the less bombing there was, the better for us. We were apprehensive about the effect of heavy attacks on London, and as our air force was only one-third the size of the German in September, 1939, we were not in a position to return blow for blow ... So long as she held that lead it was in our interests that bombing should be restricted ..."[56]

With this larger picture, Prime Minister *Chamberlain*'s speech was intended less as a British declaration of what it regarded the law to be than a continuation of British policy to limit bombing by either side until the Royal Air Force gained parity with (if not superiority to) the *Luftwaffe*. Prime Minister *Chamberlain*'s three principles were adopted in slightly different form by the League of Nations on September 30, 1938.[57]

The length, depth and breadth of Axis and Allied aerial bombardment in World War II precludes anything more than a macro view. The history has been told by many. Debates have been waged at length over the efficacy, morality and legality of the strategic bombing campaigns of World War II.[58] This paper cannot resolve those long-running debates, assuming that possible. State practice in that conflict

---

W.A. 4: the attack on German military rail, canal, and road communications (a) during the period of concentration of its armies, and (b) to delay a German invasion of the Low Countries and France.

W.A. 5: the attack on the German War Industry, including the supply of oil, with priority to that in the Ruhr, Rhineland, and Saar.

SAOG I, supra n. 29, p. 94. The Western Air Plans continued to undergo revision and refinement up to the commencement of World War II, and thereafter. Their form as of September 1, 1939, is contained in *SAOG* IV, Appendix 6, pp. 99-102.

56 *Spaight*, British Public Records Office file AIR 41/5 (June 1945), at D-1.

57 *Schindler/Toman*, supra n. 2, pp. 329-330. A Draft Convention for the Protection of Civilian Populations against New Engines of War adopted by the International Law Association on September 30, 1938, contained at *Schindler/Toman*, supra n. 2, pp. 331-336, received no acknowledgement or reference in the League of Nations resolution.

58 In addition to works previously cited, recent literature in the continuing debate includes *Olaf Groehler*, The Strategic Air War and Its Impact on the German Civilian Population, in: The Conduct of the Air War in the Second World War, supra n. 161, pp. 279-297; *Brereton Greenhous/Stephen J. Harris/William C. Johnston/William G.P. Rawling*, The Crucible of War 1939-1945, III The Official History of the Royal Canadian Air Force (1994), pp. 523-867; *Kenneth P. Werrell*, Blankets of Fire: U.S. Bombers over Japan during World War II (1996); *Robin Neillands*, The Bomber War: The Allied Air Offensive Against Nazi Germany (2001); *Henry Probert*, Bomber Harris (2001); and *Hermann Knell*, To Destroy a City: Strategic Bombing and Its Human Consequences in World War II (2003).

does offer a basis for assessment as to the law at the time.[59] But there are caveats. What was then was then, in an era of total war, with law substantially less clear than today. While State practice in that conflict offers valuable lessons as to what may constitute a military objective, State practice sixty or more years ago should not be judged by today's legal standards. Nor would military objectives of that conflict necessarily be considered so today.

- Review of World War II aerial bombardment efforts leads to an initial conclusion that pointing fingers at one State party vis-à-vis another as to adherence to the law of war contributes little to nothing to the discussion. Over the past seventeen years, I have stated that my research led me to the conclusion that the only difference between the various national aerial bombardment efforts was in capability, not intent.[60] All bombed the same categories of targets with roughly equal accuracy (or inaccuracy), without concern for civilian casualties or damage to civilian objects.[61] No historian or participant in the World War II campaigns attending conferences where I have offered this conclusion has disagreed with it, and veterans have openly agreed with it.
- There is ample evidence that the law of war principle of *distinction* was acknowledged by governments as customary law.[62] The intentional attack of the civilian population as such generally was accepted as prohibited. Except in enemy-occupied territory, however, no precaution was exercised with regard to collateral damage to civilian objects or incidental injury to the enemy civilian population.
- While there may have been a juridical lacuna as to the law of war relating to what constitutes a military objective, a shift had occurred in thinking at national levels.
- There was no geographic or range limitation related to legitimacy of targets or their attack. Targets deep within enemy-controlled territory were the object of attack by aircraft, special operations forces, and/or partisans.[63]

---

59 Portions of the text that follows are based upon this author's: The Protection of Civilians from Air Warfare, 27 Israel Yearbook on Human Rights 65-111 (1998).

60 *Parks*, Air War and the Law of War, in: Air Force Law Review (1990), pp. 1-225, at 54; id., Air War and the Laws of War, in: *Horst Boog* (ed.), The Conduct of the Air War in the Second World War (1992), pp. 310-372, at 354; The Protection of Civilians from Air Warfare, id., p. 67, and its accompanying footnote 9. The second reference, contained in "The Conduct of the Air War in the Second World War", was part of the program, "Luftkriegführung im Zweiten Weltkrieg Ein Internationaler Vergleich", Internationalen Wissenschaftlichen Tagung des Militärgeschictlichen Forschungsamtes, August 29 – September 2, 1988, Freiburg in Breisgau.

61 See this author's: 'Precision' and 'Area' Bombing: Who Did Which, and When, 18, 1 The Journal of Strategic Studies 145-174 (March 1995), comparing British and American area bombing practices, relative accuracy, and lack of concern for collateral civilian casualties other than in German-occupied territory.

62 *Parks*, Protection of Civilians, supra n. 59, p. 72.

63 A list of strategic targets as well as a notable comparison of the relative success of special operations forces vis-à-vis aerial attack – with significantly less risk to the civilian population – is contained in *M.R.D. Foot*, SOE in France (1966), at Appendix G, pp.

- Dams and dikes were regarded as military objectives by units engaged in offensive and defensive operations. When attacked, consideration of the effects of their attack (and release of their 'dangerous forces') was a factor only in protecting friendly forces or allied civilians from their effects.[64]
- The recent concept of 'dual use' was not a consideration. An object became a military objective if it was determined to contribute effectively towards the destruction of the enemy nation's means to resistance, and lowering of its determination to fight.
- *Military objective* was viewed in a strategic as well as tactical sense. For example, the 18 April 1942 joint U.S. Navy and Army Air Corps attack by twenty-six B-25 Mitchell medium bombers with very small bomb loads of military objectives in Tokyo made no "effective contribution to the *military* action" in the sense of a tactical gain, but had a major strategic effect in the Pacific War.[65] Similarly, attacks on lines of communication in the Pas de Calais area of France arguably were of limited tactical value. But they constituted a major contribution to the Allied deception plan in order to achieve a successful landing on

---

505-517. The total amount of explosives employed by the British Special Operations Executive (SOE) in attack of strategic targets in France – 3,000 pounds – was less than one-sixth the bomb load of a single Royal Air Force Lancaster bomber. In essence special operations forces were the precision munitions of World War II.

64 See *Parks*, Air War and the Law of War, supra n. 53, pp. 206-209, for a history of the attack of dams and dikes in World War II, Korea, and Viet Nam.

65 The attack is described in *Carroll Glines*, The Doolittle Raid (1988); and *D. Schultz*, The Doolittle Raid (1988). Colonel *Jermain F. Rodenhauser* concluded that the Doolittle raid had significant impact on Japanese strategy because the Japanese high command thought the raid originated in Midway, leading to the Battle of Midway, in which the Imperial Japanese Navy suffered a catastrophic defeat less than two months later. *Rodenhauser*, The Doolittle Influence on the Pacific War, 3 Air University Quarterly Review (Spring 1950), pp. 25-30. Colonel *Rodenhauser*'s analysis and conclusion was based on his interviews with key Japanese military officers as a member of the Military Analysis Division of the United States Strategic Bombing Survey (USSBS). The USSBS report concludes in part:
"The raid was too small to do substantial physical damage, but its repercussions on the planning level of the high command were considerable … [A]ttention was focused on the eastern approaches to the home islands, and additional impetus given the prewar plan to attack Midway and the Aleutians … [and] the Japanese began to implement their plans for air defense of Japan which before that time had received scant consideration …"
United States Strategic Bombing Survey, Japanese Air Power (1946), p. 10. Naval historian *Samuel Eliot Morison*, agreeing with the USSBS, commented:
"The [Doolittle raid] … did not inflict one-thousandth part of the damage it was supposed to revenge [for the Japanese attack on Pearl Harbor] … The Japanese authorities … pinned down hundreds of planes to defend Tokyo. And, what is more important, the event expedited plans for an overextension that led to the Japanese defeat at Midway."
Morison, The Two-Ocean War (1963), p. 140. Subsequent histories support this conclusion. See *Ron Spector*, Eagle Against the Sun (1985), p. 155; *John Keegan*, The Second World War (1989), p. 271.

June 6, 1944, at Normandy, and on German reinforcement once the landings were underway.

- "Attacks on morale" was at best a euphemism for relieving an attacker of any obligations with respect to collateral damage to civilian objects and incidental injury to the enemy civilian population. Notwithstanding emphasis placed on attacks on enemy civilian morale in pre-war airpower doctrine and World War II directives,[66] there is no evidence of a decisive effect on civilian morale. Marshal of the Royal Air Force Sir Arthur Harris, who commanded Royal Air Force Bomber Command from February 23, 1942, to the end of the war in Europe, concluded "The idea that the main object of bombing German industrial cities was to break the enemy morale proved to be totally unsound … [M]orale bombing was completely ineffective against so well-organized a police state as Germany."[67] *Harris*'s remarks mirror those of the post-war British Bombing Survey Unit, which concluded "[i]n so far as the offensive against German towns was designed to break the morale of the German civilian population, it clearly failed,"[68] a conclusion shared by the United States Strategic Bombing Survey.[69] A recent analysis agreed, concluding that "[o]nly when Germany was overrun and Hitler died did the will to resist finally flicker out."[70] A candid assessment is contained in a history of the postwar United States Strategic Bombing Survey:

  "The Survey's comments about many prewar assumptions that proved wanting in the test of battle were essentially unnecessary. No one, for example, needed to be reminded that unescorted bomber formations had suffered unacceptable losses. By the same token, the airmen themselves had come to realize that enemy civilian morale could be affected decisively only when the extent and

---

[66] Originally German civilian morale was not regarded as a valid objective "until widespread defeatism had been engendered by heavy air attacks against the systems which supported the means to fight and the means to live." *Hansell*, supra n. 10, p. 85. The initial Allied POINTBLANK strategic bombing plan developed at Casablanca supported this emphasis or priority of attack:
"Your primary object will be the progressive destruction and dislocation of the German military, industrial and economic system, and the undermining of the morale of the German people to a point where their capacity for armed resistance is fatally weakened." *SAOG* II, supra n. 29, pp. 12-14. As the war progressed, however, emphasis on attacks on morale increased. Id., III, pp. 52-57.

[67] Arthur Harris, *Bomber Command* (1947), at 75, 76. This view is shared by the official British history of the Allied strategic air offensive against Germany; *SAOG* III, id., pp. 302-303. For similar comments regarding the effect of *Luftwaffe* attacks on British morale, see *Richard M. Titmuss*, Problems of Social Policy (1950), p. 349.

[68] British Bombing Survey Unit, Overall Report, Air 10/3866, supra n. 1, p. 79.

[69] United States Strategic Bombing Survey (USSBS), Summary Report - European War (1945), p. 16.

[70] *Mierzejewski*, supra n. 12, p. 185. See also *Biddle*, supra n. 34, pp. 277-279.

weight of attack reached proportions altogether unacceptable to the humanitarian instincts of the governments and peoples the bombers were *defending*."[71]

* * * * * * * * *

Post-World War II conflicts. The period following World War II led not to a permanent peace, but to decades of smaller conflicts, including the Malayan Emergency, the Korean War, various wars for independence, the French and American wars in Indochina/Viet Nam, the Arab-Israeli conflicts, the civil wars in Nigeria and Angola, and numerous smaller internal conflicts. Their history is extensive, but contributes little to the development of what constitutes a *military objective*.

Policy and military reactions in the post-World War II conflicts immediately preceding and following the 1974-1977 Diplomatic Conference drove technological development of weapons systems with greater precision.[72] Technology thus has come full circle – from increasing the risk to civilians with the advent of aerial bombardment, to development of stand-off precision weapons that reduce risk to the civilian population as such, even when an opposing force has elected to use the civilian population as human shields.

This history shows that international agreement as to what constitutes a military objective – or, beyond a basic prohibition on attack of the civilian population as such, what was or should be prohibited – proved difficult.

The ICRC's Draft Rules. In 1956 the International Committee put forward its Draft Rules for the Limitation of the Dangers Incurred by the Civilian Population in Time of War. The draft rules were offered by the ICRC as a part of the Draft Rules for the Limitation of the Dangers Incurred by the Civilian Population in Time of War at the XIXth International Conference of the Red Cross in Delhi.[73]

---

71 *David MacIsaac*, Strategic Bombing in World War Two: The Story of the United States Strategic Bombing Survey (1976), p. 164 [emphasis in original]. In summarizing the discussions of the experts who complied the Strategic Bombing Survey, the author notes:
"Repeatedly they stressed their joint conclusion that enemy civilian morale was not a productive target, that while morale can be adversely affected by air attack, there can be no predictable translation of morale effects into behavior effects. And behavior, not morale, was what counted" (p. 101).
See also *David MacIsaac*, The United States Strategic Bombing Survey (Reprint, 1976), Volume IV, pp. vii-ix.

72 A comprehensive history is *Michael Russell Rip/James M. Hasik*, The Precision Revolution (2002). See also *Richard P. Hallion*, Precision Guided Munitions and the New Era of Warfare, in: Air Power History 43,3 (Fall 1996), pp. 4-21, and *Michael N. Schmitt*, The Impact of High and Low-Tech Warfare on the Principle of Distinction, Harvard Program on Humanitarian Policy and Conflict Research, International Humanitarian Law Research Initiative Briefing Paper (November 2003).

73 *Schindler/Toman*, supra n. 2, pp. 339-344.

Ushered in at the height of the Cold War, they languished for another fifteen years. The following draft articles are of interest to our discussion:

Article 1. Since the right of Parties to the conflict to adopt means of injuring the enemy is not unlimited, they shall confine their operations to the destruction of his *military resources …*
Article 6. Attacks directed against the civilian population, as such, whether with the object of terrorizing it or for any other reason, are prohibited … [I]t is also forbidden to attack dwellings, installations or means of transport, which are for the exclusive use of, and occupied by, the civilian population.
Article 7. In order to limit the dangers incurred by the civilian population, attacks may only be directed against military objectives. Only objectives belonging to the categories of objective which, in view of their essential characteristics, are generally acknowledged to be of military importance, may be considered as military objectives. Those categories are listed in an annex to the present rules.[74] However, even if they belong to one of those categories, they cannot be considered as a military objective where their total or partial destruction, in the circumstances ruling at the time, offers no military advantage.

Herein lay the approach taken and adopted by the Diplomatic Conference. I will not attempt to summarize those negotiations, particularly given the excellent negotiating histories available.[75] Choosing to define rather than list, Article 52(2) of Additional Protocol I defines *military objective* as:

"Military objectives are limited to those objects which by their nature, location, purpose or use make an effective contribution to military action and whose total or partial destruction, capture or neutralization, in the circumstances ruling at the time, offers a definite military advantage."

As the definition has been incorporated into Protocols II (mines, booby-traps and other devices) and III (incendiary weapons) of the 1980 UN Conventional Weapons Convention,[76] and the United States is a party to this treaty and its Protocol II (in original and amended form), the issue as to who and who is not a State Party to the 1977 Additional Protocol I is moot with respect to our panel's topic.[77]

---

[74] The ICRC published no appendix.

[75] In particular, see *Michael Bothe/Karl Josef Partsch/Waldemar A. Solf*, New Rules for Victims of Armed Conflicts (1982).

[76] *Schindler/Toman*, supra n. 2, pp. 181-236. Its official title is United Nations Convention on Prohibitions or Restrictions on the Use of Certain Conventional Weapons Which May be Deemed to be Excessively Injurious or to Have Indiscriminate Effects of 10 October 1980.

[77] Protocol III was submitted by the President to the United States Senate for its advice and consent to ratification, where it remains pending. Message from the President of the United States Transmitting Protocols to the 1980 Convention on Prohibitions and Restrictions on the Use of Certain Conventional Weapons Which May Be Deemed to Be Excessively Injurious or to Have Indiscriminate Effects: The Amended Protocol on Pro-

A definition for objects that may be regarded as military objectives is important only for objects other than military bases, units, equipment and forces. Each of these may be attacked at any time, wherever located, as lawful targets, without weighing the factors described below to determine whether the object in question is a military objective.

A military objective is not limited to military bases, forces or equipment, but includes other objects that contribute to an opposing state's ability to wage war. The negotiating record contains no evidence to suggest that the Protocol I definition of *military objective* alters nor was it intended to alter the statement contained in the Lieber Code that the law of war permits a commander to take "those measures which are indispensable for securing the ends of war" not expressly prohibited by the law of war.[78] This may be accomplished through intentional attack of enemy military forces or other military objectives that enable an opposing state and its military forces to wage war.

Since conclusion of the Diplomatic Conference that produced Additional Protocol I, efforts have been made to refine the definition. The first was the very comprehensive volume by *Michael Bothe*, *Karl Josef Parstch*, and *Waldemar A. Solf*, all Diplomatic Conference participants.[79] Their effort is a valuable contribution to understanding the original intent. More recent efforts by Major General *A.P.V. Rogers* and Professor *Yoram Dinstein* complement the earlier volume. In his *Law on the Battlefield*,[80] Major General *A. P. V. Rogers* offers a detailed explanation of the definition, as follows:

- If the objective is not enemy military forces and equipment, the second part of the definition limits the first. Both parts must apply before an object that is normally a civilian object can be considered a military objective. The provision deals only with intentional attack, and not with collateral damage to civilian objects incidental to the lawful attack of military objectives adjacent to the civilian objects.[81]

---

hibitions or Restrictions on the Use of Mines, Booby-Traps and Other Devices (Protocol II, or the Amended Mines Protocol); the Protocol on Prohibitions or Restrictions on the Use of Incendiary Weapons (Protocol III, or the Incendiary Weapons Protocol); and the Protocol IV on Blinding Laser Weapons (Protocol IV), Treaty Doc. 105-1, 105th Congress, 1st Session (7 January 1997).

78 But see discussion of "war-sustaining" and "war-fighting" vis-à-vis "military action", infra.

79 *Bothe/Partsch/Solf*, supra n. 75, pp. 321-326.

80 *A.P.V. Rogers*, Law on the Battlefield (1996), pp. 34-37. These have been incorporated into British Ministry of Defence, The Manual of the Law of Armed Conflict (2004), pp. 56-57, para. 5.4.5. See also *Yoram Dinstein*, Legitimate Military Objectives Under the Current *Jus in Bello*, in: Andru E. Wall (ed.), Legal and Ethical Lessons in NATO's Kosovo Campaign (2002), pp. 139-172, and *Dinstein*, The Conduct of Hostilities under the Law of International Armed Conflict (2004), pp. 84-99.

81 At the time of its ratification of Additional Protocol I, the United Kingdom deposited the following formal statement of understanding in further clarification of the intent of article 52(2): "The first sentence of paragraph 2 prohibits only such attacks as may be di-

- *Nature* refers to the type of object, for example, military transports, command and control centres, or communication stations.
- Professor *Yoram Dinstein* provides further explanation, noting *nature* denotes the intrinsic character of the military objective. To assist the discussion, he provides a non-exhaustive list of what he regards as military objectives by their nature.[82]
- *Location* includes areas which are militarily important because they must be captured or denied an enemy, or because the enemy must be made to retreat from them. An area of land, such as a mountain pass, or a like route through or around a natural or man-made obstacle, may be a military objective. A town, village or city or city may become a military objective even if it does not contain military objectives if its seizure is necessary, *e.g.*, to protect a vital line of communications, or for other legitimate military reasons.[83]
- *Purpose* means the future intended or possible use, while *use* refers to its present function. The potential dual use of a civilian object, such as a civilian air-

rected against non-military objectives; it does not deal with the question of collateral damage resulting from attacks directed against military objectives".

82 *Dinstein*, Conduct of Hostilities, supra n. 80, pp. 88-89. *Dinstein* identifies: (1) fixed military fortifications, bases, barracks, installations and emplacements, including training and war-gaming facilities; (2) temporary military camps, entrenchments, staging areas, deployment positions and embarkation points; (3) Military units... whether stationed (*sic.*) or mobile; (4) Weapon systems, military equipment and ordnance, armour and artillery, and military vehicles of all types; (5) Military aircraft and missiles of all types; (6) Military airfields and missiles of all types; (7) Warships of all types; (8) Military ports and docks; (9) Military depots, munitions dumps, warehouses or stockrooms for the storage of weapons, ordnance, military equipment and supplies (including raw materials for military use, such as petroleum); (10) industrial plants (even when privately owned) engaged in the manufacture of arms, munitions, military supplies and essential parts for military vehicles, vessels or aircraft (like ball-bearing factories); (11) laboratories or other facilities for the research and development of new weapons and military devices; (12) military repair facilities; (13) power plants (electric, hydroelectric, etc.) serving the military; (14) arteries of transportation of strategic importance, principally railroads and rail marshalling yards, major motorways, navigable rivers and canals, including the tunnels and bridges of railways and trunk roads); (15) Ministries of Defence and any national, regional or local operational or coordination centres of command, control and communication related to running the war, including computer centres, as well as telephone and telegraph exchanges, for military use; and (16) intelligence-gathering centres related to the war effort, even when not run by the military establishment.

83 See also *Dinstein*, id., pp. 91-92, and: The Manual of the Law of Armed Conflict, supra n. 80, p. 55, para. 5.4.4. At the time of its ratification the United Kingdom deposited the following formal statement of understanding in this respect: "A specific area of land may be a military objective if, because of its location or others reasons specified in … [article 52], its total or partial destruction, capture or neutralization at the time offers a definite military advantage".

port or bridge, may make it a military objective because of its future intended or potential military use.[84]

The connection of some objects to an enemy's war effort may be direct, indirect or even discrete. A decision as to classification of an object as a military objective and allocation of resources for its attack is dependent upon its value to an enemy nation's war-fighting or war-sustaining effort (including its ability to be converted to a more direct connection), and not solely to its overt or present connection or use.

For example, in considering Allied attack of military objectives in Germany during World War II, priority of attack depended upon intended effect. If the intention was to tie effects to the Allied invasion of Europe, target systems late in the production cycle would receive priority. Were the Allied invasion scheduled later than anticipated, target systems related to the general weakening of Germany's ability to wage war would receive priority over final production and stockpiles.[85] Similar evaluation was made by the Luftwaffe in its initial air assaults on Great Britain in 1940.[86] The comparison is not unlike that of the philosophy of investors in deciding whether short-term or long-term investment is better under the circumstances ruling at the time.

- The words *nature, location and purpose or use* allow wide discretion, but are subject to qualifications stated later in the definition of "effective contribution to military action" and the offering of a "definite military advantage" through its seizure or destruction. There does not have to be a geographical connection between "effective contribution" and "military advantage." Attacks on military objectives in the enemy rear, or diversionary attacks, away from the area of military operations as such (the "contact zone"),[87] are lawful.
- *Military action* is used in the ordinary sense of the words, and is not intended to encompass a limited or specific military operation. It appears to have a wide meaning, equating to general prosecution of the war.

---

84 An example is Germany's Autobahn. In addition to its possible attack as a line of communication, portions of the Autobahn were constructed for and have been used as runways and aircraft service areas in NATO exercises. Railroad construction in Europe during the Nineteenth Century had dual purposes: commerce and to facilitate the mobilization and deployment of military forces. Similarly, the U.S. interstate highway system was begun during the Eisenhower Administration in part as a critical set of lines of communication for national defence purposes; see 23 U.S. Code §§ 101, 103. It was put to that use during the 1990 deployment of Continental U.S.-based U.S. military forces to Southwest Asia for Operations DESERT SHIELD and DESERT STORM, the successful Coalition effort to liberate Kuwait from Iraqi occupation. See also discussion in *Dinstein*, supra n. 80, pp. 89-90.

85 *Mierzejewski*, supra n. 12, p. 75.

86 See, for example, *Francis K. Mason*, Battle over Britain (1969), pp. 137-274.

87 The term "contact zone" is defined in article 26(2), Additional Protocol I (referring to medical aircraft), as "any area on land where the forward elements of opposing forces are in contact with one another, where they are exposed to direct fire on the ground".

- The phrase "in the circumstances ruling at the time" is important. If, for example, enemy military forces have taken up position in buildings that otherwise would be regarded as civilian objects, such as a school, retail store, or museum, the building has become a military objective. The circumstances ruling at the time, that is, the military use of the building, permit its attack if its attack would offer a definite military advantage. If the enemy military forces abandon the building, there has been a change of circumstances that precludes its treatment as a military objective.
- *Definite* means a concrete and perceptible military advantage, rather than one that is merely hypothetical or speculative.[88] A military commander may regard this requirement as met in seeking to seize or destroy objects with a common purpose in order to deny their use to the enemy. An example is the attack of all bridges on lines of communication the enemy is using or may use as alternate lines of communication in order to reinforce or re-supply his forces.
- *Military advantage* refers to the advantage anticipated from an attack when considered as a whole, and not only from its isolated or particular parts.[89] The advantage need not be immediate. For example, the military advantage in the attack of an individual bridge may not be seen (particularly if, at the time of the attack, there is no military traffic in the area), but can be established by the overall effort against bridges in order to isolate enemy military forces on the battlefield.
- Similarly, *military advantage* is not restricted to tactical gains, but is linked to the full context of war strategy. It may involve a variety of considerations, including security of the attacking force.[90]

Military advantage refers to commander's intent in determining whether or not an object constitutes a military objective rather than actual effect as determined subsequently. One historian explains this in the context of World War II bombing and the subsequent difficulties the United States had in conducting its Strategic Bombing Survey:

"Suppose a decision is made to take out a plant producing ball bearings; suppose one hundred bombers are dispatched and succeed in utterly demolishing the plant.

---

88 An example where an object failed to meet this standard is the 25 February 1991 recommendation by the U.S. Air Force component of US Central Command for an air attack on a Baghdad statue of Saddam Hussayn and another statue, consisting of matching sets of arms with crossed swords (modelled on the arms of Saddam Hussayn), called the Victory Arch or Crossed Swords Monument, discussed infra; see also *Samir al-Khalil*, The Monument (1991).

89 At the time of its ratification of Additional Protocol I, the United Kingdom deposited the following formal statement of understanding: "The 'military advantage anticipated from an attack' is intended to refer to the advantage anticipated from the attack considered as a whole and not only from isolated or particular parts of the attack".

90 U.S. Department of Defense, Final Report to Congress: Conduct of the Persian Gulf War (1992), p. 613, where *military advantage* was weighed in terms of execution of the Coalition war plan for the liberation of Kuwait. See also *Dinstein*, supra n. 80, p. 86.

So far as the commanders and crews are concerned, the effectiveness of the mission is taken for granted to be 100 per cent – the given target was attacked and destroyed. But suppose, also, that the ball bearing output of the destroyed plant is never missed by the enemy throughout the remainder of the war – either because of huge stockpiles or alternative sources of supply. In such a case, the effectiveness of the mission in speeding up victory drops to zero; indeed. The question then arises, when one asks how the one hundred sorties might otherwise have been applied, whether or not the mission's effectiveness should be described as a negative (or minus) value. Thus, to measure effectiveness, as opposed to effects, becomes a problem of such magnitude as to be impractical, requiring an evaluation of an almost limitless number of decisions leading up to the attack order."[91]

Bearing this in mind, the United Kingdom offered the following statement of understanding at the time of its ratification of Additional Protocol I:

"In relation to Articles 51 to 58 inclusive, that military commanders and others responsible for planning, deciding upon or executing attacks necessarily have to reach decisions on the basis of their assessment of the information from all sources which is available to them at the relevant time.

In relation to paragraph 5(b) of Article 51 and paragraph (2)(a)(iii) of Article 57, that the military advantage anticipated from an attack is intended to refer to the advantage anticipated from the attack considered as a whole and not only from isolated or particular parts of the attack."[92]

Taken on its face, the definition of *military objective* in Additional Protocol I is an advancement. It has been used by States Parties and non-States Parties, including the United States, in armed conflicts since 1977. With statements of clarification similar to those of the United Kingdom and Germany, the definition of *military objective* is being incorporated into the U.S. *Department of Defense Law of War Manual*, presently in preparation.

I do not necessarily accept the conclusion of the International Committee of the Red Cross in its *Customary International Humanitarian Law Study* that the definition has attained customary law status.[93] While there are a number of States Parties to Additional Protocol I, few have taken any steps toward treaty implementa-

---

91 *MacIsaac*, supra n. 71, pp. 161-162.

92 *Schindler/Toman*, supra n. 2, p. 815. Germany offered similar declarations:
"It is the understanding of the Federal Republic of Germany that in the application of the provisions of Part IV, Section I, of Additional Protocol I, to military commanders and others responsible for planning, deciding upon or executing attacks, the decision taken by the person responsible has to be judged on the basis of all information available to him at the relevant time, and not on the basis of hindsight."
"In applying the rule of proportionality in Article 51 and Article 57, 'military advantage' is understood to refer to the advantage anticipated from the attack considered as a whole and not only from isolated or particular parts of the attack." Id, p. 802.

93 *Jean Marie Henckaerts/Louise Doswald-Beck*, Customary International Humanitarian Law, Volume I: Rules (2005), p. 29.

tion. Fewer than one-quarter of States Parties have had their military forces experience combat since 1977. As I stated in a recent critique, while the ICRC *Customary Law Study* acknowledges the importance of State practice, it suffers in its reliance on statements to the exclusion of acts. It lacks context for when and why statements it cites were made.[94] The ICRC Study relies on words possibly offered for political purposes (much like Prime Minister *Neville Chamberlain*'s 1938 proposed rules for bombing) rather than deeds – what governments *say* without understanding why it was said, rather than what they *do* in war. The study's lack of rigor in its methodology – for example, its inability to distinguish between official positions of governments and the authoritativeness (or lack thereof) of lesser official sources cited by the ICRC, such as military instruction materials or a draft law of war manual never adopted by the government in question – further diminishes its value.

War is the ultimate test of law. Government-authorized actions in war speak louder than peacetime government statements. This point has been made by Sir *Adam Roberts* in a slightly different but related context:

"There is little tradition of disciplined and reasoned assessment of how the laws of war have operated in practice. Lawyers, academics, and diplomats have often been better at interpreting the precise legal meaning of existing accords, or at devising new law, than they have been at assessing the performance of existing accords or at generalizing about the circumstances in which they can or cannot work. In short, the study of law needs to be integrated with the study of history: if not, it is inadequate."[95]

Despite being almost thirty years old, Additional Protocol I has not yet crossed the all-important threshold of having been legally applicable in an international armed conflict. Its true test remains in the future. It is true that governments and their militaries, including the United States military, has applied many of its provisions in the international armed conflicts in which they have participated. But it is premature to reach conclusions like those contained in the ICRC Customary Law Study as to whether or not Protocol I's new provisions – including the definition of military objective – may be regarded as customary international law.

While the definition of *military objective* contained in Additional Protocol I is an improvement in the law of war, more evidence of actual State practice in armed conflict will be necessary before it can be regarded as customary international law. Generally I agree with Professor *Yoram Dinstein* that the definition of *military objective* contained in Additional Protocol I might benefit through augmentation by an illustrative, non-exhaustive list of categories of objects historically regarded

---

94 *Parks*, The ICRC Customary Law Study: A Preliminary Assessment, Annual Meeting of American Society of International Law, Washington, April 1, 2005. See also *Daniel Bethlehem QC*, The ICRC Customary Law Study: An Assessment, Chatham House, 18 April 2005 (publication pending).

95 *Sir Adam Roberts*, Land Warfare: From Hague to Nuremberg, in: The Laws of War: Constraints on Warfare in the Western World, supra n. 50, p. 117.

as military objectives. There are risks, such as the potential that notwithstanding every possible disclaimer regarding its non-exhaustive character, a list soon takes on a life of its own as exclusive rather than illustrative. In this regard, I regard Professor *Dinstein*'s list as more restrictive than State practice.[96]

Following is a list of categories of objects historically regarded as military objectives. The following, exclusively military in nature, always are military objectives:

- Combatant members of the armed forces and civilian who take a direct part in hostilities without being uniformed members of the armed forces.[97]
- Military ground, air and naval equipment other than clearly identifiable medical equipment or transport, to include vehicles, ships, weapons, munitions and supplies.
- Military ground forces, air and naval bases (other than medical facilities and prisoner of war camps), whether used for training, billeting, or staging, or offensive or defensive purposes, to include headquarters or command and control centres, defence ministries or intelligence establishments.[98]

The following objects may become military objectives if they meet the definitional test set forth above.

- National command, control, computers and intelligence (C^4I).
- Economic, to include power sources, communications networks and equipment, industry (war supporting, to include industry for import or export).
- Transportation, to include equipment, lines of communication (highways, railroads, waterways, ports and airports), and petroleum, oil and lubricant (production, transportation, storage and distribution facilities) products.
- Geographic, such as known or suspected enemy avenues of approach or withdrawal.

---

96 *Dinstein*, Conduct of Hostilities, supra n. 80, p. 83, and his list recited in note 82 of this paper. In the course of the panel discussion, Professor *Wolff Heintschel von Heinegg* suggested it might be more appropriate to develop a list of objects *disqualified* as military objectives. This is an approach for consideration in military manuals. A danger is that even an item normally not regarded as a military objective, such as cultural property, may become a military objective if it meets the definition contained in Article 52(2), such as through its use by enemy forces.

97 This paper has focused on military objectives vis-à-vis the issue of what constitutes "taking a direct part in hostilities", as stated in Article 51(3), Additional Protocol I. As previously stated, the test for civilians (that is, "taking a direct part in hostilities") is too restrictive in considering whether a civilian object is a military objective.

98 Military hospitals and enemy prisoner of war or civilian internee camps are immune from attack so long as they are not used for acts harmful to the enemy, or in any other way inconsistent with their humanitarian mission. A prisoner of war camp may be the object of an attack or temporary seizure for the purpose of rescuing the prisoners of war, as the U.S. sought to do in its 21 November 1970 raid on the Son Tay prisoner of war camp in the then-Democratic Republic of North Viet Nam. The history of this mission is contained in *Benjamin F. Schemmer*, The Raid (1976).

This list is comparable to military objectives in the 1991 Coalition campaign to liberate Kuwait:[99]

- Leadership command facilities.
- Electrical production facilities powering military systems.
- Command, control and communication nodes.
- Strategic and tactical integrated air defence systems.
- Air forces and air fields.
- Known nuclear, biological and chemical weapons research and production facilities.
- Scud missile production and storage facilities, launching equipment and positions.
- Naval forces and naval (military) port facilities.
- Oil refining and distribution facilities.
- Railroads and bridges connecting Iraqi military forces with logistics depots and storage areas.
- Iraqi military units, equipment and personnel in Kuwait.
- Military storage and production sites.

Lists prepared by the ICRC[100] and international lawyers[101] are more restrictive than State practice and pre-existing treaty law,[102] raising this question: Was the definition of *military objective* in Additional Protocol I intended to reflect (if not necessarily codify) State practice (but not necessarily customary law), or is it new law? The explanation accompanying the 1994 *San Remo Manual on International Law Applicable to Armed Conflicts at Sea* identifies the definition of *military objective* as new law.[103] If the definition codifies State practice or, indeed, customary

[99] U.S. Department of Defense, Final Report to Congress: Conduct of the Persian Gulf War (1992), pp. 95-98.

[100] *Yves Sandoz/Christophe Swinarski/Bruno Zimerman*, Commentary on the Additional Protocols of 8 June 1977 to the Geneva Conventions of 12 August 1949 (1987), p. 632, n. 3; and *A.P.V. Rogers/P. Malherbe*, Model Manual on the Law of Armed Conflict (1999), p. 72.

[101] *L.C. Green*, The Contemporary Law of Armed Conflict (2nd ed., 2000), p. 191; and *Dinstein*, Conduct of Hostilities, supra n. 80, pp. 88-89, and found at footnote 82.

[102] For example, Article 8(a) of the 1954 Hague Convention for the Protection of Cultural Property in the Event of Armed Conflict in a non-exhaustive list identifies as an "important military objective ... an aerodrome, broadcasting station, establishment engaged upon work of national defense, a port or railway station of relative importance or a main line of communication." *Schindler/Toman*, supra n. 2, pp. 999-1025, at 1003.

[103] *Louise Doswald-Beck* (ed.), San Remo Manual on International Law Applicable to Armed Conflicts at Sea (1995), p. 68. This conclusion raises an interesting issue. The editor of the 1995 *San Remo Manual* was a co-editor of the 2005 International Committee of the Red Cross Customary International Humanitarian Law study, which concludes the definition of military objective in Article 52(2) of Additional Protocol I is customary international law; Customary International Humanitarian Law, supra n. 86, p. 29. This suggests one of the most rapid moves of a new law to customary law status in history.

international law, the definition of *military objective* in Article 52(2) of Additional Protocol I is broader than the interpretations proffered by the ICRC or Professors *Leslie Green* or *Yoram Dinstein*. Ultimately I believe most differences will prove situational rather than substantive. Differences between State Practice – in the historical sense of what governments *do* in wartime rather than what some governments may *say* in peacetime – and lists prepared by academicians and non-government organizations raise red flags as to the latter. International law consists primarily of what governments negotiating with other governments determine they are willing to surrender of their sovereignty for a common good. Academicians and non-governmental organizations who attempt to "push" the law further merely make the law less credible.

Time will tell whether the academic works cited assist in understanding what constitutes a military objective. Several issues remain:

May a military objective cease to be a military objective? An object that may have met the criteria to be a military objective contained in Article 52(2), may cease to be a military objective if it no longer meets the definition. But may it cease to be a military objective under other circumstances?

The question is offered as a result of arguments heard in past conferences. Some quite incorrectly have argued that inasmuch as a category of military objectives has not been attacked in recent wars, or a particular method of warfare has not been used, that each now is legally proscribed. This was a suggestion by some when the British submarine *HMS Conqueror* sank the Argentinian cruiser *General Belgrano* in the 1982 Falklands/Malvinas War.[104] Accepting this line of thought, governments would be obligated to use every method of warfare in each conflict in order to preserve the right to use it in future conflicts. The *General Belgrano* was a warship and, as such, was a military objective susceptible to attack at all times, wherever located. That no warship had been attacked by a submarine since World War II did not make submarine warfare an illegal method of warfare or cause *General Belgrano* to lose its military objective status.

The same may be said with respect to targeting. Decisions have been taken for military or policy reasons in some conflicts that particular military objectives would not be attacked, or did not merit priority in attack. In order to preserve the right to attack particular military objectives in future conflicts (that is, objectives meeting the definition), following the argument offered by some, it is necessary for at least one military objective in each possible category to be attacked in every conflict and as early in the conflict as possible lest some interpret their lack of attack as a change in State practice and, accordingly, a change in the law as to what constitutes military objectives.

Governments often exercise restraint in conflicts for diplomatic, political or other reasons. Returning to the 1982 Falklands/Malvinas War, military air bases in Argentina from which Argentina launched its attacks on British forces clearly

---

[104] The *General Belgrano* was sunk May 2, 1982, with a loss of 321 lives. *Jeffrey Ethel/ Alfred Price*, Air War South Atlantic (1983), p. 76.

were military objectives. Their attack would have been lawful. For military and policy reasons the British government decided against their attack.

Yet the argument has been offered that if military objectives are not attacked in the initial phases of an armed conflict, their subsequent attack is illegal. For example, two lawyers argued attacks of military objectives in the vicinity of Hanoi and Haiphong in the December 1972 U.S. Operation LINEBACKER II would have been illegal had the military objective criteria contained in Article 52(2) existed at the time, as they had not been attacked previously and the primary purpose for their attack was political rather than military.[105] The military objectives in question had not been authorized for attack earlier for policy reasons. Their attack was authorized in the course of a long and on-going armed conflict. A purpose for their attack was to increase destruction of line of communication targets to impede North Vietnamese movement of military personnel, equipment, and munitions to reinforce its military operations in South Viet Nam. There was also a political objective: to stop North Vietnamese leadership intransigence and encourage their return to the Paris Peace Talks. That goal was accomplished through authorization of attack of legitimate military objectives.[106] Failure to attack them before the seventh month of LINEBACKER operations did not alter their status as military objectives. Voluntary constraint in war by one side does not alter the law of war status of enemy military objectives.

"War-sustaining"and "war-fighting" versus "military action". In 1990 I expressed concern that use of "military action" in *military objective* might lead some to suggest limitations on attack of military objectives previously recognized as lawful in State practice.[107] Regrettably this has proved to be the case in discussion of the issue of "war-sustaining" and "war-fighting" objects vis-à-vis "military action", the latter being the term contained in the definition of *military objective* in Additional Protocol I. The issue was debated at the 2001 U.S. Naval War College

---

[105] *Hamilton DeSaussure/Robert Glasser*, Air Warfare – Christmas 1972, in: Peter D. Trooboff (ed.), Law and Responsibility in Warfare (1975), pp. 119-139. A rebuttal is *Norman R. Thorpe/James R. Miles*, Comments, supra, pp. 145-149. The second argument that the object of the bombing was more political than military ignores the fundamental Clausewitzian point that war is politics by other means, and merits no further response.

[106] For an overall narrative and assessment of LINEBACKER operations, see this author's "LINEBACKER and the Law of War", Air University Review XXXIV, 2 (January-February 1983), pp. 1-30. Contrary to popular view, the targets attacked by B-52s were not in Hanoi, Haiphong or other populated areas. This author's Air University Review article details target characteristics, locations and U.S. attack precautions. A leading Viet Nam War history confirms this:
"The dispatches of a lone French correspondent on the spot, cited in many American newspaper, television, and radio accounts, referred repeatedly to the "carpet bombing" of downtown areas in Haiphong and Hanoi. But Malcolm Browne of *The New York Times* reported from Hanoi soon afterward that damage had been "grossly overstated," and other foreign journalists corroborated his testimony. So did Tran Duy Hung, mayor of Hanoi ..." *Stanley Karnow*, Vietnam: A History (1983), p. 653.

[107] *Parks*, supra n. 53, p. 141.

International Law Conference.[108] It also was the subject of an excellent analysis by Rear Admiral *Horace B. Robertson, Jr.*, USN (Ret.), a former Judge Advocate General of the Navy, Professor Emeritus at Duke Law School, and former Charles H. Stockton Professor of International Law at the Naval War College.[109]

Contrary to a view expressed at a small Geneva conference last month, neither "war-fighting" nor "war-sustaining" should be regarded as a substitute for "military action."[110] *Military action* is not and was not intended to be limited to tactical effects, but as will be seen includes attacks of military objectives the effects of which are of fundamental importance for the enemy's conduct of the armed conflict, including his will to resist.

The debate over the term "war-sustaining" raised fundamental questions as to the consistency of interpretations of Additional Protocol I with the purpose of war. Notwithstanding and perhaps consistent with the definition of *military objective* in Additional Protocol I, the objective of war remains destroying the enemy's will to resist – not merely a nation's military capability, but a nation's *will.* So long as this is done through attack of military objectives, it is not prohibited. War is a coercive tool of international relations. As *Sir Michael Howard* observed:

"Wars are not simply acts of violence. They are acts of persuasion or of discussion; and although the threat of destruction is normally a necessary part of the persuading process, such destruction is only exceptionally regarded as an end in itself."[111]

The debate regarding the distinction between "war-sustaining", "war-fighting" and "military action" is not clear, and appears primarily academic. Many military objectives fulfil each as, for example, a nation's electric power grid.[112] A nation's electric power grid has been acknowledged as making an effective contribution to

---

108 *Wall*, supra n. 80, pp. 141-122.

109 The Principle of the Military Objective in the Law of Armed Conflict, in: U.S. A.F. Acad. J. Legal Studies 8 (1997-1998), pp. 35-69, at 45-51.

110 *Alexandra Boivin/Yves Sandoz*, The Legal Regime Applicable to Targeting Military Objectives in the Context of Contemporary Warfare, paper presented to Informal Meeting of Experts on Targeting Military Objectives, Geneva, 12 May 2005, p. 27.

111 Strategy and Policy in Twentieth-Century Warfare, in: Harmon Memorial Lectures in Military History 1959-1987 (1988), p. 354. The role of coercion in warfare is articulated in *Daniel L. Byman/Matthew C. Waxman/Eric Larson*, Air Power as a Coercive Instrument (RAND, 1999), and *Daniel L. Byman/Matthew C. Waxman*, Kosovo and the Great Air Power Debate, in: International Security 24, 4 (March 1, 2000), pp. 5-38. See also *Ken Watkin*, Canada/United States Military Interoperability and Humanitarian Law Issues, in: Duke Journal of Comparative & International Law 15, 2 (Winter-Spring 2005), pp. 281 et seq.

112 See, for example, *Daniel T. Kuehl*, Airpower vs. Electricity: Electric Power as a Target for Strategic Air Operations, in: The Journal of Strategic Studies 18, 1 (March 1995), pp. 237-266, at 251, which acknowledges that "Neutralization of the [Iraqi power] grid would serve two strategic purposes, one immediate and military, the other longer-term and political".

modern military action."[113] Military objectives generally are referred to as tactical or strategic rather than "war-sustaining" or "war-fighting". Clearly the terms "military objective" and "military advantage" were not intended to be limited to tactical gains.[114] A military objective may fulfil either a tactical or strategic role, or both. During Operation MARKET GARDEN, the failed September 1944 Allied effort to seize intact bridges across the Rhine, the bridge at Arnhem had both tactical and strategic importance, for example. Too strict an interpretation of the military advantage derived from attack of a military objective would undermine the credibility of Additional Protocol I. This returns to my point as to whether the definition of *military objective* was intended to reflect State practice or offer a new, limiting effect. To this end, language from the *Bothe*, *Partsch* and *Solf* treatise is instructive:

"The objects classified as military objectives under this definition include much more than strictly military objects such as military vehicles, weapons, munitions, stores of fuel and fortifications. Provided the objects meet the two-pronged test, *under the circumstances ruling at the time* (not at some hypothetical future time), military objectives include activities providing administrative and logistical support to military operations such as transportation and communications systems, railroads, airfields and port facilities and industries *of fundamental importance for the conduct of the armed conflict*."[115]

The term "war-sustaining" might constitute a "slippery slope," as some have argued, leading to attack of civilian objects.[116] But so, too, could "war-fighting" or any other term. The fear expressed by some that "war-sustaining" would lead to "justify unleashing the type of indiscriminate attacks that annihilated entire cities during [World War II]"[117] is drastically at odds with the revolution in targeting accuracy and State practice evidenced in recent conflicts in Afghanistan and Iraq. This was acknowledged in the draft report of last month's informal meeting of experts in Geneva, which concludes the argument that use of the term *war-sustaining* "is a veiled attempt to justify targeting civilians or civilian objects" is unfounded.[118] Attacking a military objective, once identified, must be carried out in accordance with other law of war provisions, including those prohibiting attacks intended to terrorize the civilian population, and indiscriminate attack, codified in Article 51 of Additional Protocol I.

To some degree the problem appears a result of recent proposals regarding attacks on civilian morale, discussed *infra*. In this regard there appears no asymme-

---

[113] *Dinstein*, Legitimate Military Objectives, supra n. 80, p. 155.

[114] *Dinstein*, Conduct of Hostilities, supra n. 80, p. 86.

[115] *Bothe/Partsch/Solf*, supra n. 75, pp. 322-323, citing Article 2, Hague Convention IX, supra n. 16, and Article 8, Hague Convention for the Protection of Cultural Property in the Event of Armed Conflict of 14 May 1954 (*Schindler/Toman*, supra n. 2, pp. 745-776) [emphasis provided].

[116] *Wall*, supra n. 80, p. 180.

[117] *Louise Doswald Beck*, as quoted in Robertson, supra n. 109, p. 46.

[118] *Boivin/Sandoz*, supra n. 110, p. 28.

try of views. As Professor *Ipsen* correctly noted during the discussion following presentation of this paper, "morale" is neither an object nor a person. But *national will* may be aimed at through attack of military objectives.

Treaty law is built not upon fear of worst-case scenarios, or a concern for its violation, but an assumption of good-faith implementation of treaty obligations. To suggest that the "military advantage" can or must be separated from the political basis for a conflict, or was intended to be, ignores the purpose of war. However disagreeable the term may be to some, "war-sustaining" is accurately descriptive of the actual practice of States in armed conflict.

In the course of the 2001 Naval War College discussion, Professor *Michael Bothe* suggested a more restrictive interpretation of *military objective* than originally contemplated by governments in 1977 "in the light of changing circumstances."[119] Given that the conference focused on the 1999 war in Kosovo and Yugoslavia, I assumed these were the "changing circumstances" to which he referred. Professor *Bothe* clarified this during our panel session on June 10th by explaining it referred to military advantage to be gained "in the circumstances ruling at the time," as stated in the definition of *military objective* in Article 52(2) of Additional Protocol I. In this respect Professor *Bothe*'s view appears to coincide with that expressed by British Field Marshal *Sir George Milne* in 1928, previously cited, but with a slightly different twist.

If I understand Professor *Bothe*'s argument, the limited nature and objective of the 1999 Kosovo conflict accordingly limited the breadth of military objectives that lawfully could be attacked, particularly those not directly battlefield-related. Nothing in the legislative history of Article 52(2) – including its assessment in the book Professor *Bothe* co-authored – or the report of the ICTY Prosecutor lends credence to this argument. If an object meets the definition of military objective contained in Article 52(2), it is a military objective, whether tactical or strategic. Political leaders have placed and may place policy limits on attack of certain military objectives depending on the political nature and strategic objectives of a particular conflict as they see it. The decision against attack of mainland Argentinian air bases during the 1982 Falklands/Malvinas War, previously cited, is a case in point.[120] But that does not alter the fact that they were military objectives and lawfully could have been attacked. Policy decisions should not be confused for law of war limitations.

---

[119] Id., p. 176.

[120] One of the most egregious examples of such policy limitations on attack of a military objective occurred during the 1965-1968 U.S. ROLLING THUNDER air campaign against the Democratic Republic of Viet Nam. North Vietnamese MiG fighter air bases were not authorized for attack by the U.S. national leadership for the first 2½ years of the war, even as they were being used by North Vietnamese fighters to attack U.S. aircraft. North Vietnamese MiG-17 and MiG-21 aircraft could not be attacked even if they were observed taking off to attack U.S. strike forces, and could not be engaged (fired upon) unless and until they fired on U.S. aircraft. *Parks*, Rolling Thunder and the Law of War, in: Air University Review XXXIII, 2 (January-February 1982), pp. 2-23, at 9, 11.

Professor *Bothe* also suggested that circumstances may have changed with respect to consideration of proportionality in attack of so-called 'dual use' targets. As I will indicate, on this point I respectfully disagree.[121] As will be noted, NATO air attacks of strategic targets in and around Belgrade were not found to violate the law of war by the ICTY Prosecutor. As I stated at that conference, bad cases make bad law, and Operation ALLIED FORCE is of limited value as a precedent for much of anything, as the comments I will offer shortly will indicate.[122]

War-sustaining and/or *war-fighting* reflect State practice. Historical evidence and the description of the target sets agreed upon by NATO governments in ALLIED FORCE support the idea that nations have, do, and will attack not only an enemy's war-fighting capability, but also his capacity to sustain the conflict. The San Remo Manual on International Law Applicable in Armed Conflicts at Sea commentary supports this view of history, declaring:

"A civilian object may become a military objective and thereby lose its immunity from deliberate attack through use which is only indirectly related to combat action, but which nevertheless provides an effective contribution to the military part of a party's overall war-fighting capability."[123]

This notwithstanding the statement under "*Innovations* in the content of the Manual" in which the commentary describes its treatment of "military objective" as:

"a *new element* of major importance ... compared with the traditional law. Based on *recent State practice*, and on the concept of military objective found in Additional Protocol I, the Round Table decided to introduce this concept into naval operations in order to *limit the lawfulness* of attacks to merchant vessels which directly help the military action of the enemy … The purpose of this measure is to take into account modern means of warfare and genuine military needs, whilst respecting the gains made since the Second World War in international humanitarian law applicable to land warfare ..."[124]

---

[121] See discussion of 'dual-use' targets, infra. Any change in the law could be accomplished only through a Diplomatic Conference and adoption by consensus, as other than the United States there is no State practice to support a re-interpretation of Article 52(2), to this effect. Given that most NATO governments spend less than 1.5% of their GDP on defense, a new legal standard along the lines argued by Professor *Bothe* would place on them a decision-making obligation few could meet with their present military capabilities. Compliance with such a new rule would paralyze their future military operations. Such a focus exclusively on the obligations of the attacker (as that term is commonly defined, as opposed to its flawed Protocol I definition) not only would encourage a defender to increase shielding, but also would constitute a return to a long-rejected Just War-type argument that suggests the entire burden adherence to the law of war and avoidance of civilian suffering is on one party to the conflict.

[122] *Boivin/Sandoz*, supra n. 110, p. 281.

[123] *Doswald Beck*, supra n. 103, p. 117.

[124] Id., p. 68.

Earlier Manual language states:

"This [Manual] should not necessarily be seen as a statement of existing law, as the manual declares that it is 'a contemporary restatement – *together with some progressive development* ... of the law applicable to armed conflicts at sea ..."[125]

By its admission, the "San Remo Manual" is an effort to establish new law, not necessarily offer a restatement of customary international law. Yet even in so doing, it does not necessarily square with objections to the term *war-sustaining*.

The principal issue in the debate appears to be export as a military objective. A common example of a "war sustaining" military objective is cotton exports during the U.S. Civil War, as the Confederacy needed cotton exports to fund the war. A modern counterpart is oil – not only for its military use but also its commercial value. It has been an historic target. Tankers carrying oil were legitimate targets during World War II perhaps primarily for the military value of the oil but certainly for economic reasons as well.[126] Tankers also were attacked during the so-called 'Tanker War' that raged in the Persian Gulf from 1980 to 1988, during the Iran-Iraq War.[127] The thirteen years of U.N. Security Council-imposed sanctions on Iraqi oil support the legitimacy of economic or export "war sustaining" objects as military objectives. Notwithstanding reservations expressed by some, an object indirectly related to military operations as such but providing an effective contribution to an enemy's war effort meets the Additional Protocol I definition of a *military objective*.[128]

Two other questions arose in the context and aftermath of the 1999 NATO War against Yugoslavia. Each will be addressed in that context.

In 1999 the North Atlantic Treaty Organization (NATO) undertook military operations against the Yugoslav regime of Slobodan Milosevic.[129] The "conflict" was interesting in many respects, beginning with a declaration by NATO Secretary General *Javier Solana* that "NATO is not waging war against Yugoslavia,"[130] undoubtedly a surprise both to aircrew flying bombing missions, Serbian forces resisting NATO air strikes, and civilians killed or injured incidental to those military operations.

ALLIED FORCE uniquely was almost exclusively an air campaign. It was executed by NATO – whose members at that time had an annual defense budget

---

125 Id., at ix [emphasis provided].

126 See, for example, *Robert Goralski/Russell E. Freeburg*, Oil & War: How the Deadly Struggle for Fuel in WWII Meant Victory or Defeat (1987).

127 See *George K. Walker*, The Tanker War, 1980-88: Law and Policy (2000).

128 *Robertson*, supra n. 109 pp. 197, 207-211; and *L.C. Green*, The Contemporary Law of Armed Conflict (2nd ed., 2000), p. 191.

129 A comprehensive discussion of the conflict and its legal issues is contained in Wall, supra n. 80, the proceedings of a colloquium of military officers and international law experts at the U.S. Naval War College, 8-10 August 2001.

130 NATO Press Statement, 23 March 1999, as cited in *Eliot A. Cohen*, Kosovo and the New American Way of War, in: Andrew J. Bacevich/Eliot A. Cohen (eds.), War Over Kosovo (2001), pp. 38-61.

twenty-five times larger than Serbia's economy. Serbia already was severely affected by United Nations sanctions imposed in 1992, essentially destroying its economy. NATO faced a disaffected Serbian population living with an inflation rate of 116 trillion per cent. Yet it took NATO airpower seventy-eight days – sixteen times longer than air planners predicted – and then only with help from the Russians, who declined to come to Milosevic's aid, and a threat of major NATO ground force operations to accomplish most, but not all, of its objectives.[131] ALLIED FORCE concluded with little damage to Serbian military forces in Kosovo due, in large measure, to their excellent use of Soviet deception measures, and weather and terrain effects on air operations. It failed in meeting one of the primary reasons for NATO intervention: Serbian forces engaged in the murder ("ethnic cleansing") of thousands and displacement of almost a million of the Albanian Kosovar population during the seventy-eight days of ALLIED FORCE.

The conflict extended outside Kosovo to attack of targets in Belgrade, prompting a complaint by some human rights groups against the United States, United Kingdom and other participating nations to the International Criminal Tribunal for the Former Yugoslavia (ICTY). While the complaint was dismissed by the ICTY Prosecutor,[132] the challenge raised issues as to what constitutes a *military objective*. While some hailed airpower's success in concluding the conflict by attack of strategic targets,[133] that thesis has been challenged by others.[134] It is not within my remit to address this debate. But it is necessary to recognize that conclusions drawn by some from the ALLIED FORCE experience are not universally accepted.

Operation ALLIED FORCE was a self-constrained military operation by the hesitant led by the reluctant, or perhaps vice-versa – a humanitarian intervention that did not quite fit the classic *jus ad bellum* mold. While it was described as a NATO operation, it had limited allied support. As one critic observed, the maintenance of the coalition became something of an object in itself.[135]

ALLIED FORCE publicly eschewed deployment of major ground forces, greatly facilitating Serbian ethnic cleansing. It was executed with acute political limitations by virtually all participating governments, including the United States. As NATO's first real military operation, it experienced what commonly is referred to as a "high learning curve" in multilateral coordination. This significantly impeded the targeting process. This was not necessarily the result of an asymmetry as to what constitutes a military objective. Many governments were on a war footing for the first time since World War II. Undoubtedly there was some reti-

---

[131] *Benjamin S. Lambeth*, NATO's Air War in Kosovo (2001).

[132] Final Report to the Prosecutor by the Committee Established to Review the NATO Bombing Campaign Against the Federal Republic of Yugoslavia, in Wall, supra n. 80, pp. 483-530.

[133] *Stephen T. Hosmer*, Why Milosevic Decided to Settle When He Did (RAND, 2001); and *Benjamin S. Lambeth*, NATO's Air War for Kosovo (RAND, 2001).

[134] *Daniel L. Byman/Matthew C. Waxman*, Kosovo and the Great Air Power Debate, in: International Security 24, 4 (March 2000), pp. 5-38.

[135] *Eliot A. Cohen*, Kosovo and the New American Way of War, supra n. 130, p. 51.

cence by some to approve certain targets for the very limited operation NATO governments agreed to undertake.

Targeting priorities were primarily military and political (rather than legal), resulting in a dispute between NATO Commander General *Wesley Clark* and Lieutenant General *Michael Short*, NATO air component commander. General *Clark* ordered a concentration of air attacks on Serb forces in Kosovo, while General *Short* sought to attack strategic targets in Belgrade, revisiting the historic American desire for a decisive battle.[136] General *Short*'s emphasis on the latter increased the politicization of the target-approval process, both in Washington and other NATO capitals.[137]

Subsequently Lieutenant General *Short* expressed his frustration with the "extraordinary restraints" placed upon his targeting ability.[138] As his comments were made at a conference of international lawyers, they appeared directed at the law and lawyers. A reading of his complete remarks shows this not to be the case. His complaints directed attention to one of the two outstanding issues I wished to discuss, so-called "dual-use" targets.

"Dual-Use" Targets. Targeting limitations experienced with respect to so-called "dual use" targets were self-imposed by U.S. Air Force doctrine, the U.S. civilian leadership and, very possibly, Air Force judge advocates advising in the target-decision process if the latter accepted the concept of "dual-use" as a legal rather than political restriction.[139]

The "dual-use" issue originated in the 1991 Coalition effort to liberate Kuwait. In the opening phases of its air campaign, attacks were launched against the highly-advanced, highly-redundant electric "super grid" serving Baghdad and central Iraq. As one of the targeting officers subsequently acknowledged, despite the highly-sophisticated U.S. target intelligence process, no one fully considered the unintended collateral effect on critical civilian life support of the electrical power grid, such as disruption of the Iraqi water supply.[140] A very belated (post-conflict) international cry arose as to the effect on the civilian population of loss of power. As now is known, much of the international furor was generated by the Iraqi government in an effort to lift or ease post-conflict sanctions imposed by the United Nations Security Council to ensure Saddam Hussayn's compliance with conditions to which he agreed in order to end Coalition operations against Iraq. Saddam's disinformation efforts were somewhat successful, leading to what became the UN's scandal-plagued "Oil-for-Food" Program, now under investigation.

Electrical power grids historically have been regarded as military objectives, notwithstanding any potential adverse effect on the civilian population.[141] Iran and

---

[136] Id., pp. 41-42.

[137] *Conrad Crane*, Bombing Yugoslavia into Submission: A Review Essay, in: Joint Forces Quarterly 35 (October 2004), pp. 143-144.

[138] Lieutenant General *Michael Short*, USAF (Ret.), Operation ALLIED FORCE from the Perspective of the NATO Air Commander, in: Wall, supra n. 80, p. 19.

[139] *Wall*, supra n. 80, pp. 218-219.

[140] *Kuehl*, supra n. 112, p. 254.

[141] See, for example, *Dinstein*, Conduct of Hostilities, supra n. 80, pp. 96-97.

Iraq attacked each other's electric power plants during their 1980-1988 war, for example.[142] The attack on the Iraqi power grid was exacerbated by callous acts by Saddam Hussayn in the aftermath of the Iraqi military defeat and retreat from Kuwait.

Post-DESERT STORM assessments by several international health teams revealed minimal damage to the power plants, due to the sophisticated U.S. targeting and weaponeering process.[143] The extent to which sustained power loss was attributable to military action vis-à-vis the United Nations-mandated embargo or Saddam's actions against his own population remains unclear. In the twelve years between the first and second Gulf Wars, Saddam spent exorbitant amounts on palaces for himself, while neglecting the Iraqi utilities infrastructure and the resultant suffering of much – but not all -- of the Iraqi population. The Ba'ath Party ensured the Sunni Mansour district had around-the-clock electricity, while the Shia-populated Sadr City would be allowed three hours electricity daily by Saddam's government.[144]

In the aftermath of the Coalition liberation of Kuwait and the "controversy" over the Baghdad power grid, the U.S. Air Force engaged in a self-inflicted wound. It incorporated into its targeting doctrine the concept of dual-use targets:

"Dual-use targets are … those targets that are used for both military and civilian purposes, such as power plants that provide electricity to both civilian institutions as well as military command and control centres."[145]

So-called "dual-use" targets are common: electric power grids, bridges, airfields and manufacturing facilities, for example. In an armed conflict, the military has first priority over the civilian population in use of objects necessary for a nation's defence. Brief points will be made with respect to each of the above other than power grids.

Bridges. Bridges on lines of communication are critical choke points for movement of military forces. Often they play additional roles. In 1991 many bridges in Iraq contained fiber-optic cable for secure communication between Baghdad and fielded forces, for example, with substantial redundancy. Severing the fiber-optic cable system would force communication with fielded Iraqi forces into other communications that could be intercepted, providing advanced warning of Iraqi forces' movement and orders to employ field-deployed weapons of mass destruction. Release authority for employment of fielded weapons of mass destruction was retained by Saddam Hussayn. Hence destruction of bridges – in the plural – was tied not only to impeding movement of Iraqi forces but to destruction of military communications.

---

[142] Id., p. 252.

[143] Id., pp. 252-254.

[144] *Richard Lowry*, What Went Right, in: National Review (May 9, 2005), pp. 29-37, at 30.

[145] U.S. Department of Air Force Pamphlet 14-210, Intelligence Targeting Guide (1 February 1998), para. A 4.2.2.

Considering attack of bridges to impede the flow of military traffic is analogous to the effect of water flowing downstream. Water finding obstacles in flowing in one direction will seek alternative paths through force and gravity. So, too, is the case with military traffic. Destruction of a single bridge on a primary line of communication (for example) from Baghdad south to fielded military forces along the border between Saudi Arabia and Iraqi-occupied Kuwait would not have prevented re-supply and reinforcement of Iraqi forces occupying Kuwait in 1991 or otherwise defending against a Coalition offensive

Attack of any bridge requires that it meet the *military objective* definition. That the bridge also may be used by civilian traffic does not make it any less a military objective. "Dual use" is not and should not become a law of war test.

Airfields/airports. There are military airfields and civilian airports and, in some nations, privately-owned airfields, all of which can be put to military use on short (or no) notice. Many civilian airports are funded in part like national highways, that is, with federal funding for possible or potential national defence purposes. Airports require no conversion to accommodate military aircraft except, perhaps, mobile capabilities for re-arming and servicing the aircraft. During the 1982 Falklands/Malvinas War, for example, control of all civilian airports and civilian aviation activity in Argentina was assumed by the *Fuerza Aerea Argentina* (Argentine Air Force). Some already were joint civil/military airports, such as the main commercial airport of Buenos Aires, used by *Comando Aviaciaon Naval Argentina units*.[146] An airport is a legitimate target if it meets the definitional test for a military objective, even if also employed for civilian use. The 1954 Hague Cultural Property Convention recognized this in listing "aerodrome" (whether military or civilian) as one of many military objectives or potential military objectives an object seeking special protection had to be separated from in order to attain special protection status.[147]

Industrial facilities. In comments offered at the 2001 U.S. Naval War College international law conference, the NATO Air Component Commander for the 1999 NATO Operation ALLIED FORCE reported difficulty in attacking a Yugoslav factory that produced civilian automobiles half the day and tank turrets the other half of the day because it was a "dual-use" target.[148] Thus the Air Force concept of a "dual-use" target was used as a basis for target denial rather than target authorization, along with an apparent concern for civilian casualties within the military objective (which it clearly was) were it attacked. These are serious errors with respect to the law of war, but also apparent evidence of the discomfort the United States and its NATO allies felt toward the humanitarian intervention operation it chose to undertake.

---

[146] *Rodney A. Burden/Michael I. Draper/Douglas A. Rough/Colin R. Smith/David L. Wilton*, Falklands – The Air War (1986), pp. 164-165.

[147] Article 8(1)(a), in: *Schindler/Toman*, supra n. 2, p. 1003.

[148] Lieutenant General *Michael Short*, in: Wall, supra n. 80, p. 30.

Comments by the Special Assistant to the President and Legal Adviser to the U.S. National Security Council in that same conference made it clear that decisions with regard to so-called "dual-use targets" were a mixture of policy decisions, errors with respect to the law of war – specifically, embracing the "dual-use" concept – and a reluctance on the part of the senior leadership in the United States and some NATO capitals to employ all legal rights provided by the law of war.[149] The U.S. Air Force unilateral adoption of the "dual-use" concept for determining whether an object is a military objective exacerbated the NATO Air Component Commander's ability to accomplish the mission assigned him.

As international law experts have acknowledged, there is no legal basis for the concept of "dual-use targets" in the law of war.[150] There never has been, and there is no basis in Additional Protocol I to support the concept. So-called "dual-use" targets are military objectives because of the military advantage gained from their seizure, destruction or neutralization.

A small, informal meeting of experts in Geneva last month weighed whether the concept of *proportionality* should be considered in attack of so-called dual-use facilities "to take into account the reverberating effects of attacks on objects that serve the military while simultaneously playing a vital role for the civilian population."[151] As I was not a participant in the meeting, I cannot report on the discussion that took place.

There are several difficulties with this idea that make it unlikely governments would accept amendment of Article 51(2). Considering *proportionality* in attack of a known or suspected 'dual use' military objective continues the trend in thinking of some of placing the burden for reducing risk and even inconvenience to the civilian population exclusively on the party to the conflict engaged in offensive operations. This is contrary to the definition of *attacks* in Additional Protocol I, which includes actions by a party engaged in offensive or defensive operations.[152] From a practical standpoint, it is counter-intuitive. If one considers an enemy's electric power grid, an attacker will have substantially less information about it than the defender, who in all likelihood constructed it to ensure redundancy for national defence and other emergencies. Similarly, an increased burden on the party engaged in offensive operations will only encourage a defender to emphasize reliance on civilian use of redundant systems to gain a propaganda advantage if they are attacked, as we have seen in the increased use of human shields – voluntary and involuntary – in armed conflicts since promulgation of Additional Protocol I. The argument that dual use should be considered "[b]ecause of the extensive long-term damage to the civilian population"[153] incorrectly assigns exclusive responsibility for all effects of an attack of a military objective, including

[149] *James E. Baker*, in: Wall, id., p. 16.

[150] *Dinstein*, in: Wall, supra n. 80, at 218-219; *Boivin/Sandoz*, supra n. 103, p. 20. The argument in behalf of consideration of 'dual use' in targeting is articulated in *H. Shue/D. Wippman*, Limiting Attacks on Dual Use Facilities Performing Indispensable Civilian Functions, in: Cornell International Law Journal 35 (2002), p. 559.

[151] *Boivin/Sandoz*, supra n. 110, p. 21.

[152] Article 49(1), Additional Protocol I.

[153] *Boivin/Sandoz*, supra n. 110, p. 21.

postwar recovery, to the attacker. There is no basis in State practice or law for such a one-sided burden.

Consideration of "dual use" is not a law of war factor in attack of military objectives, and should not be. It is commendable that the U.S. Air Force endeavoured to come up with possible ways to factor dual use into its target intelligence, weaponeering and execution. It also is something no more than one or two other governments are capable of doing. Its negative consequences surfaced in Operation ALLIED FORCE, limiting NATO attacks of legitimate military objectives and frustrating Lieutenant General Short's desire to fight the war according to his air campaign plan. "Dual use" is an example of self-inflicted political correctness, not a failure of the law.

****

General *Short*'s frustration with what he regarded as targeting constraints during ALLIED FORCE and controversies regarding targeting during that operation were revived by my distinguished co-panelist, Brigadier General *Charles J. Dunlap, Jr.*, USAF, in an article in the Summer 2000 *Strategic Review* teasingly entitled "The End of Innocence: Rethinking Noncombatancy in the Post-Kosovo Era." Let me say that I have known Brigadier General *Dunlap* for years, and I know no individual with a greater respect for the rule of law, the necessity for a military to conduct its operations in accordance with the law of war and, for that matter, for adherence to the law of war as the most effective way to fight. He also is a deep thinker on the law of war and its credibility, and is not beneath offering a thought piece to, as we say in the U.S., "stir the pot". He did so with this article. So, too, did another respected colleague, Major *Jeanne M. Meyer*, USAF, in her "Tearing Down the Façade: A Critical Look at the Current Law on Targeting the Will of the Enemy and Air Force Doctrine," in 51 The Air Force Law Review 143 (2001).

A recurrent problem with some airpower thinking lies in its objectivity. As Major General *Heywood Hansell* noted:

"Proponents of new and revolutionary weapons systems almost inevitably have the vision to see the far-reaching potential of their systems during the development phase. But that same vision seems to fade when it comes to anticipating the possible countermeasures an enemy might take …"[154]

So it was with attacks on morale in World War II which, as previously noted, led to wholly inefficient application of military resources and tragic losses of civilian lives.[155] This leads to my final point.

Civilian morale is a military objective. As has been the case since World War II, there appears near-consensus that civilian morale as such is not a legitimate military objective. Notwithstanding inarticulate language in the ICRC Commentary on

---

[154] *Hansell*, supra n. 10, p. 11.
[155] *SAOG* III, supra n. 29, p. 56.

Additional Protocol I, discussed infra, civilian morale as such does not meet the definition of *military objective* contained in Article 52(2), of Additional Protocol I. In addition, Article 51(2) of Additional Protocol I states:

"The civilian population as such, as well as individual civilians, shall not be made the object of attack. Acts or threats of violence the primary purpose of which is to spread terror among the civilian population are prohibited."

Adopted from language in United Nations General Assembly Resolution 2675 (XXV), approved 9 December 1970,[156] this provision is contained in U.S. military law of war manuals, one of which preceded both UNGA Res. 2675 and Additional Protocol I.[157]

What constitutes either an "attack on civilian morale" or "acts or threats of violence … among the civilian population" requires definition. Incorporation of the words "acts or threats of violence *the primary purpose of which* is to spread terror among the civilian population" constitutes an acknowledgement that civilians will experience fear and possibly terror as a result of lawful attacks on military objectives near them. The language prohibits attacks intended for the purpose of causing fear or terror rather than an effect that is a natural consequence of lawful military actions.[158] The prohibition remains vague, however, when one notes the *ICRC Commentary* on Additional Protocol I states "The provision is intended to prohibit acts of violence the primary purpose of which is to spread terror among the civilian population *without offering substantial military advantage*."[159] This unfortunate and rather strange choice of words [in italics] incorrectly suggests attacks to terrorize remain legally permissible if such attacks offer a substantial military advantage.

NATO military operations against the Yugoslav regime of Slobodan Milosevic in 1999 and the articles by Brigadier General *Dunlap* and Major *Meyer* resurrected the issue of attack of civilian morale. This appears one key issue for this panel.

As I noted in my tour of history, attack of a military objective, particularly one in proximity to the civilian population, was accepted as having a potential but not unlawful effect on civilian morale. One of the ironies of efforts by a very few nations to enhance the targeting process and bombing accuracy – to the extent that points of attack and weapons selection can be made to reduce risk of collateral damage to civilian objects and incidental civilian injury – is that touting of this ability has resulted in a public expectation of casualty-free war in which the civilian population is neither placed in fear nor inconvenienced in any way. This is an obvious contradiction.

---

[156] *Schindler/Toman*, supra n. 2, pp. 353-354.

[157] See, for example, U.S. Army Field Manual 27-10, The Law of Land Warfare (1956), 25; and U.S. Air Force Pamphlet 110-31, International Law – The Conduct of Armed Conflict and Air Operations (1976), para. 5-3.

[158] *Bothe/Partsch/Solf*, supra n. 75, pp. 301-302.

[159] Commentary on the Additional Protocols, supra n. 100, pp. 618 [emphasis supplied].

The issue at hand is not expectations. From the days of siege warfare, civilian morale has been an incidental but not unlawful effect of attack of legitimate military objectives.[160] This was the case in the era through World War II where collateral damage to civilian objects and incidental injury to civilians was not regarded as an attacker's responsibility.[161]

However, there is a distinction between attack of military objectives and the incidental effect on civilian morale vis-à-vis attack of civilian morale as such. There is no doubt that emphasis on civilian morale may vary in target selection. While sixty or more years in the past, examples from the Allied strategic air offensive against Germany suggest this distinction.

To some extent the argument for attack of civilian morale prior to World War II was made for deterrent purposes. Subsequently it was made late in the European Theater conflict by the Allies to suggest that one (or more) days of severe bombing of civilians would push Germany over the brink to surrender. In the closing months of World War II various proposals were made at different levels of command to use massive air bombardment to force an end to the war.

"Morale" bombing in World War II had a drug-addictive effect on its proponents: When a little failed to provide promised benefits, more was sought. It is much like an unskilled and unethical interrogator who argues that "just a little torture" will cause the person being interrogated to break down. When the torture is unsuccessful, the interrogator remains convinced – and endeavors to convince others – that "just a little more torture, or a different torture technique" will do the trick. Like morale bombing, torture seldom has gained the desired, expected or promised effect.

---

160 See, for example, *Matthew C. Waxman*, Siegecraft and Surrender: The Law and Strategy of Cites as Targets, in: Virginia Journal of International Law 39, 2 (Winter 1999), pp. 353-423, at 363.

161 Affecting civilian morale dates to siege warfare, where the morale of civilians in a besieged city (along with consumption of food and water) offered an incentive to surrender – to the extent that the besieging force had a legal right to fire upon the civilian population to drive it back into the besieged city if they attempted to depart. See, e.g., *Lester Nurick*, The Distinction Between Combatant and Noncombatant in the Law of War, in: American Journal of International Law 39 (1945), pp. 680-697, at 686. This law of war right persisted in law of war manuals until recent editions. See, for example, U.S. Army Law of War Manual 27-10, Law of Land Warfare (1956), para. 44:
"There is no rule of law which compels the commander of an investing force to permit noncombatants to leave a besieged locality. It is within the discretion of the besieging commander whether he will permit noncombatants to leave and under what conditions. Thus, if a commander of a besieged place expels the noncombatants in order to lessen the logistical burden he has to bear, it is lawful, though an extreme measure, to drive them back, so as to hasten the surrender."
See also The War Office, The Law of War on Land, being Part III of the Manual of Military Law (1958), at 98, paras. 295, 296. This provision was not carried forward in the new British manual, UK Ministry of Defence, The Manual of the Law of Armed Conflict (2004), and has been expressly deleted in the draft U.S. Department of Defense Law of War Manual, in process.

One Allied proposal, Operation THUNDERCLAP, was to be a massive Anglo-American daylight heavy bomber attack on Berlin as a *coup de grâce* to German morale.[162] The combined attack on Berlin was not approved for military reasons.[163] Another Allied proposal was Operation CLARION. Intended to "produce a stupefying effect on [civilian] morale," it was a massive air assault on transportation and communication targets in and near small German towns as a demonstration of Allied air power. General *Ira Eaker*, USAAF, writing to General *Carl Spaatz*, declared:

"[CLARION] will absolutely convince the Germans that we are the barbarians they say we are, for it would be perfectly obvious to them that this is primarily a large-scale attack on civilians as, in fact, it of course will be. Of all the people killed in this attack over 95% of then can be expected to be civilians."[164]

CLARION was executed on February 22 and 23, 1945, using more than 3,500 British and American heavy bombers and 4,900 fighters – managing to bomb the Swiss town of Schaffhausen as well in the process.[165] As the official U.S. history reports:

"High-priority military traffic continued to go through, the bombings having had only local and temporary effects. The Joint Intelligence Committee concluded CLARION had not seriously affected Germany's capacity to resist, and Royal Air Force Chief [Air Marshal Peter] Portal recommended against further CLARION

---

[162] The official Canadian history reports:

"[Royal Air Force] Air Commodore S.O. Bufton, for one … had now been persuaded that it might be useful to mount at least one massive operation (THUNDERCLAP) against the centre of Berlin in the hope of 'total devastation' of the German capital and would provide 'a spectacular and final object lesson to the German people on the consequences of … aggression' but also offer 'incontrovertible proof to all people of the power [and] the effectiveness of Anglo-American power." *Greenhous et al*, supra n. 58, p. 831.

[163] The Joint Intelligence Committee concluded that devastation of Berlin would not result in breakdown of German will to continue the war. Ultimately THUNDERCLAP re-appeared as a series of combined attacks on cities in eastern Germany, including Berlin, Chemnitz, Leipzig, Dresden and "associated cities where heavy attack will cause great confusion in civilian evacuation from the East and hamper movement of reinforcements from other fronts" as a way for Allied support of the Russian advance into Germany. *SAOG* III, supra n. 29, pp. 98-109, and *Frederick Taylor*, Dresden (2004), pp. 180-192.

[164] Letter, General *Eaker to Spaatz*, 1 January 1945, Box 20 (diary), SP, as cited by Tami Davis Biddle, The Dresden Raid of 1945: Assault, Aftermath and Legacy (unpublished paper, 2005).

[165] Actually bombing Schaffhausen again, as it had been bombed accidentally by U.S. heavy bombers the preceding year. *W.F. Craven/J.L. Cate* (eds.), The Army Air Forces in World War II, Volume III, Europe – Argument to VE Day (1951), p. 735. See also *Charles C. McBride*, Mission Failure and Survival (1989), pp. 77-79, 97, 130; and *Richard G. Davis*, Carl A. Spaatz and the Air War in Europe (1993), pp. 575, 578.

attacks. Though U.S. air chiefs did not entirely agree with Portal, no further CLARION missions were carried out."[166]

CLARION was successful in destroying a considerable amount of rolling stock, but precipitated no crisis among the railway workers, did not overwhelm the Reichsbahn's repair facilities, did not disrupt the railways enough to affect *Wehrmacht*front-line forces' capabilities, and did not lead to increased military desertion. Nor did it destroy German civilian morale.[167]

The historical record seems clear: attacks on civilian morale as such have not been effective.[168] Yet air enthusiasts continue to resurrect them, not withstanding the lessons of history or present-day law of war prohibitions.

As noted previously, effects on civilian morale from attack of legitimate military objects have not been regarded as unlawful. When the emphasis shifted in World War II from incidental effect to intentional attack, it crossed the line with respect to the fundamental law of war principle of *distinction*. Happily and rightfully, attacks on civilian morale went into the discarded file – until recently.

---

[166] Id., pp. 732-735; see also *Mierzewski*, supra n. 12, p. 170.

[167] *Davis*, supra n. 165, p. 572. What is of interest is that attacks on morale always were of lower priority than all other target categories, such as oil, transportation and military-related industry. See, e.g., *SAOG* III, supra n. 29, p. 98.

[168] *Biddle*, supra n. 34, p. 277. The discussion in the main text has focused on British and American attacks on morale in the battle for Europe. Similar attacks were proposed or executed by the Luftwaffe. Professor *Richard Muller* reports:

"Other employment of the Luftwaffe's bomber force produced a steady drain on Luftflotte 6's capabilities. In a consultation between [Generaloberst Hans] Jeschonnek and [General Robert Ritter von] Greim's chief of staff, Kless, the two officers discussed a scheme to dispatch "bomber units in formations of 20 to 30 aircraft" in "systematic terror attacks … for the breaking of Russian morale" against Soviet cities behind the front lines. "These actions … were intended to bring about the collapse of Soviet powers of resistance."

Richard Muller, The German Air War in Russia (1992), p. 140.

On February 11, 1944, General *von Greim* put forward his "Proposals for the Commencement of Strategic Air Warfare Against the Soviet War Economy." Continuing, *Muller* reports *Greim* argued:

Since Moscow was also a major population center as well as the center of Bolshevik power, Greim suggested that it should be the target of "12 to 15 repeat attacks" by the entire 300-plus aircraft strength of [General Rudilf] Meister's long-range bomber force. In a formulation strongly reminiscent of Douhet … *Greim* proposed:

"Concentrated attacks upon the military-industrial installations in Moscow may cause, alongside the destruction of industrial targets, heavy damage to the densely-packed adjoining urban areas. The working population which has been up to the present time lulled into a felling of security will suffer heavy casualties, as well as still poorer living and working conditions, and will morally be greatly affected …"

Id., pp. 195-196. In a note reminiscent of post-war British and American conclusions, General *Karl Koller* rejected *Greim*'s recommendation, noting:

"Considering the demonstrated toughness and Spartan nature of the Russian population, we cannot expect permanent and militarily decisive effects from terror attacks against residential quarters. They are, rather, more likely to give the will to resist of the Russian people new sustenance …" Id., p. 196.

General *Dunlap* places a number of prudent restrictions on application of the paradigm he offers. His proposal is to attack certain civilian objects of an "evil" (my word, not his) enemy regime if such attack would demoralize the civilian population and lead to more rapid conflict termination. Some of his arguments may be tempered. For example, as I have suggested, I do not agree with the premise of recent arguments (which he appears to accept) that "dual use" of a clearly-identified military objective requires special consideration. But re-directing attacks to purely civilian objects for the purpose of attacking civilian morale is a failed pre-World War II airpower argument that the ends justify the means.

Ignoring history, it is a temptation with which some airpower enthusiasts continue an unrequited romance. Thus on 25 February 1991, on the eve of the Coalition ground offensive to liberate Kuwait, the Commander, U.S. Central Command, announced his approval of air strikes that evening to destroy a statue of Saddam Hussayn and the Crossed Swords Monument.[169] Each was identified as a "psychological target", with the wholly implausible argument that upon learning that each had been destroyed, revealing Saddam's impotence, the Iraqi people would rise up and oust Saddam, alleviating the need for Coalition ground combat operations.[170] I was party to a portion of the subsequent deliberation process. It need not be told in detail. A neglected detail is that the two objects had been on the list of nominated targets since December 1990, but had not been approved for attack *because they were regarded as having little to no military value.*

Eventually cooler heads prevailed. The Commander, U.S. Central Command, the Secretary of Defense, and the Chairman, Joint Chiefs of Staff agreed these were not viable military objectives.[171] Yet there seems to be a continuing tempta-

[169] Destroying a single statue of Saddam Hussayn would have been of limited effect, as Saddam had installed hundreds of such statues around Baghdad. All were demolished during the Coalition's 2003-2004 occupation of Iraq following the Second Persian Gulf War. "The Crossed Swords Monument" has many names. Another is "Hands of Victory" Monument. It is described at http://www.biography.ms/Hands_of_Victory.html. It was preserved.

[170] In 1992 the U.S. Air Force's Gulf War Airpower Survey invited Colonel *Raymond C. Ruppert*, USA, Staff Judge Advocate for US Central Command during Operations DESERT SHIELD AND DESERT STORM, and me to meet with them to discuss the role of lawyers in the target decision-making process, and in particular the attack of the Saddam statue and Crossed Swords Monument. The senior Air Force psychological warfare officer for US Central Command during Operation DESERT STORM was present. He stated he advised against attack of each, not only because he doubted their attack would have the intended effect, but also because the U.S. would suffer a psychological warfare loss were the attacks to miss. Another Air Force participant agreed, stating it was not worth risking the aircraft and aircrew on such speculative and otherwise worthless targets.

[171] Cf. *Williamson Murray*, Air War in the Persian Gulf (1995), pp. 224-226. *Dr. Murray*, a military historian normally careful with his facts, was off target in his account of this episode and the role he alleges lawyers played in the decision. A participant in the Air Force's Gulf War Airpower Survey mentioned in the preceding footnote, *Dr. Murray* declined to attend the meeting at which Colonel *Ruppert* and I discussed this and other episodes in explaining the role of lawyers. General *Colin Powell*'s "My American Jour-

tion by some to exploit airpower's capabilities to attack civilian morale in the face of history and obvious policy, legal and moral issues. This penchant for some theoretical "knock-out punch" through airpower undoubtedly is the point giving many of our allies concerns about U.S. use of the terms "war-fighting" or "war-sustaining," previously discussed.

With that I return to the thesis of General *Dunlap*'s article. It is troubling for many reasons other than the historical record, and the fact that there is little distinction, if any, between morale attacks and terror attacks. As is true of the interrogator who wishes authority for just a little bit of torture, the first step down this path begins a treacherous, slippery and dangerous slope to expansion of military objectives into an area that not only has proved unsuccessful in the past but today clearly is illegal.

The article's argument is that such attacks would be reserved for wars against "morally corrupt" regimes. General *Dunlap* acknowledges this approach would run counter to constraints in war. It would do more: it would reject the treaty obligation to "respect and ensure respect" for the law of war,[172] regardless of the conduct of future enemies, while returning to a Just War Theory for respect for the law of war. General *Dunlap* argues it would place emphasis on belligerent "reprisals" against civilian objects, such as "banks and financial institutions, and factories, plants, stores, and shops that produce, sell, or distribute luxury products."

A frequent, fundamental flaw in targeting is mirror imaging, that is, looking at what would harm attacks of particular objects would have on an advanced industrial society, and assuming attack of similar targets in a less-developed society would have the same effect. Past conflicts prove this not to be the case. In addition to the fact that in recent conflicts in Viet Nam, Somalia and Afghanistan it would have been difficult to locate financial institutions or "luxury boutiques", the history of belligerent reprisal contains no known successes.[173] It is one reason governments virtually eliminated belligerent reprisals in Additional Protocol I.

Another problem with the argument offered is that it assumes all limitations on attack of military objectives are based upon the law of war. As I indicated, many limitations in Operation ALLIED FORCE were political, not legal, beginning with the decision not to employ major ground forces and, worse, to announce this intention to Milosevic. As a final comment I agree with comments by Professor *Michael Schmitt*:

"[O]ne must be careful what one wishes for. Opponents of advanced militaries have far more to gain from a relaxation of the distinction standard than those capable of fielding state-of-the-art forces. The disadvantaged side in an asymmetri-

ney" (1995, p. 496) is closer to the mark, with the exception of two key points. General *Powell*'s senior attorney, Colonel *Fred K. Green*, did not meet with General *Powell* with "a battery of lawyers," and Colonel *Green*'s discussion with General *Powell* weighed legal and policy considerations. The conversation between General *Powell* and Colonel *Green* formed the basis for the political leadership's decision against their attack.

172 Article 1 common to the Geneva Conventions for the Protection of War Victims of August 12, 1949.

173 See *Frits Kalshoven*, Belligerent Reprisals (1971).

cal fight has every incentive to strike at civilians and civilian objects because it cannot hope to prevail on the field of battle. Thus, the sole chance of victory (or chance of fending off defeat) lies in striking a center of gravity other than the military. This being so, a restrictive reading of military objective actually benefits the advantaged side by allowing it to leverage its superior military capabilities. It is only when mixing *ad bellum* and *in bello* principles by labeling one belligerent malevolent (as suggested by General Dunlap), that it makes any sense for the militarily advantaged side to adopt a less restrictive standard; so long as its cause is just, it need not fear attacks against its civilians or civilian objects. This is naïve. The difficulty of objectively determining a belligerent is in the wrong (consider the case of Iraq) means that in practice any shift of the law will apply equally to both sides."

"Boutique bombing" should not become a new category of military objective. As General *Dunlap* and Professor *Schmitt* have explained on many occasions, modern aerial warfare by advanced nations is qualitatively superior – in weapons systems, precision weapons, intelligence, and other ways – to anything ever seen. It enables careful, reasoned and timely assessment of an object to determine whether it is a military objective, and how it may be attacked to minimize risk of collateral damage to civilian objects and incidental injury to civilians not taking a direct part in hostilities. It is smarter. Smart weapons should be applied in an equally-intelligent manner. In this respect, technology-driven militaries should exploit their superiority to operate more efficiently within the law, rather than seek to violate the law.

The recent articles by Brigadier General *Dunlap* and Major *Meyer* appear to argue for a return to targeting morale. Brigadier General *Dunlap* argues for making certain civilian objects into military objectives in order to attack civilian morale, while Major *Meyer* suggests target selection with an emphasis on civilian morale. Either argument is a step back to earlier but unsuccessful airpower arguments that wars could be prevented or ended sooner with an attack on civilian morale.

Such arguments are inconsistent with the lessons not only of history but present day. Civilians and civilian morale have been subjected to terrorist attack around the world – in New York City, Washington, Riyadh, Kenya, Tanzania, Bali, Jakarta, Casablanca, Istanbul, and Madrid, to name a few. As was the case with attacks on civilian morale during World War II, while attacks initially may have struck fear into the civilian population, in the long run civilians steeled themselves against the attacks and became more defiant in their resistance.[174]

****

[174] This point was confirmed by the personal experience of two conference participants. The honoree, Professor *Ipsen*, was in Hamburg in 1943 when it was subjected to Allied bombing, while Professor *Bothe* experienced Allied attacks of Berlin. Each acknowledged fright and anger with the first experience of Allied bombing. Thereafter their fright diminished in the face of subsequent attacks.

Conclusion. Is there an asymmetry between the United States and Europe with respect to what constitutes a military objective? Perhaps some between some international lawyers on some (but not all) issues, but little to none between governments and their armed forces once specific cases are considered. For example, in the course of the discussion phase of our conference panel, debate turned specifically to attack of bridges. The debate changed measurably in agreement as to the legality of attack when reference was made to Iraqi use of bridges as conduits for fiber-optic cable for Saddam Hussayn's communication with his fielded forces. This was not so much a change of facts as a suggestion that the military commander is likely to have information at his disposal in making the decision as to whether or not an object is a military objective, and its priority if attack, that might not be available to the public.

There is no doubt disagreement increased as a result of military objectives targeted during the 1999 NATO War against the Yugoslav regime of Slobodan Milosevic. That the ICTY Prosecutor found no NATO law of war violations speaks admirably for the definition of *military objective* developed in Article 52(2), of Additional Protocol I. The ICTY Prosecutor's decision may not be a satisfactory answer to some. On this reasonable minds may disagree. This does not and should not diminish the value of the Protocol I definition of *military objective*.

Finally, I have placed emphasis on the issue of attacks on civilian morale. Wars are fought to change the will of others. Except in the most dictatorial societies, the will of the nation is affected by the will not only of its military but that of its civilian population. Attack of enemy military objectives has the collateral effect of affecting the will of the national leadership, the military and the civilian population. Nothing in the law of war prohibits influencing each ancillary to attack of objects meeting the definition of *military objective* contained in Article 52(2), of Additional Protocol I.

The advent of aviation in the last century brought a need for advocates to sell airpower as bringing something new to the battlefield in order to gain a place at the table with its older, firmly-established army and naval partners – and to achieve full-fledged independence from the former.

Beginning with *H.G. Wells*' "The War in the Air" (1907), through the between-the-wars advocates cited hereon – British, American, and German, not to mention the Italian *Giulion Douhet*[175] – there was and has continued to be an infatuation with attack of civilian morale within airpower cicles, including in some cases attack of the civilian population as such, as a way of achieving a "knock-out" punch or winning conflicts without life-consuming ground action such as was experienced by all sides in World War I.[176] Attack of the civilian population as such was acknowledged as prohibited by governments prior to World War II, while the value of attacks on morale as such was discredited by post-World War II official evaluations by Great Britain and the United States. This temptation for attacks on

[175] The Command of the Air (1921).

[176] For example, *Douhet* embraced the argument that "in the future, war will be waged essentially against the unarmed populations of the cities and great industrial centers." The Command of the Air (1942 American ed., Dino Ferrari, tr.), p. 281.

morale as such was put to rest for once and for all with the definition of *military objective* in Additional Protocol I.

Returning to the purpose of this conference – to honour Professor *Knut Ipsen* on his seventieth birthday for his lifetime of achievements on behalf of the law of war – his words during our discussion period said it best: "Morale" is neither an object nor a person. It may be affected by attack of military objectives. But morale may not in and of itself be a military objective, and civilian objects may not be attacked to affect civilian morale.

On these points there should be no asymmetry.

Targeting Hearts and Minds: National Will and Other Legitimate Military Objectives of Modern War

Charles J. Dunlap

Office of the Judge Advocate General, Headquarters U.S. Air Force, Washington, D.C.

I wish to thank the organizers of this conference in honour of *Knut Ipsen* for the kind invitation to present a few remarks about the superb work of my friend and colleague, Mr. *Hays Parks* of the U.S. Department of Defense.

At the outset, let me underline that, as with Mr. *Parks*, the views and comments we express are ours alone and do not necessarily reflect those of the United States government or any of its components, to include the Department of Defense and the U.S. Air Force.

As many of you know, *Hays Parks* is the dean of American law of war specialists. More than that, in important ways he is – literally – the father of modern air operations law in the U.S. Air Force. His book-length law review article, "Air War and the Law of War",[1] is *the* seminal piece of scholarship in the area, and mandatory reading for any serious student of the genre. What is more is that he has been a mentor to a generation of operations' lawyers of all branches, including myself.

Accordingly, it is with great pleasure – and no small amount of relief – that I can report to you that I found much with which to not just agree with in his paper, but with which to heartily endorse and, if he permits me, to expand upon somewhat. That said, we do differ to a degree on certain points. In important respects, much of this disagreement may simply be a question of semantics. Regardless, the unique opportunity this conference present and to clarify views is truly invaluable, as is the chance to receive your feedback.

As is his practice, *Hays* provides us with a fascinating *tour de force* of the evolution of international law as it applies the concept of the military objective. In doing so he makes some key points with which I firmly agree though I recognize that others may dispute one or more of his positions. One that I think we can all agree upon is his observation achieving international agreement as to what constitutes a military objective, beyond the basics, has proven difficult. Likewise, I think there is little dissent about his view that given the dynamic nature of target-

---

1 *W. Hays Parks*, Air War and the Law of War, 32 A.F. L. REV. 1 (1990).

ing, the value of a potential target may vary depending upon the circumstances prevailing at the time.

Though it is somewhat more controversial, I believe his reasoning about objects with war-sustaining value is on the mark. Specifically, in my opinion, he is very correct when he says:

"The connection of some objects to an enemy's war effort may be direct, indirect or even discrete. A decision as to classification of an object as a military objective and allocation of resources for its attack is dependent upon its value to an enemy nation's war-fighting or war-sustaining effort (including its ability to be converted to a more direct connection), and not solely to its overt or present connection or use."

This is especially true in modern conflicts where the complexities of today's engines of war often require a seemingly endless stream of logistics, much of which is of the commercial, off-the-shelf variety. Moreover, the sheer rapidity with which certain putatively "civilian" capabilities convert to military purposes is a real concern to warfighters.

I am also in complete agreement with Mr. *Parks* regarding what I gather are arguments presented at earlier conferences to the effect that inasmuch as a category of military objective has not been attacked in recent wars, it is now legally proscribed to do so now. I'm glad that *Hays* fought this absurd conclusion for many reasons, but I'll offer just one: we do not want to encourage attacks on targets in a conflict simply to ensure that no practice or custom emerges that would seem to immunize them in the future.

I find his suggestion in his longer paper, along with that of our friend *Yoram Dinstein*, about the utility of an "illustrative, non-exhaustive list of categories of objects historically regarded as military objectives" an interesting proposal. Nevertheless, while such a list could be useful, I am concerned that some may misapprehend its meaning. They might insist, despite disclaimers, that the list sets the outer limits of what is legally permissible to attack. Thus, the absence of something from the list might establish an unhelpful inference of illegality. Conversely, some operators may conclude that mere presence on the list would, *ipso facto*, automatically make it appropriate for attack regardless of other factors prevailing at the time. Still, this proposal deserves thoughtful consideration.

Having said all that, allow me to address some other areas where we may have some difference of opinion. Mr. *Parks* expresses concern about the U.S. Air Force adopting a flawed understanding of law of armed conflict (LOAC) by the use of "dual use" phraseology. I am not sure that I share that concern because I can say with some confidence that at the operational level in the Air Force, "dual use" targets do not, *per se*, enjoy any special LOAC status. It is no more than a term sometimes used to describe a fact, that is, that certain objects – power grids for example – have both military and civilian uses.

Of course, it may be that certain targets and target sets with both military and civilian uses require approvals at elevated levels, but that is an internal policy issue, not one understood by anyone in the Air Force as an international law mandate. Although I do not personally perceive there to be an actual LOAC issue in today's practice, I do agree that if it did exist, it would need to be rectified. Frankly, however, I simply do not see that phrase as being employed as some kind of limitation imposed by law as *Hays* avers.

I may, however, interpret international law somewhat differently than does Mr. *Parks* in relation to the application of a proportionality analysis. As I understand it, he rejects applying it to dual use targets, and perhaps others, that are properly characterized as military objectives. I disagree, perhaps more on practical grounds than as a matter of strict LOAC interpretation. In the American Air Force we *routinely* apply a proportionality analysis to *all* targets to the extent possible and practicable, even very obviously military ones. Why? The blast zone of a weapon perfectly aimed at an indisputably military objective may nevertheless extend to areas and objects noncombatant in nature. We take every reasonable step to consider such collateral damage prior to attack, and if the target is nevertheless to be attacked, we try to do it with weapons and tactics that minimize such losses.

Mr. *Parks* properly expresses concern about applying the proportionality analysis in cases where the defender has failed sufficiently to separate military objectives from civilians and civilian objects. We must not allow belligerents to benefit from deliberate violations of LOAC. Indeed, I believe it could be that, technically speaking, defenders doing so may actually operate to convert the civilian object into a military objective by seeking to use it, in essence, as part of a defensive scheme. For example, purposely placing military equipment near a civilian building in the hopes of creating a psychological deterrence in the mind of a conscientious attacker may obviate the legal protection the structure might otherwise enjoy.

Along similar lines, I personally do not consider voluntary human shields legally-protected "civilians" for the purposes of a proportionality analysis. When putative civilians voluntarily and directly involve themselves in protecting a bona fide military objective (dual-use or otherwise) from legitimate attack by shielding it with their bodies, in my opinion they lose their protected status while doing so. There may be political or other strategic reasons to nevertheless withhold or modify the attack in such cases but, again, such are policy considerations, *not* legal ones.

I do think there is a difference between deliberate scheming to try to exploit the protected status of civilians and civilian objects and the risk that inures to them by the fortunes of war properly waged. For example, a military force that entrenches itself within a city to take advantage of the military utility of its complex terrain (as opposed to its civilian character, *per se*), does not necessarily offend LOAC. It may be, as Mr. *Parks* suggests, that the defender is responsible for any noncombatant deaths by doing so, but I do not therefore conclude that proportionality analysis by the attacker is inappropriate or unnecessary.

Permit me to now address Mr. *Parks*' views on attacks against civilian morale. As I already alluded, much of what appears to be a difference of opinion may just be a matter of semantics. I consider civilian morale as simply a component of national will. There is no serious dispute in military thinking as to the centrality of national will in the conduct of war. U.S. Air Force doctrine, for example, states that "[w]hile physical factors are crucial in war, national will and leadership are also critical components of war. National resolve – the determination to prosecute on one side and to resist on the other – can be a decisive element."[2] Likewise, in an October 2003 article in the U.S. Naval Institute *Proceedings*, non-lawyer operators observe: "[f]rom the individual war fighter to the resolve of a nation, will is often the deciding factor in combat and war."[3]

Perhaps most persuasive is *Hays*' own description of the nature of war. He says, and I completely agree, that "[t]he object of war remains destroying the enemy's will to resist – not merely a nation's military capability, but a nation's *will*." Thus, I believe that the "object" he describes is one of *the* most important targets in war. Put another way, a nation's will is, indeed, something that makes "an effective contribution to military action and whose total or partial destruction, capture or neutralization, in the circumstances ruling at the time, offers a definite military advantage" as Article 52 of Additional Protocol 1[4] would have it.

Academicians can understandably argue that to be an "object" within the meaning of Article 52 is limited to tangible, material things. I have several thoughts on that, the first of which reflects somewhat my Jesuit education in that if purists insist on a corporeal quality, is not thought intrinsic to morale somehow the product of electrical energy in the brain? Less metaphysical, and purely practical, is the fact that regardless of what international lawyers may think, the warfighters clearly believe, as *Hays* implies, that the destruction of an enemy's national will is not just "a" military objective but in almost all cases, *the* military objective in war. Thus, conceptually, references to attacks on "civilian morale" mean attacks against those objects that will influence civilian morale in such a way that achieves a definite military advantage. To the extent that Article 52 requires another interpretation, that is just one more reason why I personally support the U.S.'s decision not to ratify the Protocol.

Again, I believe that – in the U.S. Air Force anyway – civilian morale is considered simply a constituent element of the adversary's national will that *Hays* concedes war seeks to destroy. Nevertheless, he argues, essentially, that because attacks on civilian morale allegedly were not successful in the past, attacks on civilian morale are, therefore, now somehow illegal under international law.

Lack of past success in a military effort, I respectfully offer, means little in an era transformed by new technologies of war. Consider, for example, the attacks against the Thanh Hoa Bridge during the Vietnam War. No fewer than *871* sorties were launched by the U.S. against the bridge without success. In May of 1972, however, aircraft equipped with new precision weapons, Paveway laser-guided bombs, finally destroyed it. No one would claim, I would hope, that past failure

---

2 U.S. Air Force Doctrine Document 1, Air Force Basic Doctrine, 17 November 2003, p. 15.

3 RADM *John G. Morgan*, *et al.*, Rethinking the Principles of War, in: Proceedings, October 2003, pp. 36-37.

4 Protocol Additional to the Geneva Conventions of 12 August 1949, and Relating to the Protection of Victims of International Armed Conflicts (1977) [Protocol I], art. 52. The U.S. is not a Party to Protocol I but accepts some portions as reflecting customary international law.

somehow made the successful high-tech strike unlawful as the bridge was a critical railway and truck line of communication.[5]

In arguing his position, *Hays* asserts that civilians "steeled themselves" against air attacks during World War II and "became more defiant in their resistance." *Phillip Meillinger*, in a fascinating little book published in 2003 and appropriately entitled "Airpower: Myths and Facts",[6] spends an entire chapter rebutting this persisting but faulty claim. I would also invite anyone interested to examine the oft cited but seldom actually read, "United States Strategic Bombing Survey",[7] for information counter to this familiar claim.

The "Survey" concluded that as a result of air attacks the German people's belief in "ultimate victory or satisfactory compromise, and their confidence in their leaders declined."[8] The impact of air attacks on Japanese morale was even more stunning: shortly before surrender, 68% of the Japanese were convinced that Japan could not achieve victory, and half of those attributed that belief to the conventional air attacks.[9]

While it is inaccurate to say that civilians became more defiant in their resistance, it *is* true that while the "Survey" concluded that airpower was "decisive" in World War II, Germans continued to work "efficiently" as long as the "physical means of production remained." In coming to that conclusion, the "Survey" points out that the "power of a police state over its people cannot be underestimated."[10] There is no question that Nazi Germany had a powerful internal security apparatus aimed at keep its people in line. For example, according to historian *Richard Overy*, the "German army shot fifteen thousand of their own number" in a draconian effort to maintain control over its forces.[11]

The point is that while it may be true that a police state can so dominate a society that diminished civilian morale becomes irrelevant, that fact does not speak to the relevance of civilian morale in *other* societies not so controlled. In other words, the World War II model of German and Japanese regimes has its limits. As *Hays* himself says, "what was then was then." Indeed, the "Survey" itself notes, in another overlooked passage, that airpower in World War II was in its "infancy" and, therefore, explicitly warned against applying the conclusions of the "Survey" to "other circumstances and other conditions."

Unfortunately, this is exactly what my friend does. The world has changed vastly since World War II, and so have many, if not most, societies. Where once dictators and their security apparatus might have rendered civilian morale impotent, the revolution in information technologies has informed and empowered

---

5 *Stephen Budiansky*, Air Power (Viking, 2004), p. 408.

6 *Phillip Meilinger*, Airpower: Myths and Facts (Air University, 2003), available at http://www.maxwell.af.mil/au/aul/aupress/Books/Meilinger_myths/Meilinger_myths_B91.pdf.

7 *Franklin D'Olier*, *et al.*, United States Strategic Bombing Surveys, Summary Report, September 30, 1945 (Reprint, Air University, 1987).

8 Id., p. 39.

9 Id., p. 95.

10 Op cit., p. 39.

11 *Richard Overy*, Why the Allies Won (W.W. Norton, 1996), p. 304.

populations in ways unthinkable a half-century ago. Likewise, rising economic, social, and political expectations have made grudging converts to the notion that what the people think does matter. No less an authority than the late Pulitzer Prize-winning historian and Librarian of Congress Emeritus *Daniel Boorstin* makes that case. Noting the almost bloodless collapse of the Soviet Union, he observes "history proves that ruthless rulers can be removed by popular will."[12]

Today, winning people's hearts and minds is vitally important. The reality is that regardless of what happened in World War II, the integrated and holistic nature of 21st century conflicts (itself a subject worth a separate conference) makes the morale of the people an essential element of the national will and overall war-sustaining capability of a belligerent. This is especially true for democracies, but is also increasingly determinative of the behaviour of non-democracies. Autocrats today ignore the morale of the people at their peril, as recent international events demonstrate.

I could continue the argument by debating, for example, Mr. *Parks*' interpretation of airpower's role in Operation ALLIED FORCE. He believes, as many landpower advocates contend, that it was the threat of a ground invasion that led Milosevic to capitulate. This is surely a possible ancillary factor, but incomplete, I believe, as a comprehensive theory. In the 2001 book, "Why Milosevic Decided to Settle When He Did", *Stephen Hosmer* of RAND Corporation pointed to the "psychological and physical hardships" the bombing imposed on what he called "ruling elites."[13]

In explaining the breakdown of Serb resistance, *Hosmer* cites pressure from these "ruling elites," including Milosevic's "cronies", as they were "eager to get the bombing stopped" because their assets and manufacturing facilities were being destroyed from the air.[14] According to *Hosmer*, Milosevic "had reason to doubt that the Serb people would have passively accepted the deprivation" from further air attacks so he yielded in an effort to preserve his own power from the consequences of the loss of civilian support.[15]

It is surprising that anyone steeped in military history would discount the impact of civilian morale on the outcome of the Vietnam War. Actually, Vietnam represents a textbook example of how a collapse of civilian morale – perhaps justified under the circumstances – was decisive in the U.S.'s defeat.

In fact, in *every* conflict since then, America's adversaries have made attacks on civilian morale their *principal* military objective. I doubt even the most rabid insurgent in Iraq seriously harbours any real hope of physically defeating the U.S. forces. Instead, his military objective is to erode Iraqi and American civilian morale to the point where he is able to impose his will.

I hasten to add that merely because civilian morale may be a legitimate military objective that itself is not license to attack it any and every way. For example, it is

---

12 *Daniel J. Boorstin*, Myths of Popular Innocence, U.S. News & World Report, March 4, 1991, p. 41.

13 *Stephen T. Hosmer*, Why Milosevic Decided to Settle When He Did (RAND, 2001).

14 Id., p. xv.

15 Id., p. xviii.

unthinkable to directly attack civilians. However it is unnecessary to do so to nevertheless target civilian morale. A means of doing so clearly in compliance with LOAC is via psychological warfare. This is true even where it is predictable that, as a consequence, civilian casualties result.

For example, the U.S. Army's venerable Field Manual 27-10, "The Law of Land Warfare", specifically cites as a permissible psychological stratagem, "encouraging insurrection among the enemy civilian population."[16] Yet the history of warfare sadly demonstrates that civil insurrections are often the most savage of conflicts, and frequently produce enormous noncombatant losses.

I also respectfully disagree with *Hays*' conclusion that there is "little distinction" between "morale" and "terror" bombings. True, actual terror bombings *can* cause an *immediate* collapse of civilian morale as was the case with the Madrid railway bombings. The attackers achieved the military effect of removing Spanish combat power from Iraqi battlefields as surely and completely as if the force was annihilated via traditional means. However, no one is suggesting that a civilized nation committed to the rule of law engage in any such attack.

Rather, degrading civilian morale without terror can involve controlling the information the enemy populace receives. This raises the issue of the propriety of attacks on radio, television, and other avenues of communications' employed by belligerents to preserve and enhance support for their military effort. This is where I take issue with the otherwise excellent report about the NATO bombing campaign by the prosecutor at the Internationals Criminal Tribunal for the Former Yugoslavia (ICTY).[17]

While conceding that "government propaganda may help to undermine the morale of the population and the armed forces" the ICTY report goes on to insist that "justifying an attack on a civilian [radio/television] facility on such grounds alone may not meet the 'effective contribution to military action" and 'definite military advantage' criteria required by the Additional Protocols." Without elucidating its factual basis, the ICTY insists that such attacks only offer "potential or indeterminate advantages" and fail to demonstrate a military advantage "substantial and relatively close rather than hardly perceptible and likely to appear only in the long term."

"Only likely to appear in the long term?" The 78 days it took NATO's adversary to throw in the towel is not, by the standards of modern war, a "long term" conflict. In this respect, the report demonstrates an incredible naiveté about the nature of modern war. In today's information-intensive world, events can rapidly and radically impact civilian attitudes in ways that instantly impact ongoing military operations.

---

[16] Dep't of the Army, Field Manual 27-10, The Law of Land Warfare, July 1956, at Section V, para. 49, p. 22.

[17] See e.g., International Criminal Tribunal for the Former Yugoslavia, Final Report to the Prosecutor by the Committee Established to Review the NATO Bombing Campaign Against the Federal Republic of Yugoslavia (13 June 2000) accessible at www.un.org/icty/pressreal/nato061300.htm.

Consider the immediate impact of the broadcasts and web postings as a result of the Abu Ghraib scandal. Today public opinion can turn around quickly depending upon the information it receives or, as the case may be, does not receive. Significantly, experienced military professionals, not civilian lawyers in The Hague or Geneva, most accurately determine the *military* effects of attacks.

I very much agree with Mr. *Park*'s concern about the hazards of "mirror imaging." He could not be more correct in insisting that the effective use of force requires carefully gauging the psychology of one's target; it *is* necessary to assess it from the values and perspectives of his culture, not one's own. In fact, I've spoken and written a number times making that very point in a variety of direct and indirect ways.

Accordingly, I'll offer a couple of cautions about a form of "mirror imaging" in the context of our topic today. Specifically, we ought not to assume that because of what may or may not have happened in a totalitarian European régime over fifty years ago will be replicated today in other societies in other parts of the globe. Likewise, we need to avoid underestimating the role that civilian morale plays in modern and modernizing nations with democracy or democratic features. We simply cannot assume that all 21st century opponents will be ideologically-driven zealots as was the case in World War II and often thereafter.

In closing, allow me to address some of the concerns *Hays* raised in his discussions regarding my article about rethinking noncombatancy.[18] Of course, it is true, as he suggests, that I often try to write provocative articles that "stir the pot." In this instance, the basic point I was proffering for discussion was a suggestion that we ought to look for ways for avoiding attacks on human beings, even bona fide combatants, whenever we can.

In other words, it is my view that *human life*, even of enemy soldiers, is to be valued over civilian *objects*. If it is possible to conclude an armed conflict in a way that minimizes loss of life generally, notwithstanding that doing so may be more costly in terms of the loss of civilian *objects* than might have otherwise been the case, such avenues are nevertheless worthy of consideration.

In particular, I believe that Protocol 1's prohibition of reprisals against civilian *objects* goes too far, and eviscerates any meaningful options to stopping a belligerent's commission of war crimes. If the progressive destruction of the personal property of an enemy leader directing the commission of war crimes persuades him to halt, why should it be unlawful to try to do so? Under such circumstances, why not target the personal wealth of enemy decision-making elites, *if* – and *only* "if" – doing so presents a reasonable opportunity under the circumstances to cause the adversary to cease his unlawful behaviour?

I completely agree that there may be situations, perhaps many of them, where the circumstances are such that attacks against personal property have no reasonable chance of success. In those cases, an attack would be improper.

However, I believe it is a mistake to rule out *all* such attacks, regardless of the circumstances prevailing at the time. There could be decisive elements of certain

---

18 *Charles J. Dunlap, Jr.*, The End of Innocence: Rethinking Noncombatancy in the Post-Kosovo Era, in: Strategic Review, Summer 2000, p. 9.

societies for whom avarice and the quest for material gain trumps whatever psychological pleasure or political advancement they hope to achieve through the commission of war crimes themselves (or via their armed forces on their behalf). Attacking civilian property in the context of belligerent reprisal ought to be an available, LOAC-approved tool for military commanders in such situations.

I must admit that I, speaking only for myself, would like to see a legal architecture that permits attacks on civilian objects, and especially personal property and wealth of key elites, even in the absence of circumstances warranting the application of the doctrine of belligerent reprisal. Again, my goal here is to place a greater value on the preservation of human life, even of our enemies, over the preservation of inanimate objects. Of course, we must insist upon a reasonable anticipation of success under the circumstances prevailing at the time. This is an admittedly difficult proposition but no more complex, especially, than other strategic targeting decisions.

While it may not be possible to conduct such attacks without casualties among the truly innocent, a proportionality analysis might reveal an opportunity to save more civilians in the end, not to mention combatants on both sides. In short, I believe an undifferentiated valuing of civilian property over human life does not serve the overall interests and purposes of LOAC – or human society generally.

With that I'll close by underlining again the value of conferences like this where frank views can be exchanged in an atmosphere of professional respect and a genuine, open-minded spirit of intellectual inquiry. Thank you.

The United Kingdom and Legitimate Military Objectives: Current Practice ... and Future Trends?

Steven Haines

Department of Politics and International Relations, Royal Holloway College, University of London

The identification of military objectives is a vital purpose of the law relating to the conduct of military operations during armed conflict. One might have thought that such an important element of the law would by now have been refined to the point at which universal agreement was possible. Far from it, however. As the contributions from *Hays Parks* and *Charles Dunlap* amply demonstrate, there remain a number of issues that render the identification of military objectives contentious. This chapter will concentrate on two of these. The first is to do with the extent to which there is an identifiable customary norm defining military objectives. The second is to do with the possibility of further limitations being imposed on the range of military objectives that can be legitimately targeted during future military campaigns. In between dealing with these issues, the opportunity will also be taken to outline the current legal advice on military objectives provided by the UK to its Armed Forces.

Customary Law: Rule 8 and its discontents

While the principal purpose of treaty negotiations is to achieve agreement between parties, one of the dilemmas often associated with the resultant treaties is that their wording frequently leaves considerable scope for interpretation. In the quest for negotiated agreement and ratification, the words are often crafted deliberately to accommodate states' understandably differing interests. Unfortunately, intentional vagueness, subtleties and nuances of meaning, while a route to formal agreement in the short term, can easily come back to haunt those charged with implementation over time. Within the law of armed conflict[1] there is nothing more important than the definition of 'military objective'. It is fundamental. Yet the definition we

1 Throughout this paper the author uses the term 'law of armed conflict' rather than either 'the laws of war' or 'international humanitarian law' unless one of the other terms is directly quoted.

have in treaty law, while very widely agreed and accepted in one sense, is also widely regarded as ambiguous and inadequate in another.

Let us deal with the first sense first. We know how the words contained in the ratified treaty law distinguish between 'military objectives' and 'civilian objects'. We know how a 'military objective' is defined. All should agree that what is not a 'military objective' is a 'civilian object'.[2] We are clear that 'military objectives' may contain within them 'civilian objects' (and civilians themselves) that are subject to the equally understood rules relating to distinction – and that we must apply ourselves to the issue of proportionality in relation to civilian casualties when targeting military objectives. Additional Protocol I to the 1949 Geneva Conventions provides us with a widely agreed form of words.[3] The United Kingdom ratified this in January 1998. Despite signing in 1977, the United States has since been reluctant to ratify Additional Protocol I. However, it did formally accept the Additional Protocol's definition of military objectives indirectly, through ratification of the Second Protocol Additional to the Convention on Certain Conventional Weapons,[4] which incorporates an identical form of words at Article 2(4). In one way or another, all five of the Permanent Members of the UN Security Council have ratified this definition, as have a great many other states. In relation to the basic words defining 'military objective' contained within treaty law, therefore, there is a substantial degree of agreement. So much so, in fact, that Rule 8, articulated in the recently published International Committee of the Red Cross (ICRC) sponsored study into customary law, repeats precisely the treaty definition as follows:

"... those objects which by their nature, location, purpose or use make an effective contribution to military action and whose total or partial destruction, capture or neutralization, in the circumstances ruling at the time, offers a definite military advantage."[5]

Given that this is so, it is difficult to understand why the definition of military objective contained in treaty law is not now simply accepted by all as part of the body of customary law on the subject. *Hays Parks* is one who challenges the

---

2 Notwithstanding some debate about whether combatants are included in the definition of 'military objective'. The UK's new manual (Ministry of Defence, The Manual of the Law of Armed Conflict, Oxford University Press, 2004 – hereafter UK Manual) does include combatants in its definition of 'military objective' (at Paragraph 5.4.1), although not all would agree with this approach. I am grateful for Colonel *Charles Garraway*'s comments on this point.

3 In Article 52(2).

4 Article 2(4) 1980 UN Convention on Certain Conventional Weapons: Protocol II on Prohibitions or Restrictions on the Use of Mines, Booby-Traps and Other Devices. The definition of military objectives is also included in Article 1(3) of Protocol III dealing with Incendiary Weapons.

5 *J.-M. Henckaerts/L. Doswald-Beck*, Customary International Law (in two volumes: Volume I: Rules and Volume II: Practice), Cambridge University Press for the International Committee of the Red Cross, 2005 (hereafter ICRC Customary Law Study), p.29.

status of this rule, as defined above, asserting that it is not a part of the customary law of armed conflict.[6] He relies on the argument that evidence of states' formal agreement to a rule, in this case through the ratification of treaty law, does not necessarily reflect the physical practice of states. He goes on to suggest that customary law requires evidence of actual physical practice coupled with *opinio juris*.

Physical practice undoubtedly provides the best evidence of the former. Verbal practice, in contrast, is less convincing, except as an arguably persuasive source of evidence of that with which states believe they are under a particular legal obligation to comply (ie *opinio juris*). Following this line of argument, if treaty law does not reflect physical practice, then the rule may well not meet the essential criteria leading to the development of customary law. Of course, in a great many cases this sort of argument will be persuasive. It is certainly far too easy for some states to resort to mere symbolism, formally adopting treaties and then doing very little, or even nothing, to ensure their own compliance. It is by no means unusual, for example, for treaties to be ratified without any appropriate domestic legislative action being taken to facilitate compliance. Indeed, those states that appear the most eager to ratify may well be those that in practice do precious little to reflect treaty terms in their own domestic legislation. Ratification is a process which can take considerable time if taken seriously. Those states that are the most supportive and compliant can end up being rather slow formally to accept the terms of a treaty.

Hays Parks is understandably cautious as a result of this tendency and challenges the ICRC's heavy reliance on 'verbal practice'. He quotes also *Daniel Bethlehem*'s position at the launch of the ICRC Customary Law Study in London in April 2005, which is critical of the study's heavy reliance on treaty law in the identification of customary rules.[7] Despite the difficulties, however, when it comes to the basic definition of military objective quoted above (a formal definition which is very widely accepted indeed) the ICRC position is arguably a sound one. The fact that states may not have had the opportunity to reflect their formal agreement in actual physical practice seems a somewhat pedantic reason for objecting to the content of the ICRC's Rule 8. Have we really got to wait until most states have been able to demonstrate their physical support for rules during actual combat before we declare a rule to have achieved customary law status? One hopes not, especially as this would lead, through consistency, to an unfortunate situation in which no rule contained in the law of armed conflict could ever be accepted as customary law until the vast majority of states had actually deployed their armed forces in combat and demonstrably applied the rule for all to see. Since none of us have any general desire to see states actively engaged in armed conflict, this would mean that we would all hope never to see rules of customary

---

6 See *W. Hays Parks*, Asymmetries and the Identification of Legitimate Military Objectives, in this Volume, p. 91.

7 *Parks*, Asymmetries and the Identification of Legitimate Military Objectives, supra n. 6, p. 92. See also *D. Bethlehem*, "The ICRC Customary Law Study: An Assessment" presented at the UK launch of the ICRC Customary Law Study, Royal Institute of International Affairs (Chatham House), London 18 April 2005 (at: www.chathamhouse.org.uk/pdf/research/il/ILParmedconflict.pdf, pp. 9-17).

law developed at all in this vital area of international law. This would clearly be unfortunate.

The ICRC's heavy reliance on verbal practice,[8] particularly in identifying some of the major rules of customary international humanitarian law, is understandable, therefore. That being the case, and given also that a majority of states have agreed to the definition through ratification of relevant treaty law, we have certainly identified something on which most of us can agree: the promulgated words, quoted above, used to define military objective.

However, this is by no means the end of the matter – and here we turn to the second sense, by which there is much scope for disagreement over the more detailed definition of 'military objective'. Those responsible for making decisions on targeting and the application of force actually have to apply the agreed definition above in real time situations of armed conflict. In doing this they resort to some measure of judgement. In the demanding circumstances of armed conflict itself, it may well be the case that different decision-makers will reach different conclusions about the legitimacy of particular potential targets, with some judging them to be military objectives while others judge them civilian objects. Judgement, often applied under considerable pressure (from others in the command chain, both above and below, as well as from adversaries), will be influenced a great deal by the training they have received and the formal advice they are given, either through such things as military manuals or by other immediate guidance offered through the chain of command. In the latter case, guidance will often not merely include higher level interpretation of the strictly legal issue of what is and what should not be regarded as a military objective, but may also be influenced by both general policy and the particular requirements of the campaign in progress. What impact does all of this have on the choice of a particular target in a particular set of circumstances and at a particular point in time? If there was evidence of consistency in terms of state practice relating to targeting, there might be a strong case for stating the existence of customary norms. Unfortunately, while one might argue that the precise wording of the ICRC's Rule 8 is not contentious and should be accepted as reflecting customary law, one cannot say the same about how that rule is interpreted in its application.

---

8 Examples of 'verbal practice' contained in the Introduction to the Customary International Law Study are: "military manuals, national legislation, national case-law, instructions to armed and security forces, military communiqués during war, diplomatic protests, opinions of official legal advisers, comments by governments on draft treaties, executive decisions and regulations, pleadings before international tribunals, statements in international organisations and at international conferences, and government positions taken with respect to resolutions of international organisations." (see ICRC Customary Law Study, Volume I, supra n. 5, p. xxxii). While the importance of some of these may be challenged, others will be of major significance in relation to the development of customary law. Military manuals, for example, may be especially authoritative. The author was in no doubt that the UK Manual, of which he chaired the Editorial Board, was going to be regarded internationally as a vital source of evidence of UK state practice. This was a view supported by a significant number of his former colleagues within the British Armed Forces and relevant government departments (the MoD and the FCO).

Current UK Legal Advice

The UK, as a major military power, has frequently deployed its armed forces on combat operations in recent years and is invariably a powerful voice in the processes by which the law of armed conflict is developed and interpreted. What the UK has to say about such things at any given time is, therefore, of some importance generally, not only to academic observers but also to potential allies and coalition partners whose own armed forces may well find themselves operating alongside the British Armed Forces on operations. The general British approach to defining military objectives, which has an impact on the ways in which promulgated advice is interpreted, should also be of considerable interest. This is influenced by a range of pressures, including issues of a military doctrinal nature, having a bearing on the conduct of a campaign and its constituent operations, and those related to the longer term and progressive development of the international normative environment. As *Adam Roberts* has observed – and as *Hays Parks* noted in his paper – "... the study of law needs to be integrated with the study of history; if not, it is inadequate."[9] One might add that the study of law in this area needs also to be informed by an understanding of developments in military doctrine as well as general normative pressures, which increasingly influence policymakers.

Until recently, those researching the UK's official position on various aspects of the law of armed conflict have had to refer to its classic post-Second World War manual promulgated almost half a century ago.[10] This was modified by a small number of amendments, the last of which was promulgated as long ago as 1969.[11] The 1958 Manual remained officially extant until 2004, despite its by then serious shortcomings.[12] Other sources of UK state practice have included actual physical practice in such campaigns as that against Argentina in 1982 and that against Iraq in 1991 and its reactions as a neutral during the Iran-Iraq War between 1980 and 1988. Evidence of verbal practice includes various government statements, treaty negotiating positions[13] and ratifications of various treaties and treaty protocols, together with reservations made at the time of ratification/accession. In relation to targeting and military objectives, the ICRC Customary Law Study relies partly on an official UK Government letter to the President

---

9 *Parks*, Asymmetries and the Identification of Legitimate Military Objectives, supra n. 6, p. 92.

10 The War Office, The Law of War on Land, being Part III of the Manual of Military Law, London, HMSO, 1958, as amended (hereafter referred to as the 1958 Manual). This manual was drafted by *Sir Hersch Lauterpacht* with the assistance of Colonel *Gerald Draper*.

11 There was a total of only five amendments to that date, with none since.

12 Interestingly, the index of the 1958 Manual did not even contain an entry for 'military objective', despite the interesting use of the term by British Prime Minister *Neville Chamberlain* as early as 1938 (quoted by *Hays Parks* in his paper, supra n. 6, p. 80)

13 Although, of course, negotiating positions must be regarded as dubious sources given their purpose in relation to the need to influence other states' willingness to shift their own positions.

of the UN Security Council detailing UK practice during the 1991 Gulf War.[14] The ICRC also relied on what it referred to as a UK 'manual' dating from 1981.[15] This was not, however, an officially endorsed statement of the UK position on the law. It was, rather, a short training document produced for individual servicemen. This was first produced in 1981 but has been reviewed and re-published frequently since then. It is debateable the extent to which it can be regarded as a reliable source of UK state practice and was certainly not provided to the UK's 'National Research Team' with that aim in mind.[16] Fortunately, however, the current UK position on the law of armed conflict is now much more easily and reliably located. Since July 2004 we have had the benefit of the UK's official guidance, promulgated in the new UK Manual. This was unfortunately not available to the editors of the ICRC Customary Law Study before they concluded the bulk of their work.

How does this new UK Manual deal with military objectives?[17] For a start it contains a brief introductory paragraph that states that the term 'military objective' includes combatant members of the enemy armed forces and their military weapons, vehicles, equipment and installations. It may include other objects which have military value, such as bridges, communications towers, and electricity and refined oil production facilities (examples of which were attacked during the Gulf conflict of 1991, for example).

The criteria contained in the law of armed conflict require commanders and others planning, deciding on, or launching attacks to exercise their discretion. The UK declared, on ratification of Additional Protocol I, that those concerned must "necessarily reach their decisions on the basis of their assessment of the information from all sources which is *reasonably available to them at the relevant time*".[18]

The UK Manual states that the definition of military objectives[19] contains various elements that require explanation. These are as follows:

a. The second part of the definition (definite military advantage) limits the first (effective contribution to military action). Both parts must apply before an object can be considered a military objective.
b. Attacks on military objectives that cause incidental loss or damage to civilians are not prohibited so long as the proportionality rule is complied with.

---

[14] UK Letter dated 28 January 1991; UN Doc. S/22156, 28 Jan 1991, p. 1.

[15] See, for example, Customary Law Study, Volume II, Part 1: Practice, Chapter 2, Notes 299 and 365.

[16] I am grateful to Colonel *Charles Garraway* for identifying this document (A Soldier's Guide to the Law of Armed Conflict, Army Code 71130, published by the Director General of Development and Doctrine, UK Ministry of Defence). He provided a copy of the then (1999) extant edition to *Dr Jenny Kuyper*, a member of the ICRC's UK National Research Team, when she was gathering evidence of practice for the study (although it is also understood that an even earlier version was used by the editors of the Customary Law Study).

[17] What follows is based on the UK Manual, pp. 54-57 (paras. 5.4 to 5.4.5).

[18] Emphasis added.

[19] AP I, Article 52(2).

c. The word 'nature' refers to the type of object; for example, military transports, command and control centres, or communications stations.
d. 'Location' includes areas which are militarily important because they must be captured or denied to the enemy, or because the enemy must be made to retreat from them. An area of land can, thus, be a military objective. On ratification of Additional Protocol I, the UK declared that "a specific area of land may be a military objective if, because of its location or other reasons specified in Article 52, its total or partial destruction, capture or neutralisation in the circumstances ruling at the time offers definite military advantage".
e. 'Purpose' means the future intended use of an object while 'use' means its present function.
f. The words 'nature, location, purpose or use' seem at first sight to allow a wide discretion, but they are subject to the qualifications later in the definition of 'effective contribution to military action' and the offering of a 'definite military advantage'. There does not have to be geographical proximity between 'effective contribution' and 'military advantage'. That means, for example, that attacks on military supply dumps in the rear, or diversionary attacks, away from the area of actual military operations, can be launched.
g. 'Military action' means military action generally, not a limited or specific military operation.
h. The words 'in the circumstances ruling at the time' are important. If, for example, the enemy moved a divisional headquarters into a disused textile factory, an attack on that headquarters would be permissible (even though the factory might be destroyed in the process) because of the prevailing circumstances. Once the enemy moved its headquarters away, the circumstances would change again and the immunity of the factory would be restored.
i. 'Definite' means a concrete and perceptible military advantage rather than a hypothetical and speculative one.
j. As the UK stressed in its statement on its ratification of Additional Protocol I, the 'military advantage' anticipated from an attack refers to the advantage anticipated from the attack as a whole and not only from isolated or particular parts of the attack. The advantage need not be immediate.

These rules, while very useful, are not entirely satisfactory on their own. Many scholars working in this field, as well as a great many practitioners faced with the need to apply the rules and associated guidance, have pointed to the remaining scope for interpretation and ambiguity. As *Hays Parks* points out, *Yoram Dinstein* is one of those who has quite correctly criticised the inadequacy of the rules on their own. *Dinstein* described the rules defining military objectives as "abstract and generic".[20] He went on to provide extremely valuable comment on some difficult issues, such as: retreating troops, police, industrial plants, civilian airports and maritime ports, government offices and the political leadership. He also included

---

[20] *Y. Dinstein*, The Conduct of Hostilities under the Law of International Armed Conflict, Cambridge University Press, 2004, p. 83.

comment on both maritime and air warfare.[21] As *Parks* has also noted, the ICRC Commentary on the Additional Protocols contains such a list, and he has himself provided one in his paper.[22] The need to amplify in this way is very much supported by the former UK Director of Army Legal Services, General *Tony Rogers*. In his own work (Law on the Battlefield[23]) as well as in the 'model manual' he was commissioned to write by the ICRC,[24] *Rogers* provided a list of examples. Not surprisingly, as he was also the General Editor of the UK Manual, he also proposed including such a list therein, something the Editorial Board was very happy to approve.

The UK Manual's list is not a surprising one. It stresses that the inclusion of an object on the list does not mean that it is necessarily a military objective. It must always be tested against the definition of military objective contained in Article 52(2) of Additional Protocol I, in particular by posing the question 'does it make an effective contribution to military action?' The UK Manual also, very obviously, stresses that the list is not exhaustive. Attacks on certain types of objects are clearly prohibited. These include: cities, towns and villages; buildings used by civilians and not for military purposes, such as dwellings, schools, museums, places of worship, and other buildings without military significance; foodstuffs (not intended solely for members of the armed forces) and food producing areas; and water sources for the civilian population. The full list of examples contained in the UK Manual consists of:

a. Combatant members of the armed forces and those who take a direct part in hostilities without being members of the armed forces, so long as they are not *hors de combat*.
b. Military equipment, including vehicles, weapons, munitions and fuel stocks.
c. Military works, including defensive works and fortifications.
d. Military depots and establishments, including headquarters and command and control centres, barracks, military airfields, military supply depots, defence ministries and intelligence establishments.
e. Other works producing or developing military supplies and other supplies of military value, including metallurgical, engineering, chemical, oil and power industries, and infrastructures supporting the war effort.
f. Areas of land of military significance such as hills, defiles and bridgeheads.
g. Means of transportation used for moving military supplies or other supplies of military value, including railways, ports, airfields, bridges, canals, tunnels and main roads.

---

[21] *Dinstein*, supra n. 20; see Chapter 4 on 'Legitimate Military Objectives'.

[22] *Parks*, Asymmetries and the Identification of Legitimate Military Objectives, supra n. 6, pp. 92 et seq.

[23] *A.P.V. Rogers*, Law on the Battlefield (2nd Ed), Manchester University Press, 2004, pp. 83-85.

[24] *A.P.V. Rogers/P. Malherbe*, Fight it Right: Model Manual on the Law of Armed Conflict for Armed Forces, Geneva, ICRC, 1999, p. 223.

h. Communications installations used for military purposes, including broadcasting and television stations, telephone and telegraph stations.

This effectively summarises the extent of the current advice available to the UK Armed Forces about the identification of legitimate military objectives. While the provision of amplification together with a list of examples goes a long way towards defining precisely what is and what is not a military objective, there remains, as there always will, a need for military commanders at all levels to apply responsible judgement when selecting military objectives for legitimate targeting.

It is at this point – the point of judgement – that education, training and preparation come to the fore. It is important to recognise that military training of relevance to identifying targets will consist not only of training in the law of armed conflict but also a solid grounding in military doctrine. The doctrine has to be compatible with the law but it will be influenced by a great deal besides the law of armed conflict. This leads neatly on to my final comments, which are related to the possible future development of the law relating to military objectives.

Military Objectives and the Future: Strategic Environment

Hays Parks in his paper delved very comprehensively into the issues associated with the distinction between 'war-fighting' and 'war-sustaining' in relation to military objectives.[25] As he points out, on one level the debate appears to be primarily academic. Many military objectives contribute to both and most military minds would tend towards describing targets as either tactical or strategic rather than war-fighting or war-sustaining. It should, incidentally, be stressed that tactical is not necessarily synonymous with war-fighting, nor strategic with war-sustaining. Nevertheless, the more controversial of the two categories (whether we are using the fighting/sustaining or the tactical/strategic distinction) are those objectives described as strategic or which are justified by their war-sustaining nature.

As *Hays Parks* notes, *Michael Bothe* has recently proposed a more restrictive interpretation of legitimate military objective than *Parks* himself can support. As an example, he interprets *Bothe*'s view as follows: that "the limited nature and objective of the 1999 Kosovo conflict accordingly limited the breadth of military objectives that lawfully could be attacked, particularly those not battlefield-related." *Parks*'s own response is to argue, very understandably, that the limitations imposed will have been policy rather than legally inspired and that they should emphatically not be assumed to imply any legal obligation to restrict the choice of targets. As he states:

"Political leaders have placed and may place policy limits on attack of certain military objectives depending on the political nature and strategic objectives of a

[25] *Parks*, Asymmetries and the Identification of Legitimate Military Objectives, supra n. 6, pp. 96 et seq.

particular conflict as they see it. The decision against attack of mainland Argentinian air bases during the 1982 Falklands/Malvinas War … is a case in point. But that does not alter the fact that they were military objectives and lawfully could have been attacked. Policy decisions should not be confused for law of war limitations."[26]

For *Parks*, the range of legitimate military objectives remains unaffected by policy decisions, made during the conduct of particular campaigns, not to target certain examples or types of military objective.

This debate is an important one and it raises fundamental questions about the relationship between, on the one hand, national interest and the policy that reflects it (both over time and in relation to particular circumstances) and, on the other hand, the development of international norms. There is a complex interrelationship between law, doctrine, technology and policy. Each has an influence on targeting, at both the strategic and the tactical levels. Ultimately, of course, developments in policy and doctrine will have a bearing on state practice. As a consequence, doctrinal and policy developments may well lead to shifts in customary law if the resultant practice comes to be regarded as a legal obligation.

Hays Parks also points out in his paper that mere practice does not indicate an acceptance of a legal obligation. While this is of course an extremely important point to bear in mind (and one with which this author absolutely agrees), it is equally important to recognise that one cannot simply assume that all practice will invariably be amenable to the condition that it will never come to reflect a perceived legal obligation. This is not the place to enter into a lengthy discussion of the nature of *opinio juris* and the means by which it is established or, indeed, the extent to which persistent objection to an emerging norm will exempt a state from compliance with it once it is established *vis a vis* others. However, it may be useful to explore the relationship between actual practice reflecting military doctrine and the way that this may come to be influenced by prevailing normative trends.

It is a military doctrinal truism that action taken at all levels during a military campaign must be consistent with strategic objectives. This is achieved in various ways. There is, for example, a strong relationship between tactical, operational and strategic doctrine, with the latter having a cascading influence on the operational and tactical levels. Strategic doctrine is but one of two elements that go to make up military strategy, the other being strategic (or Defence) policy. The latter states what armed force will be used for, and is politically driven; the former indicates how armed forces will go about delivering military force in support of policy, and is developed by the armed forces as a part of their professional military business. Policy is about what to do; doctrine is about how to do it. Strategic objectives arise from the policy process but those shaping them have to be aware of the capabilities and limitations of military force, which should be obvious through reference to doctrine. Strategic objectives, which can change rapidly, are pursued by reference to strategic doctrine, which is considerably more enduring. The prin-

---

[26] *Parks*, Asymmetries and the Identification of Legitimate Military Objectives, supra n. 6, p. 99.

cipal factor that influences the gradual evolution of strategic doctrine is the nature of the strategic environment. One of the dimensions of that strategic environment, recognised in British strategic doctrine, is the legal or normative dimension.[27] Strategic objectives must themselves be lawful and reflect consideration of the normative dimension of the strategic environment. Given these linkages, it must be the case that if tactical doctrine develops generally over time to reflect shifts in strategic doctrine that are themselves a consequence of changes in the normative dimension of the strategic environment, then action taken at the tactical level may eventually be associated with some measure of legal obligation. Arguably, therefore, *opinio juris* may become associated with tactical decision-making via an indirect route through the development of strategic doctrine. An example will serve to illustrate the point being made.

There has been considerable comment in recent months, in particular focusing on events in Iraq, about the conduct of military operations from initial deployment through to the post-conflict phases of a campaign. Modern military commanders and their planners have to consider campaigns in their entirety, and not merely focus on their combat phases. Experience during the campaign in Iraq has taught a number of lessons. One of the most important has been based on the extent to which the Coalition had (or had not) thought adequately through the needs of post-conflict reconstruction prior to the invasion itself. There is no need to dwell on the types of criticisms that have been levelled at political and military planners; they are well known and are to do with the transition from combat to non-combat phases and the adequacy of forces (in both quantitative and qualitative terms) to deal with the demands of post-conflict reconstruction.

The destructive capacity of modern military technology, applied in a manner intended to ensure overwhelming victory at minimum cost in lives to one's own forces during the combat phase, may have the effect of making the subsequent post-conflict phase very much more difficult to manage. It is possible to damage or destroy significant elements of a state's societal infrastructure on the grounds that they are legitimate military objectives. Unfortunately, too great a concern for rapid success during the combat phase can lead to a protracted post-conflict experience. We should not forget in this context that concentration of planning effort on the combat phase may have made subsequent internal security conditions worse than they might have been in Iraq. Ironically there have been more Coalition casualties during the post-conflict phase than were experienced during the high-intensity combat phase itself. In Iraq, importantly, there is also the highly contentious issue of the number of civilian casualties.

Within the UK Armed Forces there is a declared need, in both planning and in the actual conduct of a campaign, to ensure that all phases are conducted in a manner consistent with the needs of those phases that must inevitably follow. That is to say, the preparation for operations and the conduct of the combat phase have to take into account the longer term objectives of military action. Military force is only employed as part of a fully integrated political, economic and military ap-

---

27 UK Ministry of Defence, British Defence Doctrine (Joint Warfare Publication 0-01), 2nd Edition, 2001, p. 2-3

proach. British Defence Doctrine is at pains to point out that military action is but a part of the whole.[28] Military action has to relate to political objectives. There is nothing surprising about this, as *Clausewitz* himself would acknowledge.

The UK uses all the instruments of state power in its relations with other states within the international system. Military power, as the ultimate manifestation of state power, cannot be divorced from either political or economic power. It is vital to recognise that this means that the application of military force will not be unrestrained by considerations of a non-military nature during the combat phase of a campaign. Clearly, restraints will be imposed. The full range of restraints will include those based on perceptions of what will be required in post-conflict phases to achieve the overall success of the campaign, including its non-military measures of success. In simple terms, there may be a real need not to destroy facilities during combat if they are likely to be vital in the following phases of the operation and it may well be necessary to re-think what is actually proportionate in relation to the numbers of civilian objects – including civilians themselves – destroyed, killed or damaged during combat operations. Despite the strictly legal acceptability of defining certain elements of state infrastructure as legitimate 'military objectives' by way of the current law of armed conflict, some may well not be appropriate targets for attack, given the need to follow combat operations with post-conflict reconstruction. While this can be regarded as something of a truism, it is worth restating, nevertheless. It is likely that this sort of consideration will increasingly drive military practice during campaigns in the 21st Century.

One's thinking on this needs to relate strategy to tactics. The normative dimension of the international strategic environment, within which military forces operate, is having a steadily increasing influence on the development of what is morally acceptable in the conduct of military operations down to the tactical level. It is increasingly the case that international morality is coming to regard the need for post-conflict reconstruction as an imperative. It is no longer acceptable for wars to be waged with inadequate consideration given to what must inevitably follow. Military campaigns should not be conducted with little or no concern for the eventual end-state. The destruction of a state's military capacity to fight must not be achieved at the excessive expense of that state's ability to recover in fairly swift order. This is not merely of relevance to the ability to restore electricity and water supplies and economic activity in general. There is also a social dimension.

The extent of the suffering and displacement of populations is an increasingly important issue to take into account. The seventy-eight day air campaign against Serbia in 1999, while generally compliant with the current law relating to legitimate military objectives, failed utterly to prevent the ethnic cleansing it was meant to forestall. Of course, instead of the deliberate ethnic cleansing of the Albanian population by Serbs, NATO inadvertently created the conditions that led to the ethnic cleansing of Serbs by Albanians, as the indigenous Serb population evacuated the province for its own safety. Ethnic cleansing was still the result, however. We now have a continuing problem identifying the eventual status of Kosovo made more difficult by the ethnic mix post-conflict. Not only that, but the asser-

---

[28] British Defence Doctrine, supra n. 27, pp. 2-4 to 2-5.

tion by some, including the NATO Supreme Allied Commander, General *Wesley Clarke*, that the operation was a great success because it was achieved without a single Alliance casualty, is frankly obscene. While this particular issue is arguably not one about targeting, it does highlight the need to place the combat phase of a campaign in proper perspective – a campaign is not just about war-fighting.

Can this line of thinking be linked to the identification of legitimate military objectives? It surely must be. The moral imperatives of the modern international system that render excessively destructive elements of warfare incompatible with longer term political objectives, ought to have some influence on decisions being made about targets. In the military doctrinal sense, nothing should be done at any subordinate level that is inconsistent with the aims and objectives being pursued at the strategic; this amounts to a fundamental doctrinal principle.

Of course, one must be a little wary about linking the nature of the tactical battle to the nature of the strategic objective. As an example, effective offensive action needs to be taken at the tactical level in order to achieve strategically defensive objectives. Indeed, not to be able to do this would, for example, render the strategic right of self defence potentially meaningless. One of the principles of war contained in British Defence Doctrine is to do with the need for offensive action to achieve victory.[29] As a concrete example, the offensive tactical action that led to the sinking of the Argentine cruiser "General Belgrano" was entirely consistent with the defensive objectives of the South Atlantic campaign (which was conducted fully in accordance with Article 51 of the UN Charter). That said, one needs to consider the campaign objectives as a whole and there is a profound need to restrain military action if it would undermine strategic objectives, no matter how sensible certain actions might appear to those with a purely tactical perspective at a given point in time within the combat phase of a campaign.

This type of thinking is inherent in what this author referred to, in British Defence Doctrine, as the 'British Approach to Military Operations'. Campaigns have phases, with combat being but one in a series. In applying the manoeuvrist approach to the entire campaign – a core principle of British strategic doctrine – it becomes a military imperative to ensure that action during the combat phase be consistent with the requirements of those phases that follow on from it. The British approach to the identification of legitimate 'military objectives' is, arguably, cautious. But caution is not absolute and can be compromised. As the combat phase of a campaign extends in time beyond that originally envisaged, there may be a natural tendency to throw some of that caution to the wind. To refer to Kosovo once again, to what extent was the identification of legitimate military objectives affected by the length of the air campaign? Was there what might be referred to as 'target creep', as the original collection of legitimate military objectives ran out and consideration had to be given to including other targets to provide the air campaign with its purpose? All targets attacked throughout the seventy-eight days of the air campaign were carefully scrutinised for legitimacy against the sorts of criteria outlined above. But some early targets were hit again later in the campaign, despite the fact that the earlier targeting of them had rendered them of du-

29 British Defence Doctrine, supra n. 27, p. 3-2.

bious military capacity leading to serious doubts as to their further reduction offering a 'definite military advantage'.

One needs to be careful in the emerging strategic environment not to undermine during the combat phase of a campaign the likelihood of success in the post-conflict phases. Indeed, to do so may render the eventual outcome of the campaign unsatisfactory. There is a detectable concern for force to be used only if the outcome is to be a positive one. Humanitarian considerations alone mean that it is important now to ensure a satisfactory restoration of civil government and administration within a state following armed conflict. When one considers also the impact that human rights law is having on the conduct of military operations and campaigns generally, the possibility that what constitutes legitimate military objectives during the combat phase will be affected by post conflict concerns has to be acknowledged. While *Hays Parks* assures us that decisions of this sort are merely ones of 'policy' that will not have an impact on the range of legitimate military objectives, it is certainly appropriate to challenge that assumption. To put it simply, can something still be a legitimate 'military objective' if, by attacking it and destroying it, one undermines the ability to rebuild the state post-conflict – an ability which is arguably becoming a moral and perhaps a legal imperative?

Conclusion

There is a sense in which thinking about the whole purpose of military action is advancing and that moral and ethical issues to do with the purpose of warfare are frequently the subject of debate. While the law relating to military objectives is, on one level, reasonably clear, at other levels it is ambiguous. And it is probably going to shift as time marches on and moral and ethical concerns of a strategic nature create demands for changes in that law. Law itself must reflect the needs of the environment in which it is applied and, for military commanders, the holistic approach to campaign planning will continue to influence what is acceptable during but one of a campaign's phases; the combat phase perhaps being the shortest and least costly. As if to emphasise this point, the combat phase of the war against Iraq in 2003 was relatively short and inexpensive when compared to the length and costs of the post-conflict phases.

The final section of this paper has been no more than a collection of related thoughts about possible future influences on the development of the law relating to military objectives. *Hays Parks* is quite correct when he warns that a decision not to target something that is, and has been, regarded as a legitimate military objective does not lead inexorably to shifts in the law as to what is and what is not legitimate. He is also correct to take *Michael Bothe* to task over the assertion that limited campaign objectives must have an influence on the legality of military objectives; for the moment they do not. Some measure of policy discretion certainly has to be retained, not least because while we have to devote more thought to the longer term consequences of targeting within campaigns, decisions that are necessarily shaped by the requirements in one phase should not invariably tie our hands when it comes to the others. But what of the longer term? *Hays Parks* and others will doubtless regard this author's comments above as rather rambling, incoherent and, in some respects, just plain wrong! They are, admittedly, by no means fully worked through. However, one should not rule out for all time the possibility that shifting norms of a strategic nature might place obligations on those directing operations and selecting military objectives in the tactical context. If such considerations as the relationship of potential targets to the requirements for post-conflict operations do not as yet have an impact on our thinking about legitimate 'military objectives' (especially those of a strategic or war-sustaining nature) they probably ought to.

The System of Status Groups

The System of Status Groups in International Humanitarian Law

Yoram Dinstein

Tel Aviv University

International Humanitarian Law (IHL) is based, inter alia, on several fundamental distinctions between diverse status groups. I propose to dwell on seven IHL dichotomies (one imagined, six real) predicated on status. Since mine is an introductory presentation, I shall merely draw your attention to six out of the seven distinctions. I shall then focus at greater length on the last bifurcation, which is of great practical significance at the present juncture.

The *first* (illusory) status distinction concerns the alleged application of disparate sets of IHL norms to combatants waging a war of aggression, on the one hand, and to combatants fighting either in (individual or collective) self-defence or in an enforcement action (decreed or authorized by the United Security Council in a legally binding decision), on the other. Such a distinction is ideologically rooted in the ancient doctrine of "just war (*bellum justum*)" that was predominant in the early days of modern international law (the sixteenth through the eighteenth centuries) and – while generally regarded nowadays as *passé* – occasionally raises its head again in a variety of contexts (from "wars of national liberation" to "humanitarian intervention"). The context germane to our discussion is an attempt to project from the clear-cut contrasting status of opposing belligerent States under the *jus ad bellum* (i.e. the aggressor State vs. the victim State or any other State invoking collective self-defence or carrying out a collective security decision adopted by the Security Council) to the *jus in bello* rights and obligations of the soldiers, sailors, airmen and perhaps even civilians belonging to the respective adversary parties.

A revival of "just war" terminology might not have commanded much attention at this day and age, had it not been for a surprising pronouncement by the majority of the International Court of Justice, in its 1996 Advisory Opinion on the *Legality of the Threat or Use of Nuclear Weapons*:

"in view of the current state of international law, and of the elements of fact at its disposal, the Court cannot conclude definitively whether the threat or use of nuclear weapons would be lawful or unlawful in an extreme circumstance of self-defence, in which the very survival of a State would be at stake".[1]

This ill-advised language compels the reader "to wonder whether the Court, indeed, tangled up *ius ad bellum* and *ius in bello*",[2] inasmuch as self-defence is a paradigmatic jus ad bellum topic whereas the legality of resort to nuclear weapons is a paramount problem of the *jus in bello*. If the State fighting in "extreme circumstance" of self-defence is at liberty to resort to nuclear weapons – while its opponent is barred from doing so – the question is whether there are, perhaps, other *jus in bello* advantages that ought to be made available to the victim of aggression (thereby creating for it a preferential treatment generated by the *jus ad bellum*)?

Notwithstanding the implications that can be drawn from the Court's regrettable dictum, there is scarcely any doubt that the prevailing precept today is that of the equal application of the *jus in bello* to all belligerent parties in wartime, whatever the merits of their cause under the *jus ad bellum*. This conclusion is firmly embedded in the general practice of States; in the text of 1949 Geneva Conventions for the Protection of War Victims (now universally applicable); in entrenched case law; and in several studies in depth of the law in force (culminating in a number of resolutions of the *Institut de Droit International*).[3] There is simply no genuine spill-over from the *jus ad bellum* to the *jus in bello*, and any status distinction that purports to flow from that source is spurious.

The *second* (very real and indeed critical) distinction marking out separate status groups constitutes the very bedrock of IHL. It is *the* "principle of distinction", delineating a sharp line of division between civilians and combatants. This is the hallmark of IHL: remove the "principle of distinction" and the entire IHL system collapses. In its Advisory Opinion on *Nuclear Weapons*, the Court used the adjective "cardinal" when addressing the "principle of distinction" that sets off "combatants and non-combatants", its essence being that "States must never make civilians the object of attack".[4]

What the principle of distinction accentuates is that, while warfare is waged by and against combatants, civilians (non-combatants) should be allowed to remain as much as possible beyond the circle of hostilities. Of course, it is impossible to expect that civilians will be completely immunized from the effects of war (especially, modern war). Frequently, at times inescapably, "collateral damage" is caused to civilians. But as long as civilian losses are not inflicted deliberately or indiscriminately, and as long as they are not "excessive in relation to the concrete and direct military advantage anticipated" (to quote Article 51(5)(b) of Protocol I

---

1 Advisory Opinion on the Legality of the Threat or Use of Nuclear Weapons, [1966] ICJ Rep. 226, 266.

2 *W. Verwey*, The International Court of Justice and the Legality of Nuclear Weapons: Some Observations, in: K. Wellens (ed.), International Law: Theory and Practice, Essays in Honour of Eric Suy, 1998, pp. 751, 760.

3 For a detailed discussion with citation of sources, see *Y. Dinstein*, War, Aggression and Self-Defence, 3rd ed., 2001, pp. 140-147.

4 Advisory Opinion, supra n. 1, at. 257.

of 1977 Additional to the Geneva Conventions),[5] these losses cannot be branded as a breach of the "principle of distinction".[6]

It must be understood that the true status distinction under IHL – as formulated by the International Court of Justice – is between civilians (in the sense of non-combatants) and combatants. Unfortunately, in the Customary International Humanitarian Law Study, recently published by the International Committee of the Red Cross (ICRC), Rule 5 prescribes: "Civilians are persons who are not members of the armed forces".[7] As we shall see infra (third distinction), not every member of the armed forces is a combatant. By the same token, not every person who is not a member of the armed forces is a civilian. In particular, as we shall see when we come to the seventh distinction, by actively – or directly – participating in hostilities, a person who claims to be a civilian loses that protective mantle and becomes an unlawful combatant. Even Additional Protocol I of 1977 (that the ICRC relies on), in its "Basic rule" (Article 48) distinguishes between the civilian population and combatants; and in its definition of civilians (Article 50) – which clarifies that the civilian population comprises all persons who are civilians – prescribes that civilians are persons who do not belong to certain categories of persons, including Article 4A(2) of Geneva Convention (III) (covering irregular troops) that will be adverted to below.[8]

The *third* status distinction is between ordinary members of the armed forces and medical or religious personnel serving in military units. As confirmed by Article 43(2) of Additional Protocol I, medical and religious personnel – albeit members of the armed forces – are not combatants.[9] This leads to a different legal regime applicable if and when they are captured by the enemy. Ordinarily, members of the armed forces who fall into the hands of the adverse party are detained as prisoners of war. By contrast, captured medical or religious personnel – despite being members of the armed forces – cannot be detained as prisoners of war. At most, they may be retained, "in order to exercise their medical and spiritual functions for the benefit of prisoners of war"[10] (whose sheer numbers may overwhelm the human resources available to that belligerent party, especially after a big battle). The difference between detention and retention may sound like a theoretical refinement, but its practical consequences can be quite palpable. As a rule, prisoners of war need not be released from their detention until "the cessation of active

---

5 Protocol Additional to the Geneva Conventions of 12 August 1949, and Relating to the Protection of Victims of International Armed Conflicts (Protocol I), 1977, D. Schindler/J. Toman (eds.), The Laws of Armed Conflicts: A Collection of Conventions, Resolutions and Other Documents, 4th ed., 2004, pp. 711, 736.

6 For an examination of legitimate "collateral damage", see *Y. Dinstein*, The Conduct of Hostilities under the Law Of International Armed Conflict, 2004, pp. 123-125.

7 *J.M. Henckaerts/L. Doswald-Beck* (eds.), ICRC Customary International Humanitarian Law Study, I (2005), p. 17.

8 Protocol I, supra n. 5, p. 735.

9 Id., p. 732.

10 Article 33 of Geneva Convention (III) Relative to the Treatment of Prisoners of War, 1949, The Laws of Armed Conflicts, supra n. 5, pp. 507, 524-525.

hostilities"[11] (which may transpire years after their capture;[12] the experience of both World Wars is a stark reminder of this grim reality). For its part, retention of medical and religious personnel "must be justified by a real and pressing need"[13] and *ex hypothesi* is temporary in nature, although the specific length – dictated by the need – is not easily measurable in objective terms.

It may as well be mentioned that veterinary personnel is not assimilated to medical personnel in this crucial respect: if they are members of the armed forces, they may be treated as combatants.[14]

The *fourth* status distinction relates to ordinary combatants compared to combatants who are *hors de combat*. As far as ordinary combatants are concerned, it must be perceived that they are running a *risque du métier*. They can be attacked (and killed) wherever they are, in and out of uniform: even when they are not on active duty. There is no prohibition either of opening fire on retreating troops (who have not surrendered) or of targeting individual combatants.[15]

A drastic change in the legal situation occurs when a combatant becomes *hors de combat*, either by choice (through surrender) or by force of circumstances (having become wounded, sick or shipwrecked). When *hors de combat*, a combatant does not become a civilian; but he is entitled to special protection, and he must be accorded the privileges of a prisoner of war.[16] The regime of prisoners of war is based not only on deprivation of liberty (detention), but also – and preeminently – on substantial guarantees of life, health and dignity (as per Geneva Convention (III)).[17]

An exceptional situation arises in case of air crews and passengers parachuting from aircraft in distress (to be distinguished from airborne troops). Under article 42 of Additional Protocol I, parachutists from aircraft in distress cannot be attacked during their descent,[18] even if it is clear that as a result they will land on territory controlled by the belligerent party to which they belong and will thus live to fight another day.[19]

The *fifth* status distinction pertains to protected vs. non-protected civilians in accordance with Article 4 of Geneva Convention (IV) Relative to the Protection of

---

11 Article 118 of Geneva Convention (III), ibid., p. 551.

12 See *Y. Dinstein*, The Release of Prisoners of War, in: C. Swinarski (ed.), Studies and Essays on International Humanitarian Law and Red Cross Principles in Honour of Jean Pictet, 1984, pp. 37, 40-45.

13 *J.S. Pictet* (ed.), Commentary, Geneva Convention I, 1952, p. 241.

14 See *A.P.V. Rogers/P. Malherbe*, Model Manual on the Law of Armed Conflict, ICRC, 1999, p. 88.

15 For details, see *Dinstein*, supra n. 6, pp. 94-95.

16 For details, see id., pp. 143-146.

17 For details, see *H. Levie*, Prisoners of War in International Armed Conflict, 59 International Law Studies 1978, pp. 97-254.

18 Protocol I, supra n. 5, p. 732.

19 *Y. Sandoz* et al. (eds.), Commentary on the Additional Protocols of 8 June 1977 to the Geneva Conventions of 12 August 1949 (1987), p. 495.

Civilian Persons in Time of War.[20] Contrary to what many people believe, not every civilian is protected by Geneva Convention (IV). Protected persons within the meaning of Article 4 of the Convention are civilians (not entitled to protections under Geneva Conventions (I) through (III)) who find themselves, in case of a conflict or occupation, in the hands of a belligerent party. However, Article 4 excludes protection from any civilian who is (i) a national of the belligerent party in whose hands he is; (ii) a national of any other State not a Contracting Party to the Convention; (iii) a national of a co-belligerent State maintaining normal diplomatic relations with the belligerent in question; or (iv) a national of a neutral country maintaining normal diplomatic relations with that belligerent (but this exclusion applies only within the territory of the belligerent; not in occupied territories). Thus, the protection of Geneva Convention (IV) is only extended to foreign civilians who are either stateless; enemy nationals; nationals of co-belligerent States not maintaining normal diplomatic relations with the belligerent party; or nationals of neutral countries not maintaining such diplomatic relations (unless they are in occupied territories, in which case the condition is dropped); always provided that the State of nationality (if such exists) is a Contracting Party to the Convention. It is important to stress that no protection is conferred on the national of a Contracting Party vis-à-vis his own Government in conditions of an international armed conflict (although such protection is bestowed in circumstances of a non-international armed conflict, as per Article 3[21] common to all four Conventions). Thus, by implication, the position of stateless persons (who are not mentioned as such) is more advantageous than that of local nationals.[22]

It should be observed that, under Article 73 of Additional Protocol I,[23] the effect of Article 4 of Geneva Convention (IV) is modified by adding refugees to the list of protected persons, while explicitly confirming also the protection of stateless persons.[24]

The *sixth* status distinction concerns Government personnel vs. rebels in non-international armed conflicts (civil wars). Notwithstanding a current trend to amalgamate – whenever possible – the rules of conduct of hostilities in international and non-international armed conflicts,[25] it must be grasped that the amalgamation cannot be perfected. The reason for that is simple: the norms of the *jus in bello* simply cannot be copied undiscerningly from inter-State to intra-State armed conflicts. In a civil war there is always the built-in distinction between the combatants who fight for the central (constitutionally legal) Government and those who rise against it. The latter are viewed as traitors and, if captured, are liable to

---

20 Geneva Convention (IV) Relative to the Protection of Civilian Persons in Time of War, 1949, supra n. 5, pp. 575, 581.

21 Id., pp. 580-581.

22 See Commentary on the Additional Protocols, supra n. 19, p. 854.

23 Protocol I, supra n. 5, p. 748.

24 See Commentary on the Additional Protocols, supra n. 19, p. 854.

25 See *D. Kaye/S.A. Solomon*, The Second Review Conference of the 1980 Convention on Certain Conventional Weapons, 96 American Journal of International Law 2002, pp. 922, 927.

be prosecuted and punished for violations of the domestic law:[26] they cannot expect to be accorded the privileges of prisoners of war status.

The facile distinction between Government troops and rebels in a non-international armed conflict loses its luster in two discrete scenarios. The first is when the dimensions of the rebellion assume such large magnitude and intensity that the central Government (as happened in the course of the American Civil War in 1861-865) has no choice but to grant the rebels recognition as a belligerent party. When the central Government does that, the international *jus in bello* in its plenitude is applicable to the relations between the parties.[27] As a result, both sides must vouchsafe prisoners of war status to enemy combatants falling into their hands. The other scenario is that of a "failed State",[28] in which the central Government has completely disappeared and all that are left in the field are feuding armed forced none of which can use the trump card of constitutional legitimacy against its opponents.

The *seventh* – and, as far as this presentation is concerned, the principal - status distinction is between lawful and unlawful combatants (or, as they are sometimes called, privileged and unprivileged combatants[29]). The issue stokes the furnace of the most heated controversy between Contracting and Non-Contracting Parties to Additional Protocol I. The Protocol all but eliminates the age-old distinction between lawful and unlawful combatants in ordinary circumstances of hostilities (see *infra*). To all intents and purposes, it restricts the bounds of unlawful combatants to the special categories of spies and mercenaries (Articles 46-47).[30]

This "great schism" (as I like to call it) – between Contracting and Non-Contracting Parties to the Protocol – is spawned by a very fundamental difference of approach to what traditionalists (like myself) regard as the sole effective method of ensuring the preservation of the "principle of distinction" between combatants and civilians (discussed supra, second distinction). Customary international law has consistently required that every person choose for himself, in an unambiguous way, the relevant class of people with which he prefers to be associated: he can be either a civilian or a combatant. Having subsumed himself under that heading, he must act (and is entitled to be treated) accordingly. There is freedom of choice, but a choice must be made and it is pregnant with meaning. This is due to the fact that civilian protection from the catastrophic consequences of war is contingent on the enemy being able to tell civilians apart from combatants. If the lines separating civilians from combatants blur, there is a palpable risk that (to be on the safe side) the enemy will treat all persons encountered in or near the contact zone of military operations on land as if they were combatants, and then the "principle of distinction" will be swept aside. To preclude that eventuality, customary international

[26] See id., p. 926.

[27] See *R. Jennings/A. Watt* (eds.), Oppenheim's International Law, I, 9th ed., 1992, p. 165.

[28] On the phenomenon of "failed States", see *D. Thürer*, The 'Failed State' and International Law, 81 International Review of the Red Cross 1999, p. 731.

[29] See *R.R. Baxter*, So-Called 'Unprivileged Belligerency': Spies, Guerrillas, and Saboteurs, 28 BYBIL 1951, p. 323.

[30] Protocol I, supra n. 5, pp. 734-735.

law does not offer the option of being both a civilian (by day) and a combatant (by night). Any so-called civilian who takes a "direct" (or "active") part in hostilities, becomes *eo ipso* an unlawful combatant, that is to say, not only does he lose the status of a civilian but he fails to gain the status of an ordinary (lawful) combatant. The position of an unlawful combatant is not merely a stigma: it carries with it dire consequences entailing the loss of prisoner of war status. This dramatic reduction in entitlements, embedded in the seventh (present) distinction, is a severe sanction ensuing from the second distinction: it is imposed by customary international law in order to warrant observance of the "principle of distinction".

The distinction between lawful and unlawful combatants is relevant solely to international armed conflicts. In a non-international armed conflict, absent recognition of belligerence (which means that the conflict is governed by the same rules as those governing international armed conflicts), there is no entitlement to prisoners of war status in any case.

Customary international law is reflected in the pertinent provisions of the Geneva Conventions of 1949 (especially, Article 4A(2) of Geneva Convention (III)),[31] but it goes back to the Hague Regulations Respecting the Laws and Customs of War on Land of 1899/1907 (Article 1).[32] The Hague Regulations establish four cumulative conditions for qualifying as a lawful combatant (except in circumstances of "*levée en masse*"[33]):

a) Being commanded by a person responsible for his subordinates.
b) Having a fixed distinctive sign recognizable at a distance (paradigmatically, but not necessarily, a uniform).
c) Carrying arms openly.
d) Conducting operations in accordance with the laws and customs of war.

Article 4A(2) of Geneva Convention (III) confirms these four conditions. In effect, three additional (cumulative) conditions can be derived from its text:

e) Organization (arguably, another way of looking at Hague condition (a)).
f) Belonging to a party to the conflict.
g) Non-allegiance to the Detaining Power (a condition that came to light primarily by virtue of the 1967 Judgment of the Judicial Committee of the Privy Council in the *Koi* case[34]).

Although ostensibly – in keeping with the strict wording of the Hague and Geneva instruments – the conditions precedent to entitlement to the status of lawful combatants are confined to irregular troops, there is no doubt that in practice the same

---

31 Geneva Convention (III), supra n. 10, p. 513.

32 Hague Regulations Respecting the Laws and Customs of War on Land, Annexed to Hague Convention (II) of 1899 and Hague Convention (IV) of 1907, The Laws of Armed Conflicts, supra n. 5, pp. 55, 66.

33 On "levée en masse", see *Dinstein*, supra n. 6, p. 42.

34 Public Prosecutor v. Koi et al. (1967), [1968] Appeal Cases 829, 856-858.

conditions apply to regular troops (this is elucidated chiefly in the 1968 Privy Council *Mohamed Ali* case[35]).

The seven Geneva cumulative conditions – and even the more basic four cumulative conditions of The Hague – are not easy to satisfy in conditions of guerrilla warfare. Thus, paradoxically, the conditions are a better fit for regular troops (where the conditions are taken for granted by the texts) and a worse fit for irregular troops (to which the texts explicitly allude).

In the aftermath of World War II, attempts were made to alleviate the rigorous application of the seven conditions, for instance by turning conditions (b) and (c) (having a fixed distinctive emblem recognizable at a distance in addition to carrying one's arms openly) from cumulative to alternative requirements.[36] Unfortunately, the pendulum in Additional Protocol I has swung too far: instead of an alleviation of the conditions (which, in all likelihood, would have been met with unanimous approval), the decision fell in favour of their virtual elimination (in Article 44,[37] which is most controversial).

The seminal case in which the traditional law with respect to unlawful combatants was recapitulated is the *Quirin* Judgment of 1942, rendered unanimously by the Supreme Court of the United States (per Chief Justice *Stone*):

"By universal agreement and practice, the law of war draws a distinction between the armed forces and the peaceful populations of belligerent nations and also between those who are lawful and unlawful combatants. Lawful combatants are subject to capture and detention as prisoners of war by opposing military forces. Unlawful combatants are likewise subject to capture and detention, but in addition they are subject to trial and punishment by military tribunals for acts which render their belligerency unlawful".[38]

With the exception of the last few words, this is an accurate reflection of customary international law.

The gist of the *Quirin* decision is that, upon being captured by the enemy, an unlawful combatant – like a lawful combatant (and unlike a civilian) – is subject to detention by the enemy. The common denominator with lawful combatants (detained as prisoners of war) is that unlawful combatants may be incarcerated until the end of the armed conflict (there being no requirement to prove to the satisfaction of a court of law that they have committed any crime). Yet, in contradistinction to lawful combatants, unlawful combatants fail to benefit from the immense panoply of protection spread over prisoners of war pursuant to Geneva Convention (III). To fully grasp the enormity of the consequences, suffice it to compare the advantages of a regular prisoners of war camp with the conditions of detention prevailing in Guantanamo Bay. Obviously, the latter illustration is not

---

35 Mohamed Ali et al. v. Public Prosecutor (1968), [1969] Appeal Cases 430, 449-450.

36 See *Y. Dinstein*, Another Step in Codifying the Laws of War, 28 Year Book of World Affairs 1974, pp. 278, 284.

37 Protocol I, supra n. 5, pp. 732-733.

38 Ex parte Quirin et al. (1942), 317 United States 1, 30-31.

the sole possible model. Detention of unlawful combatants is also the subject of special legislation of Israel, passed by the Knesset in 2002.[39] This Detention of Unlawful Combatants Law defines an unlawful combatant as anyone taking part – directly or indirectly – in hostilities against the State of Israel, who is not entitled to a prisoner of war status under Geneva Convention (III).[40] Detention is based on the decision of the Chief of General Staff of the Israel Defence Forces, on grounds of State security, but it is subject to judicial review by a (civilian) District Court (both initially and every six months thereafter).[41] The Law emphasizes that detention is just one option, and that an unlawful combatant can equally be brought to trial under any criminal law.[42] An important point addressed by the Law is the maximum duration of the detention. An unlawful combatant can be held in detention as long as hostilities by the force to which he belongs have not been terminated.[43]

Although a captured unlawful combatant need not be put on trial at all, he is definitely susceptible to being prosecuted and punished by the domestic (civil or military) courts of the detaining State. What can he be prosecuted and punished for? The *Quirin* Judgment refers to trial and punishment "for acts which render their belligerency unlawful". It is true that sometimes the act that turns a person into an unlawful combatant constitutes by itself an offence (either a breach of domestic or a war crime under international law) and can be prosecuted and punished as such before a military tribunal. But the main feature of unlawful combatancy is that the judicial proceedings may be conducted – before (civil or military) domestic courts – in relation to acts other than those that divested the person of the status of lawful combatant. Even when the act negating the status of a lawful combatant does not constitute a crime *per se* (under either domestic or international law), it can expose the perpetrator to ordinary penal sanctions (pursuant to the domestic legal system) for any other act committed by him amounting to an ordinary crime under the local legal system. Unlawful combatants "may be punished under the internal criminal legislation of the adversary for having committed hostile acts in violation of its provisions (e.g., for murder), even if these acts do not constitute war crimes under international law".[44]

At bottom, warfare by its very nature consists of a series of acts of violence (like premeditated homicide, assault, battery and arson) commonly branded as criminal by the penal codes of all countries. When a combatant, John Doe, holds a rifle, aims it at Richard Roe (a soldier belonging to the enemy's armed forces) with an intent to kill, pulls the trigger, and causes Richard Roe's death, what we have is a premeditated homicide fitting the definition of murder in virtually all domestic penal codes. If, upon being captured by the enemy, John Doe is not

---

39 See Detention of Unlawful Combatants Law, 2002, 1834 Sefer Hahukim [Laws of the State of Israel, Hebrew] 192.

40 Id., (Section 2).

41 Id., (Sections 3, 5).

42 Id., 193 (Section 9).

43 Id., (Sections 7-8).

44 *A. Rosas*, The Legal Status of Prisoners of War: A Study in International Humanitarian Law Applicable in Armed Conflicts, 1976, p. 305.

prosecuted for murder, this is due to one reason only. The *jus in bello* provides John Doe with a legal shield, protecting him from trial and punishment, by conferring upon him the status of a prisoner of war. But the shield is not available unconditionally. If John Doe acts beyond the pale of lawful combatancy, the *jus in bello* removes the protective shield. Thereby, it subjects John Doe to the full rigor of the enemy's domestic legal system, and the ordinary penal sanctions provided by that law will become applicable to him.

It must be comprehended that an unlawful combatant does not necessarily act in breach of the *jus in bello* and is certainly not *per se* a war criminal. Being an unlawful combatant merely means that the person has not fulfilled certain conditions which are indispensable to the acquisition of qualification for the status (and privileges) of a prisoner of war. There are several differences between prosecution of war criminals and that of unlawful combatants.[45] The pivotal distinction is derived from the active or passive role of the *jus in bello*. War criminals are brought to trial for serious violations of the *jus in bello* itself. With unlawful combatants, the *jus in bello* refrains from branding the acts as criminal. It merely takes off a cloak of immunity from the defendant, who is therefore accessible to penal charges for any offence committed against the domestic legal system.

If an unlawful combatant does not enjoy the benefits of being an unlawful combatant, he is equally – and *a fortiori* – deprived of the benefits of civilian status. This is clearly conceded in Article 5 (first Paragraph) of Geneva Convention (IV), which specifically permits derogation from the rights of individuals "suspected of or engaged in activities hostile to the security of the State" (the derogation being less extensive in occupied territories, pursuant to the second Paragraph of Article 5).[46]

It goes without saying, perhaps, that losing the status of both a civilian and a lawful combatant does not mean that an unlawful combatant is placed beyond the ambit of the law. Even Article 5 (third Paragraph) mandates that "such persons shall nevertheless be treated with humanity and, in case of trial, shall not be deprived of the rights of fair and regular trial prescribed by the present Convention".[47] There are also certain minimum standards imposed by customary international law, which cannot be ignored. The majority of the International Court of Justice, in the *Nicaragua* case of 1986, held that "minimum rules applicable to international and to non-international conflicts" are expressed in the afore-mentioned common Article 3 of the Geneva Conventions.[48] Admittedly, the text of common Article 3 does not purport to be germane to armed conflicts of an international character. In his Dissenting Opinion, Judge *Jennings* commented that the majority's view of common Article 3 as a minimum yardstick "is not a matter free

45 See *Y. Dinstein*, The Distinction between Unlawful Combatants and War Criminals, in Y. Dinstein (ed.), International Law at a Time of Perplexity, Essays in Honour of Shabtai Rosenne, 1989, pp. 103-116.

46 Geneva Convention (IV), supra n. 20, p. 581.

47 Id., p. 582.

48 Case Concerning Military and Paramilitary Activities in and against Nicaragua (Merits), [1986] Reports of the International Court of Justice, pp. 14, 114.

from difficulty".[49] This is particularly true considering that the Court did not deem fit to produce any evidence for the conclusion that the provision reflects norms identically applicable to international and to non-international armed conflicts.[50] All the same, it can hardly be disputed that when common Article 3 prohibits "outrages upon personal dignity, in particular humiliating and degrading treatment", or establishes the need to afford in trial "all the judicial guarantees which are recognized as indispensable by civilized people",[51] the text reflects an irreducible minimum that no State is allowed to ratchet down even a notch in any armed conflict (whether international or non-international).

Fundamental guarantees to persons "who are in the power of a Party to the conflict and who do not benefit from more favourable treatment" are the subject of Article 75 of Additional Protocol I of 1977.[52] This provision is particularly important as regards unlawful combatants who are not entitled to the more favourable treatment of prisoners of war, and it is widely viewed as an expression of customary international law.[53]

Of course, the question whether a particular person actually is an unlawful combatant may be disputed. Article 5 (second Paragraph) of Geneva Convention (III) looks at the issue through the lens of doubt whether that person is entitled to a prisoner of war status (namely, is a lawful combatant):

"Should any doubt arise as to whether persons, having committed a belligerent act and having fallen into the hands of the enemy, belong to any of the categories enumerated in Article 4, such persons shall enjoy the protection of the present Convention until such time as their status has been determined by a competent tribunal".[54]

However, there is an important practical matter relating to the burden of proof. In the *Koi* case, the minority opined that the burden of proof lies on the defendant, who must show that he is entitled to a prisoner of war status.[55] The majority did not address the point. But the correct interpretation of the law in my opinion is that, if a defendant is a member of the enemy armed forces, the burden of proof that he is an unlawful combatant – not entitled to a prisoner of war status – falls on

---

49 Dissenting Opinion of Judge Jennings, id., pp. 528, 537.

50 See *T. Meron*, Human Rights and Humanitarian Norms as Customary International Law, 1989, pp. 36-37.

51 Geneva Convention (I) for the Amelioration of the Condition of the Wounded and Sick in Armed Forces in the Field, 1949, The Laws of Armed Conflicts, supra n. 5, pp. 459, 461-462; Geneva Convention (II) for the Amelioration of the Condition of Wounded, Sick and Shipwrecked Members of Armed Forces at Sea, 1949, id., pp. 485, 487-488; Geneva Convention (III), supra n. 10, pp. 512-513; Geneva Convention (IV), supra n. 20, pp. 580-581.

52 Protocol I, supra n. 5, pp. 748-750.

53 See *K. Dörmann*, The Legal Situation of 'Unlawful/Unprivileged Combatants', 85 International Review of the Red Cross 2003, pp. 45, 70.

54 Geneva Convention (III), supra n. 10, pp. 514-515.

55 *Koi* case, supra n. 34, p. 864.

the prosecution.[56] On the other hand, if the defendant is not a member of the enemy armed forces – and he was caught in an act indicating on the face of its active (or direct) participation in hostilities by a person feigning the status of a civilian – it is for him to bear the evidentiary onus that appearances in his case are deceptive.

56 See *R.R. Baxter*, The Privy Council on the Qualifications of Belligerents, 63 American Journal of International Law 1969, pp. 290, 293.

Collateral Damage, Proportionality and Individual International Criminal Responsibility

Torsten Stein

Director, Europa-Institute of the University of Saarland

I have to start with a warning: This is not really a comment on *Yoran Dinstein*'s paper, because he left certain aspects of his broad topic to the sole responsibility of the commentators, without touching them himself. Nor is this a comprehensive comment on *Stefan Oeter*'s paper[1], who rather extensively dealt with collateral damage in his comment on "asymmetries"; it serves at best as supplement. Collateral damage is neither symmetrical nor asymmetrical, unless used as a belligerent reprisal against civilians which is outlawed under current IHL because belligerent reprisals may not be directed against civilians or other non-combatants[2]. This is not to suggest that *Oeter*'s topic had nothing to do with collateral damage. He rightly deals with it under the heading that strong "classic" military powers might be (and obviously are) tempted to disregard IHL restraints in their fight against "asymmetric" enemies and thereby may create vast and disproportionate collateral damage[3]. The same is, by the way, true if "classical" military powers regard terrorism as "asymmetrical warfare" and conclude that the fight against terrorism is a "war against terror", a war that does not have to respect IHL, let alone all other guarantees under the rule of law. Lamentable examples of that attitude add up in recent times.

My approach is much more modest: I will try to show, and mostly by asking questions, that the assessment as admissible collateral damage under the principle of proportionality already poses a problem under "classic", i.e. "symmetric" circumstances. And I will try to elaborate that this problem becomes all the more relevant since we have established an international criminal responsibility of those accountable for disproportionate collateral damage.

It follows from Art. 51 (5) (b) of Protocol I Additional to the Geneva Conventions of 12 August 1949 relating to the Protection of Victims of International Armed Conflicts that collateral damage is not illegal as such and in any case; rather the doctrine of military necessity permits attacks that may cause collateral

---

1 See in this volume, at pp. 53 et seq.

2 Cf. *Stein/von Buttlar*, Völkerrecht, 11th edition, p. 496.

3 Cf. *Fidler*, The Use of White Phosphorus Munitions by U.S. Military Forces in Iraq, ASIL insight, at http://www.asil.org/insights/2005/12/insights051206.html, 6 December 2005.

damage, as long as they are imperative for the defeat of the enemy and the rule of proportionality is not breached.

As it is well known, the assessment of proportionality is not a truly new challenge in the field of humanitarian law applicable in armed conflicts. Quite on the contrary, it is a long standing rule of the law of war (the *ius in bello*) that any military action resorted to under international law must meet certain legal requirements, including necessity, proportionality and non-discrimination. Therefore, the principle of proportionality requires that military action must not be excessive in relation to the initial attack and to the action's objective. In addition, the principle of non-discrimination requires that civilians may not be attacked and that they not be disproportionately injured or killed by attacks on legitimate military targets. These preconditions are well-established rules and part of a number of multilateral treaties, part of international customary law and also part of many national military field manuals and rules of engagement. So far, so good, and agreed.

But still, it remains a permanent challenge to find out what actually is proportionate in a given case. If proportionality is today a general principle of international law (and many say it is)[4], the question still remains: "Proportionate in respect of what?"[5] And that question is valid also for the *ius in bello*. From the answer given to that question depends the amount of protection civilians will benefit from the principle according to which collateral damage may not be disproportionate. And the answer to the question "Was it actually proportionate"? will also adjudicate upon the individual disciplinary or criminal accountability of the military leader or soldier commanding or executing the military action in question in terms of individual responsibility under his national law as well as under the law of the adversary who took those responsible or acting as prisoners of war, and finally also under the Statute of the International Criminal Court[6]. Indeed, the latter may appear as the primary "new challenge" for those who are responsible for allegedly disproportionate collateral damage, because under Article 8 Sec. 2b iv) Rome Statute, it is considered as war crime to "... intentionally launching an attack in the knowledge that such attack will cause incidental loss of life or injury to civilians or damage to civilian objects or widespread, long-term and severe damage to the natural environment which would be clearly excessive in relation to the concrete and direct overall military advantage anticipated".

Interestingly, the explicit reference to "*overall* military advantage" seems to take into account interpretative declarations which a number of (mostly NATO) States have made with regard to Article 51 (5) (b) of Protocol Additional I to the Geneva Conventions of 12 August 1949 (relating to the Protection of Victims of International Armed Conflicts), hereby intending to reserve their margin of appre-

---

[4] Cf. only *Delbrück*, Proportionality, in: Bernhardt (ed.), Encyclopedia of Public International Law, Vol. III, 1997, pp. 1140 et. seq.

[5] Cf. *Higgins*, Problems and Process: International Law and How We Use it, 1994, pp. 218 et. seq. (236).

[6] Cf. *Stein*, Zur international-strafrechtlichen Verantwortung des Befehlshabers einer multinationalen Streitmacht, in: Verhandeln für den Frieden (Liber amicorum Tono Eitel), 2003, pp. 449 et. seq.

ciation as to the scale of military advantage and thus its relation to the scale of (still) acceptable collateral damage[7].

However, even if – for the sake of argument – we do accept such a margin of appreciation, there still remains a set of open questions as to the principle of proportionality in terms of admissible collateral damage:

- What are (precisely) the relative values to be assigned to the envisaged military advantage and the injury to non-combatants respectively? Is there a generally accepted standard for the classification of targets as being purely military, or of dual use, or exclusively civilian? As a matter of fact, it seems rather impossible to assure such a clear-cut division. Let us only try to rank the broadcasting station that was attacked during Operation "Allied Force": If it was destroyed because it spread "hold out" propaganda among the civilian population, then the attack was certainly illegal; but if it was attacked because there was evidence that it was also used to send disguised messages to the troops (because military communication systems had been destroyed), the fact that civilians where killed who operated that station would appear acceptable as collateral damage[8].
- What benchmark do you assign to a total of sums? Are we willing to accept 100 or more dead civilians working in or close to a munitions factory, but only a maximum of 20 in the vicinity of a lesser important military target, as it seemed to have been the rule during NATO's operation "Allied Force"?
- What benchmark do we fix for our troops? To what extent is a military commander obliged to expose his own forces to danger in order to limit (collateral) civilian casualties? NATO has been criticized for flying attacks during "Allied Force" above 15.000 ft, too high for pilots to assess possible collateral damage, or to stop the attack if disproportionate collateral damage became a so far unexpected possibility. We do remember the attack on "the bridge and the train". Now could commanders be obliged to carry out attacks at night, when no or only few civilians are around, while the risk of own casualties grows? And would that have to lead to the renouncement of attacks on important (dual use-) targets? On the one hand such a consequence seems simply unacceptable. On the other hand, taking the principle of distinction literally, the intention to reduce the risk for one's own troops shall never be realized on the backs of civilians or other non-combatants.
- These questions clearly provoke additional questions. To limit myself here, I will only mention one more striking problem: Will proportionality considerations have to take into account that intelligence information might not be cor-

[7] These interpretative declarations are listed at *Roberts/Guelff* (eds.), Documents on the Laws of War, 3rd edition, 2003, pp. 500 et. seq. For more detail compare *Stein*, Coalition Warfare and Differing Legal Obligations of Coalition Members Under International Humanitarian Law, in: Wall (ed.), Legal and Ethical Lessons of NATO's Kosovo Campaign, U.S. Naval War College, International Law Studies, 78 (2002), pp. 315, 321.

[8] Compare Banković and Others vs. Belgium and 16 Other Contracting States, Application No. 52207/99, European Court of Human Rights, 12 December 2001.

rect as to the nature of the target[9], or that appropriate weapons are at hand, but others would inflict less casualties, however being less reliable? And how do we have to calculate if the other side appears to use civilians as voluntary or involuntary "*human shields*"? Indeed, the distinction between precision-guided weapons and less smart ones serve as another striking example for the fact that there is no place for a general overarching rule in terms of what is proportionate in a given case. If a commander does dispose of smart weapons the use of which would reduce collateral damage, the decision not to use them (e.g. in order to save money) would have to be considered as disproportionate. But if he does not dispose of smart weapons, then the order to launch lesser precise ones would not be disproportionate. It is easy to finally add the notorious grey-zone scenario: How do we proceed if the commander could deploy precision-guided weapons but they are two days away from the theatre? Would he then be justified to use less accurate weapons if the military advantage of the moment would be lost in the meantime?

As a conclusion, it remains to be said, that the principle of proportionality is a difficult concept already in general international law[10], and all the more with regard to the law of war. In the principle is more easily stated than applied in practice. Not in every armed conflict do military commanders enjoy the time for due consideration as exemplified by NATO decision makers during the Kosovo campaign, discussing possible targets among 19 Ambassadors and giving up a target if only one Ambassador disagreed. And even then errors where committed by those executing the orders so carefully given. Under other circumstances, cases will most likely occur in which members of a force will not be able to make such cool calculations in the heat of the moment.

Finally, could it be said months or years later, and far away from the theatre, that a military action was not proportionate? Any tribunal scrutinizing the case retrospectively under the regime of the proportionality principle would have to assess the importance of the target in relation to the collateral damage expected. But it would also have to take into consideration the risk to own forces, and it would therefore have to put itself as best as it can in the position of the commander or soldier concerned, taking all the surrounding circumstances into account, so as to appraise the situation as experienced in real time, before considering the question of culpability. How many judges would be in a position to do that? Would any proper judgment demand that they had witnessed similar situations in place?

All these questions are qualified to cast doubt on clear cut legal judgments in the first place. However, the fact that Article 8 Sec. 2(b) Rome Statute uses the term "clearly excessive" might ensure that the Court would consider only cases in which the excessiveness of collateral damage was obvious and intended, and not

---

9 NATO always maintained that is was not aware that the building attacked in Belgrade was the Chinese Embassy, although it is difficult to imagine that the Chinese Embassy and its communications were not closely monitored during those days.

10 Cf. *Stein*, Proportionality revisited, in: Weltinnenrecht (Liber amicorum Jost Delbrück), 2005, pp. 727 et. seq.

those that involved errors of judgment by the commanders or soldiers in the field. In this respect, the report to the Prosecutor of the ICTY on "Operation Allied Force", though criticized, seems to strike a rather fair balance between normative constraints and the actual decision making situation[11].

But it may also turn out that proportionality with respect to collateral damage provides only little protection for civilians and non-combatants, while at the same time posing a considerable (individual) risk for those commanding or executing military operations.

[11] Compare the Final Report to the Prosecutor by the Committee Established to Review the NATO Bombing Campaign against the Federal Republic of Yugoslavia, ILM 39 (2000), pp. 1257 et seq. For more detail see *Fenrick*, The Law Applicable to Targeting and Proportionality after Operation Allied Force: a View from the Outside, YIHL 3 (2000), pp. 53 et seq.

Do Non-State Actors Challenge International Humanitarian Law?

Hans-Joachim Heintze

Institute for International Law of Peace and Armed Conflict, Ruhr-University Bochum

Undoubtedly, globalization has a major impact on the structure of international law and, thus; experts are convinced that this body of law is in a period of very radical transformation. To cite a few, one of these significant developments is the decline of the nation-state in the late twentieth century[1] and the rise of non-state actors as subjects of international law.[2] Non-state actors can be defined as any actor other than a sovereign state, thereby including NGOs and even individuals, involved in international affairs. In principle this development has been welcomed by the great majority of legal authors as a contribution to the democratization process in international matters. Generally, the legal status of non-state actors is determined by domestic law. So, according to the International Court of Justice (ICJ) judgment in the *Barcelona Traction*[3] case corporations have the "nationality" of the place of incorporation. The same can be said of non-state actors that are constituted under the law of a particular state. As a result, even in connection with non-state actors one can speak of the pre-eminence of the state. Yet, gradually the prominence of the non-state actors strongly challenges the power of states. Further, one realizes that private, non-state power can be as problematic as public power.[4] Therefore ECOSOC-Resolution 1296 required NGOs to adopt a democratic constitution and policy.[5] Hence, undemocratic and other criminal organizations that use violence to achieve their goals cannot be granted legal recognition as international actors.

---

1 *O. Schachter*, The Decline of the Nation-States and Its Implications for International Law, Columbia Journal of Transnational Law 36 (1997), pp. 8 et seq.

2 *J. Delbrück*, Opening Address, in: R. Hofmann (ed.), Non-State Actors as New Subjects of International Law, Berlin 1999, p. 13.

3 Barcelona Traction, Light and Power Company, Limited (Belg. v. Spain), I.C.J. Reports, The Hague 1970. pp. 42 et seq.

4 *R. Wedgwood*, Legal Personality and the Role of Non-Governmental Organizations and Non-State Entities in the United Nations System, in: R. Hofmann (ed.), Non-State Actors as New Subjects of International Law, Berlin 1999, p. 22.

5 In: UN Doc. E/4548.

Non-state actors and international humanitarian law

Whereas the development of a certain legal status of non-state actors in general international law may be seen as a positive one the appearance of non-state actors in connection with armed conflicts is a more worrying one.[6] For, international law is then confronted with armed opposition groups fighting administrations, governments and/or each other. Although very often the legal status of such groups is considered as doubtful, from a strictly international law viewpoint one must in principle consider these conflicts as of non-international nature. Consequently, Article 3 GC is applicable inasmuch as the Parties to a conflict in the sense of common Article 3 include not only governmental armed forces and insurgents, but also non-governmental armed groups fighting against each other.[7]

Although these groups are not contracting parties to the Conventions, they fall within its scope because both the State and its nationals under its jurisdiction are bound by it.[8] An example of such a binding force is Article 4 of the Optional Protocol to the Convention on the Rights of the Child on the involvement of children in armed conflict of 25 May 2000:[9]

1. Armed groups that are distinct from the armed forces of a State should not, under any circumstances, recruit or use in hostilities persons under the age of 18 years.
2. State Parties shall take all feasible measures to prevent such recruitment and use, including the adoption of legal measures necessary to prohibit and criminalize such practices.
3. The application of the present article shall not affect the legal status of any party to an armed conflict.

This article clearly underlines the responsibility of a State for all entities under its jurisdiction. Further, as means to implement this obligation States must pass laws criminalizing the recruitment or use of children under 18 years by non-state actors. International law works as an incentive for States to fulfil their obligations resulting out of their own sovereignty. Even in non-international armed conflicts the State may, for practical reasons, take into consideration the insurgency, in which case Article 3 GC is applicable. Within those states which have ratified Additional Protocol II insurgents are also governed by the protocol regulations. Yet, the application threshold is rather high because non-state actors must, among other re-

6 *J. Kellenberger*, International Humanitarian Law at the Beginning of the 21st Century, Address to 26th Roundtable on Current Problems of International Humanitarian Law, San Remo, 5 September 2002.

7 See *G. de Beco*, Compliance with International Humanitarian Law by Non-State Actors, in: Humanitäres Völkerrecht – Informationsschriften 18 (2005), pp. 190 et seq.

8 *L. Moir*, The Law of Internal Armed Conflict, Cambridge 2002, p. 53.

9 See *D. Capie/P. Policze*, 'Keeping the Promise of Protection: Holding Armed Groups to the Same Standard as States', The Armed Groups Project, University of British Columbia 2004, p. 2.

quirements, be *de facto* rulers in a state-like entity and hence able to implement the obligations of the protocol. Nevertheless, the status of non-state actors is not compatible with that of combatants so that they may be treated as insurgents and, therefore, be punished for participating in the hostilities,[10] which means that they are not entitled to the prisoners of war status. Moreover, if they violate norms of international humanitarian law they can be prosecuted by international criminal tribunals on the basis of individual liability.[11]

The acquirement of a certain legal status under international law may be an incentive for non-state actors to comply with the law even though they have never ratified any treaty. The insurgents are bound by the obligations of the state even when they are trying to bring down the government,[12] but they are on the other hand protected by the rules of IHL. However, the principle of reciprocity cannot be applied.[13]

Non-state actors and terrorism

In principle, terrorists are subjected to national criminal law.[14] Before September 11 this was also true for terrorist groups which used significant and sustained armed violence. However, already before September 11, it became clear that global non-state terrorist organizations existed. For example, the Security Council already decided in 1999, by way of Resolution 1267 (1999), to establish a Committee supervising the implementation by States of the sanctions imposed by the Security Council on individuals and entities belonging or related to the Taliban, Bin Laden and the Al-Qaida organization.

For this purpose the Committee keeps four different lists of individuals or entities associated with terrorist organizations. The names and identity information on the lists were submitted by UN Member States. After September 11 the anti-terrorism mechanism was supplemented by the Counter-Terrorism Committee (CTC) established by the Security Council according to Resolution 1373 (2001). The Committee consists of all fifteen members of the Security Council and monitors the implementation of Resolution 1373 by all States. As the aim is to increase the capability of States to fight terrorism, the Committee is entitled to use all relevant information which it may gather from States as well as any other sources.

---

10 *D. Matas*, Armed Opposition Groups, Manitoba Law Journal 24 (1997), p. 67.

11 The Prosecutor v. Dusko Tadic, Interlocutory Appeal on Jurisdiction, IT-94-1-AR72, 2 October 1995. See: *C. Greenwood*, International Humanitarian Law and the *Tadic* Case, in: European Journal of International Law 7 (1996), pp. 277 et seq.

12 *J.-M. Henckaerts*, Binding Armed Opposition Groups through Humanitarian Treaty Law and Customary Law, in: Proceedings of the Bruges Colloquium 2002, p. 127.

13 *L. Zegveld*, Accountability of Armed Opposition Groups in International Law, Cambridge 2002, p. 17.

14 See *M.E. O'Connell*, Ad Hoc War, in: H. Fischer et al. (eds.), Krisensicherung und Humanitärer Schutz – Crisis Management and Humanitarian Protection, Berlin 2004, p. 407.

Self-defence against non-state actors?

According to the principle of State responsibility a State is internationally liable for conduct in breach of its international obligations. This may be the case for acts which are directly imputable to it or for acts of private individuals, whether nationals, or aliens in the state's territory. As a result a State is obliged to take certain preventive measures, notably concerning terrorism, i.e. the State has to prevent international terrorist acts from being planned, organized or executed from within its territory or jurisdiction. In case of State responsibility, a severe act of violence by a state could be considered as an armed attack, giving rise to the right of self-defence by the victim state under Article 51 of the United Nations Charter. Under those circumstances the State is found to be legally responsible for the actions of a non-state actor.[15] However, the problem arises that non-state actors very often act internationally, i.e. that an act of terrorism is planned in one state by a group headquartered in a second state, and directed against objects in a third state by terrorists recruited in a fourth State and executed with weapons bought in a fifth State. *Stahn* argues that the Victim State has under those conditions a choice of five types of forcible response: "Military action against terrorist bases *in* another state; Military action *against* another state involved with terrorist actors; the rescue of nationals abroad; the forcible abduction of terrorists; and the killing of terrorists in another territory."[16] In practice in all of these situations armed attacks were justified as self-defence falling within the purview of Article 51. However, not all actions taken by states in so-called self-defence have been accepted by the State community. Obviously states as well as international lawyers are confronted with a significant legal gray area concerning the evaluation of terrorist attacks by non-state actors. One can argue that Article 51 may be read as a non-state centred norm today which contains the risk of uncertainty and indeterminacy.[17] One of the reasons for the general confusion has inevitably been the declaration of the 'global war on terrorism' by President Bush soon after September 11.

The global war on terrorism and non-state actors

After September 11, 2001, President *Bush* declared the United States to be involved in a global war on terrorism, which would "not end until every terrorist group of global reach has been found, stopped and defeated."[18] National Security

---

15 *M.E. O'Connell*, Enhancing the Status of Non-State Actors Through a Global War on Terror?, in: Columbia Journal of Transnational Law 43 (2005), p. 450.

16 *C. Stahn*, "Nicaragua is dead, long live Nicaragua" – the Right to Self-defence Under Art. 51 UN Charter and International Terrorism, in: C. Walter et al. (eds.), Terrorism as a Challenge for National and International Law: Security versus Liberty?, Berlin 2004, p. 862.

17 Supra n. 13, p. 876.

18 See President's Address to the Nation on the Terrorist Attacks, Sept. 11, 2001; available at www.whitehouse.gov.

Adviser *Condoleezza Rice* considered the global war on terror as a "new kind of war" to be fought on "different battlefields."[19] Leading officials of the Department of Defense explained that the existence of the "war" depends on the person targeted, not the existence of armed hostilities.[20] Accordingly, members of terrorist groups became "combatants". This classification is not only generally inconsistent with international law but has also unintended consequences for non-state actors. Generally, governments prefer to refrain from treating insurgents and terrorists as subjects of IHL, and choose to regard them as criminals. Therefore they do not consider the hostilities between their armed forces and non-state actors as armed conflicts and, subsequently, avoid granting non-state actors any sort of legitimacy[21] and the applicability of common Article 3. It is remarkable to note that in the past the USA refused to become a party to the 1977 Additional Protocol I to the 1949 Geneva Conventions on the basis that it endowed national liberation movements with the *de facto* status of a state and, accordingly, granted liberation fighters the status of combatants. In this vein, to grant combatant status to irregular forces even when they do not satisfy the traditional requirements would endanger civilians among whom terrorists and other irregulars attempt to conceal themselves.[22]

The characterization of terrorists as combatants, even as "unlawful combatants", is misleading because "the law of war draws a distinction between the armed forces and the peaceful populations of belligerent nations and also between those who are lawful and unlawful combatants."[23] Furthermore the status of "unlawful combatant" is unacceptable because it is not one of the categories envisaged by international humanitarian law.[24] An "unlawful combatant" would therefore be placed outside the regime of international humanitarian law, and hence be unprotected by that body of law. The correct position is that if a person is not a combatant in the sense of the Geneva Conventions, then he/she is a civilian subject to international criminal law and entitled to the protection of international human rights law.[25]

In the light of the confusion created by the term "unlawful combatant" and the fact that over 600 persons, who allegedly fought on the Taliban side and were taken by the US forces to Guantanamo and other prisons, one cannot support *Din-*

---

19 Quoted after *M.E. O'Connell*, supra n. 12, p. 543.

20 See *Anthony Dworkin*, Law and the Campaign Against Terrorism: The View from the Pentagon, Crimes of War Project, available at www.crimesofwar.org/print/onnews/pentagon-print.html.

21 ICRC Expert Seminars, 'Improving compliance with IHL', Report prepared by the ICRC, 10 October 2003, p. 20.

22 See *H.P. Gasser*, An Appeal for Ratification by the United States, in: American Journal of International Law 81 (1987), p. 912.

23 See the decision of the US Supreme Court in Ex parte Quirin (1942) in: J. Wieczorek, Unrechtmäßige Kombattanten und humanitäres Völkerrecht, Berlin 2005, p. 35.

24 See *K. Ipsen*, Kombattanten und Nichtkombattanten, in: D. Fleck (ed.), Handbuch des humanitären Völkerrechts in bewaffneten Konflikten, München 1994, pp. 56 et seq.

25 *B.G. Ramcharan*, Terrorism and Non-state Organizations, in: R. S. J. Macdonald/D. M. Johnston (eds.), Towards World Constitutionalism, Leiden 2005, p. 700.

stein's statement that "the term 'war on terrorism' is only a metaphor."[26] However, *Dinstein* rightly argues "that the law of the UN Charter is much clearer than most international lawyers give it credit for at this point in time."[27] Yet, this is not only true for the UN Charter but also for IHL. Therefore one can only agree with O'Connell: "Terrorism, in all its forms, must be de-legitimized. It must be disassociated from any lawful objective, such as the right of self-determination or freedom from military occupation. The United States would have been far better served if it had declared 'global law enforcement' instead of 'global war' after September 11. A far better approach would have been fostering healthy states through the principle of non-intervention, the prohibition on force, respect for proportionality in the use of coercion, and promotion of human rights."[28]

---

[26] *Y. Dinstein*, Comments on the Presentations by Nico Krisch and Carsten Stahn, in: C. Walter et al. (eds.), Terrorism as a Challenge for National and International Law: Security versus Liberty?, supra n. 15, p. 919

[27] Supra n. 25, p. 923.

[28] *O'Connell*, supra n. 14, p. 457.

The Relationship between Individual and State Responsibility

Individual and State Responsibility for Violations of the Ius in Bello: An Imperfect Balance

Dieter Fleck

Former Director of the International Legal Affairs Department,
German Federal Ministry of Defence

A. Introduction

The responsibility for violations is the key to any meaningful discussion on international humanitarian law. The topics to be dealt with are complex, as their offer an opportunity to revisit quite encouraging progress made in the field of individual (criminal) responsibility[1], and some even more important, but much slower progressing developments on the international responsibility of states[2], international

---

1 While national courts still have a dominant role to fulfil, international criminal tribunals, such as the International Criminal Tribunal for the former Yugoslavia (ICTY), established under SC Res 827 (25 May 1993) [www.un.org/icty], the International Criminal Tribunal for Rwanda (ICTR), established under SC Res 955 (8 November 1994) [www.ictr.org], the Special Court for Sierra Leone, established under the Agreement between the United Nations and Sierra Leone on the Establishment of the Special Court for Sierra Leone and Statute of 16 January 2002 [www.sierra-leone.org/specialcourtagreement.html], the Special Court for Cambodia [www.globalpolicy.org/intljustice/camindx.htm] and the International Criminal Court (ICC) [www.un.org/ law/icc/ statute, www.iccnow.org] have strengthened public awareness of the importance of individual justice for stabilising peace and security.

2 See e.g. *T. Kamenov*, The origin of state and entity responsibility for violations of international humanitarian law in armed conflicts, in: F. Kalshoven/Y. Sandoz (eds.), Implementation of International Humanitarian Law, Dordrecht et al., Martinus Nijhoff Publishers, 1989, pp. 168-227; *F. Kalshoven*, State responsibility for warlike acts of the armed forces, 40 International and Comparative Law Quarterly, 1991, pp. 847-848; *A. Randelzhofer*/*Chr. Tomuschat* (eds.), State Responsibility and the Individual. Reparation in Instances of Grave Violations of Human Rights, The Hague/London/Boston, Martinus Nijhoff Publishers, 1999; *F. Kalshoven*, The Undertaking to Respect and Ensure Respect in All Circumstances: From Tiny Seed to Ripening Fruit, 2 YIHL (1999), pp. 3-61; *D. Shelton*, Remedies in International Human Rights Law, Oxford University Press, Oxford, 1999; *D. Shelton* (ed.), Commitment and Compliance. The Role of Non-Binding Norms in the International Legal System, Oxford University Press, Oxford, 2000; *A. McDonald*, Rights to legal remedies for victims of serious violations of interntional humanitarian law, Ph.D. thesis, The Queen's University of Belfast, 2002 (unpublished); *W. Heintschel v. Heinegg*, Entschädigung für Verletzungen des humanitären

organisations[3], and armed opposition groups[4]. But still today international responsibility for wrongful acts in armed conflicts is often neglected and sometimes even not existing. As *Knut Ipsen* has stated in his textbook, internationally wrongful acts are subject to individual criminal responsibility, but not in each single case of wrongful personal conduct is responsibility of states or international organisations involved[5]. State responsibility has been reaffirmed and further developed by the International Law Commission's Draft Articles on the Responsibility of States for Internationally Wrongful Acts (DARS)[6], without affecting the *lex specialis* character of relevant provisions of humanitarian law[7]. The possible impact the ILC's Draft Articles might have on better respect for international humanitarian law in armed conflicts should not be overestimated, especially not when compared to the preventive and repressive mechanisms directed at individuals under the law already existing. But the Draft Articles do underline that states 'are not allowed to hide behind the smoke-screen labels of "globalization", "failed States" or "uncontrolled elements"' and they clarify what states should do[8]. Similar guidance may

Völkerrechts, and *St. Kadelbach*, Staatenverantwortlichkeit für Angriffskriege und Verbrechen gegen die Menschlichkeit, in: Heintschel von Heinegg/Kadelbach/ Heß/Hilf/ Benedek/Roth (eds.), Entschädigung nach bewaffneten Konflikten – Die Konstitutionalisierung der Welthandelsordnung [with English Summary], Berichte der Deutschen Gesellschaft für Völkerrecht, 27. Tagung in Frankfurt am Main vom 14. bis 17. März 2001, Band 40, Heidelberg, Verlag C.F. Müller, 2003, pp. 1-61, 63-105; *P. d'Argent*, Les réparations de guerre en droit international public: la responsabilité internationale des Etats à l'épreuve de la guerre, Bruylant, Bruxelles, 2002; *L. Zegveld*, Remedies for victims of violations of international humanitarian law, 85 (No. 851) IRRC (2003), pp. 497-527; *E.-C. Gillard*, Reparations for violations of international humanitarian law, 85 (No. 851) IRRC (2003), pp. 529-553.

3 See e.g. *I. Seidl-Hohenveldern/G. Loibl*, Das Recht der internationalen Organisationen einschließlich der supranationalen Gemeinschaften, 7. Auflage, Köln/Berlin, Carl Heymanns Verlag, 2000, paras. 0327, 0703-0709; Final Report of the Committee on Accountability of International Organisations, Recommended Rules and Practices, in: The International Law Association, Report of the Seventy-first Conference (Berlin, 16-21 August 2004), London, 2004, 164-241.

4 See *L. Zegveld*, Accountability of Armed Opposition Groups in International Law, Cambridge, Cambridge University Press, 2002.

5 *K. Ipsen*, Völkerrecht, 5th ed., München, C.H. Beck Verlag, 2004, p. 616.

6 Draft Articles on Responsibility of States for Internationally Wrongful Acts (DARS), United Nations, International Law Commission, Report on the Work of its Fifty-third Session (23 April-1 June and 2 July-10 August2001), General Assembly, Official Records, Fifty-fifth Session, Supplement No. 10 (A/56/10), http://www.un.org/law/ilc/ reports/2001/2001report.htm, U.N.doc. A/56/10; *J. Crawford*, The International Law Commission's Articles on State Responsibility, Cambridge University Press, Cambridge, 2002.

7 See Art. 55 DARS.

8 *M. Sassòli*, State responsibility for violations of international humanitarian law, 84 IRRC June 2002, No. 846, pp. 401-434 [433].

be expected from the ILC's forthcoming Draft Articles on the Responsibility of International Organizations[9].

It is not only the *lex specialis* character of international humanitarian law, but even more so the particular deficiencies of law application in international armed conflicts, non-international armed conflicts and internal disturbances which makes the exercise of individual and international responsibility a complex, difficult and often hopeless task. Lawyers, tasked to find appropriate remedies for violations of international humanitarian law, are navigating in foggy areas in which relevant provisions are not too systematic and more than often competing interests obscure what should be achieved for restoring peace and justice.

For international armed conflicts, Article 3 of the 1907 Hague Convention IV[10], reaffirmed by Article 91 of the 1977 Additional Protocol[11], provides that states are responsible for paying compensation for unlawful acts committed by their armed forces. The duty to make reparation for violations of international humanitarian law is explicitly referred to in the 1999 Second Protocol to the Hague Convention for the Protection of Cultural Property[12]. But despite courageous efforts undertaken in particular before the Tokyo District Court[13], there is still little room after armed conflicts or robust peace operations for individual claims against states, international organizations or even armed opposition groups. International responsibility of states for wounded and shipwrecked, prisoners of war and uncounted civilians is confirmed in the 1949 Geneva Conventions which underline that no state

---

9 United Nations, International Law Commission, Report on the work of its fifty-sixth session (3 May to 4 June and 5 July to 6 August 2004), General Assembly, Official Records, Fifty-ninth Session, Supplement N°. 10 (A/59/10), Chapter V: Responsibility of International Organizations (Special Rapporteur: Mr. *Giorgio Gaja*); Third Report on responsibility of international organizations, UN-Doc A/CN.4/553 (13 May 2005), www.un.org/law/ilc/sessions/57/57sess.htm.

10 1907 Hague Convention IV Respecting the Laws and Customs of War on Land [www.cicr.org/ihl]; reprinted in *A. Roberts/R. Guelff* (eds.), Documents on the Laws of War, 3rd edition, Oxford, Oxford University Press, 2000, p. 73. Article 3: "A belligerent party which violates the provisions of the said Regulations shall, if the case demands, be liable to pay compensation. It shall be responsible for all acts committed by persons forming part of its armed forces."

11 1977 Geneva Protocol I Additional to the Geneva Conventions of 12 August 1949, and Relating to the Protection of Victims of International Armed Conflicts, Article 91: "A Party to a conflict which violates the provisions of the Conventions or of this Protocol shall, if the case demands, be liable to pay compensation. It shall be responsible for all acts committed by persons forming part of its armed forces."

12 1999 Second Protocol to the Hague Convention of 1954 for the Protection of Cultural Property in the Event of Armed Conflict [www.cicr.org/ihl]; reprinted in *A. Roberts/R. Guelff* (eds.), Documents on the Laws of War, 3rd edition, Oxford, Oxford University Press, 2000, p. 698; Article 38: "No provision in this Protocol relating to individual criminal responsibility shall affect the responsibility of States under international law, including the duty to provide reparation."

13 See expert opinions by *F. Kalshoven*, *E. David* and *Chr. Greenwood* in: H. Fujita/I. Suzuki/K. Nagano (eds.), War and the Right of Individuals. Renaissance of Individual Compensation, Tokyo, Nippon Hyoron-sha Co., 1999, pp. 31-48, 49-58 and 59-71.

party to an armed conflict "shall be allowed to absolve itself … of any liability … in respect of [grave] breaches" of the Conventions.[14] But this provision does not exclude the possibility (which so often is a necessity) to postpone or limit the settlement of claims in peace treaties. There are notorious difficulties for individual victims to obtain redress.

The applicability of human rights in armed conflicts is commonplace today and human rights mechanisms are serving this purpose in a forthcoming manner. Yet the settlement of claims for wrongful acts committed in wartime is widely excluded by an inability of states and societies to restore economic welfare and security, and efforts to bring redress to victims remain subject to controversial interpretations of international responsibility and its practical effects. States, groups and individuals are escaping their responsibility for making full reparation to victims. There is a constant tendency in practice, trying to put the law into oblivion. In almost every case full settlement of atrocities committed in armed conflicts or internal disturbances is quite impossible. A spiral of claims and counterclaims would severely jeopardise any effort for post-conflict peace building, as neither the perpetrators nor the (new) government would be in a position to pay full compensation. Balanced solutions could hardly be found on the basis of individual reparation claims and the question which judicial system should govern such claims remains highly debatable[15].

While in most post-conflict situations today the right to reparation fully rests within municipal legal orders and no other means of enforcement are available except under national law, an international legal regime of reparations to be made by responsible states could support the peace process even if no more than symbolic payments can be offered. International efforts to strengthen the law of reparations could support democratic developments and also have deterrent effects for some perpetrators[16]. Hence new initiatives, centred now in the new ILA Committee on Compensation for Victims of War[17], deserve particular attention. Indeed, immate-

---

14 Arts. 51 GC I, 52 GC II, 12, 57, 131 GC III, 29, 148 GC IV.

15 *Chr. Tomuschat*, Reparations for Victims of Grave Human Rights Violations, in: Tulane Journal of International and Comparative Law, Vol. 10 (Spring 2002), pp. 157-84.

16 See *L. Fernandez*, Reparation for Human Rights Violations Committed by the Apartheid Regime in South Africa, in: A. Randelzhofer/Chr. Tomuschat (eds.), State Responsibility and the Individual: Reparation in Instances of Grave Violations of Human Rights, The Hague/London/Boston, Martinus Nijhoff Publishers, 1999, pp. 173-87; *Guatemala Memoria des Silencio* (Informe de la Comisión para el Esclarecimiento Histórico 1999 (12 volumes), see *Chr. Tomuschat*, Clarification Commission in Guatemala, in: Human Rights Quarterly 23 (2001), pp. 233-258.

17 The International Law Association has established a new Committee on Compensation for Victims of War (chair: *Dr Luke T Lee*, American Branch, rapporteurs: Professor *Rainer Hofmann*, German Branch and Professor *Shuichi Furuya*, Japanese Branch. The Mandate is as follows: "Innocent civilians are often casualties during armed conflicts, whether or not intentionally targeted. Deprived of effective protection, they are often left without any remedy if they are killed or wounded, or suffer property or other losses. It is time to systematically review the law of war and human rights with a view to focussing on the rights of victims of war to compensation – both to serve the end of justice and to inhibit wanton attack on civilian population by the military, whether or not

rial measures including the recognition of facts and responsibilities are not less important than material reparations. As experience with truth commissions has shown, a mechanism for establishing facts in individual cases may be essential for post-conflict peace building. In this context individual rights (and duties) should be promoted under international law independently from rights and duties of the particular home state which should exercise its responsibility for the victims. Too many examples of unsolved cases in the recent decades make it questionable to trust in the wisdom of national governments and continue as before.

This contribution will focus on the following questions:

1. Has the progressive development of national and international criminal jurisdiction on the crime of genocide, crimes against humanity, and war crimes during the last decade led to a full perception of individual accountability with respect to acts and omissions and of command responsibility for such acts?
2. Is the responsibility of states for violations of the *ius in bello* sufficiently regulated? What measures are required to make reparation for victims of armed conflict more effective?
3. Is there a collective responsibility of armed opposition groups in non-international armed conflicts?
4. Is state responsibility adequately mirrored today by the responsibility of transnational corporations?
5. What perspectives may be envisaged for the law of reparations? What are the prerequisites for individual claims to be accepted and adjudicated?

After a brief discussion of the larger context of individual and international responsibility within remedies to ensure compliance with international humanitarian law (B), the extent of individual responsibility and its enforcement during and after armed conflicts will be addressed (C). Critical issues of international responsibility of states and international organisations will be examined both *de lege lata* and *de lege ferenda* (D). In addition, problems of international responsibility of non-state entities will be assessed (E). Summarising statements are included at the end of each Section in Parts B-E. Finally, some conclusions will be drawn (F).

under superior order. The proposed project would have as its goal the preparation and adoption of a Draft Declaration of International Law Principles on Compensation to Victims of War, as a logical sequel to three ILA declarations already adopted: namely, on Mass Expulsion (Seoul 1986), Compensation to Refugees (Cairo 1992), and Internally Displaced Persons (London 2000). Underlying all these declarations is the principle that compensation must, under international law, be paid to victims of human rights abuses." First background reports prepared by *R. Hofmann*, *F. Riemann* and *S. Furuya* are available at http://www.ila-hq.org/html/layout_committee.htm.

B. The Larger Context of Remedies to Ensure Compliance with International Humanitarian Law

1. Rudimentary Efforts to Improve Individual and International Responsibility

The absence of a central enforcement body within the international system has positive and negative effects. It allows states and national organisations to develop interpretations and implementation practices according to their particular needs. Appropriate international reaction to breaches of humanitarian law is, however, not automatically ensured and also at the national level sanctions against violations are often far from being taken.

Considering this imperfect situation in a realistic manner, the German Manual on Humanitarian Law in Armed Conflicts[18] had devoted its last chapter to a description of the following factors which can induce the parties to a conflict to counteract disobedience of the law of armed conflict and thus enforce observance of its rules: consideration for public opinion; reciprocal interests of the parties to the conflict; maintenance of discipline; fear of reprisals; penal and disciplinary measures; fear of payment of compensation; activities of protecting powers; international fact-finding; the activities of the ICRC; diplomatic activities; national implementing measures; dissemination of humanitarian law; and personal conviction and responsibility of the individual.

Reviewing this range of implementing and enforcement measures under specific aspects of contemporary wars, the Tentative Text of the San Remo Manual on the Protection of Victims of Non-International Armed Conflicts[19] goes into further issues of individual criminal responsibility, individual and collective liability, military, economic and political consequences of violations of international rules and measures to secure and promote compliance.

However effective such measures and initiatives may be, the exercise of individual and international responsibility remains rudimentary in comparison to the many violations of international humanitarian law the world is facing today. Improvements of this situation will be subject to public attention in civil society and the necessary political support.

(1) Due to the absence of a central enforcement body, efforts to improve individual and international responsibility for violations of international humanitarian law will remain rudimentary.

---

[18] *D. Fleck* (ed.), *The Handbook of Humanitarian Law in Armed Conflicts*, Oxford, Oxford University Press, 1995.

[19] San Remo Manual on the Protection of Victims of Non-International Armed Conflicts, Tentative Text, Part III, at http://web.iihl.org/iihl/Documents/Tentative%20Text.doc.

2. The Importance of Individual Initiatives

Convincing efforts to implement international humanitarian law and ensure compliance with its rules must combine activities at various levels of decision-making. The highest degree of influence and responsibility in this respect lies with the executive branch. In comparison, the influence of courts and tribunals is rather limited, even if the role of criminal jurisdiction with respect to war crimes committed in international and non-international in armed conflicts is progressively growing. It should be borne in mind that the requirements of fair trial and the duration of criminal procedure both at national and international courts will generally exclude the possibility of using prosecution as a tool for enforcing compliance with international humanitarian law in ongoing conflicts. Rather can effective criminal jurisdiction be used for dissuading from the performance of crimes in future conflicts.

The executive branch is called to cooperate in this respect, not only with legislative and judicative branches, but also with civil society. It must also be considered that those responsible for law implementation should not limit their activities to technical aspects of treaty application, but should take a generalist approach and develop convincing policies that have to go far beyond specific provisions of humanitarian protection.

Effective initiatives to ensure compliance with international humanitarian law widely depend on individual efforts. Such efforts will often require more courage than obedience and more of a general perspective than technical expertise. To overcome negligence with respect to long-term developments and the individual fate of victims, traditional ways of thinking must be removed.

(2) **Remedies to ensure compliance with the law widely depend on individual initiatives. Such initiatives are mostly located in the executive branches of states and within civil society. To be successful, they should follow a generalist approach.**

3. International Humanitarian Law is Not a 'Self-Contained System'

In order to ensure compliance with international humanitarian law, states and non-state actors must be innovative. Sometimes they must go beyond the provisions of this specific branch of law. International humanitarian law cannot be considered as a 'self-contained system' which may be implemented only according to its own rules, assuming that it enumerates a number of possible reactions to violations and may not be extended by reference to other bodies of law[20]. A perception that international humanitarian law might be implemented only by its own mechanisms

[20] See *United States Diplomatic and Consular Staff in Teheran*, ICJ Reports 1980, p. 3, at p. 38 (para. 83) and p. 40 (para. 86): "... diplomatic law itself provides the necessary means of defence against, and sanction for, illicit activities by members of diplomatic or consular missions".

would leave it as a branch of law of a less compulsory character and with large gaps[21]. It should be noted that the ICJ, referring to the rules of diplomatic and consular law as a 'self-contained system' in the *Teheran Hostage* case, did not consider aspects of humanitarian law. It might even be argued that the concept of self-contained regimes has little significance today. Reviewing this concept for the law of diplomatic relations, the International Law Commission has convincingly limited it to the rule that a state taking countermeasures is not relieved from fulfilling its obligations to respect the inviolability of diplomatic or consular agents, premises, archives and documents[22]. Indeed, no convincing argument would exclude that compliance with a specific branch of international law might be ensured by resort to lawful measures developed within other branches of law.

This question is not only interesting for academic doctrinal discussions. It has great practical importance for political bodies and courts in their decision making. Human rights mechanisms may be successfully used as tools for better implementation of humanitarian law, as shown in the *Tablada*[23] and *Las Palmeras*[24] cases. But under existing treaty law human rights obligations only exist within the jurisdiction of the state concerned[25]. That jurisdiction may be unavailable during military operations. Its existence has been confirmed by the European Court of Human Rights in cases of military occupation[26], but denied for air attacks[27]. In the early phases of robust peace operations it will be disputable whether sending states have jurisdiction. Yet there should be no doubt on the high importance of diligent human rights application for the success of any peace operation[28]. In internal

---

21 See *Sassòli*, supra n. 8, p. 404.

22 Art. 50 (2)(b) DARS and commentary, supra n. 6, paras. (14) – (15).

23 IACHR, Tablada case, report No. 55/97, case No. 11.137, Argentina, OEA/Ser/L/V/II.97, Doc. 38 (October 30, 1997), *L. Zegveld*, The Inter-American Commission on Human Rights and international humanitarian law: A comment on the *Tablada* case, No. 324 IRRC (1998), pp. 505-511.

24 Caso Las Palmeras, Excepciones Preliminares, Sentencia de 04 Febrero de 2000, Serie C, No. 66, see *F. Kalshoven*, State sovereignty versus international concern in some recent cases of the Inter-american Court of Human rights, in: G. Kreijen (ed.), State, sovereignty, and International Governance, Oxford University Press, Oxford, 2002, pp. 259-280.

25 Art. 2 ICCPR, Art. 1 ECHR.

26 ECtHR, Loizidou v. Turkey (merits), judgment of 18 December 1996, case No. 40/1993/435/514, European Human Rights Reports (EHRR), Vol. 23, p. 513; available at: http://www.echr.coe.int.

27 ECtHR, Banković v. Belgium, the Czech Republic, Denmark, France, Germany, Greece, Hungary, Iceland, Italy, Luxembourg, the Netherlands, Norway, Poland, Portugal, Spain, Turkey and the United Kingdom, Decision as to the Admissibility of, Grand Chamber, Application No. 52207/99 of 12 December 2001, 41 ILM 517 (2002), at http://www.echr.coe.int.

28 *F. Coomans/M.T. Kamminga* (eds.), Extraterritorial Application of Human Rights Treaties, Intersentia Antwerp-Oxford 2004, http://www.intersentia.com, xiv, 281. In a recent case of Iraqi citizens who have died in provinces of Iraq under UK control, the United Kingdom High Court of Justice opined that a state party's jurisdiction within Art. 1 ECHR is essentially territorial, but that exceptionally such jurisdiction extends to out-

armed conflicts and during internal disturbances human rights obligations are even more relevant than in international armed conflicts. To ensure reparation post-conflict, the utility of human rights procedures has proven to be most effective in Latin America (IACHR and IACtHR), somewhat lesser effective in Europe (ECtHR on claims in Northern Cyprus and Chechnya), and much lesser elsewhere, where the UN Human Rights Committee exercises its limited power.

(3) International humanitarian law cannot be considered as a 'self-contained system' which may be implemented only according to its own rules. Human rights mechanisms and other means may be used as well to ensure respect of international humanitarian law and facilitate redress in case of violations.

4. The Gap between the Obligation to Make Full Reparation and Corresponding Rights of Individual Victims

The new ICRC Study on Customary International Humanitarian Law[29] underlines that a state responsible for violations of international humanitarian law 'is required to make full reparation for the loss or injury caused'. The Study describes an increasing trend in favour of enabling victims to seek reparation directly from the responsible state[30]. But it does not ignore that 'individual claimants before national courts have encountered a number of obstacles in trying to obtain compensation on the basis of Article 3 of Hague Convention (IV), although no court has explicitly ruled out such a possibility under contemporary international law'[31]. Indeed, individual victims of violations are hindered if not practically excluded by procedural and substantial problems from submitting claims. This must be described as the key question of the law of reparations which deserves an in-depth discussion[32].

posts of the state's authority abroad, such as embassies and consulates. According to the Court, this exception can apply to a prison operated by a state party in the territory of another state with the consent of that state, but it does not apply to the total territory of another state which is not itself a party to the Convention, even if that territory is in the effective control of the first state (*Al-Skeini and others v Secretary of State for Defence* [2004] EWHC 2911 [Admin], 14 December 2004, available at www.bailii.org/ew/cases/EWHC/Admin/2004/2911.html).

29 *J.M. Henckaerts*/*L. Doswald-Beck* (eds.), Customary International Humanitarian Law, 2 volumes, Vol I. Rules, Vol. II. Practice (2 Parts), Cambridge, Cambridge University Press, 2005, http://www.icrc.org/eng/customary-law and http://www.cambridge.org/CIHL; see *J.M. Henckaerts*, Study on customary international humanitarian law: A contribution to the understanding and respect for the rule of law in armed conflict, in 87 No. 857 IRRC (March 2005), pp. 175-212.

30 Id., Rule 150, Vol. I, pp. 537-550.

31 Id., Vol. I, p. 544.

32 See infra, Section D (4).

(4) The obligation to make full reparation for the loss or injury caused is based on treaty law and *opinio iuris*, but corresponding rights of individual victims of violations are limited if not practically excluded by procedural and substantial problems.

5. A Wide Definition of Victims

In order to achieve meaningful results, a wide definition of victims should be applied. A violation of the law of war may be a key element of such a definition, but it should not be considered as being essential. When it comes to reparation, it would be hardly satisfactory to propagate a limitation to victims of violations of international law (direct victims) and exclude victims of permissible collateral damages (indirect victims)[33]. Such differentiation simply could not be understood by those affected and it would not make political sense. Yet under applicable law there is no obligation to make reparation, except for internationally wrongful acts, i.e. for violations of the *ius ad bellum,* the *ius in bello* or human rights which may be clearly stated and adjudicated[34].

(5) Reparation should not be limited to violations of international humanitarian law, but include adequate redress for victims of collateral damage.

C. The Extent of Individual Responsibility

1. Unlawful Orders and the Obligation to Refuse

Under current customary law, an offender cannot be barred from claiming the defence of superior order unless he or she was aware of the illegality of the order or the order was manifestly illegal[35]. While it must be questioned whether there will be a role at all for customary law under the rule of *nulla poena sine lege scripta,* it might be worthwhile to think of a best practice manual for soldiers and their commanders in which the law could be summarised in the following terms:

---

33 *Gillard*, supra n. 2, p. 551.

34 This principle was confirmed by the Supreme Court of the Netherlands, judgment of 29 November 2002, and the Amsterdam District Court, Vierde meervoudige burgerlijke kamer, *Dedovic v. Kok et al.*, judgment of 6 July 2000, both reported by Zegveld, supra n. 2, pp. 501-502.

35 *A. Zimmermann*, Chapter 24.2. Superior Orders, in: A. Cassese/P. Gaeta/J. Jones (eds.), The Rome Statute of the International Criminal Court: A Commentary, 2002, pp. 957-955 [947]. Similar rules are described as customary in *Henckaerts/Doswald-Beck*, supra n. 29, Rules 151-155.

(6) **Orders that require subordinates to commit violations of rules of international humanitarian law are unlawful.**
(7) **Where such an order is manifestly unlawful, the subordinate must refuse to obey and cannot rely on it for excluding his or her criminal responsibility.**
(8) **Even where such an order is not manifestly unlawful, the subordinate must equally refuse the order and cannot rely upon it for excluding his or her criminal responsibility if he or she knew the order was unlawful.**
(9) **Superiors may be punished for unlawful orders and likewise for their omission to take all measures within their powers to prevent crimes of subordinates, if they knew or should have known in the circumstances that the subordinates were committing or about to commit such crimes. Once a crime has been committed, superiors may be punished for the omission to take all measures within their power to bring the offender to justice if they know or should have known that such a crime has been committed.**

In line with these principles the Tentative Text of the San Remo Manual on the Protection of Victims of Non-International Armed Conflicts[36] states:

"308. *Command and Superior Responsibility.* Superiors may be punished for their omission to take all measures within their powers to prevent crimes of subordinates if they knew or should have known in the circumstances that the subordinates were committing or about to commit such crimes. In addition, once a crime has been committed, superiors may be punished for the omission to take all measures within their power to bring the offender to justice if they know or should have known that such a crime has been committed. These principles of 'command responsibility' apply to both military and civilian authorities."

2. A Uniform Perception of Individual Accountability?

Challenges arising from the principle of command responsibility were met differently in different situations and the consequences of failure were subject not only to different criminal laws and court statutes, but also to prevailing political perceptions. Relevant jurisprudence is mostly issued post-conflict, as judgments during ongoing armed conflicts are extremely rare.

In a famous judgment, the United States Military Commission at Manila had set a questionable precedent on December 7, 1945, by sentencing General Yamashita, the Commanding General of the Fourteenth Army Group of the Imperial Japanese Army in the Philippine Islands, for atrocities and crimes committed by members of the Japanese forces under his command that "were not sporadic in nature but in many cases were methodically supervised by Japanese officers and non-commissioned officers". The Commission concluded that General Yamashita "failed to

[36] San Remo Manual, supra n. 19.

provide effective control of [his] troops as was required by the circumstances". The death sentence was confirmed by the U.S. Supreme Court in 1946[37]. In dissenting opinions Justice Rutledge had underlined that never before an enemy general was convicted and tried for action during hostilities and much less for failing to take action. Justice *Murphy* had stressed that not even knowledge of the crimes was attributed to General Yamashita, but it was simply alleged that he unlawfully disregarded and failed to discharge his duty as a commander to control the operations of the members of his command. Command responsibility was stretched in this case, but frequently neglected thereafter.

In the important 1971 *Calley* and *Medina* cases[38], decided at the height of the war in Vietnam, the issue of command responsibility of superiors was not fully addressed. In the 2005 *Graner* case[39], which dealt with gross violations of the prohibition of torture in a military prison in Abu Ghreib, Iraq, acts that had been committed over a longer period and in an organised manner, again no superior was charged, although independent inquiries, one led by former Secretary of Defense *James Schlesinger*, had pointed to institutional responsibility for those criminal acts which were as disgusting as politically counterproductive.

The duty of commanders, as summarised in Article 87 AP I, should be widely acceptable today. Military commanders must ensure that all persons under their control prevent and, where necessary, suppress and report breaches of international humanitarian law to competent authorities. States bear a responsibility that all members of their armed forces are aware of their obligations under international humanitarian law and they must initiate disciplinary or penal action against violators. This responsibility must be implemented in convincing practice and it must be enforced by policy decisions.

There are general criteria for accountability of group leaders and military commanders, such as control and authority, knowledge, and the ability to prevent or punish[40]. Such criteria should apply to both military and civilian authorities, but there is no uniform perception of these rules under different legal systems and full compliance in each single case is far from being ensured.

Issues of individual reparation are regulated under the Statutes of the International Criminal Tribunal for the former Yugoslavia (ICTY)[41], the International Criminal Tribunal for Rwanda (ICTR)[42] and the Special Court for Sierra Leone[43]. It will be interesting to see whether a uniform practice may be influenced by the

---

[37] *L. Friedman*, The Law of War. A Documentary History, New York, Random House, 1972, Vol II, pp. 1596-1623.

[38] Id., pp. 1703-1728.

[39] Warrant Officer Charles Graner was sentenced to 10 years imprisonment by a Military Commission at Fort Hood, Texas, on 16 January 2005. He had claimed to have acted by order and with full knowledge of his superiors. See also http://yaleglobal.yale.edu/ display.article?id=6079.

[40] *L. Zegveld*, supra n. 4, pp. 121-131.

[41] Art. 24(3) of the ICTY Statute, supra n. 1, Rules 105, 106 of the Rules of Procedure and Evidence.

[42] Art. 23(3) of the ICTR Statute, supra n. 1.

[43] Art. 14 of the Statute of the Special Court for Sierra Leone (2002), supra n. 1.

ICC Statute and its Article 33. It is encouraging to see that the ICC Statute provides for the participation of victims in the proceedings and requires the Court to establish principles "relating to reparations to, or in respect of, victims" (Article 75 para. 1). Such reparations may be awarded through a Trust Fund (Article 79). This Fund will include money and other property collected through fines and forfeitures imposed by the Court on perpetrators. But voluntary contributions from states, corporations, organisations and individuals remain necessary to make the settlement of claims effective.

(10) The principles of command responsibility apply to both military and civilian authorities, but there is no uniform perception of these rules under different legal systems and full compliance in each single case is far from being ensured.

3. The Immunity of State Organs

It is important to accept state immunity as an essential means to ensure unimpeded cooperation between sovereign states. As organs of their state, military forces enjoy functional immunity when deployed abroad[44]. In 1972, Article 31 of the European Convention on State Immunity expressly restated the principle that a state enjoys full immunity "in respect of anything done or omitted to be done by, or in relation to, its armed forces when on the territory of another Contracting State". The fact that this principle was not repeated in more recent texts such as the 2004 UN Convention on Jurisdictional Immunities of States and Their Property, does not diminish its continuing validity. The international immunity of state organs effectively limits reparation claims before foreign national courts. This immunity is functional in nature. It is limited to acts and omissions during official duty and cannot be invoked before national courts of the country of origin. International courts may exercise their jurisdiction with respect to sovereign states and their organs to the extent they are authorised to do so under their statute.

State immunity should not be misunderstood as offering impunity to individual soldiers; but it practically excludes claims that are not voluntarily accepted by the sending state or adjudicated by a competent international court.

(11) The international immunity of state organs applies to foreign national courts; it cannot be invoked before national courts of the country of origin. International courts may exercise their jurisdiction with respect to sovereign states and their organs, if they are authorised to do so under their statute.

---

44 *D. Fleck*, Are Foreign Military Personnel Exempt from International Criminal Jurisdiction under SOFAs?, 1 JICJ (2003), pp. 651-670 [662-664].

D. International Responsibility of States and International Organisations

1. The Background and Meaning of Art. 3 HC IV, Art. 91 AP I

It is a matter of dispute, whether Article 3 HC IV was designed only for small-scale events[45], whether civilians are sole beneficiaries[46], and whether this provision applies only to acts of regular armed forces, as opposed to the *levée en masse* and armed resistance movements in occupied territories[47]. The negotiating history of HC IV might suggest a limited approach which is, however, not reflected in the agreed text, a text which seventy years later was confirmed without much discussion in Article 91 AP I.

As these treaty provisions are clear in what they say and do not say, no limitation of general obligations under international law could convincingly be concluded from the texts themselves. Even if a restrictive interpretation would be suggested for Article 3 HC IV by its background and negotiating history, this would not necessarily influence the meaning of Article 91 AP I. Hence there is no limitation of responsibilities in armed conflicts under the *lex specialis* rule of Article 55 DARS. There should not be any doubt on the responsibility of states under general international law to make full reparation for the injury caused by any violation of international humanitarian law committed by their organs and other persons or entities empowered to act on their behalf.

The term 'compensation' which is used in Article 3 HC IV and Article 91 AP I may cause some confusion. As will be discussed later[48], this term today describes only one of various forms of reparation which include restitution, compensation, rehabilitation, satisfaction, and guarantees of non-repetition. In 1907, and still in 1977, the difference between these various forms of redress quite obviously had been neglected. Yet this cannot exclude the application of all such forms of reparation to violations of international humanitarian law. The broader term 'reparation' is used in Article 75 ICC Statute, thus avoiding practical problems that would arise, should compensation be considered as the only remedy available.

The fact that the liability to pay compensation under both Article 3 HC IV and Article 91 AP I is subject to the limiting clause 'if the case demands' may offer governments an escape clause to avoid absolute obligations, but the correct understanding should be that as part of their responsibility for all acts committed by persons forming part of their armed forces states must take serious efforts to provide redress to victims and may not neglect their liability.

(12) The background and meaning of Art. 3 HC IV is subject to controversial discussion. Even after the reaffirmation of this provision in Art. 91 AP I this discussion is still open.

---

45 *Kalshoven*, supra n. 2, p. 834; contra: *Heintschel v. Heinegg*, supra n. 2, pp. 30-31.

46 *Kalshoven*, id., p. 833; contra: *Heintschel v. Heinegg*, id., pp. 29-30.

47 *Kalshoven*, id., pp. 834-835; contra: *Heintschel v. Heinegg*, id., pp. 28-29.

48 Section D (6).

(13) These disputes, however, do not affect the responsibility of states to make full reparation for injury caused in violation of international humanitarian law.

2. The Responsibility of States to Make Full Reparation

State responsibility applies not only to wrongful acts of state, but also to acts committed contrary to orders or instructions of the state, as to omissions and to acts adopted by the state as its own conduct[49]. Principles precluding wrongfulness, as confirmed by Article 20-25 DARS, are hardly relevant for violations of international humanitarian law, as no such preclusion is applicable to breaches of peremptory norms of general international law (Article 26 DARS). Basic rights of the human person are classic examples for *ius cogens*[50].

Whereas Article 7 DARS excludes acts committed by state agents in their capacity as private individuals, even such individual acts are covered by Article 3 HC IV, Article 91 AP I, a fact which gives these latter rules a true *lex specialis* character under Article 55 DARS. If the underlying *ratio* is that members of the armed forces would never have entered the territory of operations and came into contact with its inhabitants except in their official capacity, the same applies to members of peacekeeping forces in post-conflict situations where Article 3 HC IV and Article 91 AP I do not apply *strictu sensu*. This aspect should be considered in the conduct of peace operations where sending states have a general interest to make full reparations for damages without delay as part of the peace process.

The question whether the conduct of armed forces is directed or controlled by a state within the meaning of Article 8 DARS may be a matter of dispute for paramilitary forces and forces acting under the influence of a third state. As the ICJ confirmed in *Nicaragua*, mere provision of financial and logistical support, which had been rendered in Honduras for operations of the US-backed *Contras* in Nicaragua, does not amount to an armed attack, against which acts of self-defence against the United States would be justifiable, whereas an armed attack would require "the sending by a State of armed bands to the territory of another State, if such operation, because of its scale and effects, would have been classified as an armed attack rather than a mere frontier accident had it been carried out by regular armed forces"[51]. The Court also stated that in order to establish that the United States was responsible for acts contrary to human rights and humanitarian law allegedly perpetrated by the *Contras*, it was necessary to prove that the United States had specifically directed or enforced the perpetration of those acts. Even general control over the *Contras*, with a high degree of dependency by the latter,

---

49 See Art. 2, 7, 8 DARS.

50 See *Sassòli*, supra n. 8, pp. 413-414; *L. Hannikainen*, Peremptory Norms (Jus Cogens) in International Law, Helsinki, Lakimiesliiton Kustannus, 1988.

51 Case Concerning Military and Paramilitary Activities in and Against Nicaragua (Merits), *Nicaragua* v. *United States*, ICJ Reports 1986, pp. 14-546 (para. 195), www.icj-cij.org/.

would not mean, without further evidence, that the United States had directed or enforced the perpetration of the alleged acts, contrary to human rights and humanitarian law[52].

In 1999 the ICTY Appeals Chamber in *Tadić* [53], after extensive discussion of the ICJ's decision in *Nicaragua*, accepted the evidence of 'overall control' instead of 'effective control' of insurgents in Bosnia and Herzegovina (the Bosnian Serb Army) by the Federal Republic of Yugoslavia as a sufficient criterion for qualifying the ongoing armed conflict as international[54]. Although the point of departure was similar to *Nicaragua*, i.e. to ascertain the conditions under which under international law an individual may be held to act as a *de facto* organ of another state, the ICJ had decided with a view to determining the international responsibility of that state, whereas the ICTY had to establish the necessary precondition for the grave breaches regime to apply[55]. The purpose for the ICTY Appeals Chamber to qualify the armed conflict in Bosnia and Herzegovina was not to determine whether self-defence was justified, but to decide whether the appellant was guilty of grave breaches of the Geneva Conventions. Nevertheless, it remains of general interest that the ICTY confirmed in *Tadić* that in order to attribute the acts of a military or paramilitary group to another state, it must be proved that the state wields overall control over the group, not only by equipping and financing the group, but also by coordinating or helping in the general planning of its military activities, whereas it was no longer held necessary that the state, in addition, issued instructions for the commission of specific acts contrary to international law.

Apparently, during the collective response to the September 11 attacks, an even wider principle of attributability was applied. Al Qaeda's conduct was imputed to Afghanistan on the basis that the Taliban regime had harboured and supported this terrorist group and refused to surrender its head, Osama bin Laden[56]. This should

---

52 Id., paras. 254 et seq.

53 The *Prosecutor* v. *Tadić*, Case No. IT-94-1, Appeal on the Merits, Judgment of 15 July 1999 (paras. 99-145), www.un.org/icty/judgement.htm.

54 With this decision the ICTY Appeals Chamber in a way has shadowed its more innovative earlier position, that many rules of international humanitarian law originally applicable in international armed conflict have become customary rules applicable also in internal conflict, and are binding law for all parties to the conflict: „What is inhumane, and consequently proscribed, in international wars, cannot but be inhumane and inadmissible in civil strife", see the *Prosecutor* v. *Tadić*, Case No. IT-94-1, Appeal on Jurisdiction, Judgment of 2 October 1995 (para. 119), www.un.org/icty/judgement.htm.

55 See supra n. 6, Commentary, pp. 29-365 [106-107]. Meanwhile, also war crimes committed in non-international armed conflicts are penalised under Art. 8 (2) (c) and (e) of the Rome Statute of the International Criminal Court of 17 July 1998 which is, however, not applicable to the ICTY.

56 SC Res. 1368 (2001) of 12 September 2001. Concerns which brought forward against this request were based on the participation of the United States in the voting of the Security Council and the alleged absence of fair trial for Osama Bin Laden in the United States, see *E. de Wet*, The Chapter VII Powers of the United Nations Security Council, Oxford and Portland Oregon, Hart Publishing 2004, pp. 350 f. While such concerns may be valid as far as procedures followed during the adoption of relevant Security Council Resolutions are concerned, it is beyond any dispute that the Security Council

not, however, be misunderstood as abandoning the requirement of control by the state altogether, as the Security Council had based its decision on Afghanistan's refusal to comply with a number of former Resolutions: it had requested in December 1998, "that the Taliban stop providing sanctuary and training for international terrorists and their organizations"[57]; acting under Chapter VII, it had strongly condemned support of terrorist activities by the Taliban and demanded bin Laden's extradition[58], demands which were repeated and confirmed in December 2000[59], although in vain. In the unanimously shared opinion of a large community of states and international organisations the threat to international security which derived from the situation in Afghanistan in September 2001 amounted to an armed attack. This evaluation is all the more significant as full accountability for the use of force has been forcefully stressed in recent political and legal developments, which clearly confirm that a high threshold remains applicable for acceptable responses against aggressive acts[60]. The question whether an act of terrorism can be understood as engagement in armed conflict may be difficult to answer[61]. Yet, in the case of September 11, there has been no dispute that the attacks were part of an international armed conflict with Taliban-controlled Afghanistan, a conflict which was qualified as being of non-international character from Summer 2002, when the Taliban were replaced by the Provisional Government, which authorised foreign operations on its territory.

While the three decisions referred to above should be seen in their factual and political context and not misunderstood as marking a general change in international law, it is fair to say that many examples of the use of force by non-state actors have stressed the need to take incalculable decisions on the side of the attacked state, decisions which inevitably have international ramifications. In this context, the applicability of rules of evidence has been challenged and quite often disregarded during acts of anticipatory self-defence[62]. Even claims to pre-emptive self-defence have been developed to effectively react not against an imminent at-

had convincingly and in binding form qualified the situation as a threat to international peace and security; see NATO Council, Statement of 12 September, www.nato.int/docu/pr/2001/p01-124e.htm, and that measure of self-defence were taken by a large number of states supporting Operation Enduring Freedom, see www.nato.int/docu/pr/2001/p01-124e.htm.

57 SC Res. 1214 (1998) of 8 December 1998, Preamble (third para.) and operative para. 13.

58 SC Res. 1267 (1999) of 15 October 1999, Preamble (para. 5) and operative para. 2.

59 SC Res. 1333 (2000) of 19 December 2000.

60 See *Ch. Ku/H.K. Jacobson* (eds.), Democratic Accountability and the Use of Force in International Law, Cambridge, Cambridge University Press 2003; *J.L. Holzgrefe/R. O. Keohane* (eds.), Humanitarian Intervention – Ethical, Legal, and Political Dilemmas, Cambridge, Cambridge University Press 2003; *A. Hasenclever*, Die Macht der Moral in der internationalen Politik. Militärische Interventionen westlicher Staaten in Somalia, Ruanda und Bosnien-Herzegowina, Frankfurt/New York, Campus Verlag 2001.

61 *K. Watkin*, Controlling the Use of Force: A Role for Human Rights Norms in Contemporary Armed Conflict, in 98 AJIL (2004) pp. 1-34 at 4-5.

62 *M.E. O'Connell*, Evidence of Terror, in 7 Journal of Conflict and Security Law (2002) pp. 19-26.

tack but to a state of affairs that could, under certain contingencies, develop into a dangerous situation that then would require an act of self-defence[63]. It may seem somehow paradoxical that present trends to even more critically review and strengthen political control of the use of force by states are often met with claims that would lower rather than foster the legal limitations of such use. Such trends cannot be explained by the dreadful events of September 11 alone. Changed threat perceptions, not necessarily based on verified facts, not even influenced by a change of established long-term interests, may cause political reactions as much as real imminent attacks.

Has the perception of accountability changed with respect to terrorist attacks? The difficulty (and quite often impossibility) of making non-state actors fully accountable for their conduct requires new strategies and tactics on the side of the state. But the state's accountability towards its population, towards other states and the international community as a whole remains unaffected by such events.

(14) States are responsible for acts committed by their organs and other persons or entities empowered to act on their behalf.

(15) Circumstances precluding wrongfulness are limited to specific situations (consent, self-defence, countermeasures, force majeure, distress, necessity); no such preclusion is applicable to breaches of peremptory norms of general international law.

(16) State responsibility includes responsibility for omissions if there was a duty to act. It also includes responsibility for acts committed in excess of authority or contrary to instructions and responsibility for acts adopted by the state as its own conduct.

3. A Coordinate Responsibility of International Organizations

International Organisations participating in peacekeeping and peace enforcement activities may be held liable for wrongful acts, as far as they have exclusive command and control over the conduct in question. But in practice many operations are conducted under the national command and control of sending states. In these cases international responsibility for any wrongful act is vested in the state or states conducting the operation[64]. Even when the Security Council authorizes states to take necessary measures of peace-keeping and peace enforcement outside

---

[63] The National Security Strategy of the United States of America, Part V. 'Prevent Our Enemies from Threatening Us, Our Allies, and Our Friends with Weapons of Mass Destruction', September 2002. http://www.whitehouse.gov/nsc/nss5.html; *C. Stahn,* Nicaragua is Dead, Long Live Nicaragua – the Right to Self-defence under Article 51 UN Charter and International Terrorism, with comments by *W.M. Reisman* and *Y. Dinstein*, in C. Walter/S. Vöneky/V. Röben/F. Schorkopf (eds.), Terrorism as a Challenge for National and International Law: Security versus Liberty?, Berlin et al., Springer, 2004, pp. 827-877, 909-913, 915-924.

[64] See Report of the Secretary-General on the financing of United Nations peacekeeping operations, UN-Doc A/51/389, para. 17.

a chain of command of the United Nations, conduct of these forces is attributable exclusively to the states[65]. Responsibility of states also prevails in joint operations within a regional organization, or NATO[66], as the latter, although exercising a coordinating role including operational command, in so far do not have full legal competence and responsibility and still depend on sovereign decisions taken by their member states. In most cases they not even have the budget and organisational means to process claims.

Where national contingents of a peace operation are operating under the control of the United Nations, they may be considered as subsidiary organs of the Organization and their acts are imputable to the latter. Requested by the General Assembly, the Secretary-General has developed criteria and guidelines for implementing temporal and financial limitations on UN liability.[67] According to these principles, any damage must be claimed within six months from the time of damage. UN liability is limited except in cases of gross negligence and wilful misconduct, and it is practically excluded in cases of 'operational necessity' to achieve the operational goal. Compensation for personal injury, illness, or death is limited to economic loss, measured by local standards of compensation not to exceed a ceiling of U.S. $ 50,000.[68]

Even where the United Nations or regional organisations are not directly responsible for wrongful acts of troop contributing states, they still bear a coordinate responsibility with the latter for ensuring compliance with the applicable rules of international humanitarian law in operations conducted under their control or authority. This principle has been made part of the Recommended Rules and Practices (RRPs) developed by the ILA Committee on Accountability of International Organisations[69]. It should be confirmed by the International Law Commission's forthcoming Draft Articles on the Responsibility of International Organizations[70].

---

65 See ILC 2004 Report on Responsibility of International Organizations, supra n. 9, pp. 102, 111 et seq., 122.

66 See *T. Stein*, Kosovo and the International Community. The Attribution of Possible Internationally Wrongful Acts: Responsibility of NATO or of its MemberStates?, contra: *A. Pellet*, L'imputabilité d'éventuels actes illicites – Responsabilité de l'OTAN ou des Etats membres, both in Chr. Tomuschat (ed.), Kosovo and the International Community, The Hague/London/New York, Kluwer, 2002, pp. 181-192, 193-202.

67 Administrative and budgetary aspects of the financing of the United Nations peacekeeping operations. Report of the Secretary-General, UN Doc A/51/903 (1997), adopted by GA Res 52/547 (22 June 1998).

68 *D. Shraga*, UN Peacekeeping Operations: Applicability of International Humanitarian Law and Responsibility for Operations-Related Damage, 94 AJIL (2000), pp. 408-412 [410-411].

69 Final Report of the Committee on Accountability of International Organisations, Section IV, Peacekeeping and peace enforcement activities, in The International Law Association, Report of the Seventy-first Conference (Berlin, 16-21 August 2004), London, 2004, pp. 164-241,195.

70 See supra n. 9.

(17) When the Security Council authorises states to take necessary measures of peace-keeping and peace enforcement outside a chain of command of the United Nations, conduct of these forces is attributable exclusively to the states. UN liability applies for operations under UN control, but is limited in practice.

(18) International Organisations participating in peacekeeping and peace enforcement activities bear a coordinate responsibility with troop-contributing states for ensuring compliance with the applicable rules of international humanitarian law in operations conducted under their control or authority.

4. The Responsibility of States and the Lack of Corresponding Rights of Individuals

While the law of reparation is so far limited to the international responsibility of states, the question whether there is a corresponding entitlement of individual victims of war is still subject to dispute. The development of human rights law may once remove the procedural limitation that victims of war can seek compensation only through their own governments, but there are still limitations to jurisdiction on extraterritorial application of human rights treaties[71].

The traditional view, as expressed by the ICRC in the Commentaries to the Geneva Conventions[72] and the Additional Protocol I[73] and confirmed at the 1993 Geneva Conference on the Protection of War Victims, is that application for reparation or compensation can be made only via the state, a fact which often makes the process and its outcome uncertain. It is for this reason that the ICRC has proposed to establish procedures to provide reparation for damage inflicted on the victims of violations of international humanitarian law and award compensation to them[74]. Yet even that modest practical proposal is still far from being implemented.

The German Federal Constitutional Court has held that no general rule of international law excludes individual claims for acts or omissions of a foreign state committed during wartime[75]. The Court saw in principle parallel remedies for individuals and states, but it also underlined the fact that individual claims must be forwarded by states on behalf of individual citizens. It also noted that such claims

---

71 See supra n. 25-28 and accompanying text.

72 *J.S. Pictet*, Commentary, III, Geneva Convention Relative to the Treatment of Prisoners of War, Geneva, ICRC, 1960, p. 630.

73 *Y. Sandoz/C. Swinarski/B. Zimmermann* (eds.), Commentary on the Additional Protocols, Geneva, ICRC/Nijhoff, 1987, p. 1056.

74 ICRC, Report on the Protection of War Victims, Geneva, June 1993, para. 4.3, reproduced in M. Sassòli/A. Bouvier, How Does Law Protect in War?, Geneva, ICRC, 1999, pp. 444-458 [457].

75 Forced Labour Case, BVerfGE 94, 315, 330, NJW 1996, 2717 (decision of 13 May 1996).

may be expressly excluded by peace treaties and similar treaties, such as the 1953 London Agreement on German External Debts[76].

Not exactly the same line of arguments was taken by the German Supreme Court in its 'Distomo' judgment of 26 June 2003[77], arguing that the moratorium under the London Agreement had become obsolete with the conclusion of the 2+4-Four Treaty[78], but the latter did not exclude claims of reparation by Greece as an non-party. Such claims were, however, dismissed as the case had to be decided in accordance with the law in force 1944, which prescribed that claims could not be forwarded by individual citizens, but only by states.

It should be noted in this context that the general obligation of states to make reparation to victims is often limited in peace negotiations, with a view to first re-establish an environment of public welfare and prosperity which would serve victims of war much better than any individual reparation claim possibly could. Many of such peace settlements are not free from sacrificing long-term confidence in order and justice to short-term advantages[79]. The right of parties to a peace negotiation, to limit or even exclude the compensation of claims even at the expense of their individual citizens cannot be seriously disputed. This principle was followed not only in the case of Germany, but also in the 1951 Treaty of Peace between the Allied Powers and Japan[80], the 1998 Agreement on Respect for Human Rights and International Humanitarian Law in the Philippines[81], and the 2000 Peace Agreement between Ethiopia and Eritrea[82]. The obligation under Article 3

[76] London Agreement on German External Debts of 27 February 1953, 333 UNTS 3, BGBl. 1953 II 331. Art. 5(2) of the London Agreement provided that "claims arising out of the Second World War by countries which were at war with or were occupied by Germany during that war, and by nationals of such countries, against the Reich and agencies of the Reich, including costs of German occupation, credits acquired during occupation on clearing accounts and claims against the Reichskreditkassen shall be deferred until the final settlement of the problem of reparation". The Treaty on the Final Settlement with respect to Germany (2+4-Treaty) of 12 September 1990 (BGBl. 1990 II 1317) did not address the issue and thus excludes further reparations to be paid by Germany.

[77] BGH, III ZR 245/98, http://lexetius.com/2003, 1416.

[78] Supra n. 76.

[79] Amnesty International has criticised that the new Justice and Peace Law in Colombia excludes reparation and guarantees impunity for human rights abusers, AI Index: AMR 23/012/2005, 26 April '05, http://amnesty-news.c.topica.com/maadrT9abgoppbd62tnb/.

[80] Treaty of Peace between the Allied Powers and Japan of 8 September 195,146 AJIL (1952), Supplement: Official Documents, p. 71. Under Art. 14 (a) Japan undertook to "pay reparations to the Allied Powers for the damage and suffering caused by it during the war".

[81] Comprehensive Agreement on Respect for Human Rights and International Humanitarian Law in the Philippines of 16 March 1998, www.incore.ulst.ac.uk/cds/greements/pdf/phil8.pdf. It expressly provides for indemnification of the victims of violations of international humanitarian law by both parties to the conflict.

[82] Agreement between the Government of the Federal Democratic Republic of Ethiopia and the Government of the State of Eritrea of 12 December 200, 40 ILM (2001), p. 260. A neutral claims commission was charged with deciding, through binding arbitration,

HC IV and Article 91 AP I, to pay compensation for violations of humanitarian law is not a peremptory norm. In view of the excessive civilian damages caused in modern armed conflicts the limitation of compensation must sadly be considered as one of the preconditions of a successful peace process.

Individual claims against states parties to an armed conflict have been constantly rejected by a number of national courts in the United States, Japan and Germany[83]. The most recent of such judgments are those of the Tokyo District Court of 26 and 30 November 1998[84] and the Bonn District Court of 10 December 2003[85] which was confirmed by the Regional Court of Appeals in Cologne on 28 July 2005[86]. The Amsterdam District Court, in its judgement of 6 July 2000[87], seems to have implicitly recognized the possibility of deriving individual rights from violations of international humanitarian law, as it rejected the particular claim with the argument that such violations had not occurred. But so far no judgment is known that would accept individual claims under international law and accord reparation in case such violations had been committed.

Even if international law would provide an individual right to compensation, enforcement mechanisms are not yet at hand[88] and it is open to doubt whether this could be the case in the foreseeable future[89]. Consequently, the most recent efforts of the UN Secretary-General, far from advocating individual compensation rights, are focusing on appropriately conceived combinations of reparation measures as a

---

all claims between the two governments and between private entities for loss, damage or injury related to the conflict and resulting from violations of international humanitarian law or other violations of international law. Award of any such claim is still open. See infra n. 94 and accompanying text.

83 *L. Zegveld*, Remedies for victims of violations of international humanitarian law, 85 IRRC No 851 (September 2003), pp. 497-526 [507-513].

84 Titherington et al. and Lapré et al. *v.* Government of Japan, Fujita, supra n. 13, pp. 104-117 and 118-124.

85 Bridge of Varvarin case, Landgericht (LG) Bonn, 1 O 361/02, NJW 2004, 525, HuV-I 2/2004, 111-113, http://www.uni-kassel.de/fb10/frieden/themen/NATO-Krieg/varvarin-urteil.html.

86 Oberlandesgericht (OLG) Köln, 7 U 8/04, www.olg-koeln.nrw.de, http://www.uni-kassel.de/fb5/frieden/themen/NATO-Krieg/varvarin6.html. The Court again confirmed that international humanitarian law does not provide for direct individual claims. For the first time in German jurisprudence, it generally acknowledged a right of individuals to claim official responsibility of the state (Amtshaftung) even for war damage. For this very reason, the legal remedy of revision by the German Supreme Court (Bundesgerichtshof) was admitted. But it was stated at the same time, that such claims would not be justified, as the Federal Government had no responsibility for the attack against the Varvarin bridge and it could have fully trusted in NATO targeting decisions being in conformity with international law.

87 Supra n. 34.

88 See Letter from the Secretary-General to the President of the Security Council concerning victims' compensation and participation, UN Doc S/2000/1063, App. 12 para. 22.

89 A more optimistic view is taken by *E. Schwager*, The Right to Compensation for Victims of an Armed Conflict, Vol. 4 No. 2 Chinese Journal of International Law (2005), who based her opinion on the progressing recognition of the individual as a subject of international law.

complement to proceedings of criminal tribunals and truth commissions[90]. Such steps remain fully dependent from state practice which will provide ad hoc solutions rather than generic rules for all armed conflicts and cannot be expected to provide full compensation for each single case.

Hence it must be concluded that contemporary international law does not offer rights to individuals corresponding to the duties of states to comply with international humanitarian law and make full reparation for any violation of its norms. To expect a shift of attitude and even a general regulation of this complex issue within foreseeable time would be less than realistic.

(19) State practice and jurisprudence have denied so far, that international law offers rights to individuals corresponding to the duties of states to comply with international humanitarian law. To expect a shift of attitude and even a general regulation of this complex issue within foreseeable time would be less than realistic.

5. Claims Commissions

Claims commissions, tribunals and authorities are frequently established as part of an ongoing peace process, to provide a mechanism in order to settle individual claims in a direct manner. The successful work of a number of such bodies has strengthened individual rights of war victims *vis-à-vis* foreign states, and in some cases even *vis-à-vis* their home state. Yet in many post-war situations states were and still are unable to establish claims procedures and even a successful claims settlement practice is unable to solve all open issues.

Germany has passed laws and concluded treaties to indemnify victims of the Second World War and the Holocaust[91]. Still decades later, as a result of US-German negotiations following the Printz case[92], a voluntary fund and claims review mechanism was established together with private corporations in Germany[93] to compensate former forced slave labourers and certain other victims of Nazi injus-

---

[90] The Rule of law and transitional justice in conflict and post-conflict societies. Report of the Secretary-General, S/2004/616 (23 August 2004), para. 55.

[91] See e.g. 1952 Law on the Equalization of Burdens (Lastenausgleichsgesetz); 1956 Federal Law on the Reparation of Losses (Bundesentschädigungsgesetz); 1957 Federal Restitution Law (Bundesrückerstattungsgesetz); 1994 Law on Reparation and Equalization (Entschädigungs- und Ausgleichsleistungsgesetz).

[92] *Printz v. Federal Republic of Germany,* 26 F.3d 1166 (US App. D.C. 1994), see Senate Resolution dated November 19, 1993, at http://thomas.loc.gov/cgi-bin/query/z?r103:S19NO3-B1492 and German-US Agreement dated September 19, 1995, Concerning Final Benefits to Certain United States Nationals Who Were Victims of National Socialist Measures of Persecution, http://www.virtual-institute.de/en/Prax1995/epraxb95_54.cfm, para. 321.

[93] Law on the Creation of a Foundation "Remembrance, Responsibility and Future" (Gesetz zur Errichtung einer Stiftung „Erinnerung, Verantwortung und Zukunft") of 2 August 2000 (BGBl 2000 I 1263), see www.stiftung-evz.de.

tice. An *Austrian* Reconciliation Fund was created in February 2000 to make voluntary payments to former slave and forced labourers of the Nazi Regime on the territory of present-day Austria[94].

The *United States* has launched a programme in 1988 to offer redress to compensate Canadian nationals of Japanese ancestry subjected to internment, relocation, deportation, loss of property during the Second World War, to implement recommendations of the Commission on Wartime Relocation and Internment of Civilians[95]. Similar efforts were taken by *Canada*[96].

The *Iran-United States Claims Tribunal*, established under the Algier Accords of 19 January 1981[97] to bring justice after the end of a warlike situation, has jurisdiction over claims of US nationals against Iran and of Iranian nationals against the US arising of debts, contracts, expropriations or other measures affecting property rights. It has also jurisdiction over claims of the two governments against each other arising out of contractual agreements for the purchase of goods and services. The practice of this Tribunal has provided and still provides convincing solutions for the settlement of claims resulting from violations of legal norms and humanitarian principles that had been committed outside an armed conflict.

The *United Nations Compensation Commission (UNCC)* was established under SC Res 687 (8 April 1991) to settle claims for 'any direct loss, damage, including environmental damage and the depletion of natural resources, or injury to foreign Governments, nationals and corporations, as a result of Iraq's unlawful invasion and occupation of Kuwait'. This broad mandate comprises both *ius ad bellum* and *ius in bello* claims. While not only states but also individuals were entitled, for practical reasons individual claims had to be collected by the home state of the claimant or by specified organisations (UNWRA, UNHCR, ICRC) and submitted to the UNCC which had to take decisions based on very rudimentary considerations[98].

The *Commission for Real Property of Displaced Persons and Refugees in Bosnia and Herzegovina (CRPC)* has collected claim applications for 319,220 prop-

94 See http://www.reconciliationfund.at/history.htm.

95 Civil Liberties Act (1988), 10 August 1988, Public Law 100-383, [H.R.442], paras 1, 102-104, 108.

96 Agreement between the Government of Canada and National Association of Japanese Canadians, Japanese Canadian Redress Agreement of 22 September 1988.

97 The Government of the Democratic and Popular Republic of Algeria served as intermediary in the search for a mutually acceptable solution. Having consulted extensively with the two Governments as to the commitments which each was willing to undertake in order to resolve the crisis, the Government of Algeria recorded those commitments in two Declarations made on 19 January 1981. The "General Declaration" and the "Claims Settlement Declaration" or the "Algiers Declarations," as they are often called, were then adhered to by Iran and the United States, http://www.iusct.org/.

98 *N. Wühler*, The United Nations Compensation Commission, in A. Randelzhofer/C. Tomuschat (eds.), State Responsibility and the Individual (1999), p. 213; *N. Wühler*, The Role of Ad-Hoc Claims Commissions – Background Report –, in Collection of Documents for the Expert Meeting "Remedies for victims of violations of international humanitarian law", Amsterdam Center for International Law, 9-10 May 2003, p. 50.

erties throughout Bosnia and Herzegovina (as of December 2003) and issued 302,109 decisions providing incontrovertible proof of property rights. The CRPC reconsideration body stopped its activities in December 2004[99]. A similar impartial and independent mechanism for resolving property claims was established in *Kosovo*[100]. The claims intake process closed on 1 July 2003.

The *Eritrea-Ethiopia Claims Commission*[101], established pursuant to Article 5 of the Agreement signed in Algiers on 12 December 2000 between the Governments of the State of Eritrea and the Federal Democratic Republic of Ethiopia (the "December Agreement"), is mandated to:

"decide through binding arbitration all claims for loss, damage or injury by one Government against the other, and by nationals (including both natural and juridical persons) of one party against the Government of the other party or entities owned or controlled by the other party that are

- related to the conflict that was the subject of the Framework Agreement, the Modalities for its Implementation and the Cessation of Hostilities Agreement, and
- result from violations of international humanitarian law, including the 1949 Geneva Conventions, or other violations of international law."

Under Article 5 (15) and (17), Expenses of the Commission shall be borne equally by the parties and decisions and awards be honoured by them and promptly paid. So far partial awards have been made on prisoners of war claims (1 July 2003), claims of misconduct related to the armed conflict in the central front (28 April 2004) and claims on alleged mistreatment of civilians (17 December 2004), in each case with distinct findings of liability for violations of international law, but no specific compensation has been awarded so far. The parties' remaining liability claims were heard *in camera* in April 2005. It is to be hoped that these decisions may eventually lead to a settlement of individual claims of Eritrean and Ethiopian victims.

The *Iraq Property Claims Commission (IPCC),* based on a regulation promulgated by the Coalition Provisional Authority which was entered into force as Iraqi law on July 2004[102], was established to redress certain wrongful takings of real

---

[99] Annex 7 to the Dayton Accords, Agreement on Refugees and Displaced Persons, Arts. I and XII(2); see at http://www.db.idpproject.org/Sites/IdpProjectDb/idpSurvey.nsf/wViewCountries/CB414C2EEE57A32CC1256FCD0049E577; *H. Van Houtte*, Mass property claim resolution in a post-war society: the Commission for Real Property Claims in Bosnia and Herzegovina, 48 ICLQ (1999), 632.

[100] UNMIK Regulation 1999/23; see *A. Dodson*/*A. Heiskanen*, Housing and Property Restitutions in Kosovo, in: S. Leckie (ed.), returning Home: Housing and Property Restitution Rights and Internally Displaced Persons, Transnational Publishers, New York, 2003; http://www.hpdkosovo.org.

[101] http://www.pca-cpa.org/ENGLISH/RPC/#Eritrea-Ethiopia%20Claims%20Commission.

[102] Coalition Provisional Authority Regulation Number 12, Iraq Property Claims Commission, Annex A: the Statute Establishing of the Iraq Property Claims Commission (24 June 2004), http://ipcciraq.org/08_legal.htm, see also http://ipcciraq.org/01_about.htm.

property by confiscation, seizure, expropriation, forced sale, or otherwise, in Iraq during the period 17 July 1968 to 30 June 2005.

Two other cases are still unsettled:

The *International Commission of Inquiry on Darfur*, established under SC Res 1564 (18 September 2004), has proposed the establishment of a Compensation Commission as a measure complementary to the referral to the ICC[103]. The Committee should consist of 15 members, 10 appointed by the Secretary-General and 5 by an independent Sudanese body. It should be chaired by an international member and split into five chambers, each of 3 members. Four chambers should deal with compensation for any international crime perpetrated in Darfur. A special fifth chamber should deal specifically with compensation for victims of rape, considering the widespread nature of this crime in Darfur. Funding of the Commission should be provided by the Sudanese authorities, which should be requested by the Security Council to place the necessary sum into an escrow account. Funding for compensation of victims of crimes committed by rebels should be afforded through a Trust Fund to be established on the basis of international voluntary contributions. The Security Council did not take decision on this specific proposal, but in a Resolution under Chapter VII decided to refer the situation in Darfur since 1 July 2002 to the Prosecutor of the ICC, emphasizing "the need to promote healing and reconciliation", and encouraging in this respect "the creation of institutions, involving all sectors of Sudanese society, such as truth and/or reconciliation commissions, in order to complement judicial processes". The Security Council expressly stated that none of the expense incurred shall be borne by the United Nations, but by the parties to the Rome Statute, and it invited the Prosecutor to address the Council on actions taken[104].

On 30 June 2003 the Parliament in *Northern Cyprus* had enacted the "Law on Compensation for Immovable Properties Located within the Boundaries of the Turkish Republic of Northern Cyprus (TRNC)". A commission was set up under this law with a mandate to deal with compensation claims, without, however, bringing much redress. On 22 December 2005 the European Court of Human Rights decided on the application of a Greek landowner in Northern Cyprus, Myra Xenides-Arestis, and concluded that there had been and continues to be a violation of Article 1 of Protocol No. 1 (protection of property) to the European Convention on Human Rights by virtue of the fact that the applicant is denied access to, control, use and enjoyment of her property and any compensation for the interference with her property rights. It considered that Turkey had to introduce a remedy which secured, in respect of the Convention violations identified in the judgment, genuinely effective redress for the applicant as well as in relation to all similar applications pending before the Court, in accordance with the principles for the pro-

[103] Report of the International Commission of Inquiry on Darfur to the United Nations Secretary-General, Geneva, 25 January 2005, paras. 590-603, 649.

[104] SC Res 1593 (2005) of 31 March 2005. The Prosecutor opened investigations on 6 June 2005.

tection of the rights laid down in Article 8 and Article 1 of Protocol No. 1.[105] The decision is interpreted differently by both sides. While Greek Cypriots argue that it requires an effective remedy of restoration of properties and compensation for the loss of use, Turkey holds that the case affirms the use of an internal compensation commission within the TRNC to resolve the claims.

This overview of recent and current state practice may illustrate that effective efforts to bring redress to war victims are largely depending on international cooperation and support. It may be premature to propose a general internationalisation of such efforts which so far have been developed in too many different ways. The United Nations may not be the single authority to lend its support in the interest of the victims. It is to be appreciated that work is being undertaken to evaluate the experience of the various claims settlement bodies in a more systematic way: the new ILA Committee on the Compensation of Victims of War[106] will look into main problems of procedures, including appeal mechanisms and information policies of recent and existing claims bodies, using data bases available at the Permanent Court of Arbitration in The Hague and other sources, to develop draft elements for future model solutions.

(20) There is an encouraging practice of claims commissions established by states willing or persuaded by other states or ordered by the Security Council under Chapter VII to bring redress in specific situations.

6. Forms of Reparation

Forms of reparation include restitution, compensation, rehabilitation, satisfaction, and guarantees of non-repetition[107]. Satisfaction may include an acknowledgement of the breach, an expression of regret or an official apology, and assurances of non-repetition of the violation. It may also include the undertaking of disciplinary or penal action against the actors.

Still today, the right to individual reparation mainly rests within municipal legal orders and there are no other remedies for individual victims, except under national law. An international legal regime of individual reparations could strengthen democratic developments and have deterrent effects for some perpetrators. While full reparation will be quite impossible in almost every case, honest efforts to provide reparations are essential for an effective peace process and immaterial measures including recognition of facts and responsibilities are not less important than payments and restitution[108].

It is open to doubt, whether general modalities of reparation for individual victims will ever be widely adopted by states. *Theo van Boven* and subsequently

---

[105] Judgment available at: http://ius.info/EUII/EUCHR/dokumenti%5C2005%5C12%5C CASE_OF_XENIDES-ARESTIS_v._TURKEY_22_12_2005.html.

[106] Supra n. 17.

[107] See Art. 34 DARS.

[108] Supra n. 16 and accompanying text.

Cherif Bassiouni, entrusted by the UN Commission on Human Rights with exactly that work[109], have produced relevant reports[110], following the modalities of reparation developed by the ILC in the Draft Articles on Responsibility of States for internationally wrongful acts (DARS), but neglecting the fact that these modalities were established for relationships between states and did not touch upon individual reparation claims. The Basic Principles and Guidelines proposed in these reports have not met with much support by states. Insofar as they aim at full compensation for victims, they have rightly been criticized as being unrealistic and politically flawed[111].

An international legal regime of individual reparations would have some practical value nevertheless, even if no compensation can be offered by international bodies and notwithstanding the fact that the importance of municipal solutions can hardly be disputed. International principles on reparation for violations committed in armed conflicts may strengthen democratic developments and have deterrent effects for some perpetrators. As experience with truth commissions has shown, a mechanism for establishing facts in individual cases is important for post-conflict peace building. In this context immaterial measures including recognition of facts and responsibilities are not less important than material reparations. It would certainly be in the best interest of the individual victims to develop rights (and duties) under international law independently from rights and duties of his or her home state. But a cautious approach should be taken to secure realistic results. As expressed in a former draft for Article 42 (3) DARS, 'in no case shall reparation result in depriving the population of a State of its own means of subsistence'[112]. Unfortunately that provision has disappeared from the final version. It should remain in the minds of those working for balanced post-conflict solutions.

On 19 April 2005, the UN Commission on Human Rights has adopted "Basic Principles and Guidelines on the Right to a Remedy and Reparation for Victims of Gross Violations of International Human Rights Law and Serious Violations of International Humanitarian Law"[113]. According to this document, the obligation to respect, ensure respect for and implement international human rights law and international humanitarian law, includes, inter alia, the duty: (a) to take appropriate measures to prevent violations; (b) to investigate violations effectively, promptly, thoroughly and impartially and, where appropriate, take action against those alleg-

---

109 See Sub-Commission on Prevention of Discrimination and Protection of Minorities, Resolution 1989/13, Commission on Human Rights, Resolutions 1996/35, 1998/43.

110 U.N. Doc. E/CN.4/Sub.2/1993/8 (2 July 1993); E/CN.4/Sub.2/1996/17 (24 May 1996); E/CN.4/1997/104 (16 January 1997); E/CN.4/2000/62 (18 January 2000); E/CN.4/2000/62 (18 January 2001). See also note by the secretariat E/CN.4/2002/70 and report of *Alejandro Salinas*, Chairperson-Rapporteur of the third consultative meeting on the "basic principles and guidelines on the right to a remedy and reparation for victims of violations of international human rights and humanitarian law" (E/CN.4/2005/59).

111 *Tomuschat*, supra n. 15.

112 Report of the International Law Commission on the work of its forty-eighth session, 51 U.N., GAOR Supp. (No 10), U.N. Doc. A/51/10 (1996).

113 Annex to Human Rights Resolution 2005/35, at http://ap.ohchr.org/documents/E/CHR/resolutions/E-CN_4-RES-2005-35.doc.

edly responsible in accordance with domestic and international law; (c) to provide victims with equal and effective access to justice; and (d) to provide effective remedies to victims, including reparation. This most recent result of the *van Boven/Bassiouni* project, which had been started in the Human Rights Commission fifteen years ago, vigorously confirms the responsibility of states to provide remedies and reparation for gross violations, but it does no longer address the controversial question of individual rights, except for a plea to provide equal and effective access to justice, adequate, effective and prompt reparation for harm suffered, and access to relevant information concerning violations and reparation mechanisms. Thus again the responsibility of states is invoked, to voluntarily close gaps which continue to exist in current international law. It may be realistic to support practical solutions, which should be developed rather pragmatically for each single situation, and not expect generic provisions of international law in this respect.

While a convincing general solution of the reparation problem is still not apparent, an individual complaints procedure for violations of international humanitarian law should be encouraged. It might be developed either as a new mechanism[114] or use existing human rights mechanisms. An opportunity for individual victims to apply to competent international organisations is essential for ensuring monitoring and providing remedies against violations.

(21) Forms of reparations include restitution, compensation, rehabilitation, satisfaction, and guarantees of non-repetition. If the case demands, compensation must be paid. While full reparation will be impossible in almost every case, honest efforts to provide reparations are essential for an effective peace process. Immaterial measures including recognition of facts and responsibilities are not less important than payments and restitution.

7. The Duty to Ensure Respect for International Humanitarian Law

The duty of states to respect and ensure respect for international humanitarian law, as enshrined in common Article 1 GC, has been (and certainly will be) subject to a dynamic interpretation[115]. Its relevance also for non-international armed conflicts, which had been denied decades ago, is now accepted.

---

[114] See: Hague Appeal for Peace. Draft Additional Protocol to the Geneva Conventions Establishing an Individual Complaints Procedure for Violations of International Humanitarian Law [http://www.haguepeace.org]; *Jann Kleffner*, Establishing an Individual Complaints Procedure for Violations of International Humanitarian Law, in 3 Yearbook of International Humanitarian Law (2000), 384-401; *Jann Kleffner*, Improving Compliance with International Humanitarian Law through the Establishment of an Individual Complaints Procedure, in 15 Leiden Journal of International Law (2002), 237-250.

[115] *F. Kalshoven*, The Undertaking to Respect and Ensure Respect in All Circumstances: From Tiny Seed to Ripening Fruit, in 2 YIHL (1999), pp. 1 et seq.; *B. Kessler*, Die Durchsetzung der Genfer Abkommen von 1949 in nicht-internationalen bewaffneten

Article 89 AP I confirms an obligation of states to act, jointly or individually, in co-operation with the United Nations and in conformity with the UN Charter in situations of serious violations. That obligation is as valid for non-international armed conflicts as it is in international armed conflicts, even if the ICRC Customary Law Study is silent on this issue. Security Council involvement in countermeasures is by now established practice also in non-international armed conflicts.

Whereas common Article 1 GC deals with obligations of states, it leaves states full discretion in deciding on what specific measures should be taken in accordance with international law. It is also important to note that common Article 1 does not offer any claims. Under Article 42 DARS, too, only the "injured state" is entitled to claim reparation. In the first reading the ILC had included among the injured states "any other state bound by a rule protecting human rights and all states in the case of international crime"[116]. But in the second reading this approach was explicitly abandoned. Article 42 (b) (ii) DARS now provides that a state is only considered injured if the breach is "of such a character as radically to change the position of all the other States to which the obligation is owed with respect to the further performance of the obligation". The Commentary refers to Article 60 (2)(c) of the Vienna Convention on the Law of Treaties as an analogous rule and offers as examples the Antarctic Treaty, disarmament treaties, nuclear free zones treaties, or "any other treaty where each parties" performance is effectively conditioned upon and requires the performance of each of the others[117].

Effective compliance with the duties under common Article 1 requires multilateral support for which the role of international organizations and regional arrangements must be stressed. The involvement of non-governmental organizations and civil society at large is indispensable within this process.

(22) The duty of states to ensure respect for international humanitarian law applies to both international and internal armed conflicts. Effective compliance with this duty requires multilateral efforts and the support of international organizations, regional arrangements and civil society.

Konflikten auf Grundlage ihres gemeinsamen Art. 1, Berlin, Duncker & Humblot, 2001.

116 Yearbook of the ILC 1985, Vol. II, Part Two, p. 25 (First Reading Draft Article 40 (2)(e)(iii) and (3)); *K. Sachariew*, "States" entitlement to take action to enforce international humanitarian law, IRRC, No. 270, 1989, pp. 180, 184-188.

117 See supra n. 6, Commentary, paras. (13) and (14) to Art. 42 DARS.

E. The International Responsibility for Violations Committed by Non-State Entities

1. State Responsibility in Non-international Armed Conflicts

It would be less than correct to deny international responsibility for violations of international humanitarian law committed in non-international armed conflicts altogether. The fact that both common Article 3 and AP II are silent on this issue, do not exclude that under existing international law states may be held responsible for any wrongful act attributable to them. Such acts may be committed by regular armed forces or by state-owned corporations which exercise elements of government authority within the meaning of draft Article 5 DARS. They may also be committed by *de facto* agents, i.e. persons in fact acting on the instructions of, or under the direction or control of, the state (Article 8 DARS). They may even be committed by armed opposition groups, if the state has failed to protect victims of violations.

(23) States may be held responsible for violations of international humanitarian law committed in non-international armed conflicts and attributable to these states.

(24) Such attributability exists for acts of regular armed forces, police and other state organs. It is also accepted for acts of insurgents taking over government powers post-conflict.

2. Attributability of Acts to State Organs

The 1996 version of Article 14 (3) DARS had stated that the fact that the conduct of an organ of an insurrectional movement was not be considered an act of state "is without prejudice to the attribution of the conduct of the organ of the insurrectional movement to that movement in any case in which such attribution may be made under international law". This Article was subsequently deleted because it was deemed to fall outside the scope of the subject matter under discussion. The Special Rapporteur noted that "the responsibility of such movements, for example for breaches of international humanitarian law, can certainly be envisaged"[118]. Consequently, the Special Rapporteur in his Commentary to DARS mentioned the possibility "that the insurrectional movement may itself be held responsible for its own conduct under international law, for example for a breach of international humanitarian law committed by its forces". But again he did not pursue this further, as "[t]he topic of the international responsibility of unsuccessful insurrectional or other movements … falls outside the scope of the present Articles, which

[118] ILC, First report on State responsibility by the Special Rapporteur, Addendum, UN Doc. A/CN.4/490/Add.5, 22 July 1998, § 275 (cited in *Henckaerts/Doswald-Beck*, supra n. 29, Vol. II, Part 2 (Ch. 42, § 57), p. 3517.

are concerned only with the responsibility of States"[119]. The conduct of successful insurrectional movements is, however, fully attributable to the state when government powers have been taken over after successful insurgence[120], as explicitly described in DARS, in which the two alternatives: insurrectional movements which become the new government of a state and movements which succeed in establishing a new state are both addressed and treated likewise[121]. In his Commentary, the Special Rapporteur shows some confusion in defining the term "insurrectional movement" according to the extraordinary high threshold of AP II[122]. He may have simply overlooked the much lower threshold under Article 3 common to the Geneva Conventions and the wealth of literature related thereto. But he did offer excellent sources of state practice and jurisprudence, including the classical statement made in the 1903 *Bolivar Railway Company* arbitration:

"The nation is responsible for the obligations of a successful revolution from its beginning, because in theory, it represented *ab initio* a changing national will, crystallizing in the finally successful result"[123].

Hence despite some critical views in literature[124] at least for the conduct of successful insurrectional movements, it is not correct to conclude that an obligation of the state to pay compensation for violations of the law of non-international armed conflicts does not exist.

But is there an international responsibility for atrocities committed by unsuccessful insurrectional movements? The Special Rapporteur's expectation, that relevant provisions might be found in the *lex specialis* rules of international humanitarian law[125] may prove to be wrong, but a general rule stems from his own consideration, that a state may be responsible for the effects of the conduct of private parties, if it failed to take necessary measures to prevent those effects[126]. The ICRC Customary Law Study refers to a 'widespread and representative practice in which States have made efforts to compensate victims of violations of interna-

---

119 United Nations, International Law Commission, Report on the Work of its Fifty-third Session (23 April - 1 June and 2 July - 10 August 2001), General Assembly, Official Records, Fifty-sixth Session, Supplement No. 10 (A/56/10), chapter IV, at www.un.org/law/ilc/reports/2001/2001report.htm, Draft Article 10, Commentary, para. 16.

120 *Zegveld*, supra n. 4.

121 Art. 10 (1) and (2) DARS.

122 See supra n. 6, Art. 10 DARS, Commentary, para. 9.

123 UNRIAA, Vol. IV, p. 445 (1903), at p. 453, cited supra n. 6, Art. 10 DARS, Commentary, para. 12.

124 *Heintschel v. Heinegg*, supra n. 2, pp. 52-56, 60 who had based this conclusion not only on the absence of relevant treaty provisions in common Art. 3 and AP II, but also on an alleged lack of relevant custom. The opposite position was taken by *Zegveld*, supra n. 4.

125 See supra n. 6, Commentary, para. (16) to Art. 10 DARS.

126 See supra n. 6, Chapter II, general comments, para. (4) with reference to the *Teheran Hostage* case, I.C.J. Reports 1980, p. 3.

tional humanitarian law committed in non-international armed conflicts'[127]. Such practice may have been voluntary rather than stemming from an international obligation. States may be held responsible for omissions, in particular where they have failed to exercise due diligence in preventing breaches of international humanitarian law by non-state actors (see Articles 2, 23 DARS), if they failed to make efforts possible for them to protect victims of violations[128]. Yet such possibilities may vanish with the intensity and duration of an armed conflict.

(25) States may be held responsible also for omissions, if they have failed to protect the civilian population against violations committed by armed opposition groups.

3. Individual Responsibility of Non-State Actors

Non-state actors including members of armed opposition groups may be held individually responsible for compensation of serious crimes in accordance with Article 75 of the ICC Statute. The ICC may decide on reparations also in cases where no international responsibility exists, as in accordance with Article 8(2)(c)(iv) it has jurisdiction also for war crimes committed in non-international armed conflicts.

Victims of violations may also bring a civil suit for damages against the offenders before national courts post-conflict. Claims may be directed against leaders and members of the group and against the group as such.

The UN Secretary-General, in his 1998 report on the causes of conflict and the promotion of durable peace and sustainable development in Africa, recommended that "in order to make warring parties more accountable for their actions ... combatants [should] be held financially liable to their victims under international law where civilians are made the deliberate target of aggression". He further recommended that "international legal machinery be developed to facilitate efforts to find, attach and seize the assets of transgressing parties and their leaders"[129].

The ICRC Customary Law Study also points to "some practice to the effect that armed opposition groups are required to provide appropriate reparation for the damage resulting from violations of international humanitarian law"[130].

---

[127] *Henckaerts/Doswald-Beck*, supra n. 29, Vol I (Ch. 42 Rule 150), p. 548 with reference to practice in Guatemala, the Philippines, Chechnya, Chile, El Salvador, Sri Lanka, Rwanda, and Zimbabwe.

[128] *H. Blomeyer-Bartenstein*, Due Diligence, in R. Bernhardt (ed.), Encyclopedia of Public International Law, Volume I (1992), pp. 1110-1115.

[129] UN-Doc A/52/871-S/1998/318, 13 April 1998. See also Report on the Protection of Civilians in Armed Conflict, UN-Doc S/1999/957, 8 September 1999, para. 38.

[130] Id., pp. 549-550 with reference to practice by armed opposition groups in Colombia, and to SC Res 1071 (1996) with respect to 'the leaders of the factions in Liberia' and a Resolution of the UN Commission on Human Rights with respect to "all the Afghan parties" (UNCHR Res. 1998/70).

(26) Non-state actors including members of armed opposition groups may be held individually responsible for compensation of serious crimes.

4. Accountability of Transnational Corporations

Transnational corporations should be held responsible for wrongful acts committed on their behalf. While such responsibility is an obligation under civil law, states should cooperate in sanctioning unlawful behaviour of transnational corporations and ensure that the victims will be offered redress[131].

(27) Transnational corporations should be held accountable for violations of international humanitarian principles committed on their behalf.

F. Conclusions

1. A Balance Yet to Be Achieved

This report shows a considerable imbalance between individual and state responsibility. Successful efforts have been made in recent years to strengthen individual criminal accountability for violations of international humanitarian law, but much more remains to be done to ensure that states comply with their obligation to make reparations as appropriate. While there is a relatively well established legal responsibility of individuals under international and national law, existing rules to ensure effective implementation of the responsibility of states for internationally wrongful acts are much less perfect and the responsibilities states have under international and national law are not consistent. This is all the more significant as individual perpetrators in most cases cannot be expected to financially fulfil their full liability for violations of human rights and international humanitarian law they have committed.

Strong efforts are necessary to ensure that the responsibility of states to make reparation for losses or injuries caused will not remain theoretical. Political steps are required by states and international organizations to close existing gaps. They may not be limited to violations of the *ius in bello* and exclude a responsibility for violations of the *ius ad bellum* altogether. A comprehensive approach to consequences of state responsibility would be in conformity with the Martens clause[132] which in a very farsighted and generalist way ensures humanitarian protection in

---

[131] *L. Komarova*, Illegal Activity of Transnational Corporations and the Problem of Responsibility for International Crimes and Offences, SYIL 1985, p. 153.

[132] Preamble (para. 8) HC IV, Art. 1 (2) AP I, Preamble (para. 4) AP II; see *D. Fleck*, Friedrich von Martens: A Great International Lawyer from Pärnu, in 10 Baltic Defence Review 2/2003, 19-26, http://www.bdcol.ee/content/pdf_files/bdreview/bdr-2003-10-section2-article1.pdf.

cases not covered by treaty law. While general legal provisions may be difficult to reach, the impact should be laid to practical solutions in each specific case.

2. The Duty of States

States have a duty under common Article 1 GC to ensure respect for international humanitarian law and to protect victims of violations. This duty is subject to a dynamic interpretation. It applies today also in non-international armed conflicts. Whereas common Article 1 GC provides for a general obligation of states, it does not offer them claims to raise in the interest of victims of foreign nationality which do not live in their territory.

Effective compliance with the duties under common Article 1 requires multilateral support for which the role of international organizations and regional arrangements must be stressed. Non-governmental organisations have an important mission to seek redress for victims of war where governments fail to meet their responsibility.

3. State Responsibility in Non-international Armed Conflicts

In non-international armed conflicts states are responsible for gross violations of human rights and international humanitarian law attributable to them. State responsibility does not exclude acts committed by armed opposition groups. This in particular relevant for cases, where states have violated a duty to protect victims of violations or where government powers have been taken over after successful insurgence.

4. Individual Rights

International law offers no individual rights of compensation corresponding to the duties of states to comply with the law. To expect a shift of consensus in this respect would not be realistic. Efforts *de lege ferenda* should concentrate on the development of general procedures that might facilitate post-conflict claims under municipal law.

5. Claims Commissions

Claims commissions may be the most effective means to provide redress for war victims. They will hardly follow generic solutions, but must be adapted to requirements and possibilities of the specific conflict. Ideally, claims commissions should operate under international mandate and with international control.

6. Responsibilities of Non-State Actors

Members of armed opposition groups may be held individually responsible for compensation of serious crimes. Transnational corporations should be held accountable for violations of international humanitarian principles committed on their behalf. States should cooperate in sanctioning unlawful behaviour of non-state actors and ensure that the victims will be offered redress.

7. Preventive Action

As activities to provide reparation remain retroactive and will be largely insufficient, preventive action is required to enforce international responsibility for better compliance with human rights and international humanitarian law.

Retroactive measures against violations of the *ius in bello* cannot replace preventive action to ensure compliance in the future and they will not be convincing without due consideration of what had been done in the past to implement relevant rules.

A convincing response to violations of international humanitarian law is owed to the victims of all armed conflicts and the international community.

Some Comments on the International Responsibility of States

Frits Kalshoven

University Leiden

First, I should like to thank the organizers of this symposium in honour of Professor *Knut Ipsen*, for having invited me to participate in it. My first meetings with Professor *Ipsen* date back to the nineteen seventies, when we were both engaged in the efforts to "reaffirm and develop the international humanitarian law of armed conflict", and I have held him in high esteem ever since.

After the very complete and rich introduction by *Dieter Fleck* to this panel's broad subject of the relations between individual and international responsibility for violations of IHL, I shall restrict my comments to one specific and much narrower topic, viz., the responsibility of states.

It may now be regarded as axiomatic that a state is responsible for any acts or omissions attributable to it and that constitute violations of the law of armed conflict. This actually is no more than an application of the principles, expressed in Articles 1 and 2 of the ILC Draft Articles on State Responsibility, that "every wrongful act of a State entails the international responsibility of that State" and "there is an internationally wrongful act of a State when conduct consisting of an action or omission … is attributable to the State under international law and … constitutes a breach of an international obligation of the State." Already a century ago, Article 3 of the 1907 Hague Convention on land warfare stated the rule with respect to acts of the armed forces of a belligerent state in particular: "A belligerent Party … shall be responsible for all acts committed by persons forming part of its armed forces." The Article specified one consequence of violation of the rules set forth in the Regulations annexed to the Convention: the belligerent state "shall, if the case demands, be liable to pay compensation." (Actually, in the negotiating history, the secondary rule on compensation had come first and the principle of responsibility was added for completeness sake.) The ILC Draft Articles elaborate the legal consequences of an internationally wrongful act in much greater detail. In particular, they list restitution and satisfaction alongside compensation.

Article 3 of the 1907 Hague Convention is a typical product of a conference that had other matters on its mind. It bluntly states principle and rule, does not specify whether "acts" will encompass omissions, and entirely leaves open who may invoke a state's responsibility for a violation of applicable rules, and when, where and how. As to this, the ILC Draft Articles obviously deal only with invocation by another state. The question is whether under Article 3 as well, states are the only ones entitled to invoke the responsibility of another state; or might individual persons share this right? I shall revert to this issue later on.

I take the question of inter-state claims first. Even prior to 1907, the right of belligerent states to invoke an enemy state's responsibility for violations of the law of armed conflict was well established. Obviously, no international court existed at the time where states could lodge their complaint. Legal means at their disposal included unilateral protest and recourse to measures of reprisal (a topic I have written about more than once and that I need not discuss now). Belligerent states might even attempt to enter into a bilateral process of negotiations to settle a dispute, although it was never very likely that negotiations between belligerent parties about alleged unlawful wartime behaviour would lead to a settlement during the conflict.

In theory, a post-war bilateral agreement settling reciprocal claims for compensation might stand a better chance. In this context, I should mention the so-called lump-sum agreements concluded in the wake of several of last century's major wars. Although on the face of it concluded with the consent of all the (ex-belligerent) parties, these agreements were imposed by the victors on the vanquished state. This state was made to pay an amount of money, ostensibly in compensation for the losses victor states claimed they and their nationals had suffered. These claims could actually include damages caused by alleged violations of the law of armed conflict committed on the side of the vanquished party. But even to the extent this has been the case, the sum claimed in compensation did not rest on an accurate calculation nor on any verification of the justness of individual claims. In truth, the size of the "lump sum" was the outcome of a political calculation, driven by the effect the victor wanted to achieve in, or in relation to, the vanquished party. – Needless to say, lump-sum agreements by definition are one-sided and do not take into account the harm suffered by the vanquished party and its inhabitants, whether from the war itself or specifically from violations of the law of armed conflict that might have been committed by the victorious armed forces.

Post-war bilateral settlements for wartime losses have also come about between belligerent parties and neutral states. In the course of World War Two, Allied bombs occasionally fell on Swiss soil, just across the German border; or the shock wave of bombs dropped on German territory did damage to objects on the Swiss side (windows broken, and all that). Negotiations after the war between Switzerland and the ex-belligerents led to the grant of compensation, depending on the factual circumstances of each case. Thus, the United States in an exchange of notes of 21 October 1949 agreed to pay Switzerland 62 million Swiss francs, in "full and final settlement" for all Swiss claims arising out of such incidents involving a violation of neutral rights by U.S. armed forces.

After unilateral and bilateral methods, third-party involvement is another road that may lead to the settlement of outstanding issues. The only formal forum originally available to states was arbitration. Taking the law of armed conflict in a broad sense, the well-known "Alabama" arbitration stands out as an early example. The arbitral award of 1872 held Great Britain guilty of having violated its obligations as a neutral state in respect of the parties to the American Civil War, and Britain had to pay 15.5 million dollars to the United States.

As of today, the most authoritative legal forum available is the International Court of Justice. One early instance of the Court being seized of an armed conflict-connected case was the short-lived application Pakistan filed on 11 May 1973, accusing India of maltreatment of Pakistani prisoners of war. Seven months later, by a letter of 14 December 1973, Pakistan was happy to inform the Court that bilateral negotiations between the two parties were under way, and it asked for closure of the proceedings; a request the Court honoured the next day.

A recent case involving, inter alia, violations of the law of armed conflict arose from the complaint filed by the Federal Republic of Yugoslavia on 29 April 1999 against a number of NATO states for violations allegedly committed in the bombing campaign these states had started a month earlier, on 24 March 1999. The Court lacked jurisdiction in respect of the United States of America and some other states by virtue of the reservations limiting their acceptances of the Court's jurisdiction. And on 15 December 2004, the Court dismissed the remaining eight cases, having found that on the date of filing its application, the Federal Republic of Yugoslavia had lacked standing to sue before the Court. (I note in passing that Yugoslavia obviously could not accost the Court with a complaint against NATO, the latter organisation not being a state.)

A famous Court case concerning one state's involvement in an internal armed conflict being waged in another state is the case of Nicaragua versus the United States. In the early 1980s, the latter state had supported the *contras*, an armed opposition group operating in the territory of Nicaragua against the Sandinista government. The Court held that the United States was not responsible for violations of the law of armed conflict allegedly committed by the *contras*, for want of what it termed effective control over their activities. On the other hand, the Court by its judgment of 1986 held the United States responsible for its mine laying activities in Nicaragua's territorial waters.

One case before the Court that involves alleged gross violations of the law of armed conflict in a situation of international armed conflict concerns the application Bosnia-Herzegovina filed in 1993 against the then Federal Republic of Yugoslavia. The application alleges violations of the Genocide Convention, apparently as the only conceivable treaty base for jurisdiction of the Court. Today, twelve years later, the case is still pending. A Court press release of 8 December 2004 has announced that public hearings on the merits will open on Monday 27 February 2006. Given the changed political constellation in the region, it remains to be seen how much effort the parties to the dispute will still be willing to spend on the further proceedings.

Another theatre of frequent (armed and political) conflict that occasionally leads to moves in the direction of the ICJ is the Democratic Republic of the Congo with its neighbours. Cases were brought and rapidly withdrawn. One pending case was filed on 28 May 2002 by the Congo against Rwanda. The application lists a series of horrendous acts asserted to have been committed by Rwandan forces operating in the territory of the Congo. It qualifies these acts as violations of human rights as well as of humanitarian law. In effect, I found one fleeting reference to the 1949 Geneva Conventions and the Additional Protocols of 1977. However, the instruments on which the application seeks to base the jurisdiction of the Court all belong to the human rights family. As announced, public hearings in the case were held from 4 to 8 July 2005. The Court is presently writing a judgment which, as it has announced, will deal solely with the issues of its jurisdiction and admissibility of the application, not with the merits of the case.

I may note in passing that reliance on a mixture of human rights law and the law of armed conflict is quite common in current discourse. Although particularly apposite in relation to situations of internal armed conflict, the mix may be helpful in cases of international armed conflict as well. Especially in respect of these latter cases, the scope of application of rules of either body of law needs to be taken into account (as demonstrated by the European Court of Human Rights in the *Bankovic* case). Having said this, the so-called *lex specialis* argument advanced by the United States of America, *inter alia* in the Guantánamo Bay affair, to the effect that applicability of the law of armed conflict excludes the application of human rights norms, is untenable. The law of armed conflict is a *lex specialis* in the sense that many of its rules apply solely in situations of armed conflict. Human rights law, in its own way a *lex specialis* as well, applies to some degree irrespective of whether there is peace or war. The normative similarity if not identity between a number of the principles and rules of the two bodies of law should lead to an insight of complementarity, not to mutual exclusion.

I next turn to a category of cases involving claims of individuals who have incurred damages as a result of violations of the law of armed conflict attributable to a belligerent state. Well-known in this category is the *Nottebohm* case, initiated in 1951 by an application filed by Liechtenstein against Guatemala. Originally of German descent, *Nottebohm* had long lived and worked in Guatemala. In 1939, just before the outbreak of World War Two, he visited Liechtenstein and was rapidly granted the nationality of that state. Even so, Guatemala in the course of the war confiscated as enemy property the goods he had in that country. The claim brought by Liechtenstein on behalf of *Nottebohm* was in compensation for the losses he sustained from the confiscation of his goods. However, the Court found that *Nottebohm*'s remarkably rapid naturalisation in 1939 provided insufficient grounds to override his close bonds with Guatemala and hence held the claim of Liechtenstein inadmissible. Regrettably, the question whether Guatemala's mode of acting had been in conformity with international law thus remained undecided.

Of greater practical significance for the settlement of individual claims have been the claims commissions that operated in the first half of the twentieth century on the basis of bilateral agreements, e.g., between Mexico on the one hand and Great Britain or the United States of America on the other. The cases often involved injury or damage incurred by individuals at the hands of the Mexican police or violent rebel groups. Whenever Mexico was held responsible, either directly for acts of its organs or indirectly for lack of due diligence, it had to pay compensation.

These claims commissions predated Article 3 common to the 1949 Geneva Conventions. As well, neither the notions of internal armed conflict nor of human rights had been introduced into the body of international law. The law applicable in the cases submitted to these claims commissions was a set of rules of international law governing the treatment of foreigners. In the body of international law of the time, it may be said to have stood apart as a sort of *lex specialis*, but without the overtones of conflict of opinion that, as we saw, presently make for some problems in the debate about human rights vs. law of armed conflict.

International commissions for the settlement of individual claims arising out of wartime events have been set up in recent times as well. I mention just two. One is the United Nations Compensation Commission (or UNCC), established in 1991 to deal with claims, both of governments and individuals, arising out of Iraq's invasion and occupation of Kuwait. The claims of individuals were collected and submitted to the UNCC by their home states. Claims needed not concern alleged violations of the law of armed conflict. Rather, the basis of Iraq's responsibility was seen in its unlawful act of aggression against Kuwait, and claims could be submitted for any damage incurred at the hands of the invader. One factor explaining this generosity is the availability of an important sum of Iraqi money seized at the time of the invasion and out of which the payments are made. As so often in inter-state arrangements, the arrangement is noteworthy for its one-sidedness: the commission has no competence over any damage, whether as a result of violations of the law of war or otherwise, caused by the allied forces that came to the defence of Kuwait.

The other, very different example is the Eritrea-Ethiopia Claims Commission. Based on a bilateral agreement of 12 December 2000 between the two parties, the commission is unique in that it is competent to deal with claims, whether from the governments or nationals, for compensation arising from alleged violations of the law of armed conflict committed on either side. A number of claims have been heard and decisions about accountability for violations of the law of armed conflict or general international law have been taken. There remains the matter of actual compensation. A major difference with the UNCC is that Eritrea and Ethiopia are extremely poor countries. One commissioner could be heard wondering what funds would become available to pay the sums allotted in compensation for established violations. In the meantime, he said, the commission would simply continue its work, examining evidence, assessing damage or injury and awarding amounts in compensation.

These two recent examples may suffice to point up some aspects that may temper the at times high expectations of the institution of compensation commissions. A first major point is that, rare exceptions apart, mandates are one-sided, so that violations of the law of armed conflict committed on the other side will remain unaccounted for. Another is the inclination to expand the mandate to cover all war damage (as was the usual practice in lump-sum agreements and as was specifically done in the UNCC). This may be appreciated by those on the receiving end but has nothing to do with the felt need of attribution of responsibility for violations of the law of armed conflict. The third problem is that a majority of present-day armed conflicts are waged in or among poor countries, and they may not easily find the means out of which to pay sums awarded in compensation – unless these were to be reduced to token amounts.

This may be the right place for me to offer some comments on an idea that appears to enjoy widespread popularity and, in effect, was advocated by *Dieter Fleck* in his introduction as well. It is often expressed in the terms that compensation should not only be given for violations of the law of armed conflict but for collateral damage as well. This has a ring of reasonableness to it: when two houses are destroyed, one by an unlawful attack and the other by the side effects of that attack, it would beat comprehension if compensation were provided for the destruction of one house and not for the other.

However, collateral damage may arise as well as the side effect of a perfectly lawful attack. Suppose one of the two houses in our example was in military use and the other not: since the attacker is not liable to pay compensation for the destruction of the first house, I fail to see on what grounds he should be obliged to compensate for the equally lawful damage to the other house. In actual fact, collateral damage is as likely – if not more so – to occur as a result of an attack that is lawful according to the applicable rules of the law of armed conflict, than of an unlawful one.

Conceivably, the collateral damage argument simply reflects the feeling that civilians should not have to suffer the hardships of war. With all the sympathy this feeling deserves, one may comment: (1) that compensation of civilian losses on this ground is not a matter of law, at least not under the existing rules of the law of armed conflict; (2) there is no particular reason why the party causing the damage should pay the compensation, and (3) a simpler and more practical solution would be for either party to bear its own losses.

As noted, the legal grounds for holding Iraq accountable for all damage resulting from its attack and occupation of Kuwait was the illegality of the attack. In combination with the availability of the requisite capital, this provides a comfortable situation. Yet the point should be made that views on the legality or illegality of the opening of hostilities usually differ starkly. Take the attack of the United States of America and its allies on Iraq: this split the world into two parties, with each side equally firmly convinced of the correctness of its judgment that the attack was/was not justifiable under the rules governing recourse to armed force. Who then will determine whether losses should be compensated?

In sum, therefore, I am not convinced that "collateral damage" should be added to the agenda of promotion of individual rights to compensation for violation of the law of armed conflict.

My last point, somewhat connected with the foregoing, concerns the question whether individuals can directly claim compensation from a belligerent or ex-belligerent state for the effects they suffered from violations of the law of armed conflict. As noted at the outset, Article 3 of the 1907 Hague Convention on land warfare does not specify who may be the claimant. States obviously have this right, and there is nothing in the text of Article 3 that contradicts this. Nor is there anything in the text that excludes the possibility for individuals to have this capacity as well (although not, obviously, by bringing a claim on the international plane). In effect, the drafting history of the article suggests that it was written first of all out of a perceived need to facilitate access for individuals to the authorities of the belligerent party at whose hands they suffered damage.

One practical way for belligerent states to fill the gap left in 1907 is to open a counter where day-to-day matters of compensation are directly settled. It appears to be the case that the U.S. armed forces regularly apply this method in their operations on other states' territories. This appears to be exactly what the initiators of Article 3 of 1907 had in mind in the first place.

However, once the war over and the troops out of the territory, this easy method no longer obtains. The question then arises whether individuals can submit their claims to any domestic court. *Shimoda* is a famous case where Japanese nationals claimed damages from their own state for the effects they had suffered from the use by the United States of atomic bombs against Hiroshima and Nagasaki. While the Tokyo District Court in its judgment of December 1963 held the use of the bombs unlawful, the action of the plaintiffs failed, mainly as a result of the doctrine of sovereign immunity.

More logical is for an individual to try his or her luck at the courts of the ex-enemy state. Individuals have access to foreign domestic courts for any number of affairs. This may be on the basis of the domestic law of the court or of a rule of international law the court applies either directly (when the national legal system and the character of the rule permit this) or after the legislator has incorporated it into the national legal order. Issues of violation of the law of armed conflict might belong in the category of tort cases, and an individual victim might find an argument supporting his or her claim under this heading in Article 3 of the 1907 Hague Convention. Obviously, our claimant will encounter a number of obstacles, and the chances of success seem slim. The point to be made is, however, that the obstacles are a matter of domestic law and, indeed, politics: there is nothing in Article 3, nor in the position of individuals, that would prevent a domestic court from deciding in favour of the individual claimant.

Some years ago I was involved as an expert witness in the "comfort women" cases before the Tokyo District Court. I learned one important thing. These women, victims of multiple rape by members of the Japanese armed forces in territories under Japanese occupation, were not seeking financial retribution: what they really wanted was to be able to tell their story – a thing many of them had not been able to do for long years after the war. Hence their disappointment at the extremely limited number of witnesses called to give testimony before the Japanese courts (and, of course, at the negative outcome of the proceedings). Hence also their enthusiasm and thankfulness for the mock trial staged in Tokyo somewhat later. Under the presidency of Judge Gabrielle Kirk McDonald, the "Women's International War Crimes Tribunal for the Trial of Japan's Military Sexual Slavery" sat in public session from 8 to 10 December 2000. The tribunal, and the several hundred Japanese who attended the session, heard the voices and saw the tears of survivors from all the countries where the "comfort women" system had worked. Later, on 4 December 2001, the tribunal published its judgment, as long and detailed and as replete with evidence as are the judgments of the ICTY or the ICTR. For the women, however, the important thing was that their voices had been heard – in terms of the ILC Draft Articles: they had been given satisfaction.

I should add that in another set of cases I was involved in before the Tokyo courts and that concerned claims of ex-prisoners of war and civilian detainees, monetary compensation was in fact the satisfaction the claimants were seeking. This was motivated as much by a desire to make Japan pay for their past sufferings as by dissatisfaction with their own authorities for having accepted lump-sum agreements that were insufficient to compensate all individual suffering and were more suited to help the Japanese economy make a new start.

The upshot of my remarks about past and present events is that too much should not be expected of official legal institutions created or mandated to enforce the responsibility of states for violations of the law of armed conflict attributable to them. Individuals depend entirely on the goodwill of governments, whether to espouse their claim in the exercise of diplomatic protection, to set up *ad hoc* international machinery mandated to entertain their case, or to open up the domestic courts for their claims. True, the Commission on Human Rights in April 2005 adopted the *Van Boven/Bassiouni* "basic principles and guidelines on the right to a remedy and reparation for victims of gross violations of international human rights law and serious violations of international humanitarian law". I am afraid, however, that the adoption of these principles, even if confirmed later this year at the next session of the General Assembly, will not change the world: it will still be the governments that, on a case-by-case basis, determine whether to do something for the individual and, if so, what.

The legal means available to the states on the international plane are not much better. The International Court of Justice is a most honourable institution but it rarely has jurisdiction in a contentious case involving a belligerent state's international responsibility under the law of armed conflict. Arbitration might hold out somewhat greater promise, in view of its greater flexibility. But recourse to arbitration depends on consent of both sides. Eritrea-Ethiopia is a fortunate, yet rare, recent case where a variant of arbitration was agreed.

What remains for states is the political process. Whether individually (if they are strong) or collectively, in *ad hoc* alliances or through established bodies such as the Security Council, they may, and should, pursue the cause of respect for the law of armed conflict, if need be, by holding belligerent states publicly responsible for their violations of this body of law.

Comment: Responsibility for Violations of International Humanitarian Law, International Criminal Law and Human Rights Law – Synergy and Conflict?

Andreas Zimmermann

Walther-Schücking-Institute of International Law, University of Kiel

I. Introductory remarks

It is a great pleasure for me to be able to participate in this symposium in honour of Professor *Knut Ipsen* and it is even a greater pleasure to comment on the excellent paper presented by my colleague *Dieter Fleck*. I was asked to focus on the interrelationship of violations of international humanitarian law, international criminal law and human rights law, and even with regard to this somewhat limited topic, I will only make some temptative remarks, which should therefore be more considered as 'food for thought and discussion' rather than as a fully developed paper.

II. Interrelationship between the law of State responsibility and international criminal law

My first point concerns the interconnection between State responsibility with regard to violations of international humanitarian law on the one hand, and individual criminal responsibility on the other. Let me start with an obvious remark already made by *Frits Kalshoven* in his presentation, namely that violations of international humanitarian law, when committed by individuals whose behaviour may be attributed to a given State within the meaning of Chapter II of the ILC Articles on State Responsibility[1], entail the State responsibility of that given State[2] – a principle reiterated in both, Art. 3 of Hague IV[3] and Art. 91 of the First Addi-

---

1 Cf. generally on the ILC (Draft) Articles on State Responsibility *C. Tams*, All's well that ends well – Comments on the ILC's articles on state responsibility, in Zeitschrift für ausländisches öffentliches Recht und Völkerrecht 2003, pp. 759 et seq.

2 Cf. supra *F. Kalshoven*, pp. 207 et seq.

3 Said provision stipulates:

tional Protocol of 1977[4]. This is even true where a given combatant acts in contravention of instructions given to him or her by his or her superiors[5], be it in the form of individualized orders, be it in the form of generalized field manuals such as the German "Zentrale Dienstvorschrift: Humanitäres Völkerrecht in bewaffneten Konflikten"[6]. This principle of attribution applies to both, international and non-international armed conflicts, but in the latter form of conflicts for purposes of *State* responsibility[7] solely extends to those persons, whose acts may either be attributed to the State *ex ante* by virtue of Arts. 4-9 of the ILC Articles on State Responsibility[8], or where the acts of a successful insurrectional movement are to be attributed to a State *ex post facto* by virtue of Art. 10 of the ILC Articles[9]. And given that war crimes, which carry with them individual criminal responsibility, do constitute the worst form of violations of international humanitarian law, the commission of them by persons whose acts are attributable to a State therefore by the same token also entail State responsibility. This fact does constitute the more

"A belligerent party which violates the provisions of the said Regulations shall, if the case demands, be liable to pay compensation. It shall be responsible for all acts committed by persons forming part of its armed forces".

4 Art. 91 of the First Additional Protocol quite similarly provides:
"A Party to the conflict which violates the provisions of the Conventions or of this Protocol shall, if the case demands, be liable to pay compensation. It shall be responsible for all acts committed by persons forming part of its armed forces".

5 See for such proposition Art. 7 of the ILC Articles on State responsibility which provides:
"The conduct of an organ of a State or of a person or entity empowered to exercise elements of the governmental authority shall be considered an act of the State under international law if the organ, person or entity acts in that capacity, even if it exceeds its authority or contravenes instructions".

6 Bundesministerium der Verteidigung (ed.), Zentrale Dienstvorschrift 15/2: Humanitäres Völkerrecht in bewaffneten Konflikten, 1992; text to be found inter alia in *D. Fleck* (ed.), Handbuch Humanitäres Völkerrecht, München 1994.

7 It is another matter, yet, whether an insurrectional or other movement may incur responsibility under international law for violations committed by its troops. This issue, which is outside the scope of this comment is, inter alia, dealt with by *L. Zegved*, Accountability of Armed Opposition Groups in International Law, Cambridge 2002, p. 133 et seq.

8 Cf. generally *A. de Hoogh*, Articles 4 and 8 of the 2001 ILC Articles on state responsibility, the Tadić case and attribution of acts of Bosnian Serb authorities to the Federal Republic of Yugoslavia, Brit. YB. Int. L. 72 (2001), pp. 255 et seq.

9 Art. 10 of the ILC Articles reads:
"1. The conduct of an insurrectional movement which becomes the new government of a State shall be considered an act of that State under international law.
2. The conduct of a movement, insurrectional or other, which succeeds in establishing a new State in part of the territory of a pre-existing State or in a territory under its administration shall be considered an act of the new State under international law.
3. This article is without prejudice to the attribution to a State of any conduct, however related to that of the movement concerned, which is to be considered an act of that State by virtue of articles 4 to 9".

or less obvious first interrelationship between international humanitarian law and international criminal law.

This obvious and at first glance clear-cut principle has to be however nuanced in several ways. *First*, while the criminal responsibility of an individual might be excluded by virtue of a defence, as now codified in Arts. 31-32 of the Rome Statute[10] or the lack of a respective *mens rea*[11], this fact does not exclude that the very same acts would still entail the State responsibility of the State concerned on whose behalf the individual concerned was acting.

Second, the question might arise whether any determination of individual criminal responsibility does not presuppose an, at least implicit, determination of a violation of an applicable norm of international humanitarian law by the State on whose behalf the person concerned has acted. This might be exemplified by an example: When ratifying the First Additional Protocol of 1977 in 1998 the United Kingdom submitted a reservation whereby it reserved the right to take countermeasures with regard to acts which would otherwise violate Arts. 51-55 of the First Additional Protocol in case the adverse party itself previously committed violations of Arts. 51 through 55 of the Protocol[12]. Provided one assumes that this reservation is legal and does not contradict the very object and purpose of the treaty as contemplated in Art. 19 of the Vienna Convention on the Law of Treaties (which in turn has codified customary international law on the matter[13]) despite the specific prohibitions of reprisals contained in the First Additional Protocol it-

---

[10] Cf. generally as to the content of the various defences as contained in Arts. 31 and 32 of the Rome Statute inter alia *A. Eser*, Art. 31, in: O. Triffterer, Commentary on the Rome Statute of the International Criminal Court, Baden-Baden 1999 and *O. Triffterer*, Art. 32, in: id.

[11] See generally *G. Werle*, International Criminal Law (2005), pp. 104 et seq.

[12] This reservation reads:
"The obligations of Articles 51 and 55 are accepted on the basis that any adverse party against which the United Kingdom might be engaged will itself scrupulously observe those obligations. If an adverse party makes serious and deliberate attacks, in violation of Article 51 or Article 52 against the civilian population or civilians or against civilian objects, or, in violation of Articles 53, 54 and 55, on objects or items protected by those Articles, the United Kingdom will regard itself as entitled to take measures otherwise prohibited by the Articles in question to the extent that it considers such measures necessary for the sole purpose of compelling the adverse party to cease committing violations under those Articles, but only after formal warning to the adverse party requiring cessation of the violations has been disregarded and then only after a decision taken at the highest level of government. Any measures thus taken by the United Kingdom will not be disproportionate to the violations giving rise there to and will not involve any action prohibited by the Geneva Conventions of 1949 nor will such measures be continued after the violations have ceased. The United Kingdom will notify the Protecting Powers of any such formal warning given to an adverse party, and if that warning has been disregarded, of any measures taken as a result".

[13] Advisory Opinion of 28 May 1951, Reservations to the Convention on the Prevention and Punishment of the Crime of Genocide, ICJ Rep. 1951, pp. 23 et seq.

self[14], this would raise the question whether a soldier who commits a violation of Art. 8, para. 2, lit. b), i) or ii) of the Rome Statute[15], which *mutatis mutandis* reiterates certain prohibitions of the just mentioned provisions of the first Additional Protocol, as part of a counter-measure covered by the just-mentioned British reservation, could face criminal prosecution. I would argue that not since otherwise such State would otherwise *de facto* not be in a position to take measures which are permitted by the applicable treaty regime. If one shares this view the declaration made by the British government on the occasion on its ratification of the Rome Statute[16], which pointed to this interrelationship would be purely declaratory. Accordingly said declaration would not raise the issue whether or not it could be considered a reservation explicitly prohibited by Art. 120 of the Rome Statute[17].

Similar issues could arise under customary law. Once again an example might demonstrate what I have in mind: If one were to assume that the type of military conflicts envisaged by Art. 1, para. 4 of the First Additional Protocol and their qualification as international armed conflicts by now forms part of customary law[18], States such as Israel, which qualify as persistent objectors in that regard[19], are not bound to apply the rules applicable in international armed conflict in such type of conflict. The question arises, however, what effect that might have upon their soldiers when eventually facing criminal responsibility for having committed violations of norms of international humanitarian law in such a type of conflict, which are only applicable in *international* armed conflicts. One should, consistent with the argument made above, consider that from the very beginning they would *per se* not be subject to the respective rules providing for individual criminal responsibility without the need to rely on any form of defence such as, for example,

---

14 See e.g. Arts. 20, 51 para. 8, 54 para. 4, 55, para. 2, and 56 para. 4 of the First Additional Protocol.

15 For a detailed analysis of said provision see *W.J. Fenrick*, Art. 8 para. 2 lit. b) i) and ii) in: Triffterer, supra n. 10.

16 The declaration reads:
"The United Kingdom understands the term ‚the established framework of international law', used in article 8 (2) (b) and (e), to include customary international law as established by State practice and opinio iuris. In that context the United Kingdom confirms and draws to the attention of the Court its views as expressed, inter alia, in its statements made on ratification of relevant instruments of international law, including the Protocol Additional to the Geneva Conventions of 12th August 1949, and relating to the Protection of Victims of International Armed Conflicts (Protocol I) of 8th June 1977".

17 As to the content and effect of Art. 120 of the Rome Statute see *G. Hafner*, Art. 120, in: Triffterer, supra n. 10.

18 See for such a proposition inter alia *A. Cassese*, The Geneva Protocols of 1977 on the Humanitarian Law of Armed Conflict and Customary International Law, in: 3 UCLA Pacific Basin Law Journal 1984, pp. 55 et seq.

19 Cf. generally as to the very concept of persistent objectors *T.L. Stein*, The Approach of the Different Drummer: The Principle of the Persistent Objector in International Law, in: Harvard International Law Journal 1985, pp. 457 et seq.; as well as *E. Olufemi*, Some remarks on the persistent objector rule in customary international law, in: Denning Law Journal 1991, pp. 37 et seq.

the defence of superior order. Thus, if one takes the codification of international criminal law in the Rome Statute as a starting point[20], the respective soldier would accordingly only face criminal prosecution for acts prohibited in all types of armed conflict, *i.e.* only for those acts which also constitute war crimes when committed within the context of a non-international armed conflict[21].

The thrust of my argument therefore is that, at least with regard to international armed conflicts, but also with regard to the 'governmental side' of non-international armed conflicts, individual criminal responsibility of a person acting on behalf of their State necessarily requires that his or her home State by the same token is also bound by the parallel primary rule for matters of State responsibility and that it would therefore normally also be responsible under the law of State responsibility. Accordingly, both international and domestic courts, when applying norms of international criminal law, would have to always take into consideration the question whether at all, and if so to what extent, the State concerned is itself bound by the respective rule of international law. With regard to the Rome Statute, this does not raise any significant problem, since the chapeau of Art. 8 para. 2 lit. b) of the Statute of the International Criminal Court explicitly states that the Court shall have jurisdiction in respect of violations of the laws and customs of war "within the established framework of international law", thereby linking the Rome Statute to the corpus of international humanitarian law as it applies for purposes of State responsibility. Besides, it is also important to note that Art. 10 of the Rome Statute further states that the definition of crimes shall not be interpreted as limiting or prejudicing in any way existing rules of international law *for purposes other than this Statute* thus making it clear that the Rome Statute does not interfere with issues of State responsibility.

This result only holds true, however, for those persons whose acts may be attributed to a given State within the meaning of the ILC Articles on State Responsibility. It would therefore, in particular, neither apply to individuals fighting on the side of insurgents or rivalizing armed groups in non-international armed conflicts, the acts of which are not attributable to a given State, nor to civilians committing war crimes in international armed conflicts, the acts of which may neither be attributed to a party to the conflict[22]. Finally this principle just outlined would not

---

[20] Cf. also already the position of the Secretary-General of the United Nations, who, in its report on the establishment of the ICTY stated that the ICTY was to apply only such norms "which (...) beyond doubt [form] part of customary international law", UN Doc. S/25704 (3 May 1993). Similar considerations hold true for the Statute of the ICC; but see also for a more reluctant position *W. Heintschel v. Heinegg*, Criminal International Law and Customary International Law, in: A. Zimmermann (ed.), International Criminal Law and the Current Development of Public International Law (2002), pp. 27 et seq.

[21] Cf. as to the criminalization of war crimes in non-international armed conflict: *C. Kreß*, War crimes committed in non-international armed conflict and the emerging system of international criminal justice, in: Israel Yearbook on Human Rights 30 (2000/2001), pp. 103 et seq.

[22] But cf. generally Arts. 9 and 11 ILC Articles on State Responsibility which might provide for attribution of certain acts of private individuals for purposes of State responsibility.

apply in situations of a failed State, provided one takes the position that in a failed State situation attribution for purposes of State responsibility is no longer possible, anyway[23].

Let me now come to my second point which is rather brief.

III. Interrelationship between the law of State responsibility and the rights of individuals

The subject-matter of our panel was described by our organizers as dealing with the relationship between individual and international *responsibility*. Somewhat in contrast thereto *Dieter Fleck* in his paper, however, also focused, and I believe rightly so, on *rights* of victims of violations of international humanitarian law to claim compensation[24] and he also pointed, to put it bluntly, to the reluctance of States to accept such rights[25]. While one might agree with that finding as a matter of *lex lata*[26], it is most striking that it is taken for granted that *those who commit violations* of international humanitarian law are governed by a by now rather developed and detailed set of norms of international law, while in contrast thereto the *victims* still have to rely on their respective home State exercising diplomatic protection, *i.e.* that while we are willing to lift the veil of State sovereignty for the first purpose, we are not willing to do so for the latter. *Dieter Fleck* has in his paper argued that finding otherwise "a spiral of claims and counterclaims would severely jeopardise any effort for post-conflict peace building".[27]

But one wonders whether one could not make the very same argument for individualized *prosecutions* of war crimes, which could bar more general attempts to settle an overall situation, by *e.g.* providing for amnesties or by establishing truth and reconciliation commissions. Still, the Rome Statute as the most recent attempt by the international community to deal with war crimes, provides that even the Security Council, acting under Chapter VII of the Charter, may only *interrupt* ongoing proceedings for a limited period of time, but may not stop them for good[28]. Indeed this might be considered a contradiction.

---

23 Cf. for a detailed analysis *R. Geiss*, "Failed States" – die normative Erfassung gescheiterter Staaten (2005), pp. 251 et seq.

24 *Fleck*, supra pp. 171 et seq. (179 et seq.).

25 Id.

26 See generally for a detailed discussion of the overall issue *W. Heintschel v. Heinegg*, Entschädigung für die Verletzung des humanitären Völkerrechts, in: Berichte der DGVR, vol. 40, pp. 1-62.

27 *Fleck*, supra p. 174.

28 For an analysis of Art. 16 of the Rome Statute and the practice of the Security Council (and the legal problems involved) see *A. Zimmermann*, 'Acting under Chapter VII (...)' – Resolution 1422 and possible limits of the powers of the Security Council, in: J.A. Frowein et al. (eds.), Verhandeln für den Frieden/Negotiating for Peace – Liber Amicorum Tono Eitel, 2003, pp. 253 et seq.

The underlying reason why granting such individual rights is considered to be dangerous solely lies in the fact that we are mostly concerned by the fact that such issues of compensation are dealt with in domestic *fora* eventually even applying domestic law but not by the very idea of providing for a remedy as such. Maybe, one could at least perceive a norm of international law obliging States to set up appropriate international mechanisms after the end of hostilities such as most recently the Ethiopian-Eritrean Claims Commission[29], which in turn would then also provide for compensation for serious violations of international humanitarian law, a solution that was indeed alluded to in the recently adopted Resolution of the United Nations Human Rights Commission on "Basic Principles and Guidelines on the Right to a Remedy and Reparation for Victims of Gross Violations of International Human Rights Law and Serious Violations of International Humanitarian Law" of 10 April 2005[30].

Besides, if one considers that the scope of application of human rights treaties and applicable norms of international humanitarian law overlap to a large extent, a tendency recently confirmed by the International Court of Justice in its advisory opinion on the Legal Consequences of the Construction of a Wall in the Occupied Palestinian Territory subject to *lex specialis*-considerations[31], one wonders why an individual might be considered, at least conceptually, to be the bearer of individual rights as to those human rights violations, but not with regard to violations of international humanitarian law, even where the underlying facts are identical, the case of Northern Cyprus involving violations of both, the European Convention of Human Rights and applicable norms of international humanitarian law, being one example.

Indeed if the main argument against granting individual rights for violations of international humanitarian law is that it would bring with it thousands of individualized claims which could not be appropriately settled without endangering overall peace, the very same argument could be made with regard to violations of *e.g.* the European Convention of Human Rights in situations of massive and widespread violations such as in the just mentioned case of Northern Cyprus – still it is generally believed that it is appropriate that such individual rights continue to exist, but which, as part of an overall political solution could and indeed should nevertheless form part of a settlement.

The crucial point is that the very fact that such individual rights do exist as such influences the outcome of any such general settlement providing for at least some kind of reparation, be it only in form of a lump sum. One wonders therefore,

---

29 Cf. for further details *N. Klein*, State responsibility for International Humanitarian Law Violations and the Work of the Eritrea Ethiopia Claims Commission So Far, 47 GYIL (2004), pp. 214 et seq.

30 C.H.R. Res. 2005/35, Un Doc. E/CN.4/2005/L. 10/Add. 11 (19 April 2005). It is also worth noting that this resolution also interpreted both, Art. 3 of Hague IV and Art. 91 of the First Additional Protocol, as providing a right to a remedy for individual victims of violations of international humanitarian law.

31 Legal Consequences of the Construction of a Wall in the Occupied Palestinian Territory, Advisory Opinion of 9 July 2004, paras. 104 et seq., to be found at http://www.icj-cij.org/.

whether a parallel approach might not be helpful with regard to serious violations of international humanitarian law. Thus any such acknowledgment of individual rights in case of violations of international humanitarian law could serve as an empowerment for the victims so that they can play a more important role in any overall political settlement.

IV. Individual Civil Responsibility for Violations of International Humanitarian Law

Another brief *third* remark takes the first part of the title of our panel as a starting point, namely the notion of 'individual *responsibility*'. In that regard we have so far only or at least mainly focused on individual *criminal* responsibility, while State responsibility is, if one considers its legal consequences and in particular the duty to make reparation[32], rather of a 'civil character'. Thus the question arises whether we should not focus also, and indeed eventually even lay more emphasis on, strengthening the regime of civil liability of individuals committing or ordering to have committed violations of international humanitarian law. This might be particularly helpful where such violations are attributable to international legal entities, such as armed groups or corporations providing military services. So far we only perceive such tendencies in selected national jurisdictions and namely in the United States under the Alien Tort Statute[33], a more restrictive of the jurisprudence of the United States Supreme Court in Sosa v. Alvarez-Machin notwithstanding[34], the recent Agent Orange case (even after having been dismissed)[35] being one example at hand.

Given that such unilateral approaches and the exercise of universal jurisdiction by national tribunals carry with them certain risks and dangers, it is certainly once again to be welcomed that Art. 75 of the Rome Statute empowers the International Criminal Court to also make binding orders against a convicted persons providing for reparations to be paid directly to victims or the Trust Fund established under Art. 79 of the Rome Statute[36], orders which States parties to the Rome Statute are under an obligation to carry out.

---

[32] For further details as to the legal effects of a violation of international law under the law of State responsibility see Part Two (Arts. 28 et seq.) of the ILC Articles on State Responsibility.

[33] 28 U.S.C. § 1350.

[34] Sosa *v.* Alvarez Machain and United States *v.* Alvarez-Machain, Judgment of 29. June 2004, 124 S.Ct. 2739 (2004).

[35] The Vietnam Association for Victims of Agent Orange/Dioxin et al. *v.* The Dow Chemical Company et al., Judgment and Order of the 10th of March 2005, MDL 381 (04-CV-400).

[36] For further details cf. *D. Donat-Cattin*, Art. 75, in: Triffterer, supra n. 10.

V. Concluding remarks

This brings me to the end of my comment. Summarising one might say that the interrelationship between international humanitarian law, international criminal law and human rights law raises a whole series of interesting issues all of which deserve significant more analysis in the future. It is to be therefore hoped that the 75th, 80^{th,} or 85th birthday of *Knut Ipsen* would provide us with further opportunities to discuss these and other issues of international humanitarian law – the development of which has in the past been significantly influenced by him.

Dissemination and Monitoring Compliance

Dissemination and Monitoring Compliance of International Humanitarian Law

Knut Dörmann

International Committee of the Red Cross (ICRC), Geneva

International humanitarian law, when respected, affords vital protection to the lives and dignity of those who are vulnerable in times of armed conflict. Parties to an armed conflict have the responsibility to implement and respect this law[1] and the States not involved in the armed conflict have the responsibility, or one could speak of obligation[2], to ensure individually or collectively this respect[3].

When international humanitarian law is not respected, human suffering becomes all the more severe and the consequences become all the more difficult to overcome, reconciliation between former adversaries more problematic. Deliberate targeting of civilians, indiscriminate attacks, the use of civilians as human shields, destruction of infrastructure vital to civilian populations, torture, rape and other forms of sexual violence, hostage taking, forced displacement of populations, destruction of civilian property and looting – these and other violations of international humanitarian law cause untold suffering in armed conflicts throughout the world.

One of the main challenges of today's armed conflicts relates to the prevention of these atrocities from happening and thus to the question of how to improve compliance with international humanitarian law.

In this contribution the question of how to improve compliance will be tackled in two steps. In a first part preventive measures to be taken essentially in peacetime will be discussed: Dissemination, which is specifically mentioned in the title of this contribution is one crucial tool in this regard, but certainly not the only one. In a second part, monitoring compliance with the provisions of international humanitarian law during armed conflicts will be addressed.

---

1 Article 1 common of the Geneva Conventions of 1949 (Geneva Convention for the Amelioration of the Condition of the Wounded and Sick in Armies in the Field, 12 August, 1949 (hereafter: First Geneva Convention); Geneva Convention for the Amelioration of the Condition of Wounded, Sick and Shipwrecked Members of Armed Forces at Sea, 12 August, 1949 (hereafter: Second Geneva Convention); Geneva Convention Relative to the Treatment of Prisoners of War, 12 August, 1949 (hereafter: Third Geneva Convention); Geneva Convention Relative to the Protection of Civilian Persons in Time of War, 12 August, 1949 (hereafter: Fourth Geneva Convention)).

2 See in more detail infra B.IV, in particular fn. 59 and accompanying text.

3 See supra n. 1.

A. Preventive measures, in particular dissemination

I. Dissemination

Since the early codifications of international humanitarian law, various treaties of international humanitarian law contain provisions requiring dissemination of the law to the armed forces and also to the civilian population, thus recognizing the importance of promoting knowledge of international humanitarian law. Although it is primarily the responsibility of the States to make the law known, other organizations, such as the ICRC, working in cooperation with the National Red Cross and Red Crescent Societies and their International Federation, have a mandate to assist the States in this task and are encouraged to take initiatives to that effect.[4] As will be seen later on, also armed opposition groups bear a responsibility in this regard.

1. Teaching of armed forces

The importance of training armed forces in international humanitarian law is obvious: it is not very likely that a body of law is being observed unless those whose duty it is to respect and apply it know it and are familiar with it. Sound acquaintance of the rules set forth in the law is essential for their effective application and, consequently, for the protection of the victims of armed conflicts.

This is recognized in various treaties of international humanitarian law. The duty of States to teach international humanitarian law to their armed forces was first codified in the 1906 and 1929 Geneva Conventions.[5] It was subsequently re-

---

4 The ICRC, for its part, has a mandate to work for the understanding and dissemination of international humanitarian law with the cooperation of the National Societies (Art. 5 Statutes of the International Red Cross and Red Crescent Movement, 1986 (hereafter: Movement Statutes), and Art. 4 Statutes of the International Committee of the Red Cross). It has delegates who are specialized in this field and who are assigned to dissemination tasks in the various regions of the world, it draws up dissemination programmes and special teaching material for the armed and security forces, academic circles and young people, and it runs campaigns to heighten public awareness of the law. The ICRC Advisory Service on International Humanitarian Law regularly updates a collection of documents on implementation of the law in individual countries; this collection, which is part of a database that can be accessed through the ICRC web site (http://www.icrc.org/ihl-nat), contains, inter alia, information on the measures taken by the States to spread knowledge of IHL.
The National Societies have a mandate to disseminate and to help their governments to disseminate knowledge of the law. They must take initiatives to that effect and recruit, train and assign the necessary staff (Art. 3 Movement Statutes). Their International Federation also helps promote IHL and cooperates with them in this field (Art. 6 Movement Statutes and Art. 3 Constitution of the International Federation of the Red Cross and Red Crescent Societies).

5 Geneva Convention for the Amelioration of the Condition of the Wounded and Sick in Armies in the Field, 6 July 1906 (hereafter: 1906 Geneva Convention for the Protection of Wounded and Sick), Article 26; Geneva Convention for the Amelioration of the

stated in the four 1949 Geneva Conventions[6] and their 1977 Additional Protocols,[7] in the 1954 Hague Convention for the Protection of Cultural Property[8] and its Second Protocol of 1999,[9] and in the 1980 Convention on Certain Conventional Weapons and its annexed protocols.[10] These treaties all specify that the obligation to teach to armed forces applies in time of peace as well as in time of armed conflict. Peacetime teaching is clearly of particular importance. If teaching only starts during an armed conflict in the heat of an ongoing battle, this is often too late for influencing the behaviour of the soldiers. They clearly must be aware of what is required from them in terms of international humanitarian law respect before a conflict starts. In addition, States which provide troops for peace-keeping or peace-enforcement operations conducted by the United Nations, regional organizations or under their auspices should ensure that the military personnel belonging to their contingent are instructed in the provisions of the law.

Condition of the Wounded and Sick in Armies in the Field, 27 July 1929 (hereafter: 1929 Geneva Convention for the Protection of Wounded and Sick), Article 27.

6 Article 47 of the First Geneva Convention; Article 48 of the Second Geneva Convention; Article 127 of the Third Geneva Convention; Article 144 of the Fourth Geneva Convention. The Third and Fourth Geneva Conventions contain some more specific provisions. The Third Convention adds that any military or other authorities who in time of war are responsible for prisoners of war must possess the text of the Convention and be specially instructed as to its provisions (Art. 127(2)). The officers in charge of prisoner-of-war camps must ensure that these provisions are known to the camp staff and the guards and are held responsible for their application (Art. 39). The Fourth Geneva Convention provides the same obligations with regard to any civilian, military, police or other authorities who assume responsibilities in respect of civilians, particularly in places of internment (Arts. 99 and 144(2)).

7 Protocol Additional to the Geneva Conventions of 1949, and relating to the Protection of Victims of International Armed Conflicts, 8 June 1977 (hereafter: Additional Protocol I), Article 83; Protocol Additional to the Geneva Conventions of 1949, and relating to the Protection of Victims of Non-International Armed Conflicts, 8 June 1977 (hereafter: Additional Protocol II), Article 19.

8 Convention for the Protection of Cultural Property in the Event of Armed Conflict, The Hague, 14 May, 1954 (hereafter: Hague Convention for the Protection of Cultural Property), Article 25.

9 Second Protocol to the Hague Convention of 1954 for the Protection of Cultural Property in the Event of Armed Conflict, The Hague, 26 March, 1999 (hereafter: Second Protocol to the Hague Convention on Cultural Property), Article 30.

10 Convention on Prohibitions or Restrictions on the Use of Certain Conventional Weapons Which May be Deemed to be Excessively Injurious or to Have Indiscriminate Effects, Geneva, 10 October, 1980 (hereafter: Convention on Certain Conventional Weapons), Article 6; its Second Amended Protocol on Prohibitions or Restrictions on the Use of Mines, Booby-Traps and Other Devices specifies that each State must require its armed forces to issue relevant military instructions and operating procedures and to provide training for armed forces personnel that is commensurate with their respective duties and responsibilities (Art. 14). Protocol IV on Blinding Laser Weapons stipulates that the States shall provide training for their armed forces (Art. 2).

The obligation to teach the armed forces is mentioned explicitly in several military manuals.[11] The legislation of several States provides that members of the armed forces must receive instruction in their duties under international humanitarian law or includes provisions that directly aim to fulfil this requirement by introducing such training programmes.[12] A closer look at this practice shows that it is not required that all members of the armed forces be totally familiar with every detail of international humanitarian law, but rather that they should know the essential rules of the law that are relevant to their actual functions.[13]

Based on the practice available, it seems that much of the teaching is carried out primarily or exclusively in the form of written instruction or classroom teaching. One may wonder whether this is sufficient to ensure effective compliance during the stress of combat. As explained by South Africa's Law of Armed Conflict (LOAC) Manual, "in the circumstances of combat, soldiers may often not have time to consider the principles of the LOAC before acting. Soldiers must therefore not only know these principles but must be trained so that the proper response to specific situations is second nature".[14]

It is therefore suggested that international humanitarian law should not only be treated as a separate subject matter in military training, but that an international humanitarian law dimension be integrated in military exercises and military doctrine.

2. *Obligation of commanders to instruct the armed forces under their command*

Article 87(2) of Additional Protocol I sets forth the obligation of commanders to ensure that members of the armed forces under their command are aware of their obligations under international humanitarian law. The rationale of this provision is that the most effective way to ensure compliance with States' obligation to instruct their armed forces is by making commanders responsible for the instruction of the armed forces under their command. The obligation of commanders is also contained in numerous military manuals.[15] Some of these mention this obligation at the same time as commanders' responsibility to ensure that their troops respect international humanitarian law.[16]

---

11 See *Jean-Marie Henckaerts/Louise Doswald-Beck*, Customary International Humanitarian Law, Volume I: Rules (2005), p. 502 with the references of practice that could be collected.

12 See id. with the references of practice that could be collected.

13 Canada, Code of Conduct for CF Personnel, Office of the Judge Advocate General, Edition of 4 June 2001, Introduction, § 8, Rule 11, § 1.

14 South Africa, Presentation on the South African Approach to International Humanitarian Law, Appendix A, Chapter 4: International Humanitarian Law (The Law of Armed Conflict), National Defence Force, 1996. This manual is also included in Chapter 4 of the Draft Civic Education Manual of 1997, § 14.

15 See *Henckaerts/Doswald-Beck*, supra n. 11, p. 504 with the references.

16 Id.

3. *Availability of legal advice*

Given the complexity of modern international humanitarian law, the role of legal advisers is probably most important for advising military commanders during an armed conflict on legal matters related to specific operations or reminding them of their obligations under Article 87 of Additional Protocol I. They may however also have a role in peacetime and be called upon to cooperate in the instruction of international humanitarian law through for example instruction in military academies and instruction of troops, particularly in the context of operational exercises.

Additional Protocol I therefore contains the obligation that:

"The High Contracting Parties at all times, and the Parties to the conflict in time of armed conflict, shall ensure that legal advisers are available, when necessary, to advise military commanders at the appropriate level on the application of the Conventions and this Protocol and on the appropriate instruction to be given to the armed forces on this subject".[17]

4. *Teaching of international humanitarian law to the civilian population*

While instructions in international humanitarian law remains a priority for the armed forces, it is just as important to familiarize the civilian population with the essential rules. Three reasons can be identified for why this is important:

- First, civilians are protected under international humanitarian law and therefore benefit from its rules. Therefore knowledge of the protections and their limits are important. Furthermore, they may also have a role in providing protection without adverse distinction to the wounded and sick during an armed conflict.
- Second, it is clear that the attitude of the civilian population has an influence on the behaviour of armed forces, whether by inducing greater restraint and better observance of the rules or, on the contrary, by further inflaming passions and fuelling violence. Knowledge of the basic principles and values of international humanitarian law can prevent the latter and favour the former.
- Third, members of regular armed forces are no longer the only ones to commit violent acts in today's armed conflicts; indeed, in many contexts, civilians have become potential participants in hostilities.

Dissemination to the civilian population is dealt with in treaties of international humanitarian law in less strict terms than teaching to the armed forces. However, the obligation dates back to the beginning of the last century. The 1906 and 1929 Geneva Conventions required States to take the steps necessary to make the con-

[17] Article 82 of Additional Protocol I.

ventions known to the population at large.[18] In accordance with the 1949 Geneva Conventions and the Hague Convention for the Protection of Cultural Property States are required to include the study of international humanitarian law in their programmes of civilian training "if possible".[19] The qualifier "if possible" was not included to make civilian instruction optional but was added to take into account the possibility that in federal countries the central government may not have authority in educational matters.[20] Additional Protocol I obliges States to disseminate international humanitarian law as widely as possible and, in particular, to "encourage the study thereof by the civilian population".[21] It thus implies that States should at least take measures conducive to the study of international humanitarian law by the civilian population. It is submitted that instruction in IHL should be provided primarily to the public authorities responsible for its application. It should thus be stepped up in universities, specifically in faculties of law, and the general principles of the law should be taught in secondary schools. Members of the medical corps and of the media should also be given training commensurate with their activities.

Many military manuals emphasise States' obligation to encourage the study of international humanitarian law by the civilian population and to disseminate international humanitarian law as widely as possible so that it becomes known to the civilian population.[22] The legislation of several States also provides that the civilian population must receive instruction in international humanitarian law or includes provisions that directly aim to fulfil this requirement by introducing such training programmes.[23]

In practice, many States facilitate courses in international humanitarian law, often through the provision of funds to organisations such as the National Red Cross or Red Crescent Society.[24] It is encouraging that an increasing number of institutions of higher education have started to offer courses in international humanitarian law in recent years.[25] In this regard the important work initiated, supported and conducted by Prof. *Knut Ipsen* over many years at the university and German Red Cross level deserves to be highlighted.

---

18 Article 26 of the 1906 Geneva Convention for the Protection of Wounded and Sick; Article 27 of the 1929 Geneva Convention for the Protection of Wounded and Sick.

19 Article 47 of the First Geneva Convention; Article 48 of the Second Geneva Convention; Article 127 of the Third Geneva Convention; Article 144 of the Fourth Geneva Convention; Article 25 of the Hague Convention for the Protection of Cultural Property.

20 *Jean S. Pictet* (ed.), Commentary on the First Geneva Convention, Geneva, International Committee of the Red Cross, 1952, p. 349.

21 Article 83 of Additional Protocol I.

22 See *Henckaerts/Doswald-Beck*, supra n. 11, p. 506 with the references of practice that could be collected.

23 See id.

24 For the basis of their activities, supra n. 4.

25 See *Henckaerts/Doswald-Beck*, supra n. 11, pp. 506 et seq. with the references of practice that could be collected.

5. Instruction within armed opposition groups parties to a non-international armed conflict

Not only State armed forces but also armed opposition groups must respect and ensure respect for international humanitarian law in a non-international armed conflict. In this respect, dissemination is generally seen as an indispensable tool. Again, without proper knowledge of the requirements of international humanitarian law, it is not very likely that the rules will be applied in practice. Article 19 of Additional Protocol II, which also binds armed opposition groups,[26] states that the Protocol "shall be disseminated as widely as possible". In practice, the ICRC has been frequently allowed by armed opposition groups to disseminate international humanitarian law among their members. The ICRC itself has called upon parties to non-international armed conflicts to ensure dissemination of international humanitarian law to their troops, or to allow or facilitate ICRC efforts to do so.

Although practice with respect to the obligation of armed opposition groups to encourage the teaching of international humanitarian law to the civilian population under their control is limited, it is important – as pointed out by the UN General Assembly already in 1973 – that "information concerning [rules of international humanitarian law] be given to civilians everywhere, with a view to securing their strict observance".[27] It is noteworthy to mention that armed opposition groups have in many instances given permission to the ICRC to disseminate international humanitarian law to civilians living in areas they controlled.

6. Assessment

Over the years, States, supported by other actors, have devoted considerable effort to devising and implementing peacetime measures, as required in various humanitarian law treaties. Dissemination of international humanitarian law among armed forces and armed groups has been reinforced. In addition, international humanitarian law has been increasingly incorporated into military manuals and doctrine.

The ICRC on the basis of the mandate given to it by the international community regularly assists with dissemination activities for armed forces and in efforts to develop an awareness of international humanitarian law within academic circles and civil society. For example in 2003 30 specialised delegates conducted or took part in some 424 courses, workshops, round tables or exercises involving some 21,600 police and military personnel in 141 countries.

While there have been positive developments in many states during the last years, there is still a lot to be done. Teaching within the armed forces can still be improved in order to make respect for international humanitarian law a reflex even in the heat of the battle. It seems obvious that there is an enormous responsibility on higher levels of the military hierarchy. Their attitude towards international hu-

---

26 *Yves Sandoz/Christophe Swinarski/Bruno Zimmermann* (eds.), Commentary on the Additional Protocols, ICRC, Geneva, 1987, p. 1488, § 4909.

27 UN General Assembly, Res. 3102 (XXVIII), 2197th Plenary meeting, 12 December 1973.

manitarian law needs to be exemplary, their support for its training must be secured and their orders must be in full compliance with international humanitarian law. This is probably most important for ensuring that also their subordinates behave in accordance with the rules. Any ambiguity stemming from the superiors may have a negative impact. Of equal importance seems to be the positive role that the political leadership should play and the emphasis it gives on respect for international humanitarian law.

A new challenge in contemporary armed conflicts is the fact that more and more private contractors – private military companies and security companies – perform tasks that are governed by international humanitarian law. In particular if they are used for activities that previously have been in practice reserved to or undertaken by the military, it is crucial that they are aware of their obligations under international humanitarian law. If the staff of such companies have not been incorporated or belonging to the armed forces, only the less stringent obligation to disseminate the law to the civilian population would apply to them. However, States using these companies are obliged to ensure that the companies' employees respect international humanitarian law where relevant. States should therefore ensure that the employees are properly trained in international humanitarian law.[28] If they are not, there is an important risk that violations of international humanitarian law may be committed and that these would be attributable to States hiring the companies, thus engaging the State's international responsibility for wrongful acts. It is also in the interest of the employees themselves to be properly trained in order to avoid the risk of facing individual criminal responsibility.

Another challenge in the field of dissemination and training lies in reaching armed opposition groups and other non-State armed actors. It is possible that knowledge of international humanitarian law is not well developed among them, since, contrary to members of armed forces, they did not benefit from specific peacetime international humanitarian law training unless these groups are constituted of former or dissident members of armed forces. Therefore, much depends on whether dissemination to the population at large had reached them or whether they were trained by their group during the armed conflict. The latter is certainly difficult to accomplish. The ICRC undertakes efforts to do so, but all depends on establishing contact with these groups in a secure environment and their willingness to let the ICRC conduct dissemination activities. Again the attitude of the political and military leaders and superiors towards respect for international humanitarian law is crucial for ensuring compliance.

---

[28] One could arguably derive an obligation train to disseminate/train based on the obligation contained in common Article 1 of the four Geneva Conventions to ensure respect for international humanitarian law that also covers measures to be taken with regard to persons operating under their control. Other provisions of the Geneva Conventions contain specific provisions on instruction during armed conflict that would apply to employees of private military or security companies in the same ways as to members of the armed forces. Arts. 127 (2) of the Third Geneva Convention and 144 (2) of the Fourth Geneva Convention should at least serve as a guidance.

In addition, the best dissemination will not improve compliance if the aims that are pursued with an armed conflict are contrary to the bases of international humanitarian law, such as conflicts with an ethnic cleansing-objective.

II. Other essential preventive measures

Dissemination of or training in international humanitarian law are certainly not the only preventive measures for ensuring compliance with that law. Of equal importance is the adoption of legislative and statutory provisions. For example with regard to criminal repression, treaties of international humanitarian law contain specific provisions. This aspect and other possible preventive measures will not be further addressed given the scope of this contribution.

B. Monitoring compliance with the provisions of humanitarian law during armed conflicts

I. Existing Mechanisms under the Geneva Conventions and Additional Protocols

In the following section existing monitoring mechanisms will be assessed and the potential for improvement analysed. The Geneva Conventions and their Additional Protocols contain the following:

- Protecting Powers and their substitutes,
- the enquiry procedure,
- the International Fact-finding Commission,
- meetings of the High Contracting Parties and
- action by the ICRC.

Among these mechanisms mentioned in the Conventions and Protocols, only ICRC Action is specifically envisaged – albeit in different terms – for both international and non-international armed conflicts.

1. Action by Protecting Powers[29]

The role and function of Protecting Powers as well as their substitutes are defined in the Geneva Conventions and Additional Protocol I. Art. 8/8/8/9 common to the four Geneva Conventions state that "[t]he present Convention shall be applied

[29] See generally and with specific references *François Bugnion*, The International Committee of the Red Cross and the Protection of War Victims, 2003, pp. 847 et seq.

with the cooperation and the scrutiny of the Protecting Powers whose duty it is to safeguard the interests of the Parties to the conflict."

A Protecting Power is normally a State, which is mandated by a State party to a conflict in order to safeguard its interests vis-à-vis the other State party to the conflict. It exercises essentially two functions:

- first of all, a control function, examples are access to prisoners of war and civilian internees and detainees protected by the Fourth Geneva Convention as well as monitoring of trials of such persons;
- second, a liaison function between the parties to a conflict.

The designation of a Protecting Power is an obligation; if none is nominated, the ICRC can offer its good offices with a view to the designation of a Protecting Power. If there is still no Protecting Power designated, States Parties to a conflict shall ask the ICRC to act as a substitute.

Despite the obligation foreseen in the Geneva Conventions and the First Additional Protocol to designate a Protecting Power, this mechanism has seldom been used. Protecting Powers have been appointed since World War II only in the following situations:

- in 1956, Protecting Powers were used in the so-called "Suez conflict" between Egypt and its adversaries Great Britain and France,[30]
- in 1961, in the conflict between France and Tunisia overt Bizerta,[31]
- in 1961, during the Goa crisis between India and Portugal,[32]
- in 1971, during the conflict between India and Pakistan[33],
- in 1982, during the South Atlantic conflict between the UK and Argentina.[34]

Reasons for the failure to designate a Protecting Power may be the following: (1) the perception that very few States are considered "neutral" and either able or willing to carry out the role of Protecting Power; (2) the majority of current conflicts are non-international armed conflicts, where Protecting Powers are not foreseen by the treaties; (3) States may not recognize the existence of the armed con-

---

30 Switzerland represented British and French interests in Egypt, whereas India represented Egyptian interests in the United Kingdom and France. There was no Protecting Power representing Egyptian interests in Israel or Israeli interests in Egypt. (See more in: Keesing's Contemporary Archives, 1956, p. 15181.)

31 Sweden protected Tunisian interests in France and Switzerland protected French interests in Tunisia. (See id., p. 18343)

32 Egypt protected Indian interests in Portugal and Brazil protected Portuguese interests in India. (See id., p. 18635.)

33 Both states appointed Switzerland as Protecting Power. (See id., p. 25054.)

34 Switzerland represented British interests in Argentina and Brazil represented Argentine interests in the United Kingdom. (See *Sylvie-Stoyanka Junod*, Protection of the Victims of Armed Conflict Falkland/Malvinas Islands (1982): International Humanitarian Law and Humanitarian Action, ICRC, Geneva, 1984, p. 20.)

flict; (4) sometimes diplomatic relations are maintained despite the conflict; (5) often the ICRC *de facto* undertakes most of the functions of a Protecting Power.

One remark about the ICRC acting as a substitute of a Protecting Power, which is possible under the Geneva Conventions and Additional Protocol I: In the past it has preferred to use its other bases for action (they will be mentioned them later on) rather than being a substitute of a Protecting Power. The reason for this is that with the other bases it can more easily adhere to its neutrality and independence.

Although potentially beneficial for ensuring better respect for international humanitarian law, it is not foreseeable that the protecting power regime will or can be resuscitated.

2. Enquiry Procedure

Under the Geneva Conventions each Party to an international armed conflict can request an enquiry concerning any violation of the conventions (possibility for a unilateral activation). In a second step, the belligerents need to agree on the procedure. If there is no agreement, the parties should agree on the choice of an umpire who will decide upon the procedure to be followed.[35]

While the Conventions refer to an enquiry "concerning any alleged violation", the ICRC Commentary to the Fourth Geneva Convention points out that the enquiry procedure would only involve violations of a certain degree of seriousness which cause disagreement between the Parties.[36] Thus the enquiry procedure should only be relevant for important problems which cannot be settled in the normal way through the Protecting Powers or through an official enquiry carried out by the Detaining Power itself for example under Article 131 of the Fourth Geneva Convention.

The findings of the enquiry will assess the reality of the alleged facts. Once the violation has been established, the Parties to the conflict must put an end to it.

The enquiry procedure has not been used in practice. The main reason consists probably in the difficulty to reach an agreement between the parties in situations of armed conflict, when the tensions are extremely high. To agree on a procedure in such extreme circumstances is hardly realistic.

3. International Fact-Finding Commission

The International Fact-Finding Commission was established in 1991 pursuant to Article 90 of Additional Protocol I and formally accepted by 68 States as of 31 December 2005. Under the provisions of Additional Protocol I the Commission's competence can be accepted in two ways:

---

35 Articles 52/53/132/149 common of the Geneva Conventions of 1949 (see supra n. 5).

36 Commentary to Article 149 of the Fourth Geneva Convention, ICRC, Geneva, 1958, p. 604.

- States can either accept the Commission's competence in relation to any High Contracting Party accepting the same obligation based on a declaration when adhering to Additional Protocol I[37] or
- they can give *ad hoc* consent for a particular situation.[38]

The Commission has a twofold competence: first, to enquire into alleged grave breaches or other serious violations of the Geneva Conventions or Additional Protocol I, and second, to facilitate through its good offices the restoration of an attitude of respect for these treaties.[39]

Although its formal competence extends only to situations of international armed conflict, the Commission has expressed a willingness to conduct investigations into non-international armed conflicts.[40]

Once the procedure of the gathering of evidence is complete and the findings made, the Commission itself submits to the parties confidentially a report on those findings, along with such recommendations as it may consider appropriate. The Commission may only report its findings publicly if all the parties to the conflict agree.[41]

Despite the Commission's own efforts, and the support of the ICRC and others, no cases have yet been referred to it. This is due, in large part, to a lack of willingness by the parties to an armed conflict to request or give their consent to an investigation, which is required before the Commission can act. Additionally, still a rather small number of States has accepted the commission's competence and armed conflicts often take place in regions where States have not accepted its competence.

The potential influence of the Commission must not be dismissed prematurely, before it has been given the opportunity to show what it can provide. As has been seen in some recent conflicts (e.g. Darfour), there is clearly a need for fact-finding – not only to establish violations, but also to show that certain allegations are due to a distortion of facts. However, when fact-finding missions were undertaken in the recent past, they were in most cases specifically set up by the UN.[42] The International Fact-Finding Commission was not considered. Despite some negative views expressed, it is still worth continuing to strive to increase awareness of the Commission and advocate its use. Third States or others with influence over parties to an armed conflict should encourage the parties to agree to a Commission investigation. It is also advocated by some that the United Nations should be en-

---

37 Article 90, paragraph 2 a) of Additional Protocol I.

38 Article 90, paragraph 2 d) of Additional Protocol I.

39 Article 90, paragraph 2 c) of Additional Protocol I.

40 Report of the International Humanitarian Fact-Finding Commission: 1991-1996, p. 2. and accordingly the Report of the International Humanitarian Fact-Finding Commission: 1997-2001, p. 1.

41 Article 90, paragraph 5 a) and c) of Additional Protocol I.

42 E.g. for Darfur, Sudan, see Letter dated 31 January 2005 from the Secretary-General addressed to the President of the Security Council, 1 February 2005 (UN. Doc. S/2005/60); for the former Yugoslavia, see Security Council Resolution 780 (1992), 6 October 1992, UN Doc. S/RES/780 (1992).

couraged to utilize the Commission, perhaps through a Security Council mandate pursuant to Chapter VII of the UN Charter.

Finally, more emphasis could be placed on the second potential role of the Commission – its "good offices" function.[43] Through its good offices, the Commission's efforts to restore respect for international humanitarian law have the advantage of being "forward-looking" and may be welcomed by the parties to a conflict as less threatening to State sovereignty.

4. Meeting of High Contracting Parties

Article 7 of Additional Protocol I provides for the possibility of convening meetings of the High Contracting Parties: "The depositary of this Protocol shall convene a meeting of the High Contracting Parties, at the request of one or more of the said Parties and upon the approval of the majority of the said Parties, to consider general problems concerning the application of the Conventions and of the Protocol." The reference to "general problems" seems to exclude that this mechanism could play an important monitoring function in specific conflict situations. However, although some might consider that a discussion of specific situations of violation would have more potential impact, a discussion of "general problems" could nonetheless provide a significant opportunity to achieve State consensus on interpretations of general issues of international humanitarian law. Thus far, however, no such meeting has been convened.

5. ICRC action

In accordance with the Statutes of the Red Cross and Red Crescent Movement the ICRC has the mandate "to undertake the tasks incumbent upon it under the Geneva Conventions, to work for the faithful application of international humanitarian law applicable in armed conflicts and to take cognizance on any complaints based on alleged breaches of that law."[44] The Statutes have been adopted by an International Red Cross and Red Crescent Conference, which includes members of all State Parties to the Geneva Conventions.[45]

The Geneva Conventions and Additional Protocols describe the functions of the ICRC in the following terms. In international armed conflicts the Geneva Conventions and Additional Protocol I foresee two roles: an autonomous role, and the

---

43 Article 90, paragraph (2) c) (ii) of Additional Protocol I.

44 Article 5 (2) c) Movement Statutes. For a comprehensive overview, see *Yves Sandoz*, The International Committee of the Red Cross as Guardian of International Humanitarian Law, ICRC, 1998, available at: http://www.icrc.org/WEB/ENG/siteeng0.nsf/htmlall/p0700?OpenDocument&style=Custo_Final.4&View=defaultBody2; *Toni Pfanner*, Le rôle du Comité International de la Croix-Rouge dans la mise en oeuvre du droit international, in: Le droit face aux crises humanitaires: de l'efficacité du droit international humanitaire dans les conflits armés, Luxemburg, Office des publications officielles des Communautés européennes, 1995, pp. 177-248.

45 The Statutes of the International Red Cross and Red Crescent Movement were adopted by the 25th International Conference of the Red Cross at Geneva in October 1986.

role of a substitute of a Protecting Power.[46] Since the latter has been mentioned above, only a few remarks on the ICRC's autonomous role will be made here. Two points should be highlighted:

- First, the Geneva Conventions confer a right of initiative to the ICRC: it may thus undertake any humanitarian action with the agreement of the Parties to an international armed conflict.[47]
- Second, the ICRC is given specific functions under the Geneva Conventions: for example the right to visit prisoners of war and civilian internees,[48] it may conduct relief activities in the field of aid to prisoners of war and protected persons,[49] and functions as the Central Tracing Agency.[50]

For non-international armed conflicts, common Article 3 of the four Geneva Conventions contains a conventional right of initiative for the ICRC, but does not specify the functions.[51]

These provisions serve as a basis for the ICRC's work in monitoring compliance with international humanitarian law by parties to international and non-international armed conflicts.

A few figures may illustrate the dimensions of ICRC's detention work: In 2004 the ICRC visited 571,503 detainees held in 2,435 places of detention in nearly 80 countries.[52]

6. Mode of action

ICRC action in cases of violations of international humanitarian law is mainly based on confidential and bilateral representations. In its direct contacts with the

---

46 See page 221 et seq.

47 Articles 9/9/9/10 of the four Geneva Conventions of 1949 and Article 81 (1) of Additional Protocol I. According to the referred articles "The provisions of the present Convention constitute no obstacle to the humanitarian activities which the International Committee of the Red Cross or any other impartial humanitarian organization may, subject to the consent of the Parties to the conflict concerned, undertake for the protection (…)" of persons protected by the various Geneva Conventions. It is noteworthy to mention though that the wording of Article 81 (1) of Additional Protocol I more demanding when, describing the obligations of states, it uses the term "shall grant" instead of the terms "may" and "consent to".

48 Article 126 of the Third Geneva Convention and Article 143 of the Fourth Geneva Convention.

49 Article 125 (3) of the Third Geneva Convention and Article 142 (3) of the Fourth Geneva Convention.

50 Article 123 of the Third Geneva Convention and Article 140 of the Fourth Geneva Convention.

51 "An impartial humanitarian body, such as the International Committee of the Red Cross, may offer its services to the Parties to the conflict.", Article 3 (2) common to the four Geneva Conventions of 1949.

52 Annual Report 2004, ICRC, June 2005, p. 45.

parties to an armed conflict, the ICRC tries first and foremost to influence them through persuasion. In accordance with its doctrine, it only resorts to public communication on violations under very exceptional and strict conditions if its confidential and bilateral representations have not been successful.[53]

Among the specific mechanisms that are foreseen in the Geneva Conventions and Additional Protocols and which aim at monitoring compliance, ICRC action has been the only one that has been available in armed conflicts throughout the years and it has thus become quite important for ensuring compliance with international humanitarian law. Because it is essentially restricted to trying to persuade parties to an armed conflict and has no enforcement powers, the ICRC's ability to influence them is somewhat limited.

While only the ICRC has received a specific mandate from the international community, in today's armed conflicts, ICRC action is in practice complemented by activities of mechanisms dealt with in the next section and a number of initiatives taken by a range of other humanitarian and human rights organizations that have become more and more active in situations of armed conflict.[54] In their activities, they have more flexibility as regards the publicity of their findings. However, in the end, all enforcement action rests with the States themselves.

II. Other mechanisms not based on international humanitarian law treaties for monitoring compliance with international humanitarian law

Throughout the last years human rights bodies have increasingly taken up issues of international humanitarian law. In particular in the inter-American system reference has often been made to the international humanitarian law regime when assessing the behaviour of parties to an armed conflict.[55] The High Commissioner

---

[53] Action by the International Committee of the Red Cross in the event of violations of international humanitarian law or of other fundamental rules protecting persons in situations of violence, International Review of the Red Cross, No, 858, pp. 393-400.

[54] Without the intention of providing an exhaustive list, as examples one can mention non governmental organizations such as Human Rights Watch, Amnesty International, Médecins Sans Frontières.

[55] See for example the Inter-American Commission on Human Rights's Report on Human Rights and Terrorism, OEA/Ser.L/V/II.116, Doc. 5 rev. 1 corr., 22 October 2002 see in particular para. 29, (http://www.cidh.oas.org/Terrorism/Eng/toc.htm). *Liesbeth Zegveld*, The Inter-American Commission on human Rights and International Humanitarian Law – A Comment on the Tablada Case, International Review of the Red Cross, No. 324, 1998, pp. 505-512; *Fanny Martin*, Application du droit international humanitaire par la Court interaméricaine des droits de l'homme, International Review of the Red Cross, No. 844, 2001, pp. 1037-1066; *Christina M. Cerna*, Extraterritorial Application of the Human Rights Instruments of the Inter-American System, in Menno T. Kamminga and Fons Coomans, Extraterritorial Application of Human Rights Treaties, 2004, pp. 141-174.

for Human Rights is also more and more active in international humanitarian law matters.

For the purposes of this contribution, this tendency is only mentioned without going into the details since it is developed in *Rainer Hofmann*'s contribution. While generally speaking such an approach may have merits and has sometimes also proved useful, there are however two main limitations:

- Human Rights mechanisms do not have a specific competence to examine issues of international humanitarian law, except where some fundamental human rights and international humanitarian law intersect.
- Human Rights law only entails obligations for States and not for armed opposition groups.

Furthermore, sometimes international humanitarian law expertise is not as developed in these fora as human rights expertise.

III. New proposals for mechanisms aiming at improving compliance with international humanitarian law – the ICRC regional seminars

As we have seen from the preceding sections, most of the existing monitoring compliance mechanisms are rather weak or have not been used in practice. This led the ICRC to conduct a series of regional expert meetings in Cairo, Pretoria, Kuala Lumpur, Mexico City, and Bruges in 2003 on the subject "Improving Compliance with International Humanitarian Law".

Participants discussed a range of measures, including existing international humanitarian law mechanisms and what new proposals might be considered. Proposals for new measures or mechanisms for improving respect for humanitarian law included a system of either *ad hoc* or periodic reporting and the institution of an individual complaints mechanism; the creation of a committee of States or of independent international humanitarian law experts to serve as a "Diplomatic Forum" for addressing situations of humanitarian law violations; and the establishment of an Office of a High Commissioner for international humanitarian law that could be created as a "treaty body" to the Geneva Conventions and their Additional Protocols.[56]

Although it is possible that these and other proposals will provide inspiration for future developments, participants nonetheless expressed some concern that the general international atmosphere at present is not conducive to the establishment of new mechanisms. Probably a majority of the participants – despite the rather limited effectiveness of existing mechanisms – felt that they were not defective, but rather suffered from lack of political will by States to use them.

---

[56] For further detail see Improving Compliance with International Humanitarian Law, ICRC Expert Seminars, Report prepared by the International Committee of the Red Cross, Geneva, October 2003, (www.icrc.org/Web/eng/siteeng0.nsf/htmlall/5TAM64/$File/Improving%20compliance%20with%20ihl-Oct%202003.pdf).

During the debates significant emphasis was placed on ensuring better compliance with the law in non-international armed conflicts. Given that the majority of contemporary armed conflicts are waged within the boundaries of States, the lack of respect for international humanitarian law in situations of non-international armed conflict by both the government and the armed opposition side is of particular concern. As we have seen, under Article 3 common to the four Geneva Conventions and Article 18 of the Second Additional Protocol, the ICRC or other relief organizations may offer their services in non-international armed conflicts. In addition, the International Fact Finding Commission has expressed its willingness to conduct an enquiry related to a non-international armed conflict. There are no other specific mechanisms for non-international armed conflicts foreseen in international humanitarian law treaties.

Therefore, the ICRC decided to focus its reflection on improving compliance in non-international armed conflicts. It has decided to look into past practices and to identify which tools and approaches have proved successful in influencing parties to a non-international armed conflict to respect international humanitarian law. A few examples:

- First, encourage the conclusion of special agreements, as provided for in paragraph 3 of Article 3 common to the four Geneva Conventions. Through such agreements, the parties may make an explicit commitment to comply with a broader range of rules of international humanitarian law. This may provide parties with added incentive to comply with the law, based on their mutual consent and express commitment.
- Second, encourage armed groups to issue unilateral declarations, stating clearly their commitment to comply with humanitarian law. The aim of such declarations is to provide a self-disciplining effect on the armed groups, in particular where groups are concerned about their public image and reputation.
- Third, encourage armed groups to adopt internal codes of conduct on respect for international humanitarian law – in the same way as States develop for example military manuals.
- Fourth, depending on the context, a possible grant of immunity from prosecution or amnesty for mere participation in hostilities.[57] Given that armed group members are likely to face maximum penalties for their participation in a non-international armed conflict – even if they respect international humanitarian law – they have little legal incentive to abide by the norms. A State grant of immunity to armed group members for participating in the hostilities – which of course could never include an amnesty or immunity for alleged war crimes – might provide armed groups with an incentive to comply with humanitarian law.

57 Article 6 (5) of Additional Protocol II encourages states parties to "endavour to grant the broadest possible amnesty (...)", however without guaranteeing a certain status whatsoever to those "who have participated in the armed conflict, or those deprived of their liberty for reasons related to the armed conflict, whether they are interned or detained".

IV. Role of States not involved in an armed conflict

Any discussion on how to improve and strengthen measures promoting respect for international humanitarian law during armed conflicts must begin with a reflection on the obligation contained in Article 1 common to the four Geneva Conventions and Additional Protocol I – that is, States' responsibility to "respect and ensure respect" for these instruments in all circumstances.

In addition to a clear legal obligation on States to "respect and ensure respect" for international humanitarian law within their own domestic context, common Article 1 also requires States not involved in an ongoing armed conflict neither to encourage a party to an armed conflict to violate international humanitarian law nor take action that would assist in such violations.[58] Furthermore, as recently affirmed by the International Court of Justice in an Advisory Opinion, common Article 1 is generally interpreted as laying down a responsibility on States not involved in armed conflict to ensure respect for international humanitarian law by the parties to an armed conflict, by means of positive action.[59] Third States have a responsibility, therefore, to take appropriate steps – unilaterally or collectively – against parties to a conflict which are violating international humanitarian law, in

[58] Military and Paramilitary Activities in and against Nicaragua (Nicaragua v. United States of America), Merits, ICJ Reports 1986, p. 14, para. 115; see also Article 16 Draft Articles on Responsibility of States for internationally wrongful acts (International Law Commission, 53rd Sessions, 2001); *Marco Sassòli,* State responsibility for violations of international humanitarian law, International Review of the Red Cross, No. 846, p. 412 et seq.

[59] Advisory Opinion of the International Court of Justice on the Legal Consequences of the Construction of a Wall in the Occupied Palestinian Territory, 9 July, 2004, General list No. 131., paras. 158, 163; The Prosecutor v. Zoran Kupreskic and others, ICTY Trial Chamber, Judgment, The Hague, 14 January 2000, Case No. IT-95-16-T, para. 519: "[as] a consequence of their absolute character, these norms of international humanitarian law do not pose synallagmatic obligations, i.e. obligations of a State vis-à-vis another State. Rather (...) they lay down obligations towards the international community as a whole, with the consequence that each and every member of the international community has a 'legal interest' in their observance and consequently a legal entitlement to demand respect for such obligations". See also *Theodor Meron*, Human Rights and Humanitarian Norms as Customary Law, 1989, pp. 30-31; *Laurence Boisson de Chazournes* and *Luigi Condorelli*, Common Article 1 of the Geneva Conventions revisited: Protecting collective interests, International Review of the Red Cross No. 837 (2000), pp. 67-87; *François Bugnion*, The International Committee of the Red Cross and the Protection of War Victims, 2003, p. 924, with further references; *Yves Sandoz*, "Droit" or "devoir d'ingérence" and the right to assistance: the issues involved, International Review of the Red Cross, No. 288, 1992, pp. 215-227; *Yves Sandoz*, Appel du C.I.C.R. dans le cadre du conflit entre l'Iran et l'Irak, Annuaire Français de Droit International 1983, p. 167; *Hans-Peter Gasser*, Ensuring Respect for the Geneva Conventions and Protocols: The Role of Third States and the United Nations, in: Hazel Fox/Michael A. Meyer, Effecting Compliance, British Institute of International and Comparative Law, 1993, p. 32; *Umesh Palwankar*, Measures available to States for fulfilling their obligation to ensure respect for international humanitarian law, International Review of the Red Cross, No. 298, 1994, pp. 9-25.

particular to intervene with States or armed groups over which they might have some influence to stop the violations. In this way they may contribute to enhancing compliance and possibly also fulfil an important monitoring function.

A couple of questions remain: Building on this understanding of common Article 1, how can this "positive" responsibility be put into practice? How can third States be stimulated to take appropriate action to ensure compliance with international humanitarian law by parties to an armed conflict? In particular, how can third States be encouraged to intervene with States or armed groups over which they might have some influence to stop the violations, in both international and non-international armed conflicts? Finally, what measures or steps for improving compliance with international humanitarian law have third States can be envisaged and would be successful?

Cases where States are prepared to take action to secure respect for international humanitarian law in conflicts in which they are not involved are still rare (at least those that were made known), but not unheard of. Most public are calls to respect the law. Are the cases rare because we are not doing enough to motivate them, or are they rare because other interests carry more weight for States? In the absence of a more efficient enforcement system, for its part, the ICRC is convinced of the significant role third States can play, and continues to encourage States to consider taking such positive action.

In this regard one should not forget the important role that the UN or regional organizations can play in monitoring compliance with international humanitarian law and influencing the behaviour of parties to an armed conflict. The role of the UN is specifically mentioned in Art. 89 of Additional Protocol I[60]. During the last 15 years or so (maybe since the first Gulf war in 1990/1991) the UN have become a very important actor in the field of international humanitarian law.

Just a few examples:

- appeals by the SC to respect international humanitarian law,
- establishment of ad hoc criminal tribunals,
- sending of fact-finding missions,
- the attention given to the protection of the civilian population in situations or armed conflict (production of several reports),
- also the General Assembly has dealt with several issues of international humanitarian law.

Quite recently – at the end of 2005 – the European Union has adopted Guidelines on promoting compliance with international humanitarian law.[61] They aim at setting out operational tools for the European Union and its institutions and bodies to

60 "In situations of serious violations of the Conventions or of this Protocol, the High Contracting Parties undertake to act, jointly or individually, in cooperation with the United Nations and in conformity with the United Nations Charter".

61 European Union Guidelines on promoting compliance with international humanitarian law (IHL), 2005/C 327/04, Official Journal of the European Union, 23.12.2005, C 327/4 et seq.

promote compliance with international humanitarian law and underline its commitment to promote such compliance in a visible and consistent manner. The adoption of these guidelines is a very significant step. Other regional organizations should follow that initiative. The challenge will now be the implementation in practice.

In conclusion, it is hoped that, in addition to a more determined role of third States not involved in an armed conflict, both the UN and regional organizations will become more active and effective as well as less selective in the field of monitoring and enhancing compliance with international humanitarian law.

C. Concluding remarks

Dissemination and compliance monitoring can contribute to better respect of international humanitarian law. While quite a lot of progress has been made in the field of preventive measures, such as dissemination and national legislation aiming at implementing international humanitarian law, as well as in the field of repressive action with the development of international criminal law, this cannot be said for monitoring and measures taken to improve compliance during armed conflict. Relatively weak mechanisms and tools foreseen in international humanitarian law treaties coupled with a lack of political will to seize them remains a challenge. Much depends therefore on serious efforts of the parties to an armed conflict themselves to ensure respect and the international community to pressure for that. The UN and regional organizations have still acted more on an ad hoc basis and often very selectively.

In this context one should not forget that the media and civil society, in particular the activities of certain NGOs, can and do play more and more often a major role in monitoring compliance. Publicly speaking out about alleged violations may have a powerful effect and, as stressed in the new British Military Manual, may often lead to the taking of other action.[62]

A number of new or aggravated characteristics of armed conflict make it increasingly difficult to uphold international humanitarian law and to protect human dignity. Among these characteristics one may mention: new actors capable of engaging in violence; the fragmented nature of conflicts in weak or failed States; the overlap between political and private aims; asymmetrical warfare; an uncontrolled availability of large quantities and categories of weapons; and an increasing involvement of civilians in armed conflict.

In addition to these, there are other challenges in contemporary armed conflicts to a better respect for international humanitarian law that need to be considered in assessing the current situation. Just a few bullet points:

- If certain armed actors show no willingness to respect even the most fundamental rules of international humanitarian law, it seems questionable whether the

62 The Manual of the Law of Armed Conflict, UK Ministry of Defence, 2004, p. 410.

traditional and even new means of ensuring compliance may change their attitudes and behaviours. The same is true when certain of the very objectives of parties to an armed conflict are in contradiction with rules of international humanitarian law, e.g. campaigns of ethnic cleansing or acts of violence the main aim of which is to directly target the civilian population.

- It is often quite difficult to locate, engage in a dialogue and then influence certain armed actors in contemporary armed conflicts, in particular if deemed terrorists from the outset.
- The somewhat growing tendency to dehumanise or demonise the adversary is equally not conducive to ensure compliance with international humanitarian law. Opponents are being described as not deserving the protections of the law and dealt with accordingly.
- Lastly, while international humanitarian law is not based on reciprocity, i.e. compliance is required even if the other side does not respect the law, expectations of reciprocity in terms of respect for international humanitarian law were always very important as disciplining factor. The expectation that one's own people will be respected and properly treated when in enemy hands if oneself respects and treats enemy prisoners or civilians well was always very prominent. In some of today's armed conflicts this expectation has unfortunately become far less important and thus no longer plays an important disciplining role.

Some characteristics of today's armed conflicts might contain the potential for clarification of existing law in order to render it more efficient and to better respond to new challenges. Fields for such efforts include the notion of direct participation in hostilities and related conduct of hostilities issues, the application of existing international humanitarian law to private military or security companies and the responsibility of States, air warfare or the concept of occupation. Nevertheless, the ICRC is convinced that the existing provisions of international humanitarian law form an adequate basis to meet the challenges raised by modern conflicts. A view shared by the participants of the last International Conference of the Red Cross and Red Crescent.[63] The problem of respect for the law is not primarily related to the adequacy of the rules themselves, but is mainly the result of a lack of political will on the part of the parties to armed conflicts to adhere to the law.

---

63 Declaration "Protecting human dignity", adopted by the 28th International Conference of the Red Cross and Red Crescent, Geneva, 2-6 December 2003.

Fact-finding as a means of ensuring respect for international humanitarian law

Michael Bothe

Johann Wolfgang Goethe-University Frankfurt am Main

I. Fact-finding – a general introduction

Fact-finding plays a major role in today's international relations, but not only in international relations. In many contexts, it is an important element of procedures serving to secure compliance and/or to settle disputes. For uncertainty about facts, diverging claims about what "really happened" often constitutes a substantial part of a dispute. Certainty about actual facts often is a first step in ensuring compliance with an obligation. This is true for many types of disputes, be they of a social, political or legal character. But as the contexts differ, the function of ascertaining facts (commonly called "fact-finding") varies, and so do the rules governing the process of ascertaining facts.

This paper tries to elaborate some specific characteristics of ascertaining facts in international relations and in particular in the framework of procedures designed to ensure a better implementation and respect of international humanitarian law. In order to do this and to put some order into the multiplicity of procedures which can be observed, an abstract framework of analysis is proposed.

On a relatively high level of abstraction, it is possible to describe the course of fact-finding procedures by a common scheme:[1]

Initiation (suspicion/unilateral claim, routine)

↓

Determination of a mandate

↓

Taking evidence (problem of access and reliability)

↓

Evaluating evidence

↓

Statement of facts (report, judgment)

↓

Reaction

---

1 See also the various steps of the procedure described by *Sylvain Vité*, Les procédures internationales d'établissement des faits dans la mise en œuvre du droit international humanitaire, 1999, pp. 187 et seq.

This general scheme is helpful as a framework of comparative analysis. As already indicated, procedures for ascertaining facts serve different purposes. This can be seen in each of these procedural steps. Both the actors and the rules governing the process vary according to the context.

What matters most is, of course, the last phase, or the end result. It is directly related to the ultimate purpose or function of the procedure. Why fact-finding? Any fact-finding procedure is undertaken with a view to measures which might be taken as a result of it, or with a view to a certain effect produced by it. This is what motivates relevant actors to initiate fact-finding procedures. It sets the agenda of various actors. Furthermore, the intended result also determines the design of the various phases of the procedure.

This applies to very different procedural forms of "fact-finding". Fact-finding in a narrow sense, also called "inquiry", may constitute a specific separate or self-contained procedure. But it serves nevertheless a purpose beyond that procedure, mostly the settlement of a dispute or the creation of trust in another actor's behaviour (confidence-building). Where fact-finding is used within the context of measures taken to monitor and ensure compliance with a treaty regime (so-called "verification", in particular within the framework of arms control and disarmament regimes) its purpose is to detect violations, deter violations and to create confidence. The structures of the relevant procedures are geared to that purpose.

It is with this general perspective in mind that our analysis deals with different actors in this field.

II. Fact-finding – actors, institutions and functions

There are essentially four different types of institutions or bodies engaged in ascertaining facts: States, organs established in common by two or more States, inter-governmental organisations (or specific organs of these organisations) and non-governmental organisations. In some cases, individuals may also undertake fact-finding without being an organ of one of these four types of entities. Fact finding by intergovernmental institutions may include permanent international organisations (e.g. the United Nations) and treaty-based organs (e.g. the IHFFC[2]). The ICRC is a particular institution having inter alia fact-finding functions.

Before or within these bodies or institutions, fact-finding procedures relating to facts which are of international legal relevance may be initiated by various actors and may be pursued in various ways.

1. Fact-finding by the State concerned

There is, first, unilateral fact-finding by the State concerned, i.e. the State where relevant facts happened or are still happening. It has its own agenda for clarifying

2 For details see below III.2.

facts. It may just engage in a "lessons learned" process. A more fundamental example are "truth and reconciliation commissions" or the like. This type of fact-finding often occurs in a post conflict situation as part of a process of re-establishing normalcy in a conflict-torn society. Establishing the truth may be part of a normalisation process. In recent years, it has become an important element of post-conflict peace building.[3]

In these cases, usually the government and/or the parliament of the country in question sets up a commission for the purpose of inquiring into violations of human rights and international humanitarian law with a view to put an end to impunity and to create, by clarifying the past, a basis for future peaceful living together of different groups in the society. Whether this clarification then leads to any criminal prosecution is a question which varies from case to case.

A decisive question is whether the result achieved is really accepted as the truth and can serve as a basis of reconciliation. This depends on the political context and the personalities chosen for the purpose of fact-finding. Foreign participation in such an exercise may add to its credibility. This was, for instance, the case of the truth commissions in Sierra Leone and Guatemala. In the case of the former, the Commission was appointed by the President of Sierra Leone, but the United Nations High Commissioner for Human Rights was involved in the selection of non-citizens.[4] The chair of the latter was a person appointed by the UN Secretary-General.[5] The foreign participation gave additional authority to that commission. But on the other hand, foreign participation may in other cases be considered an unwelcome infringement on the State's sovereignty.

Where such international input is welcome or even considered essential, the State concerned may even seize international bodies for the purpose of establishing relevant facts. An example is the Commission on the Truth in El Salvador, created on the basis of the peace agreements between the parties to the internal conflict, which consisted exclusively of foreign nationals.[6]

2. Fact-finding as a means of interstate dispute settlement

The second major function of fact-finding is its use as a means of dispute settlement between States, be it by bodies created *ad hoc* for a particular controversy or by referring this task to an existing institution. States create enquiry commissions or the like to clarify facts which are the object of, or relevant for, disputes existing between them.

3 The rule of law and transitional justice in conflict and post-conflict societies, Report of the Secretary-General, UN Doc. S/2004/616; see also the statement of the Secretary-General before the Security Council on September 24, 2003, S/PV.4833, p. 3.

4 Sierra Leone Truth and Reconciliation Commission Act, 2000, sec. 3.

5 The German professor *Christian Tomuschat*, see *Christian Tomuschat*, Friedenssicherung durch Wahrheitsfindung. Die Kommission zur Aufklärung der Vergangenheit in Guatemala, Vereinte Nationen 47 (1999), p. 192.

6 See the report "From Madness to Hope": The Twelve-Year War in El Salvador, UN Doc. S/25500, Annex.

In these cases, a procedure for ascertaining facts is created, or seized, on the basis of an agreement between the parties to a dispute. There may be a preceding agreement in a general form providing for such a procedure. Then, it is possible that one party unilaterally triggers the process. If there is no provision for such unilateral initiation of the procedure, there must be an *ad hoc* agreement between the parties. The result of the procedure usually is a statement of the facts. But it is assumed that the clarification of the facts will facilitate the solution of a dispute.

Under the name of "inquiry", procedures of this type are a traditional means of dispute settlement. This is witnessed by the treaties adopted by the Hague Peace Conferences, the First Hague Convention of 1899 and Second Hague Convention of 1907.[7] Commissions of inquiry were a major feature of the so-called Bryan Treaties, a series of bilateral dispute settlement agreements concluded by the United States 1913 and 1914.[8] As a means of dispute settlement, inquiry is mentioned in Art. 33 of the United Nations Charter and in the "Principles for Dispute Settlement" adopted by the Conference for Security and Co-operation in Europe.[9]

Under the Hague Convention of 1907, the fact-finding body is created *ad hoc* according to procedures established by this treaty. But States may also create permanent bodies to ascertain relevant facts. A body of this type is the International Humanitarian Fact-Finding Commission (IHFFC) established pursuant to Art. 90 of Protocol I Additional to the Geneva Conventions. It is competent to ascertain the relevant facts where there are allegations of grave breaches or other serious violation of the Conventions and the Additional Protocols.[10] But it may also offer its good offices.

In these cases, the procedure is triggered by one party to the dispute or by both of them if they agree beforehand on using it. The latter is the only possibility under the Second Hague Convention,[11] the former is possible under Art. 90 AP I.

The result is a statement of facts. Art. 35 of the Second Hague Convention reads:

"The report of the commission is limited to a statement of facts, and has in no way the character of an award. It leaves to the parties entire freedom as to the effect to be given to the statement."

It is apparently this openness which, in the view of the drafters of the Second Hague Convention, constitutes the appeal of this type of procedure. Similar con-

---

7 Hague Convention for the Pacific Settlement of Disputes, 29 July 1899; 18 October 1907 (Second Hague Convention), Art. 9 et seq.; published in *Karin Oellers-Frahm/ Andreas Zimmermann*, Dispute Settlement in Public International Law, 2nd ed. 2001, p. 6; Report of the Secretary-General on methods of fact-finding, 1 May 1964, UN Doc. A/5694, paras. 11 et seq.

8 *Hans-Jürgen Schlochauer*, Bryan Treaties (1913/1914) in: EPIL vol. I, pp. 509 et seq.

9 Report of the CSCE Meeting of Experts on Peaceful Settlement of Disputes Adopted at La Valetta, February 8, 1991, *Oellers-Frahm/Zimmermann*, supra n. 7, p. 163.

10 Although the text of Art. 90 only relates to AP I, the Commission is of the view that it can also accept the task of enquiry in violations of AP II.

11 Art. 10.

siderations may have prompted the drafters of the provision of the Geneva Conventions on enquiry[12] and of Art. 90 AP I.[13] But there is bound to be a purpose behind an inquiry. Inquiry procedures considered as successful have indeed served as a basis for solving a conflict.[14] The Geneva Conventions and Art. 90 make it clear that there is a definite purpose behind the fact-finding procedure, namely to ensure respect for international humanitarian law. This was made explicit already in the First Convention of 1929 (Art. 30):

"On the request of a belligerent, an enquiry shall be instituted, in a manner to be decided between the interested parties, concerning any alleged violation of the Convention; *when such violation has been established the belligerents shall put an end to and repress it as promptly as possible.*"[15]

Similar language is used in the common article of the 1949 Conventions. Art. 90 AP I is less explicit as to the expected result. But it, too, contains a kind of opening towards a result beyond the actual statement of the facts. Para. 5 (a) reads:

"The Commission shall submit to the Parties a report of the findings of fact of the Chamber, *with such recommendations as it may deem appropriate.*"[16]

While other fact-finding procedures are booming (as will be shown), there has only been scarce use of fact-finding or inquiry as a means of interstate dispute settlement in the first half of the 20th century and even less so after the 2nd World War.[17] The case most often cited is that of the *Dogger Bank* of 1904 between Great Britain and Russia. That dispute was resolved on the basis of an enquiry by experts, leading to compensation being paid by Russia.[18] Two cases of application of the 1907 Hague Convention are reported, none of them having led to any kind of result.[19] As to the time after the 2nd World War, two cases are reported, one of them, the *Red Crusader Incident* between the United Kingdom and Denmark, was indeed resolved on the basis of the report of the commission enquiry.[20] Neither the inquiry procedure established by the Geneva Conventions nor the IHFFC have ever been used. In the light of allegations made in the aftermath of the hostilities between Israel and Arab States of October 1993, the ICRC indeed proposed an in-

12 First Convention of 1929, art. 30; Conventions of 1949, common article 52/53/132/149.

13 See *Karl Josef Partsch*, in; Bothe, Michael/Karl Josef Partsch/Waldemar A. Solf, New Rules for Victims of Armed Conflicts, 1982, p. 544.

14 See for instance the *Dogger Bank* and *Red Crusader* cases, below notes 18 and 20.

15 Emphasis added.

16 Emphasis added.

17 For an elaborate analysis, see *Vité*, supra n. 1, pp. 15 et seq.

18 *Peter Schneider*, Dogger Bank Incident, in EPIL vol. I, p. 1090.

19 Report of the Secretary-General on methods of fact-finding, supra n. 7, paras. 42 et seq.; Permanent court of Arbitration, Annual Report 2004, p. 49.

20 *Jörg Polakiewicz*, Red Crusader Incident, in EPIL vol. IV, p. 63.

quiry on the basis of common article 52/53/132/149, but no agreement on it could be achieved.[21]

The reasons for this apparent lack of interest in fact-finding or inquiry as an independent means of international dispute settlement remains to be discussed after a presentation of other types of fact-finding.[22]

Fact-finding as an independent, so to say self-contained procedure has to be distinguished from procedures for ascertaining facts which are a part of other dispute settlement procedures, in particular international conciliation or judicial proceedings.

3. Fact-finding and international conciliation

Conciliation or mediation is not so much concerned with what happened in the past, but more directly with the solution of a controversy for the future. However, clarification of facts, still existing or having occurred in the past, may indeed contribute to solutions for the future. This is why fact-finding is indeed a possible element of conciliation procedures.

Thus, the so-called Geneva General Act of 1928[23] refers to inquiry as a possible part of a conciliation procedure (Art. 15 para. 1):

"The task of the Conciliation Commission shall be to elucidate the questions in dispute, to collect with that object all necessary information by means of enquiry or otherwise, and to endeavour to bring the parties to an agreement."

That concept of inquiry as a part of conciliation procedures is well developed by the American Treaty on Pacific Settlement (Pact of Bogotá) of April 13, 1948.[24] It creates, inter alia, a "procedure of investigation and conciliation" (Articles XV et seq.). As to the role of fact-finding in the conciliation procedure, Art. XXII states:

"... The Commission shall institute such investigations of the acts involved in the controversy as it may deem necessary for the purpose of proposing acceptable bases of settlement."

This shows quite clearly the subordinate character of fact-finding in relation to conciliation. In this context, its only function is achieving a settlement. This being so, the conciliation procedure can nevertheless be limited to fact-finding (Art. XXVI) if the circumstances so require:

---

21 *François Bugnion*, Le Comité international de la Croix-Rouge et la protection des vicitmes de la guerre, 1994, pp. 1099 et seq.

22 See below III.1.

23 LNTS 93, 343; *Oellers-Frahm/Zimmermann*, supra n. 7, p. 93.

24 *Oellers-Frahm/Zimmermann*, id., p. 231.

"If, in the opinion of the parties, the controversy relates exclusively to questions of fact, the Commission shall limit itself to investigating such questions, and shall conclude its activities with an appropriate report."

Conciliation procedures have been included in the dispute settlement clauses of a considerable number of international treaties.[25] They are a major element in the dispute settlement system created by the CSCE/OSCE.[26] They were introduced in the Geneva Conventions in 1929[27] and maintained and expanded in 1949.[28] Conciliation has fared a little better than inquiry as a means of international dispute settlement, but not very much.[29] There is at least one *cause célèbre* in recent years, namely the mediation by the Holy See between Argentina and Chile concerning the Beagle Channel.[30] But on the other hand, neither the OSCE procedures nor those established by the Geneva Conventions have been used so far.

4. Fact-finding and international adjudication

Ascertaining facts, i.e. taking evidence constitutes a major component of the judicial settlement of disputes.[31] It is beyond the scope of the present paper to analyse this in greater detail. What matters in the present context is the comparison with other procedures for ascertaining facts. For that purpose, it has to be recalled that international adjudication is performed by a great variety of institutions having very different structures.[32] There are permanent international tribunals competent for interstate disputes (ICJ, ITLOS), quasi-judicial bodies for the same purpose (WTO Panels and the Appellate Body), and arbitral tribunals. In the field of the protection of human rights, there are regional courts and a number of other bodies also dealing with specific cases in a manner which at least resembles adjudication, such as the procedure governed by the Optional Protocol to the ICCPR. There are interstate procedures before human rights bodies, but mostly the procedures relate to claims put forward by victims of human rights violations against a State allegedly having violated these rights. The structure of this type of procedure varies from that of the interstate processes. A further and differently structured type of international adjudication are international criminal tribunals.

---

25 *Rudolf Bindschedler*, Conciliation and Mediation, in: EPIL vol. I, pp. 721 et seq.

26 Supra n. 9.

27 Art. 87 of the Prisoners of War Convention.

28 Common article 11/11/11/12.

29 For a review of the earlier practice, see *Hans von Mangoldt*, Arbitration and Conciliation, in: Hermann Mosler/Rudolf Bernhardt (eds.), Judicial Settlement of International Disputes, 1974, pp. 417 et seq., at 484 et seq.

30 *Karin Oellers-Frahm*, Beagle Channel Arbitration, in EPIL vol. I, p. 363 et seq., at 366.

31 *Vité*, supra n. 1, pp. 18 et seq.

32 See *Pemmaraju Sreenivasa Rao*, Multiple International Judicial Forums: A Reflection of the Growing Strength of International Law or Its Fragmentation, Michigan Journal of International Law 25 (2004), pp. 929 et seq.

In contradistinction to the procedures of inquiry and conciliation, the use of international adjudication in all its forms has tremendously developed during the last decades. In 1972, the President of the ICJ, in an address on the occasion of the fiftieth anniversary of the creation of the international judicial system stated: "There is an observable decline in the number of cases submitted not only to this Court, but to international arbitration in any form". And he explained: "All States have the sovereign power to use or to bypass the Court".[33] The idea to perpetuate the example of the tribunals of Nuremberg and Tokyo and to establish an international criminal jurisdiction had at that time become the victim of the political circumstances of the Cold War.

These negative trends have definitely been reversed, both as to the ICJ and as to other institutions of international adjudication. The ICJ has become a very busy court. WTO dispute settlement is booming. International arbitration has regained momentum.[34] The European Court of Human Rights is in danger of cracking down under its heavy case load. The 1990ies have seen the re-establishment of international and "hybrid" criminal jurisdictions, culminating in the establishment of the International Criminal Court. On the other hand, not all the institutions which exist are actually used. The OSCE Court has yet to receive its first case. In the field of human rights, the interstate procedures which do exist under various treaty regimes only play a marginal role, if any. The affected individuals, supported by organisations of the civil society, are those who create the heavy case load of these courts and institutions. But in general, one can state that reliance on adjudication has greatly increased in the international system. This may be one explanation for the relatively scarce use of non-judicial procedures, including procedures for ascertaining facts.

It is the common element of the judicial procedures that they result in a legally binding statement on what the law is in a given situation. Taking evidence is geared towards that result and limited to what is necessary for that purpose. In contradistinction to the other procedures just described, the result is not open. The judgement declares how the parties are expected to behave as a matter of law.

The procedural structure of interstate judicial settlement, of human rights courts and of criminal tribunals is of course different, and so are there rules on taking evidence. It presents different problems depending on the type of proceedings. There are essentially three different types of international judicial proceedings:

- interstate proceedings, before the ICJ or arbitration tribunals;
- proceedings instituted by individuals against a State before human rights courts or quasi-judicial human rights bodies;
- proceedings instituted against individuals before international criminal courts.

---

33 See *Hermann Mosler*, Introduction, in: Mosler/Bernhardt, supra n. 29, p. 3. For an analysis of this decrease, see *Helmut Steinberger*, The International Court of Justice, id., pp. 193 et seq., at pp. 211 et seq.

34 See for example the statistics of the Permanent Court of Arbitration. There were no interstate cases before that arbitral institution between the end of the 2nd World War and 1988; since then, 12 interstate cases have been submitted for arbitration.

The interstate proceedings, as a matter of principle, are of the adversarial type. This means that the tribunal in question has to rely on the evidence put forward by the parties. The ICJ, however, is not strictly bound in this way. It may ask the parties to supply specific evidence or to give explanations (Art. 49 of the Statute) and it may *motu proprio* entrust an individual or an organisation to make an enquiry (Art. 50). This is without prejudice to the rule that any party must prove the facts on which it relies to found its legal claim. If it does not succeed in doing so, the burden of proof becomes relevant, which has indeed played a major role in cases before the ICJ. Examples are, in particular, cases relating to the circumstances of the use of armed force, beginning with the *Corfu Channel* case,[35] continuing with *Nicaragua*,[36] *Oil Platforms*[37] and the *Congo*.[38]

Proceedings before human rights courts are also to a large extent of the adversarial type.[39] It is up to the complaining victim to furnish the relevant facts to the satisfaction of the court in question. But the European Court of Human Rights may in addition take evidence, also *motu proprio*, "which it considers capable of providing clarification of the facts of the case".[40] There is also a duty of the defendant State to cooperate with the Court which to some degree mitigates the deficiencies of the adversarial system.[41] Another element is the role of NGOs which may assist victims in presenting the evidence or which may themselves present such evidence in the form of *amicus curiae* briefs.

The process before the *ad hoc* international criminal tribunals, too, is at least to a large extent of the adversarial type, one of the parties being the public prosecutor. What has been said for the human rights courts applies *mutatis mutandis* here. A major problem of taking evidence before international criminal tribunals is the fact that this occurs quite often a long time after the facts, and far away from the place of the crime.

---

35 ICJ Reports 1949, p. 4.

36 Military and Paramilitary Activities in and against Nicaragua (Nicaragua v. United States of America), ICJ Reports 1986, p. 14.

37 Case Concerning Oil Platforms (Islamic Republic of Iran v. United States of America), Judgement of 6 November 2003, paras. 57 et seq.

38 Case Concerning Armed Activities in the Territory of the Congo (Democratic Republic of the Congo v. Uganda), Judgement of 19 December 2005, paras. 57 et seq.

39 *W.J. Ganshof van der Meersch*, European Court of Human Rights, in EPIL vol. II, p. 201 et seq., at 209.

40 Rule 42 of the Rules of the European Court of Human Rights, November 4, 1998, *Oellers-Frahm/Zimmermann*, supra n. 7, p. 456.

41 See also *Jörg Nowak*, Staatliche Mitwirkung in Tatsachenfeststellungsverfahren zum Schutz vor Folter, 1997.

5. Fact-finding by intergovernmental organisations

Ascertaining facts also plays an important role in the activities of intergovernmental organisations.[42] International organisations frequently use fact-finding as a genuine means to perform their various tasks. First the League of Nations, and then the United Nations have used fact-finding in various contexts as part of their activities for the maintenance of international peace and security. This is also the case with the OAS[43] and the OAU/AU. Usually, the purpose is to find a reliable factual basis for further measures to be taken by the Organisation. Since the very beginning of the United Nations, both the General assembly and the Security Council have used inquiry commissions for that purpose. A few recent examples may suffice to state the case.

In 1992, the Security Council created a fact-finding mission for Yugoslavia to enquire into the allegations of massive violations of international humanitarian law.[44] After its chairman, the commission became known as Kalshoven Commission. The result of its appalling findings was the creation of the ICTY by the Security Council.[45]

In 2002, there were allegations of violations of human rights and international humanitarian law when Israeli troupes had forcefully entered the Palestinian city of Jenin. The Secretary-General established a fact finding mission, which was welcomed by the Security Council.[46] Unfortunately, that commission, although it had become operational, was finally not admitted on site.

In 2004, when there were horrible reports about massive human rights violation in the Darfur region of Sudan, the Security Council requested the Secretary-General to established a fact-finding mission, which then was to be headed by Professor *Antonio Cassese*, former President of the ICTY, to enquire into the violations of human rights and international humanitarian law and also into the nature of the crimes allegedly committed in the area.[47] The result of its report was that the Security Council referred the case to the Prosecutor of the International Criminal Court.[48]

---

42 *Vité*, supra n. 1, pp. 55 et seq.; Report of the Secretary-General, supra n. 7, paras. 22 et seq., 149 et seq.

43 Report of the Secretary-General, supra n. 7, paras. 330 et seq.

44 Resolution 780 of 6 October 1992. The relevant part of the resolution reads: "The Security Council … requests the Secretary-General to establish, as a matter of urgency, an impartial Commission of Experts to examine and analyse the information submitted … together with such other information as the Commission of Experts may obtain through its own investigations or efforts, …, with a view to providing the Secretary-General with its conclusions on the evidence of grave breaches of the Geneva Conventions and other violations of international humanitarian law committed in the territory of the former Yugoslavia".

45 Resolution 827 of 25 May 1993.

46 Resolution 1405 of 19 April 2002.

47 Resolution 1564 18 September 2004.

48 Resolution 1593 of 31 March 2005.

The examples show that a prominent function of fact-finding is to provide a basis for further measures to be taken by the organisation. This means that the results must be given into the hands of the organ which has instituted the fact-finding process. Certain limitations in this regard, however, are to be observed. The Darfur fact-finding mission, right from the beginning, was undertaken with a view to criminal prosecutions to be instituted later. This meant that part of the information had to be treated as confidential in order not to compromise the later criminal proceedings.

While these examples taken from the practice of the United Nations took place *ad hoc* and were related to a specific controversy, fact-finding is also undertaken by international organisation as a part of their routine monitoring or supervisory activities. In the field of human rights, the thematic and the country rapporteurs of the Human Rights Commission[49] have to be mentioned. In this case, fact-finding is part of a political process of building a scenario of pressure designed to promote better respect for human rights. The process is triggered by the Commission, according to its usual procedures. It does not depend on the consent of the State concerned, only on site activities of the rapporteurs do.

Other examples are the routine verification processes of the OPCW[50] and monitoring by the IAEA on the basis of the safeguards system.[51] Both are treaty based and have a specific structure tailor made for the specific purposes of the procedures. In these cases, the function of fact-finding is transparency, in particular transparency about compliance, detection of violations and confidence building. In this context, already the mere existence of fact-finding procedures is a means to ensure compliance. Transparency means that the State in question has to justify before a relevant public what it does or does not do. This also means that transparency, under certain conditions, must be limited. This is, for example, the case of verification measures in the field of disarmament. The information obtained, as a rule, remains in the hand of the Secretariat of the organisation in charge. This is as a rule enough to build confidence.

6. Fact-finding by the ICRC

An important actor in fact-finding relating to international humanitarian law is the ICRC. Technically, it is not an intergovernmental organisation. But it resembles IGOs in that it derives its functions from the Geneva Conventions and the Protocols additional thereto, i.e. from international treaties. An important aspect of its activities in favour of the victims of armed conflicts consists indeed of fact-finding. It serves two different purposes. First, fact-finding is needed to assess the

---

49 See *Henry J. Steiner/Philip Alston*, International Human Rights in Context, 2nd ed. 2000, pp. 641 et seq.

50 Convention on the Prohibition and Development, Production, Stockpiling and Use of Chemical Weapons and on their Destruction, 13 January 1993, Art. VI.

51 Non-Proliferation Treaty, Art. III.

needs of different kinds of victims. In this respect, it is an important preliminary measure for relief operations.

Secondly, it is part of the activities of the ICRC to ensure compliance with international humanitarian Law. The purpose of that fact-finding, too, is a limited transparency, i.e. limited to the ICRC, as the results are generally treated as confidential. It is only where access is consistently denied or where violations observed by the ICRC are not stopped that the ICRC goes public and uses the general transparency as a means to induce compliance.

For both purposes, the ICRC's right of access to victims, in particular to prisoners of war is very important. This right is treaty based, in the case of prisoners of war on explicit provisions of the Third Convention[52], generally on the "right of initiative"[53].

All this is a core element of the implementation of international humanitarian law.

7. Fact-finding by non-governmental organisations

Last but not least, non-governmental organisations play a major role in international fact-finding, in particular in the fields of environmental protection (Greenpeace) and of human rights (Amnesty International, Human Rights Watch). Amnesty International has published numerous reports concerning alleged violations of international humanitarian law.[54] Human Rights Watch recently published the well researched report "Off Target" concerning the respect for international humanitarian law by both sides during the American and British intervention in Iraq.

III. Fact-finding as a means to implement and enforce international humanitarian law

1. Overview and development

On the basis of these reflections, the role of the different fact-finding procedures for a better implementation and enforcement of international humanitarian law can be clarified.

The role of international courts and quasi-judicial bodies varies greatly, and so does the fact-finding undertaken by these bodies. There is, first of all, the International Court of Justice whose role has greatly increased in recent years. Its function is to state in a legally binding way violations of international law and (if so requested) to award damages for these violations. This also applies to international

---

52 Art. 126 of the IIIrd Convention.

53 Common article 9/9/9/10 of the Conventions, art. 81 (1) AP I, see the ICRC Commentary to the Additional Protocols, Art. 81, marg. notes 3309 et seq.

54 Examples are recent reports concerning the detainees at Guantanamo Bay.

humanitarian law. The Court has fulfilled these functions in the Nicaragua[55] and the recent Congo case[56]. These judgments were the result of extensive fact-finding by the Court. The two cases show the potential of the Court in this field.

Arbitration similarly plays an increasing role. A recent example is the Eritrea-Ethiopia Claims Commission dealing with violations of international humanitarian law during the conflict between these two States.[57] On the basis of extensive fact-finding, it has rendered a number of awards, stating either that violations of international humanitarian law had happened or could not be proved, and that one of the States was liable to pay compensation for a particular case of damage.

Whether and to what extent human rights bodies play a role in enforcing international humanitarian law, which applies in parallel to human rights law, still is a matter of some controversy, but it has been recognised as a matter of principle by the International Court of Justice.[58] This means that a violation of a human right can at the same time constitute a violation of international humanitarian law, and that the human rights remedy (a complaint by the individual victim before a human rights tribunal) also covers the violation of international humanitarian law.[59] Thus, taking evidence, i.e. fact-finding done by and for international human rights tribunals may also be relevant for international humanitarian law. This has become increasingly important in recent years.

Another important development is that of international criminal courts. The establishment of the two *ad hoc* tribunals for the former Yugoslavia and for Rwanda have opened a new chapter as to the ways and means of ensuring respect of international humanitarian law. They have done a great amount of fact-finding under difficult circumstances. The ICC has its own procedure of investigation which is in the hands of the Office of the Prosecutor.

As the Security Council has stated on several occasions that systematic violations of international humanitarian law constitute a threat to the peace,[60] the entire array of measures within the power of the Security Council can be triggered by fact-finding relating to violations of international humanitarian law. Examples are the creation of the International Criminal Tribunal for the Former Yugoslavia and that for Rwanda, both preceded by a fact-finding mission. A recent example of this practice is the case of Darfur. Other UN organs or bodies play different roles in the field, in particular the rapporteurs of the Human Rights Commission and the High Commissioner for Human Rights.

The role of fact-finding by the ICRC and by NGOs has already been explained.

---

55 Case Concerning Military and Paramilitary Activities in and against Nicaragua, Nicaragua v. United States of America, Judgement of 27 June 1986.

56 Case Concerning Armed Activities on the Territory of the Congo, Democratic Republic of the Congo v. Uganda, Judgement of 19 December 2005.

57 See for example the award rendered 28 April 2004, 43 ILM 1249 (2004).

58 Legal Consequences of the Construction of a Wall in the Occupied Palestinian Territory, Advisory Opinion, 9 July 2004, paras. 102 et seq.

59 As to the inter-American practice, see the *Tablada* case decided by the Inter-American Commission of Human Rights, IACHR Report No. 55/97.

60 Resolutions 827 (1993) (former Yugoslavia); 955 (1994) (Rwanda); 1564 (2004) (Darfur).

Fact finding is indeed a major tool for a better implementation and enforcement of international humanitarian law, yet it has become multifaceted and complex.

This development of these various institutions involved in ascertaining fact in international relations generally and in respect of international humanitarian law in particular was bound to have an impact on fact-finding as a means of interstate dispute settlement and on the procedures created for that purpose by the Geneva Conventions and the Additional Protocols. In order to understand that phenomenon of non-use of certain dispute settlement procedures, it is necessary to recall it is not limited to fact-finding. It also applies, albeit to a lesser extent, to conciliation and also to certain judicial and quasi-judicial institutions. Examples are the non-use of OSCE dispute settlement and of the interstate complaints in the field of human rights. Interstate cases before the institutions of the European Convention on Human Rights have only played a marginal role.[61] The same holds true for the interstate procedure under art. 26 of the ILO Constitution.[62] The interstate procedures existing under other treaties (ICCPR, ACHR, CERD, CAT) have not been used at all.[63] One of the reasons of the non-use of these procedures may be that the decision to seize an interstate dispute settlement body means overcoming a threshold. As a rule, the necessary effort is not made where the issue is essentially an altruistic one as in the case of human rights and international humanitarian law. States have been extremely reluctant to lodge complaints as a kind of *action popularis* in the "public", in the common interest. Generally speaking, the booming of international judicial dispute settlement relates to other matters. Where issues of human rights and/or international humanitarian law are submitted to an interstate dispute settlement body, the "plaintiff" State must have a rather strong political motivation to do so. In most of the interstate cases before the institutions of the European Convention, there was a serious political conflict between the plaintiff and the defendant State (Cyprus v. U.K.; Austria v. Italy; Ireland v. U.K.; Greece v. Turkey).[64] If this political motivation exists, (as in the cases of Nicaragua and Iran v. the United States, Congo v. Uganda, Rwanda and Burundi, or the cases concerning the application of the Genocide Convention against Yugoslavia/Serbia-Montenegro), States have apparently preferred to use judicial procedures instead of just fact-finding or conciliation. This accounts for the increasing role of the ICJ in this field. It is not really at odds with the traditional wisdom that fact-finding is more acceptable to States because it is less offensive to State sovereignty. This is seen from the perspective of the potential defendant. If a plaintiff thinks that it has a good case, it will use the stronger judicial forum.

---

61 In the 55 years of the existence of the European Convention, there have been, technically speaking, 18 cases, in reality only 6: Greece v. U.K. (Cyprus, 1956, 1957), Greece v. Turkey (Cyprus, 1974, 1975, 1977); Austria v. Italy (South Tyrol, 1960), Ireland v. U.K. (Northern Ireland, 1978), [several States] v. Greece (internal situation in Greece, 1968, 1970), [several States] v. Turkey (internal situation in Turkey, 1982).

62 See *Manfred Nowak*, U.N. Covenant on Civil and Political Rights, 2nd ed. 2005, Art. 41 marg. note 2.

63 *Nowak*, id.; *Christian Tomuschat*, International Covenant on Civil and Political Rights, Human Rights Committee, in EPIL vol. II, pp. 1115 et seq.

64 *Nowak*, id.

Where fact-finding is initiated by third parties, in particular IGOs and NGOs, which have an agenda of their own, these actors usually have that sufficient impetus to engage in such procedures which is lacking where the States just decide on their own. This accounts for the widespread use of fact-finding by international organisations and NGOs. The costs involved in a bilateral fact-finding procedure also constitute a restraining factor.

2. Fact-finding as a means of implementing and enforcing international humanitarian law – current situation and the role of the IHFFC

On the basis of these reflections, it will now be attempted to specify the possible role of the IHFFC as a means of ensuring a better respect for international humanitarian law. At the outset, the particular context in which the relevant text, i.e. art. 90 AP I, was negotiated has to be recalled. Apart from dissemination, the attention of the negotiators of the Protocols, as far as ensuring respect for international humanitarian law is concerned, concentrated on two traditional instruments already found in the Conventions: the Protecting Powers and inquiry.

As to inquiry, this traditional instrument was considered as useful by many States despite the fact that it had not been used. The negotiators wanted to improve the situation by eliminating the need to establish the inquiry body *ad hoc* by a special compromise, a need which might account for the non-use of the inquiry procedure found in the Conventions since 1929. Thus, it was proposed to create a standing commission. The proposals which were made, however, went far beyond what is now in Art. 90. It was proposed to create a body with obligatory monitoring functions which it could even trigger on its own initiative.[65] This was bitterly opposed by a number of delegations.[66] Even a general obligation to accept an inquiry initiated at the request of a State party was not acceptable. The compromise was to adopt a copy of the optional clause of Art. 36 of the Statute of the International Court of Justice.[67]

As has just been shown, the possibilities and practices of fact-finding in the field of international humanitarian law have since then considerably developed. What is, in this complex new context, the role of the IHFFC as an institution specifically created for the purpose of ascertaining facts where there are allegations of violations of international humanitarian law? When the Commission was created by the Diplomatic Conference 1974-77, the multiplicity of procedures just described was not imagined. The functions of the Security Council were hampered by the phenomenon of the so-called automatic veto. Resort to the International Court of Justice was rather rare. No international criminal tribunal existed, and those who advocated its establishment were regarded as utopians. The enforcement of international humanitarian law by human rights tribunals was certainly

---

65 See *Partsch*, supra n. 13, pp. 539 et seq.

66 See also *Vité*, supra n. 1, p. 203.

67 *Partsch*, supra n. 13, p. 240.

not a perspective which came to mind of the negotiators. It was assumed and hoped that the maximum acceptable for States in terms of a third party dispute settlement procedure was that Commission with a limited jurisdiction.

Does the fact that the circumstances have changed mean that the IHFFC has become superfluous, in particular in the light of the fact that it has so far not been seized by any State and that there are so many "competing" institutions? An answer to this question, which this author thinks is negative, has to single out what are the specific traits the IHFFC presents for the States to take advantage of, which the other procedures do not have. These specific characteristics are

- that it is an interstate procedure which is very much influenced and even shaped by the States concerned;
- that the procedure is confidential;
- that its result stops short of a statement of the law.

All three elements are important, in particular in the light of the situation described above.

State influence on the procedure: The parties to the procedure, not a fact-finding body coming with the authority of the Security Council or that of the Prosecutor of the ICC, determine the scope of the case. This is obvious where the Commission offers its good offices (Art. 90 par. 2 (c)(ii)). But although the scope of an enquiry will be determined by the allegation (Art. 90 par. 2 (c)(i)), the procedure possesses a cooperative character. It is up to the parties, both parties (!), to decide whether the report is rendered public.

Confidentiality: This element is related to the first one. It is important for States that there is no naming and shaming involved as is the case with many other procedures.

No statement of the law: This remains important in relation to the various judicial procedures. Once the facts are stated, the parties can agree on what follows. If the ICJ has jurisdiction in the case, one party can still go to the ICJ for a declaration of the law and an award of damages. But this is highly improbable. The facts being ascertained will as a rule facilitate an agreement among the parties on the question of just compensation. The Commission may even offer its good offices to arrive at such an agreement. This may be less expensive and less time consuming than going to the ICJ or to arbitration. Thus, although the Commission can and will deal with questions of law, it can do so in a more flexible way than any court.

Similar considerations apply concerning the question of whether the Commission might pronounce itself on individual responsibility for certain violations. As a matter of principle, this is not the Commission's function. But depending on the case which is submitted to it, i.e. depending on the wishes of the parties, it may be called upon to do so. It is then up to the parties to draw the necessary conclusions and to decide on appropriate consequences.

In relation to the ICC, an early functioning of the Commission may render superfluous the need to call upon the Prosecutor of the ICC. The stated facts may facilitate a party's decision itself to prosecute, which would exclude the jurisdiction of the ICC.

The IHFFC is not the only institution charged with fact-finding for the purpose of a better implementation of international humanitarian law. There remains, however, a considerable potential for it, in particular in cases where the States concerned want to retain a control of the procedure which either the Security Council or the ICC Prosecutor might take away from them.

There remains the question whether and how the Commission could overcome its dependence on States deciding to use it. The answer depends on the concept of "good offices". On the one hand, as has been explained, the Commission has no right to initiate a fact-finding mission *motu proprio*. On the other hand, it may "facilitate, through its good offices, the restoration of an attitude of respect for the Conventions and this Protocol" (Art. 90 (2)(b)(ii)). Art. 90 does not say that it can do so only within the framework of an ongoing procedure initiated by a State against another State. In other words, the Commission is able to offer its good offices without being asked to do so, while the State to whom they are offered is of course free to refuse them. The good offices clause, thus, is the key which opens the door for a proactive role of the Commission.[68]

3. Perspectives: the relationship between different bodies involved in ascertaining facts

Having elaborated the specific role the IHFFC in the overall complex of ascertaining facts in current international relations, a few comments must be added concerning its relationship to other bodies tasked with ascertaining facts relevant for their functions which have been mentioned.

The first question is that of the relationship between the Commission and the United Nations. Assuming that the Security Council requests the assistance of the Commission, the situation presents particular problems. When the Security Council acts under Ch. VII of the Charter, it may adopt decisions which are binding on the member States and probably also on intergovernmental organisations. It may create fact-finding bodies as its subsidiary organs or oblige the Secretary-General to establish such bodies as part of the Secretariat, but it may also task existing bodies, including the IHFFC. In doing so, the Council is bound by the Charter and also, according to a prevailing view, by customary norms relating to the protection of human rights,[69] but arguably not by the details of the AP I concerning the confi-

68 *Vité*, supra n. 1, pp. 214, et seq.

69 The exact scope of the obligation of the Security Council to respect human rights is controversial. The Court of First Instance of the European Communities limits this obligation to the core guarantees which constitute *ius cogens*: Kadi v. Council and Commission, Judgement of 21 September 2005, Case T-315/01, paras. 226 et seq.; Yusuf et al. v. Council and Commission, Judgement of 21 September 2005, Case 306/01, paras. 277 et seq. For a somewhat broader view, see *Hans-Peter Gasser*, Collective Economic Sanctions and International Humanitarian Law, Heidelberg Journal of International Law 56 (1996), pp. 871, at 880 et seq.

dentiality of the work of the Commission. As a matter of expediency, however, there is no reason why the Council should disregard these rules. If the Council wants to establish a fact-finding procedure of a different nature, it can do so, and it has done so, without having recourse to the services of the Commission. If the Council wants to mandate the Commission to undertake a fact-finding mission, it will, as a rule, do so because it wants to use the particular advantages the Commission has to offer, which have been described above.

As to the ICC, it has already been pointed out that findings of the Commission may be used in subsequent criminal proceedings. This can cause a problem even where the State concerned itself institutes criminal proceedings. In the course of public proceedings, that State may use the findings which the Commission submits if all the parties to the Commission proceedings agree on them being made public (article 90 (5)(c) AP I). If that agreement is lacking, the findings may not be so used.

Where there is the necessary agreement, the question of how the findings are used in those proceedings is a matter of the law of criminal procedure of the State in question. From the point of view of the law governing the work of the Commission, there is no objection against members of the Commission or experts or investigators engaged by the Commission testifying before the national court. From the point of view of the procedural rights of an alleged perpetrator, it is, however, important that the findings of the Commission do not deprive that person of his or her right to challenge any evidence used against him or her.

These considerations apply *mutatis mutandis* to the ICC. The ICC is an institution tasked to ensure the application of international humanitarian law. This means that the ICC has to accept international humanitarian law as it is as a whole – which includes the rules concerning to confidentiality of the investigations of the Commission. Thus, unless there is an agreement by all parties to a Commission proceeding, its findings may not be used by the ICC, nor may members or investigators of the Commission be obliged to testify before the ICC. This limitation is implied in article 87 (6) of the ICC Statute which deals with assistance by intergovernmental organisations. On the other hand, if the use of this information is permissible from the point of view of the confidentiality of the Commission's proceedings, the rights of the defence have to be respected, as indicated.

IV. Conclusions

The ways and means to ensure respect of international humanitarian law are diverse. Various actors play various roles on this scene. There are various actors representing the "public" interest, the international community. First, there is the ICRC, impartial, experienced, of high moral standing, mostly using a diplomatic approach. There are public prosecutors, albeit not in all cases, depending on details of the rules concerning jurisdiction. There is the Security Council, powerful, sometimes high-handed, and sometimes inefficient. There are the victims, having more and more access to remedies. However, a decentralised procedure being to a larger extent in the hands of the States directly concerned has a necessary function in this complex mix of procedures. This, it is submitted, is provided by the International Humanitarian Fact-finding Commission.

Human Rights Treaty Bodies and Their Potential Role in Monitoring

Rainer Hofmann

Johann Wolfgang Goethe-University Frankfurt am Main

1. In his excellent paper a draft of which I had the pleasure to read before this Conference, *Knut Dörmann*, rightly pointed out that, as concerns IHL and other branches of International Law, the major problem is not a shortage of applicable rules but the lack of sufficiently effective mechanisms to monitor, and if need be to enforce, compliance with such rules. Notwithstanding his correct conclusion that while some of the new characteristics of armed conflicts might result in the need to clarify the contents of existing law, he is – and I should like to stress: correctly so – of the opinion, also shared by the ICRC, that the existing provisions of IHL form an adequate basis to meet challenges raised by modern types of armed conflict.

In his paper, *Knut Dörmann*, examines a range of measures which eventually might add to, and improve, the monitoring and enforcement of compliance. He specifically mentioned the potential role of mechanisms not based on IHL treaties, in particular human rights bodies and the UN in general. He also invited commentators to look more closely into this issue – and that is what I should like to do, namely to briefly present my views on what human rights treaty bodies and the more general human rights machinery of the UN might achieve as regards the possible improvement of the situation of participants and victims of armed conflicts.

I propose to do so by examining various scenarios in which human rights treaties and monitoring activities of the respective treaty bodies might have an impact on the human rights situation of those involved in armed conflicts. At the outset, I should like to stress, however, that it is important to keep in mind that the monitoring competence of any such treaty body is, *ratione materiae*, limited to the provisions of the respective human rights treaty and does not include IHL norms as such.

This, however, presupposes – and that is the first and quite fundamental issue to be dealt with – that the application of human rights law, on the one hand, and IHL, on the other hand, is not mutually exclusive. To this audience, I do not have to elaborate on the point that the previously dominant view according to which in a situation of armed conflict, i.e. in a situation where the rules of IHL are applicable, the rules of human rights law cease to be applicable, does not reflect any longer the current state of international law. So, *ratione materiae*, both IHL and human rights norms are, in principle, applicable in a situation of armed conflict. However, the rules of human rights law are only applicable insofar as they are not superseded by the rules of IHL; to a certain degree, IHL could, thus, be considered as *lex specialis* with respect to human rights law. This means that, and I should like to stress that as being the starting point of my comment, human rights law is, in principle, applicable in situations of armed conflicts.

2. Now, I should like to briefly present the various scenarios which I shall deal with:

a) The armed conflict is a truly non-international armed conflict with no intervention from outside.

Now, if the state concerned is a member to any universally or regionally applicable human rights treaty which provides for a system of compliance monitoring based on state reports or triggered by individual complaints, I think the conclusion is quite obvious: The competent treaty organs are entitled to continue their monitoring activities insofar as the applicability of the relevant treaty provisions has not ceased due to a formal declaration of derogation or because it has been superseded by a corresponding IHL rule.

However, this conclusion does not solve one of the major – if not the major – problems in such situations and this is the question how to monitor and to enforce compliance with human rights obligations by all parties to such a non-international armed conflict. In particular in a situation where the armed forces of the government – which are clearly bound by the human rights treaty obligations by the state concerned – do not control all parts of the territory of that state, we are faced with the question how to ensure respect of such human rights treaty norms by the insurgents or the non-state party to that non-international armed conflict exercising effective control over a part of the territory of the state concerned. While it might rightly be argued that such non-state actors are bound by customary human rights law, and while I find it difficult but possible to argue that they are also bound by the substantive human rights norms of treaties ratified by the state in question, they are clearly not bound by any reporting obligation or other procedural rules in such treaties. Moreover, it might very well be argued that any international human rights treaty supervisory body which would accept to deal with an individual complaint concerning an alleged human rights violation attributable to such a non-state actor, would disrespect the sovereignty and, depending on the case, also the territorial integrity of the state concerned and, thus, act in violation of most fundamental international law norms.

In my opinion, two kinds of measures might be considered: First, we should think about ways and means to clarify and to ensure that also insurgent forces are bound, with respect to human rights, by the rules of customary and treaty law; in this regard, inspiration might be found in the norms of IHL which, since quite some time, are considered, under certain conditions, to be binding upon, as well as protecting, members of such insurgent forces. Second, we should explore ways and means how the general UN machinery might contribute to improve both the compliance by insurgent forces with human rights law as well as the international control of such compliance. Here, as in other fields of international law, non-international armed conflicts still remain far from being sufficiently and satisfactorily regulated by international law – not to mention the even more complex issue of implementing the pertinent rules.

b) The armed conflict is a truly international armed conflict between two or more states.

Here, it is important to make a distinction as to who are the actors of alleged human rights violations: With respect to actors exercising state authority of that state on the territory of which the alleged violation has taken place, they remain, in principle, bound by the human rights obligations which "their" state has incurred and, thus, also subject to compliance monitoring by those treaty bodies operating under the respective treaties provided, again, that the applicability of such human rights treaty provisions has not ceased as a result of a lawful declaration of derogation or by virtue of the superseding effect of IHL.

The major problem, however, exists as concerns the actors exercising state authority on the territory of another state. This is, as you all know, the situation which resulted in the *Bankovic* decision of the ECtHR: I should like to state that the criterion of "exercising effective control" developed by the ECtHR in that judgment, could and should serve as a guideline also to other treaty bodies such as the UN Human Rights Committee, the Inter-American institutions or the African Commission as well as bodies acting under specific human rights treaties such as Anti-Torture Conventions. You are probably all aware of the recent judgment of the English High Court of Justice in the *Al-Skeini* case in which it had to deal with several allegations of violations of rights guaranteed under the ECHR by British troops in and around Basra. Without wishing to go into the details, I should just like to point to two findings: As regards the allegation of a violation of the right to life of an Iraqi civilian being shot to death by British soldiers at a road control, the Court held that in such a situation there was no exercise of effective control. In contrast thereto, and quite convincingly, the Court held that the United Kingdom was responsible for a violation of the right to life and the freedom from torture in a case where an Iraqi civilian had been arrested by British troops, then held in British detention where he died as a result of what appeared to have been torture or inhuman treatment; here, the Court was of the opinion that the British troops clearly exercised "effective control".

In order somehow to fuel our ensuing discussion, I should like to formulate the following thesis: If the effective control – criterion constitutes indeed, as I think, the best, or at least a viable, means to decide on the applicability of a given human rights treaty, it seems that human rights treaty provisions will not be applicable in zones of actual combat. They might, however, be applicable in zones which are in fact occupied by foreign troops, irrespective of whether the armed conflict as such continues elsewhere or has been formally ended by a cease-fire or armistice. Again, it needs to be stressed that this general applicability of human rights treaty provisions, and the corresponding competence of the treaty organs concerned to exercise their competences of compliance control, is subject to declarations of derogations or the effects of the prevalence of specific IHL rules.

c) Finally, I should like to briefly identify another scenario of high potential relevance, i.e. a situation of a belligerent occupation by an international organisation.

Here we are faced with the currently intensively discussed problem whether and to what extent such international administrations, established with a view to secure and enforce peace in a given territory such as, e.g., the Kosovo, are bound by international human rights law. To make a very long story short: I think that, whereas such international administrations are bound by customary human rights law, they are not bound by any treaty law (international organisations have not yet become members of human rights treaties and the provisions of those treaties to which the state the territory of which is under occupation /administration, is a party do not apply because this state does not exercise any authority). This means that, from a more *de lege ferenda* – point of view, it would be highly desirable if, in the act establishing such international administrations, the human rights treaties to be respected by the international administration would be clearly spelled out – that is the case as concerns UNMIK. Even more important seems to be, however, the establishment of specific mechanisms which would allow for the treaty bodies concerned to exercise their monitoring tasks even with respect to acts attributable to such international administrations – as UNMIK has done with respect to the European Convention for the Protection against Torture and the Framework Convention for the Protection of National Minorities.

d) To conclude, I should like to refer to that situation in which none of the states involved is a party to a human rights treaty.

Here, the only – and as to its effects rather weak – possibility consists in the involvement of either the Office of the UN High Commissioner on Human Rights (OHCHR), or the UN Human Rights Commission. In view of the on-going discussion as to the means of considerably improving the human rights profile and record of the UN, in particular proposals on a substantial increase of OHCHR activities in monitoring of human rights obligations – and not only standards-setting – or thoughts on the future establishment of a Human Rights Council as an organ of the UN, it might be worthwhile to further pursue this avenue: One could, in particular, discuss the advantages and disadvantages of including IHL rules into the norms the compliance of which should, in the future, be monitored by such bodies which would, obviously, presuppose a rather wide understanding of the term "human rights".

3. Having said all this, I must admit that I find my conclusion rather discouraging: Except from situations which fulfil the "effective control" – criterion, I see only a very limited, if any, role for human rights treaty bodies as concerns compliance control of human rights norms in situations of armed conflict. If, and to what extent, the current discussion on UN reforms will yield any feasible result as to the need for strengthening compliance control of IHL norms remains to be seen. In the end, it all boils down to the old question as to whether states have the political will to accept an effective international control of their compliance with their obligations under international law – and to contribute to the strengthening of such an attitude has been the major goal of the professional activities of *Knut Ipsen* in honour of whom we have come together and in whose spirit we shall continue to work.

Contributors

Bill Boothby

Group Captain Bill Boothby is a serving officer in the Royal Air Force Legal Branch. He joined the Royal Air Force in 1981 and has served in Germany, Hong Kong, Cyprus, Croatia and in the United Kingdom. He has been increasingly involved in recent years in international and operational law work. He was a member of the UK delegation to the diplomatic conference in Oslo which negotiated the 1997 Ottawa Convention. He was similarly a member of the UK delegation to the UN Conventional Weapons Convention negotiations in Geneva which led to Protocol V to that Convention on Explosive Remnants of War. He has advised and written on a broad range of international law issues, including in particular matters relating to weapons.

Michael Bothe

Professor emeritus, Dr. iur. – born 1938. Studied Law at the Universities of Heidelberg and Hamburg and International Relations at the Graduate Institute of International Studies, Geneva. Research Assistant/Fellow at the Max Planck Institute for Comparative Public Law and International Law, Heidelberg, 1964-1979. Professor of Public Law, in particular International Law at the Universities of Heidelberg, Hannover and Frankfurt 1977-2003. Visiting professor/lecturer at the following universities: Université de Montréal, University of Florida (Gainesville), Moscow State Institute of International Relations, Rijksuniversiteit Groningen, Université Paris II, Georgia State University (Atlanta), University of Tasmania (Hobart). Vice-President and President, European Environmental Law Association 1993-1998; President of the German Society for International Law 2001-2005; Chair of the Commission for International Humanitarian Law, German Red Cross; Vice-President of the International Humanitarian Fact-Finding Commission. Counsel in various cases before the International Court of Justice and the German Federal Constitutional Court. Author of numerous publications on international law and the use of force, international humanitarian law, international, European and comparative environmental law, comparative constitutional law.

Yoram Dinstein

Dr. Yoram Dinstein is Professor Emeritus at Tel Aviv University (Israel), where he is a past President, Rector and Dean of the Faculty of Law. Professor Dinstein served two terms as a Stockton Professor of International Law at U.S. Naval War College (2002/2003, 1999/2000). He was also a Humboldt Fellow at the Max Planck Institute for International Law at Heidelberg (Germany), 2000/2001; a Meltzer Visiting Professor of Law at New York University (1985/1987); and a Visiting Professor of Law at the University of Toronto (1976/1977). Professor Dinstein is a Member of the Institute of International Law. He has written extensively on subjects relating to international law, human rights and the law of armed conflict. He is the founder and Editor of the *Israel Yearbook on Human Rights* (36 volumes of which have been issued - in English - since 1971). His latest books in English are *The Conduct of Hostilities under the Law of International Armed Conflict* (2004) and *War, Aggression and Self-Defence* (4th ed., 2005), both published by Cambridge University Press.

Knut Dörmann

Dr. Knut Dörmann is Deputy Head of the Legal Division of the International Committee of the Red Cross (ICRC), Geneva, since June 2004. Before he had been Legal Adviser at the ICRC Legal Division between December 1998 and May 2004, he was inter alia Member of the ICRC Delegation to the Preparatory Commission of the International Criminal Court. Prior to joining the ICRC, he had been Research Assistant (1988-1993) and Research Associate (1993-1997) at the Institute for International Law of Peace and Armed Conflict, University of Bochum, as well as Managing Editor of *Humanitäres Völkerrecht – Informationsschriften*, 1991-1997. He holds a Doctor of Laws (Dr. iur.) of the University of Bochum (2001). Dr. Dörmann is and has been a member of several groups of experts working on the current challenges of international humanitarian law. He has extensively presented and published on international law of peace, international humanitarian law and international criminal law. He received the 2005 Certificate of Merit of the American Society of International Law for his book *Elements of War Crimes under the Rome Statute of the International Criminal Court.*

Charles J. Dunlap Jr.

Maj. Gen. Charles J. Dunlap Jr. is Deputy Judge Advocate General, Headquarters U.S. Air Force, Washington, D.C. General Dunlap assists the Judge Advocate General in the professional oversight of more than 2,200 judge advocates, 350 civilian attorneys, 1,400 enlisted paralegals and 550 civilians assigned worldwide. In addition to overseeing an array of military justice, operational, international and civil law functions, General Dunlap provides legal advice to the Air Staff and commanders at all levels. He is a graduate of St. Joseph's University (1972) and Villanova University School of Law (1975). He has deployed to support various operations in the Middle East and Africa, including Provide Relief, Restore Hope, Vigilant Warrior, Desert Fox, Bright Star and Enduring Freedom. Additionally, he has led military-to-military delegations to Uruguay, the Czech Republic, South

Africa and Colombia. The general speaks widely on legal and national security issues, and he is published in Armed Forces Journal, the Washington Post, Air and Space Power Journal, Peacekeeping & International Relations, Parameters, Proceedings, the Military Review, the Fetcher Forum of World Affairs, the Air Force Times, the Wake Forest Law Review, the Air Force Law Review, the Tennessee Law Review, and the Strategic Review, among others.

Volker Epping

Professor Dr. Volker Epping has studied at the Ruhr-University of Bochum, Germany. After his second State Examination in 1989, he worked as a research assistant for Knut Ipsen at the Ruhr-University of Bochum. In 1994 he was conferred his doctorate and in 1996 he was granted his venia legendi for Public Law by the Law Faculty of the Ruhr-University of Bochum. Volker Epping has lectured at the University of Bochum, Münster, Köln, Freiburg as well as at the University of Regensburg. From 1999 until 2001 he was professor of Public Law at the Westfälische Wilhelms-University of Münster. Since December 2001 he has the chair for Public Law, Public International Law and European Law at the Leibniz Universität of Hannover, Germany. Since April 2004 Volker Epping is dean of the Law Faculty of the Leibniz University of Hannover. Prof. Epping's research interests mainly focus on general issues of German Constitutional Law, European Law and of Public International Law. In particular, he has given special attention to the subjects of Public International Law, especially the state and international organisations. He is also engaged in law of academic institutions. For more detailed information see: http://www.volker-epping.de

Dieter Fleck

Dieter Fleck, Dr. iur. (Cologne), formerly Director of the Department of International Agreements and Policy, Federal Ministry of Defence, Germany, is Honorary President of the International Society for Military Law and the Law of War and Member of the Council of the International Institute of Humanitarian Law. He is widely published on the law of peace and security, arms control and disarmament law, international humanitarian law, and the law of visiting forces.

Steven Haines

Steven Haines is Professor of Strategy and the Law of Military Operations at Royal Holloway College, University of London and served as Head of the Department of Politics and International Relations in the College from 2003-6. A former Royal Navy officer and UK Ministry of Defence staff officer, he has operational experience on UN maritime embargo operations, on maritime counter-terrorist operations, in fishery protection and, most recently, from brief attachments to the British led Multi-National Brigade (Centre) in Pristina, Kosovo and the UK Joint Task Force HQ in Freetown, Sierra Leone. He was the Hudson Senior Fellow at St Antony's College, Oxford in 2001 and has been Visiting Fellow in Cranfield University's Security Studies Institute since 2003. He is a member of the UK Committee of the International Society for Military Law and the Law of War and has been nominated to serve on the Society's international council. Most recently he has been a member of the specialist working group compiling a British academic response to the ICRC's *Customary IHL Study* and is, in particular, the author of the commentary on Weapons Law. Uniquely, he has been a leading contributor to both military strategic development and thinking on operational law within the British Armed Forces. He was the lead author of the Royal Navy's military strategic doctrine (*British Maritime Doctrine*, 2nd Edition, 1999), the author of the UK's strategic doctrine (*British Defence Doctrine*, 2001), the author of the Royal Navy's interim *Handbook on the Law of Maritime Operations*, produced for use during the war against Iraq in 2003, and he chaired the editorial board of the UK's official *Manual of the Law of Armed Conflict* (Oxford University Press, 2004), co-authoring its chapter on "Maritime Warfare". For more detailed information see www.rhul.ac.uk/politics-and-ir/about-us/haines/index.html

Wolff Heintschel von Heinegg

Professor Dr. Wolff Heintschel von Heinegg is Professor of Public Law, especially Public International Law, European Law and Foreign Constitutional Law at the Europa-Universität Viadrina in Frankfurt (Oder), Germany. Since October 2004 he is the dean of the law faculty of the Europa-Universität. Previously, he served as Professor of Public International Law at the University of Augsburg. In the academic year 2003/2004 he was the Charles H. Stockton Professor of International Law at the U.S. Naval War College in Newport, R.I., USA. He had been a Visiting Professor at the Universities of Kaliningrad (Russia), Almaty (Kazachstan), Santiago de Cuba (Cuba) and Nice (France). He was the Rapporteur of the International Law Association Committee on Maritime Neutrality and was the Vice-President of the German Society of Military Law and the Law of War. Professor Heintschel von Heinegg was among a group of international lawyers and naval experts who produced the San Remo Manual on International Law Applicable to Armed Conflicts at Sea, in 2002 he published the German Navy's Commander's Handbook on the Law of Naval Operations. Professor Heintschel von Heinegg is a member of several groups of experts working on the current state and progressive development of international humanitarian law. He is a widely published author of articles and books on public international law and German constitutional law. For more detailed information see: http://voelkerrecht.euv-frankfurt-o.de.

Hans-Joachim Heintze

Hans-Joachim Heintze Dr. habil., Senior Researcher at the Ruhr-University of Bochum (Germany), has been working at the Institute of International law of Peace and Armed Conflict since 1990. His publications and research fields include, besides human rights law and international humanitarian law, also minority protection and issues if self-determination. He is one of the co-authors of Marc Weller's Commentary on the Framework Convention on Minorities and of Markku Suksi's collection on Autonomy Issues. He took also part in the elaboration of the Lund Recommendations of the OSCE High Commissioner on National Minorities concerning the political participation of minorities. His teaching activities comprise all aspects of international law. He regularly teaches "Human Rights Law and Humanitarian Law" at the European Master Programmes "Network of Humanitarian Action" in Bochum, "European Master in Human Rights and Democratization" in Venice and "Human Rights and Democratization in South East Europe" in Sarajevo. In co-operation with the ICRC he took part in several teaching activities of the ICRC in Central Asia. He is a member of the German-French Commission on the Rights of Indigenous Peoples and of the international working group on autonomy regulations which is co-ordinated by the Columbia University. From 2001 to 2005 he was the president of the international organization on the study of the World Refugee Problem.

Rainer Hofmann

Since 2004, Professor Dr. Dr. Rainer Hofmann is Professor of Public, Public International Law and European Law at the Johann Wolfgang Goethe-University at Frankfurt am Main (Germany) and Co-Director of the Wilhelm-Merton-Centre for European Integration and International Economic Law. Before, he was Professor of Public Law and Public International Law at the Christian-Albrechts-University in Kiel and Co-Director of the Walther-Schücking-Institute for International Law. He is Co-Rapporteur of the International Law Association Committee on Compensation for Victims of War (since 2003) and was Co-Rapporteur of its Committee on Internally Displaced Persons (1992-2000). He was a Member and President of the Advisory Committee under the Council of Europe Framework Convention for the Protection of National Minorities (1998-2004). Since 2001 he is a member of the Advisory Council on Public International Law of the German Ministry of Foreign Affairs. He has published widely in the field of human rights law. For more detailed information see www.merton-zentrum.uni-frankfurt.de.

Frits Kalshoven

Frits Kalshoven (1924, The Hague) is Professor emeritus of general international and humanitarian law. He was an Officer in the Royal Netherlands Navy, 1945-1967. From 1958, having obtained his Master's degree at Leiden University, he taught the law of war at the Dutch Royal Naval Academy. From 1967, he taught international law at Leiden University, where in 1971 he defended his doctoral thesis on *Belligerent Reprisals* (with honours). From 1975, he also held a Chair on international humanitarian law, until his retirement in 1989. From 1999-2003, he was a Visiting Professor of international humanitarian law at Groningen University. From 1991, he was a member, and from 1997 the president of the International Humanitarian Fact-Finding Commission ex Article 90 of Additional Protocol I, until 2001. In 1992-1993 he acted as Chairman of the Commission of experts ex Security Council Resolution 780 (1992), to report on violations of international humanitarian law in the territory of the former Yugoslavia. In 1997 he was an Expert witness for claimants in cases of comfort women, prisoners of war and civilian detainees, vs. Japan, before the Tokyo District Court. In 2003, the International Red Cross and Red Crescent Movement awarded him the Henry Dunant Medal.

Stefan Oeter

Stefan Oeter is Professor of German and Comparative Public Law and Public International Law, Managing Director of the Institute of International Affairs, University of Hamburg Law School (since April 1999); Chairman of the Independent Committee of Experts of the European Charter for Regional or Minority Languages (Council of Europe); 1987-1999 Senior Fellow, Max-Planck-Institute for International Law and Comparative Law, Heidelberg; 1990 Dr. iur. utr., University of Heidelberg. Author of "Integration und Subsidiarität im deutschen Bundesstaatsrecht", Tübingen (Mohr Siebeck) 1998, and numerous books and articles on issues of German and Comparative Public Law, Public International Law and European Law.

W. Hays Parks

Office of General Counsel, Department of Defense, Washington, DC, 2003-present. Special Assistant to The Judge Advocate General of the Army, 1979-2003; Charles H. Stockton Chair of International Law, Naval War College, 1984-1985; Colonel, U.S. Marine Corps Reserve, Retired; Adjunct Professor of International Law, Washington College of Law, American University, 1995-present.

Michael Schmitt

Professor Michael Schmitt is Director, Program in Advanced Security Studies, and Professor of International Law at the George C. Marshall European Center for Security Studies in Garmisch-Partenkirchen, Germany. In 2006 he was the Sir Ninian Stephen Visiting Scholar at Melbourne University Law School and in 2005-06 a Visiting Scholar at Yale University Law School. Professor Schmitt is scheduled to assume the Charles H. Stockton Chair of International Law at the United States Naval War College in 2007. A retired US Air Force judge advocate with extensive operational experience, he is also the member of several groups of international experts working on the current state and progressive development of international humanitarian law. Professor Schmitt is a widely published author on international humanitarian law and operational law.

Torsten Stein

Dr. Torsten Stein is Professor of International, European Union and Comparative Constitutional Law and Director of the Institute of European Studies (Law Department), University of Saarland (Germany), since 1991. Before, he spent many years as Senior Research Fellow at the Max-Planck-Institute of Comparative Public and Public International Law, Heidelberg (Germany), and as Professor at the Heidelberg Law Faculty. After serving in the German Air Force, he received his legal education at the Universities of Heidelberg and Berlin, and his Doctorate and Ph.D. from the Law Faculty in Heidelberg. He is the President of the German Branch of the International Law Association (ILA) and member of ILA's Executive Council. He was Rapporteur of ILA's International Committees on "Legal Problems of Extradition in Relation to Terrorist Offences" and on "International Law before National Courts" and is currently Chairman of ILA's Committee on the International Criminal Court. Prof. Stein is a frequent guest lecturer at universities in Latin America and consultant there for governments and NGOs in constitutional questions. He has also advised a number of other countries in that field and was instrumental in the drafting of the new constitution of Mongolia in 1991. He has published several books and numerous articles in his fields of law and is the editor of a European Law Journal and of a series of monographs on European Union Law. Being also a Colonel in the German Air Force Reserve, he takes in his writings special interest in legal problems relating to international security and the use of the military. For more detailed information see: http://Stein.jura.uni-sb.de.

Andreas Zimmermann

Prof. Dr. Andreas Zimmermann, Professor of Law and Director of the Walter-Schücking Institute for International Law, University of Kiel, Germany. Visiting professorships at the University of Michigan (1995), Regensburg (1999/2000), Hannover (2000) and Copenhagen (2001), as well as in Tartu and Johannesburg. He holds a Doctorate in Law from the University of Heidelberg, an LLM from Harvard Law School and a Law Degree from the University of Tübingen. From 1999 to 2001 member of the expert commission for the drafting of a Code of Offences against International Law at the German Ministry of Justice. In 1997/1998 member and legal adviser of the German delegation at the Preparatory Committee for-, and at the United Nations Diplomatic Conference of plenipotentiaries on the Establishment of an International Criminal Court. Member of the Advisory Committee on International Humanitarian Law of the German Red Cross. Numerous publications in public international law (in particular refugees law, State succession and international criminal law), European Community Law and German and Comparative Constitutional Law. He is, inter alia, co-editor of the *Statute of the International Court of Justice – A Commentary* (Oxford University Press, 2006). Since 2001 counsel in various cases before the International Court of Justice. 2006 Judge ad hoc at the European Court of Human Rights.

FSC
www.fsc.org
MIX
Papier | Fördert
gute Waldnutzung
FSC® C083411

Kolibri 360 GmbH
Ferdinand-Jühlke-Straße 7
99095 Erfurt, Deutschland
produktsicherheit@kolibri360.de